Behar al-Anwar Volume 43

English Translation

Behar al-Anwar Volume 43

English Translation

First Edition

Compiled by
Allamah Muhammad Baqir al-Majlisi

He is also addressed by writers & orators as:
Al-'Alam al-'Allamah al-Hujjah Fakhr
al-Ummah al-Mawla' al-Shaykh Muhammad
Baqir al-Majlisi

Translated by
Muhammad Sarwar

Published by
The Islamic Seminary Inc.
www.theislamicseminary.org

The Islamic Seminary Inc., New York
© 2015 by The Islamic Seminary Inc.
All rights reserved
First Edition 2015
Printed in the United States of America.

ISBN: 978-0-9914308-4-0

Behar al-Anwar: Volume 43. English Translation - 1st ed.
Rabi' al-Awwal 1436
January 2015

This Edition was Sponsored by Sajjad Foundation

رَبِّ زِدْنِي عِلْمًا ۝

"My Lord, grant me more knowledge." (20:114)

* * * * *

طالب العلم حبيب الله ،

ومن أحب العلم وجبت له الجنة

One who seeks knowledge is beloved to Allah and whoever loves knowledge, for him paradise becomes obligatory.

(Behar Al-Anwar, Volume 1, H 183, Ch. 1, h 60)

**Sajjad Foundation
Tanglin Post Office
PO BOX 319,
Singapore 912411,
Singapore**

Note to Readers

Dear respected readers, please note the following:

The English translation of this Volume from Behar al-Anwar is now, by the will of Allah, in your hands. It was only because of the beauty of the words of Ahl al-Bayt *'Alayhim al-Salam* that made it all possible. The magnitude of this project had become quite large and complex due to two language texts and it was sometimes difficult to handle.

All comments, suggestions and corrections will be very much appreciated. In fact it will be your participation in the good cause and rewarding in the sight of Allah, most Majestic, most Glorious. Please e-mail your comments, suggestions or corrections to: info@theislamicseminary.org.

With thanks,

The Islamic Seminary
www.theislamicseminary.org

Contents

i

Translator's Introduction

Fatimah al-Zahra' *'Alayha al-Salam* - The Hawra' of human Beings

O Allah, please, grant compensation to her, her father, her husband and sons, throughout the length of the life of the earth and the skies, worthy of their services to your cause.

In this volume of Behar al-Anwar, namely volume 43 according to the currently printed edition, the readers learn about the history and biography of a personality who was called "The Hawra' of human Beings (الحوراء الانسية)" by the Holy Prophet, *'Alayhi al-Salam*.

The name (the term) 'al-Hawra' in al-Quran and the Islamic literature stands for one kind of the immortal creatures of Paradise. Fatimah, *'Alayha al-Salam,* is called 'The Hawra' of human Beings.' This expression states that she was a human individual as well as of one kind of the immortal creatures of Paradise. The fact that she is addressed as a human individual is partially because she was the mother of five children and other relationships with her family and a supremely pious female servant of Allah, most Majestic, most Glorious.

The information presented in this volume also proves that she was a creature of one kind of immortal beings of Paradise as well as free of all sins and mistakes as a supremely pious human being according to the following verse of al-Quran, "O People of the house, Allah wills to remove all kinds of uncleanness from you and to purify you thoroughly. (33:33)"

H 58, Ch. 3, h 22
'Amali al-Tusi:

Hamawayh has narrated from abu al-Husayn from abu Khalifah from al-'Abbas ibn Fadl from 'Uthman ibn 'Umar from Israel from Maysarah ibn Habib from al-Minhal ibn 'Amr from 'A'ishah daughter of Talhah from 'A'ishah who has said the following:

"'A'ishah has said that she had never seen anyone as similar to the Messenger of Allah, in speaking and conversation, as Fatimah, *'Alayha al-Salam,* was. When she would visit him he would welcome her, kiss her hands and make her sit in his own seat and whenever he would visit her she would welcome him, and kiss his hands. Once during his illness she visited him and he spoke secretly to her and she began to weep, then he spoke to her secretly and she laughed. I (the narrator) then said, "I thought she was more excellent than other women but she weeps when she laughs and I then asked about why she wept and then laughed. She then said, 'If I tell you I will be of those who destroy the trusteeship of secrets.'

"When the Messenger of Allah, passed away I then asked her about it and she told me that when he at first spoke to me secretly, he told me about his leaving this world (his death) very soon, I wept and then he spoke to me secretly to tell me that I will be the first one from his *Ahl al-Bayt* (family) to meet him, meaning that I will die very soon and for this reason I laughed."

The following is about her strict Hijab

H 195, Ch. 7, h 19
Kashf al-Ghummah:

It is narrated from ibn 'Abbas who has said the following:

Fatimah, *'Alayha al-Salam,* became seriously ill. She said to 'Asma' the daughter of 'Umays, "As you see my condition and what has become of it. You must not carry me on an open bed." She then said, "No, by Allah, however, I will make a coffin as I had seen in Ethiopia." Fatimah, *'Alayha al-Salam,* then asked her to show how it looks. I, 'Asma' then sent for wet twigs then bent them on a bed that formed a *Na'sh* (a box with its open side downward on the bed) and it was the coffin used in that place. Fatimah, *'Alayha al-Salam,* after looking at it smiled. She was not seen smiling except on that day. We then carried her and buried in the night. Al-'Abbas ibn 'Abd al-Muttalib performed the funeral *Salat* (formal prayer) and she was taken down in her grave; he, Ali, and al-Fadl ibn 'Abbas climbed down in the grave.

It is narrated from 'Asma' the daughter of 'Umays who has said that Fatimah, *'Alayha al-Salam,* the daughter of the Messenger of Allah, said, "I detest people's placing a sheet on the women from behind which people can see the figure of the women, the contour (outline) of her body." Asma' then said, "O daughter of the Messenger of Allah, I can show something which I have seen in Ethiopia." She has said that she then sent for palm tree twigs and formed a 'u' shaped structure facing down by bending the twigs then spread a sheet over it. Fatimah, *'Alayha al-Salam,* said, "This is very good and beautiful, one cannot see the figure if it is a man or a woman."

More about her Hijab

H 118, Ch. 4, h 16
Nawadir by al-Rawandi:

Through the chain of his narrators he has narrated from Musa ibn Ja'far from his ancestors, 'Alayhim al-Salam, who have said the following:

Once a blind man asked permission to come in and Fatimah, *'Alayha al-Salam,* wore her complete *Hijab* (modest dress for women). The Messenger of Allah, *O Allah grant compensation to Muhammad and his family worthy of their services to your cause,* asked her, "Why did you wear complete *Hijab* when he cannot see you (he is blind)?" She replied, "He cannot see me but I can see him and he can sense the scent."

The Messenger of Allah, *O Allah grant compensation to Muhammad and his family worthy of their services to your cause,* then said, "I testify that you are a part of myself."

Through the same chain of narrators as that of the previous Hadith the following is narrated:

He (the narrator) has said that the Messenger of Allah, *O Allah grant compensation to Muhammad and his family worthy of their services to your cause,* asked his companions about the woman and what she is. They replied, "She is a privacy." He then asked, "When is she nearest to her Lord?" They could not answer. When Fatimah, *'Alayha al-Salam,* heard this question, she said, "A woman is closest to her Lord when she is in the deepest private place of her house (where no stranger can see her)."

The Messenger of Allah, *O Allah grant compensation to Muhammad and his family worthy of their services to your cause,* then said, "Fatimah, *'Alayha al-Salam,* is a part of myself."

The Speech of Fatimah, *'Alayha al-Salam,* in the Masjid:

Shaykh Ahmad ibn abu Talib al-Tabarsi has narrated in the book al-Ihtijaj in a Mursal manner. We write down according to his words then will point out the areas of differences of the narrations when explaining certain passages:

He (rh) has said that 'Abd Allah ibn al-Hassan through the chain of his narrators, narrated from his ancestors, *'Alayhim al-Salam,* that abu Bakr decided to prevent Fatimah, *'Alayha al-Salam,* from the benefits of Fidak and when she was informed about it, she then dressed up herself as such that covered her from head down to the ground and in the company of a group of women of her relatives and helpers moved toward the Masjid and the train of their dresses touched the ground. Her walking did not miss even slightly the way the Messenger of Allah walked, *O Allah, grant compensation to him and his family worthy of their services to your cause,* until she arrived in the office of abu Bakr where he was in a crowd of Muhajir (immigrants) and al-Ansar (people of al-Madinah) and others. A curtain was then put in place between her and the people present. She then sighed deeply struggling with tears that made the whole gathering shake in sobbing and wailing. She then remained calm for a while until the sobbing of the crowd settled in calmness from the outburst of moaning, weeping and gasping.

She then commenced her speech with thanking and praising Allah and praying to Allah to grant blessings upon His Messenger, *'Alayhi al-Salam.* The people turned to weeping again and when they held back their weeping she resumed her speech and said, "All praise belongs to Allah who has granted bounties, and all thanks are due to Him for his granting inspiration. He is admired for His universal grants which He initiated, which are abundantly pleasant gifts that are there all in continued manners. Such bounties which are greater than can be enumerated and attaining the limits of compensation for the same is far away, beyond reach and beyond comprehension. He has instructed to appreciate the same to receive additional ones in continuation and that the creatures must praise Him for His grants and admire Him for similar ones. I testify that no one other than Allah alone, who has no partners, deserves worship and I testify no one deserves worship except Allah. This is the statement for which He has set sincerity as its interpretation which is placed in the hearts, and has placed light in the heart to understand it. It is not possible for the eyes to see Him, for the tongues to describe Him, and for the imagination to figure out how is He.

"He has invented things but not from something that existed before, and without any models to follow its example. He brought them in existence by His power, then spread them as He wished without being in need of inventing them or any benefit to give their shape, except to establish His wisdom and to provide awareness for the need to obey Him and to submit to His Lordship and cherisher-ship and to honor His call (praying before Him). He has placed the rewards in obedience to Him and suffering in disobedience to Him, to keep His servants away thereby from His anger and to attract them to His Paradise.

"I testify that Muhammad, my father, is His servant and His messenger, who He had chosen and selected before sending him to the people (for their guidance). He had named him before creating him, and had chosen him before sending him (as His messenger) in which time the creatures were hidden in the unseen, safe from the covering of fears, and very close to the limits of nothingness, while knowledge of Allah is thorough and complete about the limits of all things, encompassing the events of all times and with the locations of the measured things thoroughly distinguished in His knowledge.

"Allah, most High, sent him as His messenger to complete His commandments by His firm decision to approve His wisdom and to execute inevitably what He had measured.

"He saw the nations forming sects in their religion, attending the fires of their religion, worshipping their idols, denying the existence of Allah despite knowing Him.

vii

"Allah through Muhammad, *O Allah, grant compensation to him and his family worthy of their services to your cause*, made the light to shine to turn its darkness to light and to bring ease against its difficulties and clear up the saddened, clouded eyes. He rose with guidance among the people, saved them from misguidance, gave them eyesight in blindness, taught them the upright religion, and called them to the straight path.

"Allah then took him to His self with compassion and choice, interest and His preference for Muhammad, *O Allah, grant compensation to him and his family worthy of their services to your cause*, to relieve him from the fatigue of this world to receive comfort, surrounded by the virtuous angels and the pleasure of the forgiving Lord, in the neighborhood of the powerful King. May Allah, grant compensation to my father, His Holy Prophet, trustee of His revelation, His chosen one and His selected from among the people, the accepted one. May the greeting of peace, kindness and blessings of Allah be with him."

She then turned to the people in the gathering and said, "You are the people who are addressed by His commandments and prohibited, the carriers of His religion and revelations and the Trustees of Allah over your own souls and His preachers among other nations. You believe that all of this belongs to you; in fact, all of this is a covenant from Allah which He has presented to you, with that which remains as successors among you. There is the speaking book of Allah, the truthful al-Quran, the shining light, the blazing brightness in which understanding is evidently clear, with open secrets, out worldly clear (face meaning), whose followers are proud of it and it leads its followers to His pleasure and listening to which takes one to salvation. With it the bright authority of Allah is gained as well as His interpreted commands, His warned off prohibited matters, His clear evidence, His sufficient argumentations, His preferred excellence, His allowable gifts, and His written laws.

"Allah has made belief to cleanse you from paganism, the Salat (formal prayer) to keep you away from arrogance, Zakat, (charity) to cleanse the soul (self) and to increase wealth, fasting to establish sincerity, al-Hajj to propagate the religion, justice to harmonize the hearts, *obedience to us to keep the nation organized, our Imamat (leadership with divine authority) for protection against schism.*

At this point this introduction must be concluded, although this not the end of her speech. (The complete speech can be found at the end of this book in the Addendum)

The Arabic expression for the italicized words above:

وطاعتنا نظاما للملة ، وإمامتنا أمانا من الفرقة

This is said by a personality whom is called, "The Hawra' of human Beings (الحوراء الانسية)" by the Holy Prophet, *'Alayhi al-Salam.*

If a person as stated earlier above, only eighteen years old [See H 1, Ch. 1, h 1, about the special rate of growth of Fatimah, *'Alayha al-Salam*], and a mother of four children with the oldest among them only about eight years old, on being informed by the Holy Prophet of her death very soon, joyfully laughs then who else can she be other than a partly immortal creature of one kind of the creatures of Paradise.

Therefore obedience to Ahl al-Bayt (family) of the Holy Prophet as the Imams with true love is the secret behind have a loving united nation to enjoy peace and harmony.

A thorough reading of this volume of Behar al-Anwar enlightens one much more about Ahl al-Bayt (family) of the Holy Prophet and their excellence in religion.

Muhammad Sarwar

January 5, 2015

* * *

Bismillah (in the name of Allah, most Beneficent, most Merciful)

Chapters on the history of the master of women of the worlds, a piece of the self of the master of the messengers (of Allah) and the source and the original location of the lights of 'A'immah, *'Alayhim al-Salam,* who are the leaders of religion, the wife of the most honorable among the Executors of the Wills of the Holy Prophets, *al-Batul al-'Adhra* (a title ascribed to the Holy Prophet's daughter and the Virgin Mary), the Hawra' of human Beings, Fatimah al-Zahra', *'Alayha al-Salam*

O Allah, please, grant compensation to her, her father, her husband and sons, throughout the length of the life of the earth and the skies, worthy of their services to your cause.

Chapter 1 - The date of birth of Fatimah, *'Alayha al-Salam*, Her ornaments, household items and the general issues of the history of her life

H 1, Ch. 1, h 1
'Amali of al-Saduq:

Ahmad ibn Muhammad al-Khalili has narrated from Muhammad ibn Bakr al-Faqih from Ahmad ibn Muhammad al-Nawfali from Ishaq ibn Yazid from Hammad ibn 'Isa from Zur'ah ibn Muhammad from al-Mufaddal ibn 'Umar who has narrated the following:

I (the narrator) asked Abu 'Abd Allah, al-Sadiq about how the birth of Fatimah, *'Alayha al-Salam* had taken place.

He (the Imam) said, "Yes, when Khadijah, *'Alayha al-Salam* married the Messenger of Allah, *O Allah grant compensation to Muhammad and his family worthy of their services to your cause,* the women of Makkah boycotted her. They would not visit her, greet her or allow other women to visit her.

Khadijah then became depressed and lonely. This had become the cause of cautiousness about her for the Messenger of Allah, *O Allah, please; grant compensation to Muhammad and his family worthy of their services to your cause.*

When she conceived Fatimah, *'Alayha al-Salam,* Fatimah, *'Alayha al-Salam* would speak to her from inside Khadijah, and tell her to exercise patience but Khadijah *'Alayha al-Salam* would not tell the Messenger of Allah, *O Allah, please, grant compensation to Muhammad and his family worthy of their services to your cause,* until one day the Messenger of Allah entered the chamber of Khadijah and heard Khadijah speaking to Fatimah, *'Alayha al-Salam.* He (the Messenger of Allah), asked, "To whom were you speaking, O Khadijah?" She then replied, "This fetus inside me speaks to me to comfort me."

He (the Messenger of Allah), *O Allah, please, grant compensation to Muhammad and his family worthy of their services to your cause,* then said, "O Khadijah, this is Jibril (the Arch angel) who gives me the glad news that it is a baby girl, that she is a blessed purified descendant and that Allah, the most blessed most High, will continue my descendants through her and from her descendants Allah will make *'A'immah* (religious leaders) whom He will make His deputy on His earth after the time of His discontinuing sending *wahy* (divine revelations)."

Khadijah, *'Alayha al-Salam,* continued with her experience up to the time for the delivery of the baby girl. She then asked the women of al-Quraysh and Banu Hashim for help as women do to help each other.

They responded by sending her a message that said, "You have ignored our advice, refused to heed to our call not to marry Muhammad, the orphan of abu Talib who is very poor who has no wealth, therefore, we do not help you. Khadijah *'Alayha al-Salam,* became very sad and at such time four tall women of brownish complexion looking similar to the women of banu Hashim, entered her chamber, from whose presence Khadijah *'Alayha al-Salam,* became scared but one of them said, "Do not be scared, O Khadijah *'Alayha al-Salam;* we are messengers from your Lord to you and we are your sisters. I am Sarah, she is Assiyah, daughter of Muzaham who will be your companion in the garden (paradise), and this one is Mary daughter of 'Imran and this one is Kulthum sister of Musa, son of 'Imran *'Alayhi al-Salam.* Allah has sent us to help you as women help other women."

One of them then sat on her right side, one on her left the third one in front of her and the fourth one behind her. Fatimah, *'Alayha al-Salam* was born clean and purified.

When she was on the ground a light shone from her; it then reached the houses of Makkah and there no place remained in the east or the west of the earth without the arrival of the shine of that light to it. Ten *Hawra' al-'In* came in each with a water container and a wash basin in her hand; all from the garden (paradise) filled with water from al-Kawthar water. The woman in front of Khadijah *'Alayha al-Salam,* took the water container and washed her clean, then she took out two pieces of white garments from the garden (paradise) which were whiter than milk and of sweeter fragrance than the most excellent musk and ambergris. She than wrapped her in one of the garments and used the other one as her head scarf and she made her to speak. Fatimah, *'Alayha al-Salam* then spoke the two testimonies of faith saying, "I testify that only Allah deserves worship, He is one and has no partners and I testify that my father, Muhammad is His servant and Messenger, the master of the Holy Prophets and that my husband, Ali is al-Sayyid (master) of the Executors of the Wills of the Holy Prophets, and my children are the masters of the descendants (of the Holy Prophets). She then said *Salam* (the phrase of offering greeting of peace) to them mentioning each one's name and they each one said *Salam* (the phrase of offering greeting of peace) to her. They all smiled with joys and *al-Hawra'* and the inhabitant of the skies congratulated each other for the birth of Fatimah, *'Alayha al-Salam.*

In the sky a shining light emerged, the angels had not seen such light before. The four ladies then said to Khadijah *'Alayha al-Salam,* "You can take her now purified, blessed with blessed descendants.

She (Khadijah *'Alayha al-Salam*) then holding the new born in her lap began to breastfeed her. The baby would grow in one day as much as babies normally grow in a month and in one month she would grow in a month as much as children grow in one year.

Misbah al-Anwar:

It is narrated from abu al-Mufaddal al-Shaybani from Musa ibn Muhammad al-Ash'ariy son of the daughter of Sa'd ibn 'Abd Allah from al-Hassan ibn

Muhammad ibn 'Isma'il known as ibn abu al-Shawarib from 'Ubayd Allah ibn Ali ibn 'Ushaym from Ya'qub ibn Yazid from Hammad a similar Hadith.

H 2, Ch. 1, h 2
'Amali of al-Saduq, 'Yun Akhbar al-Rida':

Al-Hamadani has narrated from Ali from his father from al-Harawi from al-Rida':

Al-Rida', *'Alayhi al-Salam,* has said that the Holy Prophet, *O Allah, please, grant compensation to Muhammad and his family worthy of their services to your cause,* has said that when I was taken to the sky Jibril, held my hand then admitted me in the garden (paradise). He then passed to me (some) of its fresh dates which I then ate and it then turn into the seed in my back (reproducing system) and after my return from the sky I slept with Khadijah *'Alayha al-Salam,* then she conceived Fatimah, *'Alayha al-Salam.* Fatimah, *'Alayha al-Salam* is *Hawra'* of human Beings. Whenever I desire to smell the fragrance of the garden (paradise) I sense the fragrance of the garden (paradise) from Fatimah, *'Alayha al-Salam.*

Al-Ihtijaj:

In a Mursal manner a similar Hadith is narrated.

H 3, Ch. 1, h 3
Ma'ani al-Akhbar:

Ibn Al-Mutawakkalh has narrated from al-Himyari from ibn Yazid from ibn Faddal from 'Abd al-Rahman ibn al-Hajjaj from Sadir al-Sayrafi from 'Abu 'Abd Allah, from his ancestors, 'Alayhim al-Salam, who has said the following:

The Messenger of Allah, *O Allah grant compensation to Muhammad and his family worthy of their services to your cause,* had said that the light of Fatimah, *'Alayha al-Salam,* was created before the creation of the earth and the sky. Certain people then asked, "O Messenger of Allah is it that she is not a human being?" He (the Messenger of Allah) replied, "Fatimah, *'Alayha al-Salam,* is *al-Hawra'* human being. "

They then asked, "O Messenger of Allah, what is the meaning of 'Fatimah, *'Alayha al-Salam,* is *al-Hawra'* human being?'"

He (the Messenger of Allah) replied, "It means that Allah, most Majestic, most Glorious, created Fatimah, 'Alayha al-Salam from His own light before His creating Adam, 'Alayhi al-Salam, in the realm of the spirits. When Allah most Majestic, most Glorious, created Adam, they (spirits) were introduced to Adam, 'Alayhi al-Salam."

It was asked, "O Messenger of Allah, where was Fatimah, 'Alayha al-Salam?" He (the Messenger of Allah) replied, "She was in 'al-Huqqah' (a special container) below the leg of the Throne." They then asked, "O Messenger of Allah, what was her food?" He (the Messenger of Allah) replied, "It was Tasbih (Allah is free of all defects), Taqdis, to speak of the Holiness of the name of Allah, Tahlil, (no one deserves worship except Allah). And Tahmid, (all praise belongs to Allah). When Allah, most Majestic, most Glorious, created Adam, and brought me out from his back He made her an apple in the garden (paradise) and Jibril 'Alayhi al-Salam, brought it for me saying, "May the greeting of peace and the blessings of Allah be upon you, O Muhammad," and I responded likewise calling him my beloved friend. He then said, "O Muhammad, your Lord sends you greeting of peace." I then said, "From Him is peace and to Him returns peace." He then said, "O Muhammad, this is an apple which Allah, most Majestic, most Glorious, has sent to you as a gift from the garden (paradise)." I then took it and held it against my chest." He then said, "O Muhammad, Allah, most Majestic, most Glorious, says that you must eat it." I then opened it and I saw a shining light which shocked me. He then asked, "O Muhammad, why do you not eat all of it? You must not become frightened thereby; it is the light of victorious one in the sky and she on earth is Fatimah, 'Alayha al-Salam." I then asked, "My dear friend, Jibril, why is she called victorious in the sky and Fatimah, 'Alayha al-Salam?"

He replied, "She is called Fatimah, 'Alayha al-Salam on earth because she will protect her (Shi'a, followers of Ahl al-Bayt) against the fire and she moves away her enemies from caring for her and she is called victorious in the sky because of the words of Allah, most Majestic, most Glorious, "All matters of the past (to command) and future (to judge) are in the hands of Allah. The believers will enjoy the help of Allah on that day (of victory over the Persians). (30:4) He helps whomever He wants. He is Majestic and All-merciful. (30:5) This is the promise of Allah. Allah does not ignore His promise, but many people do not know. (30:6)" It means Allah will grant victory to Fatimah, *'Alayha al-Salam* in favor of those who honor and respect her."

(Note: This interpretation is applicable if the word 'that day' points to the Day of Judgment.)

H 4, Ch. 1, h 4
'Ilal al-Shara'i':

Al-Qattan has narrated from al-Sukkary from al-Jawhari from ibn 'Amarah from his father from 'Abd al-Jabbar from abu Ja'far, 'Alayhi al-Salam from 'Abd al-Jabbar ibn 'Abd Allah who has said the following:

It was said, "O Messenger of Allah, why is it that you make Fatimah, *'Alayha al-Salam* wear the veil, hold her against yourself and keep her close to yourself and do such things for her which you do not do for anyone of your other daughters?" He (the Messenger of Allah) replied, "Jibril *'Alayhi al-Salam,* brought an apple for me from the garden (paradise) which I ate and it changed into the seed in my back and then I went to bed with Khadijah *'Alayha al-Salam,* then she conceived Fatimah, *'Alayha al-Salam.* I sense the fragrance of the garden (paradise) from her (Fatimah, *'Alayhi al-Salam*)."

H 5, Ch. 1, h 5
'Ilal al-Shara'i':

Al-Qattan has narrated from al-Sukkary from al-Jawhari from 'Umar ibn 'Imran from 'Ubayd Allah ibn Musa al-'Abasi from Jubalah al-Makki from Tawus al-Yamani from ibn 'Abbas who has said the following:

He (the narrator) has said that once 'A'ishah entered in her chamber and saw the Messenger of Allah kiss Fatimah, *'Alayha al-Salam,* and she asked, "Do you love her, O Messenger of Allah?" He (the Messenger of Allah) said, "By Allah had you known why I love her you would love her more. When I was taken to the fourth sky Jibril said *Adhan* and Michael said *Iqamah* then it was said to me, "Move ahead, O Muhammad, (to lead)." I then said, "How can I move ahead when you, O Jibril, are present?" He said, "That is so but Allah, most Majestic, most Glorious, has granted preference to the messenger Prophets over the very close angels and the preference granted to you is special." I then moved ahead and led the *Salat* (prayer) with the inhabitants of the fourth sky then I turned to my right and I found Ibrahim *'Alayhi al-Salam* in a garden of the gardens of paradise surrounded by a group of angels.

Thereafter I was in the fifth sky, then in the sixth sky where I was called, "O Muhammad. Your father Ibrahim is the best father and your brother is the best brother." When I found myself near the curtains, Jibril, *'Alayhi al-Salam* held my hand and took me to the garden (paradise) where I found a tree of light under which there were two angels who were folding garments and arranging ornaments. I then asked my beloved friend Jibril, "Whose is this tree?" He replied, "This is for your brother Ali ibn abu Talib, *'Alayhi al-Salam* and these two angels fold dresses and arrange ornaments for him up to the Day of Judgment." I moved ahead where I found a piece of fresh date softer than butter with the fragrance of musk and sweeter than honey. I then took it and ate it. It then turned into a seed in my reproductive system. When I descended back to earth I went to bed with Khadijah *'Alayha al-Salam* and she conceived Fatimah, *'Alayha al-Salam,* thus, Fatimah, *'Alayha al-Salam,* is *al-Hawra' al-'in* human Being. Whenever I yearn for the garden (paradise) I then find the fragrance of the garden (paradise) from Fatimah, *'Alayha al-Salam.*

H 6, Ch. 1, h 6
Tafsir of Ali ibn Ibrahim:

My father has narrated from ibn Mahbub from ibn Ri'ab from abu 'Ubaydah from 'Abu 'Abd Allah, 'Alayhi al-Salam who has said the following:

The Messenger of Allah, *O Allah grant compensation to Muhammad and his family worthy of their services to your cause,* would kiss Fatimah, *'Alayha al-Salam,* very often but 'A'ishah would dislike it. The Messenger of Allah, *O Allah grant compensation to Muhammad and his family worthy of their services to your cause,* speaking to 'A'ishah said to her, "O 'A'ishah, when I was taken to the sky for the night journey I entered the garden (paradise) and Jibril accompanied me to the Tree of *Tuba* (the tree in the garden (paradise)) and gave me of the fruits of that tree which I ate and from which the seed formed in my back. When I returned back to earth I went to bed with Khadijah, *'Alayha al-Salam,* and she then conceived Fatimah, *'Alayha al-Salam.* Whenever, I kiss Fatimah, *'Alayha al-Salam,* I sense the fragrance of the Tree of *Tuba* (the tree in the garden (paradise)) from her."

H 7, Ch. 1, h 7
Manaqib of ibn Shahr Ashub:

Anas ibn Malik has narrated that he asked his mother about the person of Fatimah, *'Alayha al-Salam*. His mother told him that Fatimah, *'Alayha al-Salam,* is very handsome and distinguished like the full moon or the sun away from or coming out of the cloud. She is white and of very fine complexion.

'Ata' has narrated from abu Ribah who has said the following:

When Fatimah, *'Alayha al-Salam*, daughter the Messenger of Allah, would prepare dough, her braid of hair would touch the basin containing the dough.

It is narrated that Fatimah, *'Alayha al-Salam,* had a bright and not very tall figure.

Jabir ibn 'Abd Allah has said that whenever I would see Fatimah, *'Alayha al-Salam,* walking her walking reminded me of the walking of the Messenger of Allah whose body would slightly incline to the right, then to the left.

Fatimah, *'Alayha al-Salam,* was born in Makkah five years after the Holy Prophet, announced his mission as the Prophet of Allah and it was three years after the taking place of his night journey on the twentieth of the month of Jamadi Al-'Akhirah. She lived with her father in Makkah for eight years then she migrated with him to al-Madinah, then was married to Ali two years after her arrival in al-Madinah from Makkah on the first of the month of Dhil Hajjah. It is also narrated that it was on the sixth of this month. She moved to the house of her husband on Tuesday on the sixth of the month of Dhil-Hajjah after the battle of Badr. When the Holy Prophet, passed away she was eighteen years old. When al-Hassan was born she was twelve years old. [See H 1, Ch. 1, h 1, about the special rate of growth of Fatimah, *'Alayha al-Salam*.]

H 8, Ch. 1, h 8
Kashf al-Ghummah:

Ibn al- Khashshab has narrated from his Shaykhs in a marfu' manner from abu Ja'far, Muhammad ibn Ali 'Alayhima al-Salam, who have said the following:

Fatimah, *'Alayha al-Salam,* was born five years after the announcement of Allah of the mission of His Prophet by sending divine revelations to him and at such time al-Quraysh was rebuilding the Sacred House. She passed away when she was eighteen years and seventy five days old. According to the narration of Sadaqah (a narrator of hadith) she was eighteen years and forty five days old. She lived with her father in Makkah for eight years. She migrated to al-Madinah to join the Messenger of Allah, *O Allah, please, grant compensation to Muhammad and his family worthy of their services to your cause,* in al-Madinah, where she lived with her father for ten years and after the death of her father she lived with 'Amir al-Mu'minin (commander of the believers) for seventy five days and according to another Hadith it was forty days.

Al-Dhari' has said that according to the above Hadith she lived eighteen years and forty days. Al-Hassan was born three years after the migration when she was eleven years old.

In the book on the birth of Fatimah, *'Alayha al-Salam,* by ibn Babwayh in a marfu' manner from 'Asma' daughter of 'Umays who has said that the Messenger, *O Allah, please, grant compensation to Muhammad and his family worthy of their services to your cause,* once said to her; after she had served Fatimah, *'Alayha al-Salam,* as a nurse at the time of the birth of some of her children but she had not seen any bleeding; Fatimah, *'Alayha al-Salam,* was created as *al-Hawra' al-'in* in the form of a human Being.

H 9, Ch. 1, h 9
Rawdatul Wa''izin:

Fatimah, *'Alayha al-Salam,* was born five years after the announcement of the mission of the Holy Prophet and three years after the event of the night journey. She lived in Makkah for eight years with the Messenger of Allah, *O Allah, please, grant compensation to Muhammad and his family worthy of their services to your cause,* then she migrated to join the Messenger of Allah, *'Alayhi al-Salam* in al-Madinah where He (the Messenger of Allah) gave her in marriage to Ali *'Alayhi al-Salam* one year after their arrival to al-Madinah. When the Messenger of Allah, *'Alayhi al-Salam* passed away she was eighteen years old then she lived only seventy two days after the death of her father.

H 10, Ch. 1, h 10
Al-Kafi:

Al-Kulayni has said, "*Fatimah, 'Alayha al-Salam,* was born five years after the Messenger of Allah declared his message. She died when she was eighteen years and seventy-five days old. She lived for seventy-five days after the death of her father, *'Alayhi al-Salam.*"

H 11, Ch. 1, h 11
'Uyun al-Mu'jizat:

It is narrated from Harithah ibn Qudamah who has said that Salman (Rh) narrated to him who has said that 'Ammar narrated to him saying:

"I, 'Ammar want to inform you, O Salman (Rh) of something astonishing." I, Salman (Rh), then said please do so. He 'Ammar then said, "I saw Ali ibn abu Talib, *'Alayhi al-Salam,* enter the chamber of Fatimah, *'Alayha al-Salam,* and she said, 'come closer so I can tell you about all that will exist and what will not exist up to the Day of judgment when the Hour will take place.'"

"Ali *'Alayhi al-Salam* moved backwards facing inside of the house and I also returned back with him until he arrived in the presence of the Holy Prophet, *'Alayhi al-Salam* who said, 'Come closer O abu al-Hassan.' When he moved closer to him (the Messenger of Allah) and settled in his seat, he (the Messenger of Allah) said, 'Do you like to tell your story or should I tell you about it?' He (Ali *'Alayhi al-Salam* replied, 'To hear it from you is better, O Messenger of Allah.' He (the Messenger of Allah) then said, 'I saw that you entered the chamber of Fatimah, *'Alayha al-Salam,* and she said to you so and so and you returned backwards.' Ali *'Alayhi al-Salam* asked, 'Is the light of Fatimah, *'Alayha al-Salam,* from our light?' He (the Messenger of Allah) asked, 'Did you not know that that is correct?' Ali *'Alayhi al-Salam,* fell down in *Sujud* (prostrations) in thanks giving to Allah, most High."

'Ammar has said that "'Amir al-Mu'minin *'Alayhi al-Salam* came out and I also came out with him and he then entered the chamber of Fatimah, *'Alayha al-Salam,* and I entered along with him. She said, 'It seems that you returned back to my father, *O Allah, please, grant compensation to Muhammad and his family worthy of their services to your cause,* to inform him about what I had said to you?' He replied, 'That is correct, O Fatimah, *'Alayha al-Salam.'*

"She then said, 'O abu al-Hassan, I like to tell you that Allah, the most High, created my light, who would say *Tasbih* (Allah is free of all defects) about Allah, most Majestic, most Glorious, and then He placed my light in a tree of the trees of the garden (paradise) which it turned bright and when my father went to the garden (paradise) Allah sent him revelation to pick from the fruits of that tree and allow it to turn in his mouth. When he did so Allah, the most High, deposited me in the back of my father, *'Alayhi al-Salam,* then He placed me with Khadijah *'Alayha al-Salam,* daughter of Khuwaylid and then she gave birth. I am of that light and I know what was there and what will be there and what will not be there. O abu al-Hassan, a *Mu'min* (believing person) sees with the light of Allah, the most High.'"

H 12, Ch. 1, h 12
Iqbal:

Shaykh al-Mufid in the Hada'iq al-Riyad has said that on the twentieth of the month of Jamadi al-'Akhar Fatimah, *'Alayha al-Salam,* in the second year after Mab'th (Rise of divine revelations) was born. From the books of certain non-*Shi'a* Muslims through the chain of his narrators he has narrated from 'Abd Allah ibn Muhammad ibn Sulayman al-Hashimi from his father from his grandfather who has said the following:

Fatimah, *'Alayha al-Salam,* was born forty one years after the birth of the Holy Prophet, *O Allah, please, grant compensation to Muhammad and his family worthy of their services to your cause.* Muhammad ibn Ishaq has thought that Fatimah, *'Alayha al-Salam,* was born before the coming of divine revelation to the Holy Prophet, *'Alayhi al-Salam* and so also was the case about the birth of his other children from Khadijah *'Alayha al-Salam.* In a narration from al-Hafiz in the book of "Knowing the companions of the Holy Prophet" it is said that Fatimah, *'Alayha al-Salam,* was the youngest of the daughters of the Messenger of Allah and she was born when al-Quraysh was rebuilding al-Ka'bah and previously she was called by the nickname 'Um-'Asma'.

Abu al-Faraj in the book 'Muqatil al-Talibiyin has said that Fatimah, *'Alayha al-Salam,* was born before the commencement of divine revelation to the Holy Prophet, and at that time al-Quraysh was rebuilding al-Ka'bah. Her marriage to Ali ibn abu Talib took place in the month of Safar after the arrival of the Messenger of Allah, *O Allah, please, grant compensation to Muhammad and his family worthy of their services to your cause,* in al-Madinah and she moved to the house of Ali ibn abu Talib after the return of the Holy Prophet,

11

from the battle of Badr and at that time she was eighteen years old and this is narrated to me by al-Hassan ibn Ali from al-Harith from ibn Sa'd from al-Waqidi from abu Bakr ibn 'Abd Allah ibn abu Sabrah from Ishaq ibn 'Abd Allah abu Farwah from Ja'far ibn Muhammad ibn Ali, 'Alayhi al-Salam.

H 13, Ch. 1, h 13
Al-Kafi: [H 1232, Ch. 113, h 10, from al-Kafi]

'Abd Allah ibn Ja'far and Sa'd ibn 'Abd Allah both have narrated from Ibrahim ibn Mahziyar from his brother, Ali ibn Mahziyar from al-Hassan ibn Mahbub from Hisham ibn Salim from Habib al-Sajistani who has said the following:

"I heard abu Ja'far, *'Alayhi al-Salam,* say, 'Fatimah, daughter of the Holy Prophet, *'Alayhi al-Salam,* was born five years after he proclaimed his being the Messenger of Allah and she passed away when she was eighteen years and seventy-five days old.'"

H 14, Ch. 1, h 14
Misbah of al-Kaf'ami:

Fatimah, *'Alayha al-Salam,* was born on the twentieth of the month of Jamadi al-'Akhir on Friday in the second year after the commencement of the mission of the Holy Prophet, and it is said that she was born five years thereafter. The insignia of her ring said, 'Whoever trusts (Allah) is secure'. Her secretary was Fizzah her housemaid.

H 15, Ch. 1, h 15
Al-Misbahayn:

Fatimah, *'Alayha al-Salam,* was born on the twentieth of the month of Jamadi al-'Akhir on a Friday, two years after the commencement of divine revelation to the Holy Prophet, *'Alayhi al-Salam.* According to some of the narrations and another narration, she was born five years after the commencement of divine revelation to the Holy Prophet, the *'Ammah,* (non-Shi'a Muslims) narrate that she was born five years before the commencement of divine revelation to the Holy Prophet.

H 16, Ch. 1, h 16
Kitab Dala'il al-Imamat (leadership with divine authority):

Muhammad ibn Jarir al-Tabari, al-Imami from al-Mufaddal al-Shaybani from Muhammad ibn Hammam from Ahmad ibn Muhammad al-Barqiy from Ahmad ibn Muhammad ibn 'Isa from 'Abd al-Rahman ibn abu Najran from ibn Sinan from ibn Muskan from abu Basir from 'Abu 'Abd Allah, 'Alayhi al-Salam who has said the following:

Fatimah, *'Alayha al-Salam*, was born on the twentieth of the month of Jamadi al-'Akhir forty-five years after the birth of the Holy Prophet, *O Allah, please, grant compensation to Muhammad and his family worthy of their services to your cause.* She lived in Makkah for eight years and ten years in al-Madinah. She passed away on a Tuesday on the third of the month of Jamadi al-'Akhir in the year eleven (A.H).

It is narrated from him (the above narrator) from Muhammad ibn Harun ibn Musa Tal'akbari from Ahmad ibn Muhammad al-Dabbi from Muhammad ibn Zakariya al-Ghallabi from Shu'ayb ibn Waqid from Ja'far ibn Muhammad from his father from his grandfather from ibn 'Abbas who has said the following:

Fatimah, *'Alayha al-Salam*, would grow in one day as normally children would grow in one week, in one week she would grow as others do in one month, and in one month she would grow as others did in one year. When the Messenger of Allah, *O Allah, please, grant compensation to Muhammad and his family worthy of their services to your cause,* migrated from Makkah to al-Madinah, built a Masjid, people of al-Madinah became comfortable with him, his words spread, people realized his blessing, they on horses journeyed toward him, belief became public, al-Quran was taught, the kings and nobles spoke about it, and great people feared from the sword of his anger, Fatimah, *'Alayha al-Salam*, along with 'Amir al-Mu'minin and women migrated. Along with them was 'A'ishah. She then arrived in al-Madinah in the presence of the Holy Prophet, *'Alayhi al-Salam* in the house of 'Umm abu Ayyub al-Ansar (people of al-Madinah). The Messenger of Allah addressed the women and married Sawdah in the beginning of his arrival in al-Madinah, then he moved Fatimah, *'Alayha al-Salam*, with her and then he married 'Umm Salamah who said that the Messenger of Allah married her and made her the person in charge to look after his daughter, Fatimah, *'Alayha al-Salam*, to teach her proper discipline, but she by Allah was more properly disciplined than me and she knew all things.

13

Chapter 2 - The names of Fatimah, *'Alayha al-Salam,* and some of the matters of Her excellence

H 17, Ch. 2, h 1
'Amali of al-Saduq: 'Ilal al-Shara'i': Al-Khisal:

>*Ibn al-Mutawakkal has narrated from al-Sa'd 'Abadi from al-Barqiy from 'Abd al-'Azim al-Hassani from al-Hassan ibn 'Abd Allah ibn Yunus from 'Yunus ibn Zabayan who has said the following:*

'Abu 'Abd Allah, *'Alayhi al-Salam* has said that Fatimah, *'Alayha al-Salam,* has nine names with Allah, most Majestic, most Glorious: Fatimah, al-Siddiqah, al-Mubarakah, al-Tahirah, al-Zakiyah, al-Radiyah, al-Marziyah, al-Muhaddathah and al-Zahra'.

He (the Imam) then asked, "Do you know what the meaning of 'Fatimah' is?" I said, "My master, please teach me what it means." He (the Imam) said, "It means that she is free and away from all evil." He (the Imam) then said, "If 'Amir al-Mu'minin, *'Alayhi al-Salam* did not exist for her marriage no one on earth from Adam, *'Alayhi al-Salam,* and thereafter to the Day of Judgment, could ever have been a match for her in marriage."

Kitab Dala'il al-Imamat (leadership with divine authority) of Muhammad ibn Jarir al-Tabari, al-Imami:

Fom al-Hassan ibn Ahmad al-'Alawi from al-Saduq a similar Hadith is narrated.

Note: . . . the above facts can be considered the basis to prove that she is more excellent than all the Prophets.

H 18, Ch. 2, h 2
My father has narrated from Sa'd from Ja'far ibn Sahl al-Sayqal from al-Darami from the one who narrated to him from Muhammad ibn Ja'far al-Hurmuzani from Aban ibn Taghlib who has said the following:

I (the narrator) asked 'Abu 'Abd Allah, *'Alayhi al-Salam,* "Why is al-Zahra' called al-Zahra'?" He (the Imam), *'Alayhi al-Salam* replied, "It is because her figure would become a source of delightful light for 'Amir al-Mu'minin, *'Alayhi al-Salam* three times every day. Such light would appear from her face in the time of morning *Salat* (prayer) when people were sleeping in their beds and such light would reach their rooms in al-Madinah and their walls would become white and they with astonishment would come to the Holy Prophet, *O Allah, please, grant compensation to Muhammad and his family worthy of their services to your cause,* and tell him about what they had seen. He would send them to the house of Fatimah, *'Alayha al-Salam,* where they would see her sitting in her place for *Salat* (prayer) praying and the light spreading from her *Mihrab* (place of prayer) from her face.

Also in the midday when she would ready herself for *Salat* (prayer) in which time a yellowish light appear from her face and reach the rooms of the people because of which their clothes turn of yellow color as well as their own colors and they would ask about it. Then he (the Messenger of Allah) send them to the house of Fatimah, *'Alayha al-Salam,* where they could see her standing in her *Mihrab* (place for prayer) with the light emerging from her face, *O Allah, please, grant compensation to her, her father, her husband and the her two sons worthy of their services to your cause.* People then would learn that that light was because of the light emerging from her face. At the end of the day at sunset a red light would appear from the face of Fatimah, *'Alayha al-Salam,* and her face would glow with redness due to her happiness and giving thanks to Allah, most Majestic, most Glorious. Such redness would reach the rooms of the people and their walls would turn red. They in their astonishment would go to the Holy Prophet, *O Allah, please, grant compensation to Muhammad and his family worthy of their services to your cause,* and ask about the light and he would send them to the house of Fatimah, *'Alayha al-Salam,* where they would find her sitting in the place for her *Salat* (prayer) doing *Tasbih* (Allah is free of all defects) of Allah, speak of His greatness with red light emerging from her face with a reddish color which would make them realize that what they were seeing was from the light of the face of Fatimah, *'Alayha al-Salam.* This continued to emerge until the birth of al-Husayn, and this light continues existing in our, *'A'immah* from *Ahl al-Bayt's* (family), faces up to the Day of Judgment with one Imam after the other Imam.

H 19, Ch. 2, h 3
'Yun Akhbar al-Rida':

Through the chain of his narrators to al-Daram who has said that narrated to him Ali ibn Musa al-Rida', and Muhammad ibn Ali *'Alayhima al-Salam* who have said that they heard Ma'mun narrate from al- Rashid from al-Mahdi from al-Mansur from his father from his grandfather who has said that ibn 'Abbas asked Mu'awiyah, "Do you know why Fatimah, *'Alayha al-Salam,* is called Fatimah?" He replied, "No, I do not know." Ibn 'Abbas said, "It is because she has separated herself and her followers from the fire and I heard the Messenger of Allah, *O Allah, please, grant compensation to Muhammad and his family worthy of their services to your cause,* say this."

H 20, Ch. 2, h 4
'Yun Akhbar al-Rida':

It is narrated through the three chains of narrators from al-Rida', from his ancestors who has said the following:

The Messenger of Allah, *O Allah grant compensation to Muhammad and his family worthy of their services to your cause,* has said, "I have named my daughter Fatimah, *'Alayha al-Salam,* because Allah, most Majestic, most Glorious, has kept her and those who honor and respect her away from the fire."

Sahifah al-Rida':

It is narrated from al-Rida', from his ancestors a similar Hadith is it is narrated.

H 21, Ch. 2, h 5
'Ilal al-Shara'i':

My father has narrated from Muhammad ibn Ma'qil al-Qirmisini from Muhammad ibn Yazid al-Jazari from Ibrahim ibn Ishaq al-Nahawandi from 'Abd Allah ibn Hammad from 'Amr ibn Shimr from 'Abd al-Jabbar from 'Abu 'Abd Allah, who has said the following:

He (the narrator) has said that he asked him (the Imam), "Why is Fatimah, al-Zahra', *'Alayha al-Salam,* named al-Zahra'?" He (the Imam), *'Alayhi al-Salam* replied, "It is because Allah, most Majestic, most Glorious, created her from the light of His greatness and when this light shined the sky and earth became bright because of her light and the eyes of the angels were overwhelmed. The angels bowed in *Sujud* (prostrations) before Allah and they asked, "O our Lord and master what is this light?" Allah then sent to them inspiration that said, "This is a light from my light. I have placed this light in

17

My sky and I have created this light from my greatness and will take this light out from the back of one of my Prophets to whom I will give preference over all of my Prophets and then I will bring in the world from this light *'A'immah*, (leaders with divine authority and knowledge) who will carry out my commands and guide to my rights and I will appoint them as my deputies on my earth after my sending divine revelation is complete."

Al-Misbah al-Anwar:

From abu Ja'far, a similar Hadith is narrated.

H 22, Ch. 2, h 6
Ma'ani al-Akhbar: 'Ilal al-Shara'i':

Al-Taliqani has narrated from al-Jalludi from al-Jawhari from ibn 'Ammarah from his father who has said the following:

I (the narrator) asked 'Abu 'Abd Allah, about why Fatimah, *'Alayha al-Salam,* is named al-Zahra'? He (the Imam) *'Alayhi al-Salam* replied, "It is because when she would stand up in the place of her *Salat* (prayer) her light shined for the inhabitants of the sky just as the lights of the stars shine for inhabitants of the earth."

H 23, Ch. 2, h 7
'Ilal al-Shara'i':

My father has narrated from Ali ibn Ibrahim from al-Yaqtini from Muhammad ibn Ziyad Mawla' Banu Hashim who has said that narrated to us our Shaykh who was trustworthy and was called Najibah ibn Ishaq al-Farazi saying that narrated to us 'Abd Allah ibn al-Hassan ibn Hassan who has said the following:

Abu al-Hassan, *'Alayhi al-Salam* asked, "Why is Fatimah, *'Alayha al-Salam,* named Fatimah?" I (the narrator) replied, "It is to distinguish it from other names." He (the Imam) *'Alayha al-Salam,* said, "That is one of the names which people use, however, Allah, the most High, knew whatever was before and He knew that the Messenger of Allah, *O Allah, please, grant compensation to Muhammad and his family worthy of their services to your cause,* will marry from the towns and they will entertain greed for inheriting from him (the Messenger of Allah) this *'Amr* (leadership with divine authority). When Fatimah, *'Alayha al-Salam,* was born Allah, the most High, named her

Fatimah, *'Alayha al-Salam,* and because of her their greed as such was cut off. Fatimah means 'cutting off'.

H 24, Ch. 2, h 8
Ma'ani al-Akhbar: 'Ilal al-Shara'i':

Al-Qattan has narrated from al-Sukkari from al-Jawhari from Mukhdaj ibn 'Umayr al-Hanafi from Bashir ibn Ibrahim al-Ansari from al-Awza'i from Yahya' ibn abu Kathir from his father from abu Hurayrah who has said the following:

He (the narrator) has narrated that Fatimah, *'Alayha al-Salam,* is named Fatimah, *'Alayha al-Salam,* because she keeps away from the fire those who honor and respect her.

H 25, Ch. 2, h 9
'Ilal al-Shara'i':

Majiluwayh has narrated from Muhammad al-'Attar from Muhammad ibn al-Husayn, from Muhammad ibn Salih ibn 'Uqbah from Yazid ibn father al-Malik from abu Ja'far who has said the following:

When Fatimah, *'Alayha al-Salam,* was born Allah, most Majestic, most Glorious, sent revelation to an angel who caused the tongue of Muhammad, *O Allah, please, grant compensation to Muhammad and his family worthy of their services to your cause,* to name her Fatimah, *'Alayha al-Salam.* He then said, "I have made you distinct (from others) with knowledge and I have kept you away from menses." Abu Ja'far, *'Alayhi al-Salam* then said, "I swear by Allah that Allah, most Blessed, most high, had made her distinct from others with knowledge and had kept her away from menses during the time of the grand covenant."

Al-Misbah al-Anwar:

In this book a similar Hadith is narrated from him.

H 26, Ch. 2, h 10
'Ilal al-Shara'i':

Ibn al-Walid has narrated from Ahmad ibn al-'Alawiyah al-Isbahani from Ibrahim ibn Muhammad al-Thaqafi from Jandal ibn Waliq from Muhammad ibn 'Umar al-Basri from Ja'far ibn Muhammad ibn Ali from his father 'Alayhim al-Salam who has said the following:

The Messenger of Allah, *O Allah grant compensation to Muhammad and his family worthy of their services to your cause,* once asked, "Do you know, O Fatimah, *'Alayha al-Salam,* why I have named you Fatimah?" Ali, then asked, "O Messenger of Allah, why have you named her so?" He (the Messenger of Allah) replied, "It is because she and her (*Shi'a,* followers of *Ahl al-Bayt*) are kept away from the fire."

Misbah al-Anwar:

From the narrator of the previous Hadith a similar Hadith is narrated.

H 27, Ch. 2, h 11
'Ilal al-Shara'i':

Ibn al-Mutawakkal has narrated Sa'd from ibn 'Isa from Muhammad ibn Sinan from ibn Muskan from Muhammad ibn Muslim al-Thaqafi who has said the following:

I (the narrator) heard Ja'far ibn Muhammad *'Alayhi al-Salam* say, "Fatimah, *'Alayha al-Salam,* will have a stop at the gate of hell. When it will be the Day of Judgment, between the eyes of everyone there will be a writing that will say "an unbeliever" or it will say "a believing person".

Then a person honoring and respecting *Ahl al-Bayt* (family Muhammad) who has sinned a great deal will be ordered to hellfire, then Fatimah, *'Alayha al-Salam,* will read the writing between the eyes of that person as a person honoring and respecting *Ahl al-Bayt* (family Muhammad). She then will say, "O Lord, my master, you have named me Fatimah, *'Alayha al-Salam,* and you have kept me and those who honor and respect me away from the fire as well as those who love my descendants; your promise is true and you do not disregard your promise." Allah, the most High, will say, "You have spoken the truth, O Fatimah, *'Alayha al-Salam.* I have named you Fatimah, *'Alayha al-Salam,* and because of you I have kept away from the fire those who honor and respect your (guardianship with divine authority and knowledge) and love your descendants and submit (to their divine authority and knowledge.) My promise is true and I do not disregard my promise. I have ordered this person to be sent to hell so that you will intercede on behalf of this person. You now can intercede on behalf of this person and so that my angels, Prophets, messengers and the people of the field of resurrection notice your prominent status and position before Me. Whoever you find with the writing between his eyes saying "a believing person" you may take that person to the garden (paradise)."

H 28, Ch. 2, h 12
'Amali al-Tusi:

Al-Fahham has narrated from al-Mansuri from his uncle from abu al-Hassan al-Thalith from his ancestors from the Messenger of Allah, O Allah, please; grant compensation to Muhammad and his family worthy of their services to your cause, who has said the following:

I have named my daughter Fatimah, *'Alayha al-Salam,* because Allah, the most High, has kept her and those who honor and respect away from the fire."

H 29, Ch. 2, h 13
Ma'ani al-Akhbar: 'Ilal al-Shara'i':

Through the chain of al-'Alawi from Ali, 'Alayhi al-Salam who has said the following:

The Holy Prophet, *O Allah, please, grant compensation to Muhammad and his family worthy of their services to your cause,* was asked, "What is al-Batul, because we hear you, O Messenger of Allah, say, "Mary is Batul and Fatimah, *'Alayha al-Salam,* is Batul." He (the Messenger of Allah) replied, "Al-Batul is one who never experiences menses because it is detestable in the case of the daughters of the Prophets."

Al-Misbah al-Anwar:

From Ali, *'Alayhi al-Salam* a similar Hadith is narrated.

H 30, Ch. 2, h 14
Manaqib of ibn Shahr Ashub:

Ibn Babwayh in the book "Birth of Fatimah", 'Alayha al-Salam, and al-Kharkushi in the book "the honor of the Holy Prophet, O Allah, please, grant compensation to Muhammad and his family worthy of their services to your cause, and ibn Battah in the book "al-Ibanah from al-Kalbi from Ja'far ibn Muhammad, 'Alayhi al-Salam, has said the following:

The Messenger of Allah, *O Allah grant compensation to Muhammad and his family worthy of their services to your cause*, asked Ali "Do you know why Fatimah, *'Alayha al-Salam*, is named Fatimah?" Ali *'Alayhi al-Salam* then asked, "Why is she named Fatimah, *'Alayha al-Salam*, O Messenger of Allah?" He (the Messenger of Allah), *'Alayhi al-Salam* replied, "It is because she and her (*Shi'a*, followers) are kept away from the fire."

Abu Ali al-Salami in his book of history through the chain of his narrators from al-Awza'i from Yahya' ibn abu Kathir from abu Hurayrah who has said the following:

Ali, has said that Fatimah, *'Alayha al-Salam*, is named Fatimah, because Allah keeps away from the fire those who honor and respect her."

Shirwayh in al-Firdaws has narrated from 'Abd al-Jabbar al-Ansari who has said the following:

The Holy Prophet, *O Allah, please, grant compensation to Muhammad and his family worthy of their services to your cause*, has said that my daughter Fatimah, *'Alayha al-Salam*, is named Fatimah, because Allah keeps away from the fire those who honor and respect her."

Al-Sadiq, *'Alayhi al-Salam* was asked, "Are you aware what the interpretation of Fatimah is?" He (the Imam) *'Alayhi al-Salam* replied, "It means that evil is kept away from her. It is also said menses is kept away from her."

Abu Salih al-Mu'dhdhin in the book "Al-Arba'in has said that the Messenger of Allah, *O Allah, please, grant compensation to Muhammad and his family worthy of their services to your cause*, was asked, "What is the meaning of al-Batul?" The Messenger of Allah, *O Allah grant compensation to Muhammad and his family worthy of their services to your cause*, replied, "It stands for one who never experience menses; menses are detestable for the daughters of the Prophets." He (the Messenger of Allah) said to 'A'ishah, "O Humayrah, Fatimah, *'Alayha al-Salam*, is not like the women of the human beings. Fatimah, *'Alayha al-Salam*, does not suffer from what women experience (menses)."

'Abu 'Abd Allah, has said that Allah made it unlawful for Ali to marry other women during the lifetime of Fatimah, *'Alayha al-Salam,* because she is purified and would not experience menses.

'Ubayd al-Harawi has narrated in al-Gharibayn that Mary is called Batul because she disregarded men and Fatimah, *'Alayha al-Salam,* is called Batul because she was peerless.

Abu Hashim al-'Askari has said that he asked Saheb al-'Askar about why Fatimah, *'Alayha al-Salam,* is named al-Zahra'?" He (the Imam) *'Alayhi al-Salam* replied, "It is because her face would become bright for 'Amir al-Mu'minin, *'Alayhi al-Salam* in the beginning of the day like the midday sun, at the time of the moving of the sun from a point in the middle of the sky to the west like the full moon and at the time of sunset like a bright star."

Al-Hassan ibn Yazid has said that he (the narrator) asked 'Abu 'Abd Allah, *'Alayhi al-Salam* about why Fatimah, *'Alayha al-Salam,* is named al-Zahra'?"

He (the Imam), *'Alayhi al-Salam* replied, "It is because in the garden (paradise) there is a dome of red ruby which is standing in space as tall as the distance of one year's journey and is suspended by the power of the almighty. It is not suspended from the above or supported by any pillars from below. It has one hundred thousand gates and a thousand angels as guards at each gate and the people of the garden (paradise) will see it as you see a bright star shining in the horizon of the sky. They will say this bright shining dome belongs to Fatimah, *'Alayha al-Salam.*

H 31, Ch. 2, h 15
Manaqib of ibn Shahr Ashub:

Fatimah, *'Alayha al-Salam,* was addressed with the nicknames like 'Umm al-Hassan, 'Umm al-Husayn, 'Umm al-Muhsin, 'Umm 'A'immah, and 'Umm Abiha' (the mother for her father).

Her names, as abu Ja'far al-Qummiy has mentioned, are Fatimah, *'Alayha al-Salam,* al-Batul, al-Hisan, (well-protected) al-Hurrah, (the free) al-Sayyidah, (the leader) al-'Adhra', (free from what women experience) al-Zahra' (the lady of light), al-Hawra' (the blossoming lady of the garden (paradise)), al-Mubarakah, (the blessed one) al-Tahirah, (the purified one) al-

Zakiyah, (the cleansed one) al-Radiyah, (the contented) al-Mardiyah, (the one made happy) al-Muhaddahtrhah, (the one to whom the angels spoke) Maryam al-Kubra', (the great Mary) al-Siddiqah al-Kubra', (the great truthful one) and in the sky she is called al-Nuriyah al-Sama'wiyah (the heavenly light) al-H'aniyah (the affectionate one to her family).

H 32, Ch. 2, h 16
Al-Irshad al-Qulub:

It is narrated in a marfu' manner *from Salman al-Farsi (Rh) who has said the following:*

He (the narrator) has said that he was sitting with the Holy Prophet, *O Allah, please, grant compensation to Muhammad and his family worthy of their services to your cause,* in the Masjid of the Holy Prophet, *'Alayhi al-Salam.* At this time 'Abbas ibn 'Abd al-Muttalib came and offered Salam (the phrase of offering greeting of peace) and the Holy Prophet, responded likewise and welcomed him. He then asked, "O Messenger of Allah, why is it that Allah has given preference to Ali ibn abu Talib over other members of our family, when our genealogical lineage is the same. The Holy Prophet, *O Allah, please, grant compensation to Muhammad and his family worthy of their services to your cause,* said, "Now I must inform you, O uncle: Allah created me and He created Ali when there was no sky, earth, the garden (paradise), the fire, the tablet and the pen. When Allah, the most High, willed to commence our creation He spoke a word and it was a light, then He spoke another word and there was a spirit and He then mixed them which made them balanced, then He created me and Ali from the two. Then He split from my light another light to create the Throne, thus I am more exalted than the Throne. He then split from the light of Ali the light of the skies. He then split from the light of al-Hassan the light of the sun and from the light of al-Husayn, He split the light of the moon, thus they are more exalted than the sun and the moon and the angels said *Tasbih* (Allah is free of all defects) to speak of the glory of Allah, the most High, and in their *Tasbih* (Allah is free of all defects) they said, 'Free of all defects is Allah. He is the most Holy for His creating such lights who are very honorable in the sight of Allah, the most High.' When Allah, the most high, willed to examine the angels He sent to them a cloud from darkness and the angels could not see its beginning and its end. The angels then said, 'O Lord, our master, from the time we were created until now we had not seen the kind of condition we are in. We ask you through these lights to grant us relief from our condition.'

"Allah, most Majestic, most Glorious, then said, 'I swear by my majesty and glory that I will do so.' He created the light of Fatimah, *'Alayha al-Salam, al-Zahra'* on that day like a chandelier and hanged it from the earing of the Throne whereby the seven skies and seven earths shone and for this reason Fatimah, *'Alayha al-Salam,* is name al-Zahra'. The angels said *Tasbih* (Allah is free of all defects) and spoke of His Holiness. Allah then said, 'I swear by my majesty and glory that I will make the reward, for your saying *Tasbih* (Allah is free of all defects) and your speaking of my glory until the Day of Judgment, for those who honor and respect her and for those who love her father and her husband and her two sons.'" Salman (Rh) has said that then 'Abbas left and met Ali ibn abu Talib, *'Alayhi al-Salam.* He then embraced him and kissed between his eyes and said, "I pray to Allah to keep my soul in service for your cause, the *Ahl al-Bayt* (family) of al-Mustafa' (the purified one). How honorable are you in the sight of Allah, the most High!"

H 33, Ch. 2, h 17
Tafsir of Furat ibn Ibrahim:

Musa ibn Ali ibn Musa has narrated from 'Abd al-Rahman al-Muhariby in a Mu'an'an manner from 'Abu 'Abd Allah, Ja'far ibn Muhammad ibn Ali 'Alayhim al-Salam from his father from his grandfather who has said the following:

The Messenger of Allah, *O Allah grant compensation to Muhammad and his family worthy of their services to your cause,* asked, "O the community of the people do you know out of what Fatimah, *'Alayha al-Salam,* is created?" They replied, "Allah and the Messenger of Allah know best." He (the Messenger of Allah) said, "Fatimah, *'Alayha al-Salam,* was created as *al-Hawra'* Human being and not a human being." He (the Messenger of Allah) said that she was created out of the perspiration and fluffs of Jibril, *'Alayhi al-Salam.*" People then said, "O Messenger of Allah, it has become difficult for us to grasp, because you just said that she was created *al-Hawra'* Human being and not a human being. Then you said that she was created from the perspiration and the fluffs of Jibril, *'Alayhi al-Salam.*" He (the Messenger of Allah) then said, "Now I can explain it for you. Allah granted me a gift in the form of an apple from the garden (paradise) which Jibril brought for me and

25

he held it against his chest and perspired and the apple also perspired and the perspiration of both of them became one thing. Then Jibril offered me *Salam* (the phrase of offering greeting of peace and blessings and mercy) from Allah and I responded likewise. He then said, 'Allah has granted you a gift in the form of an apple from the garden (paradise).' I then took it and kissed and placed it over my eyes and held it against my chest.

"He Jibril then said, 'O Muhammad you must eat it.' I then said, 'My beloved Jibril, can the gift of my Lord be eaten?' He replied, 'Yes, you are commanded to eat it.' I then sliced it and I saw a light shining from it which scared me. He then said, 'You must eat it and that light is the light of al-Mansurah, Fatimah, *'Alayha al-Salam.*' I then asked, 'Who is al-Mansurah?' He replied, 'She is the girl who will be born from you and her name in the sky is Mansurah and on earth her name is Fatimah, *'Alayha al-Salam.*'

"I then asked, 'O Jibril is she named Mansurah in the sky and Fatimah, *'Alayha al-Salam,* on earth?' He replied, "'She is named Fatimah, *'Alayha al-Salam,* on earth because her *Shi'a* are kept away from the fire and her enemies are kept away from honoring and respecting her and this is because of the meaning of the words of Allah, most Majestic, most Glorious, ". . . All matters of the past (to command) and future (to judge) are in the hands of Allah. The believers will enjoy the help of Allah on that day (of victory over the Persians) [because of help through Fatimah, *'Alayha al-Salam*]. (30:4) He helps whomever He wants. He is Majestic and All-merciful. (30:5) This is the promise of Allah. Allah does not ignore His promise, but many people do not know." (30:6)'"

H 33, Ch. 2, h 18
'Amali al-Tusi:

A group has narrated from abu al-Mufaddal from Ja'far ibn Muhammad al-'Alawi from Muhammad ibn Ali ibn al-Husayn, ibn Zayd from al-Rida', from his ancestors from Ali, 'Alayhim al-Salam, who has said the following:

I (the narrator) heard the Messenger of Allah, *O Allah, please, grant compensation to Muhammad and his family worthy of their services to your cause,* say that Fatimah, *'Alayha al-Salam,* is named Fatimah, *'Alayha al-Salam,* because Allah keeps her descendants away from the fire and this

26

applies to those of them who will meet Allah with *al-Tawhid* (belief in oneness of Allah) as well as in what I have brought from Allah.

H 34, Ch. 2, h 19

I ('Allamah Majlisi) say that in the book 'Muqatil al-Talibiyin through the chain of his narrators from Ja'far ibn Muhammad from his father, *'Alayhima al-Salam,* it is narrated that one of the nicknames of Fatimah, *'Alayha al-Salam,* was *'Umma Abiha'* (the mother of her father).

H 35, Ch. 2, h 20
Misbah al-Anwar:

It is narrated from abu Ja'far from his ancestors *'Alayhim al-Salam,* who have said that Fatimah, *'Alayha al-Salam,* daughter of Muhammad was named purified because of her being clean from all forms of uncleanliness, and because of her complete freedom from all forms of menses or such issues during child birth.

Chapter 3 - Her excellence and merits and certain issues of her life and her miracles

H 36, Ch. 3, h 1

I ('Allamah Majlisi) say that it was mentioned in the chapter about the riders on the Day of Judgment as narrated from the Holy Prophet, *O Allah, please, grant compensation to Muhammad and his family worthy of their services to your cause,* in the narration of ibn 'Abbas who has said that no one will ever ride on that day (the Day of Judgment) except four people: Myself, Ali, Fatimah, *'Alayha al-Salam,* and the Prophet of Allah Salih. I however, will ride on al-Buraq, my daughter Fatimah, *'Alayha al-Salam,* will have my camel al-'Adba' . . . to the end of the Hadith.

H 37, Ch. 3, h 2
Majalis al-Mufid:

'Umar ibn Muhammad al-Sayrafi has narrated from Muhammad ibn Hammam from Muhammad ibn Qasim from 'Isma'il ibn Ishaq from Muhammad ibn Ali from Muhammad ibn al-Fudayl from al-Thumali from Al-Baqir, from his father from his grandfather, 'Alayhim al-Salam, who has said the following:

The Messenger of Allah, *O Allah grant compensation to Muhammad and his family worthy of their services to your cause,* has said that Allah becomes angry if Fatimah, *'Alayha al-Salam,* becomes angry and He becomes happy if she becomes happy.

H 38, Ch. 3, h 3
Al-Khisal:

Ibn Idris has narrated from his father from al-Ash'ariy from 'Abu 'Abd Allah, al-Razi from ibn abu 'Uthman from Musa ibn Bakr from abu al-Hassan al-Awwal, 'Alayhi al-Salam who has said the following:

The Messenger of Allah, *O Allah grant compensation to Muhammad and his family worthy of their services to your cause,* has said that Allah has from among the women chosen four: they are Maryam (Mary), Assiyah, Khadijah and *Fatimah, 'Alayha al-Salam* . . . to the end of Hadith.

H 39, Ch. 3, h 4
'Yun Akhbar al-Rida', 'Alayhi al-Salam:

Through three chains of narrators from al-Rida', 'Alayhi al-Salam from his ancestors who has said the following:

The Messenger of Allah, *O Allah grant compensation to Muhammad and his family worthy of their services to your cause,* has said that Allah becomes angry if Fatimah, *'Alayha al-Salam,* becomes angry and He becomes happy if Fatimah, *'Alayha al-Salam,* becomes happy.

Sahifah of al-Rida:

From al-Rida', *'Alayhi al-Salam,* a similar Hadith is narrated.

H 40, Ch. 3, h 5
'Yun Akhbar al-Rida':

Through the chain of the narrators of al-Tamimi from al-Rida', from his ancestors 'Alayhim al-Salam the following is narrated:

The Messenger of Allah, *O Allah grant compensation to Muhammad and his family worthy of their services to your cause,* has said that al-Hassan and al-Husayn, *'Alayhima al-Salam,* are the best of the inhabitants of the earth after me and after their father and their mother is the best of the women of the inhabitants of the earth.

H 41, Ch. 3, h 6
'Yun Akhbar al-Rida':

Through the chain of the narrators of al-Tamimi from al-Rida', from his ancestors, 'Alayhim al-Salam, the following is narrated:

The Messenger of Allah, *O Allah grant compensation to Muhammad and his family worthy of their services to your cause,* has said that Fatimah, *'Alayha al-Salam,* maintained chastity so Allah made the fire forbidden to her descendants.

H 42, Ch. 3, h 7
'Amali of al-Saduq:

Al-Hassan ibn Muhammad ibn Sa'id al-Hashimi has narrated Ja'far ibn Muhammad ibn Ja'far al-'Alawi from Muhammad ibn Ali ibn Khalaf from Hassan ibn Salih ibn abu al-Aswad from abu Masher from Muhammad ibn Qays who has said the following:

Whenever the Holy Prophet, O *Allah, please, grant compensation to Muhammad and his family worthy of their services to your cause,* would come back from a journey he would first visit Fatimah, *'Alayha al-Salam.* He (the Messenger of Allah) would visit her and stay with her for a long time. Once He (the Messenger of Allah) went on a journey. Fatimah, *'Alayha al-Salam,* had made a pair of bracelets of silver, a necklace, a pair of earrings and a curtain for the door in preparation for the arrival of her father. When the Messenger of Allah, *O Allah, please, grant compensation to Muhammad and his family worthy of their services to your cause,* arrived he visited her and his companions waited at the door not knowing to wait or move because of his long stay with her. The Messenger of Allah, *O Allah grant compensation to Muhammad and his family worthy of their services to your cause,* came out and anger was apparent from his face until he sat near the pulpit and Fatimah, *'Alayha al-Salam,* thought that it was only because of his seeing the bracelets, the necklace, the earrings and the curtain. She then removed, her earrings, the bracelets, the necklace and the curtain and sent them to the Messenger of Allah, *O Allah, please, grant compensation to Muhammad and his family worthy of their services to your cause,* with the message of *Salam* (the phrase of offering greeting of peace) and saying that your daughter says, "You may spend these items in the way of Allah." He (the Messenger of Allah) then said, "She has done it, may her father be made a ransom for her." He (the Messenger of Allah) said it three times. He (the Messenger of Allah) then said, "The worldly things are not from Muhammad and *Ale* (family) Muhammad. Had the worldly things been worthy in the sight of Allah more than the wings of a fly, the unbelievers could not benefit from one sip of water thereof. He (the Messenger of Allah) then stood up to go and visit Fatimah, *'Alayha al-Salam.*

H 43, Ch. 3, h 8
Al-Ihtijaj:

Al-Husayn ibn Yazid has narrated from Ja'far al-Sadiq, 'Alayhi al-Salam who has said the following:

"The Messenger of Allah, *O Allah grant compensation to Muhammad and his family worthy of their services to your cause,* would say to Fatimah, *'Alayha al-Salam,* 'O Fatimah, *'Alayha al-Salam,* Allah, most Majestic, most Glorious, becomes angry whenever you become angry and He becomes happy because of your happiness.'"

He (the narrator) has said that then the narrators of Hadith narrated this Hadith to people. He (the narrator) has said that then ibn Jarih came to him and said, "O 'Abu 'Abd Allah, today we have narrated a Hadith but people consider it very unpopular." He (the Imam) *'Alayhi al-Salam* then asked, "What is that Hadith?" He (Jarih) then replied, "It is what you narrated that the Messenger of Allah, *O Allah, please, grant compensation to Muhammad and his family worthy of their services to your cause,* would say to Fatimah, *'Alayha al-Salam,* 'Allah becomes angry whenever you become angry and He becomes happy because of your happiness.'"

He (the Imam), *'Alayhi al-Salam* said to Jarih, "Is it not true that you narrate a Hadith which says that Allah becomes angry when His believing servant becomes angry and He becomes happy when His believing servant becomes happy?" Jarih (Jarij) then replied, "That is correct, we do narrate such Hadith."

He (the Imam), *'Alayhi al-Salam* then said, "Why then you deny in the case of the daughter the Messenger of Allah, *O Allah, please, grant compensation to Muhammad and his family worthy of their services to your cause,* and her being a believing person, and Allah's becoming angry for her anger and His becoming happy because of her happiness?"

Jarih then said, "You have spoken the truth. Allah knows best where to place His message."

H 44, Ch. 3, h 9
'Amali of al-Saduq:

Al-Qattan has narrated from Sukkary from al-Jawhari from 'Abbas ibn Bakar from 'Abd Allah ibn al-Muthanna' from his uncle Thumamah ibn 'Abd Allah from Anas ibn Malik from his mother who has said the following:

"Fatimah, 'Alayha al-Salam, never experienced any menses or any discharges women experience during their child birth."

H 45, Ch. 3, h 10
'Amali of al-Saduq:

Ibn al-Walid has narrated al-Saffar from ibn Ma'ruf from abu Ishaq from al-Hassan ibn Ziyad al-'Attar who has said the following:

I (the narrator) asked 'Abu 'Abd Allah, *'Alayhi al-Salam,* about the words of the Messenger of Allah, *O Allah, please, grant compensation to Muhammad and his family worthy of their services to your cause,* "'Fatimah, *'Alayha al-Salam,* is the leader of the women of the garden (paradise).' Is she the leader of the women of her world?" He (the Imam), *'Alayhi al-Salam* said, "That is Maryam (Mary). Fatimah, *'Alayha al-Salam,* however, is the leader of the women of the garden (paradise) of the past and future generations." I then asked about the words of the Messenger of Allah, *O Allah, please, grant compensation to Muhammad and his family worthy of their services to your cause,* "Al-Hassan and al-Husayn, *'Alayhima al-Salam,* are the leaders of the young people of the garden (paradise)." He (the Imam), *'Alayhi al-Salam* said, "They, by Allah, are the leaders of the young people of the garden (paradise) of the past and future generations."

H 46, Ch. 3, h 11
'Amali of al-Saduq:

Al-Taliqani has narrated from Muhammad ibn Ishaq al-Madara'I from abu Qalabah from Ghanim ibn al-Hassan al-Sa'difm Muslim ibn Khalid al-Makki from Ja'far ibn Muhammad from his ancestors 'Alayhim al-Salam, from Jabir ibn 'Abd Allah al-Ansari from Ali ibn abu Talib, 'Alayhi al-Salam who has said the following:

"Fatimah, *'Alayha al-Salam,* asked her father the Messenger of Allah, *O Allah, please, grant compensation to Muhammad and his family worthy of their services to your cause,* "O father, where will I find you on the station of the great resurrection on the Day of Judgment, the day of horror and the great fear?"

The Messenger of Allah, *O Allah grant compensation to Muhammad and his family worthy of their services to your cause,* replied, "You will find me, O Fatimah, *'Alayha al-Salam,* near the gate of the garden (paradise) with the banner of *al-Hamd* in my hand and I will be interceding on behalf of my followers before my Lord." She then asked, "What will happen if I will not find you there?" He (the Messenger of Allah), said, "You will find me near the pond where I will be giving water to my followers." She then said, "What if I will not find you there also?" He (the Messenger of Allah), said, "You will find me on the bridge standing and saying, 'O Lord, please save my followers.'" She then said, "What if I will not find you there also?" He (the

33

Messenger of Allah), said, "You will find me near the Balance saying, 'O Lord, please save my followers.'" She then said, "What if I will not find you there also?" He (the Messenger of Allah) said, "You will find me at the edge of hell where I will be diverting the shooting flames of the fire from my followers."

Fatimah, *'Alayha al-Salam,* received it as a glad news. O Allah, please, grant compensation to *Fatimah, 'Alayha al-Salam,* her father, husband and sons worthy of their services to your cause.

H 47, Ch. 3, h 12
'Amali of al-Saduq:

Yahya' ibn Zayd ibn 'Abbas has narrated from his uncle Ali ibn 'Abbas from Ali ibn al-Mudhir from 'Abd Allah ibn Salim from Husayn ibn Zayd from Ali ibn 'Umar ibn Ali from al-Sadiq, Ja'far ibn Muhammad from his father from Ali ibn al-Husayn, ibn Ali ibn abu Talib from the Messenger of Allah, O Allah, please, grant compensation to Muhammad and his family worthy of their services to your cause:

"The Messenger of Allah, *O Allah grant compensation to Muhammad and his family worthy of their services to your cause,* would say to Fatimah, *'Alayha al-Salam,* 'O Fatimah, *'Alayha al-Salam,* Allah, most Majestic, most Glorious, becomes angry whenever you become angry and He becomes happy because of your happiness.'"

He (the narrator) has said that then Sandal came to Ja'far ibn Muhammad *'Alayhima al-Salam,* and said, "O 'Abu 'Abd Allah, these young people come and narrate from you unpopular Hadith." He (the Imam) *'Alayhi al-Salam* then asked, "What is that Hadith?" He (Sandal) then replied, "It is what you narrated that the Messenger of Allah, *O Allah, please, grant compensation to Muhammad and his family worthy of their services to your cause,* had said to Fatimah, *'Alayha al-Salam,* 'Allah becomes angry whenever you become angry and He becomes happy because of your happiness.'"

He (the Imam), *'Alayhi al-Salam* said to Sandal, "Is it not true that you narrate a Hadith which says that Allah becomes angry when His believing servant becomes angry and He becomes happy when His believing servant becomes happy?" Sandal then replied, "That is correct, we do narrate such Hadith."

He (the Imam), *'Alayhi al-Salam* then said, "Why then you deny in the case of the daughter the Messenger of Allah, *O Allah, please, grant compensation to Muhammad and his family worthy of their services to your cause,* as her being a believing person, and Allah's becoming angry for her anger and His becoming happy because of her happiness?"

Sandal then said, "You have spoken the truth. Allah knows best where to place His message."

'Amali al-Tusi:

Al-Ghada'iri has narrated from al-Saduq from Yahya' a similar Hadith.

H 48, Ch. 3, h 13
'Amali of al-Saduq:

Ibn Musa has narrated from al-Asadi from al-Barmaki from Ja'far ibn Ahmad al-Tamim from his father from 'Abd al-Malik ibn 'Umayr from his father from his grandfather from ibn 'Abbas from the Holy Prophet, O Allah, please, grant compensation to Muhammad and his family worthy of their services to your cause, who has said the following:

"My daughter is the leader of the women of the worlds . . ." to the end of the Hadith.

H 49, Ch. 3, h 14
'Amali of al-Saduq:

Al-Taliqani has narrated from al-Jalludi from Hisham ibn Ja'far from Ahmad from 'Abd Allah ibn Sulayman who has said the following:

He (the narrator) has said that he has read in the Injil (the Gospel) of the information about the Holy Prophet, and about his marrying women and about the small number of his children. However, his offspring continues through a blessed female who has a house in the garden (paradise) and she will never experience any of what other females experience or menses that she will live with a guardian just as your mother lived under the guardian-ship of Zakariya. She will have two child who will be martyred . . . This Hadith was mentioned in a complete form in the book of the biography of the Holy Prophet, *O Allah, please, grant compensation to Muhammad and his family worthy of their services to your cause.*

H 50, Ch. 3, h 15
'Amali of al-Saduq:

Ibn Idris has narrated from his father from ibn 'Isa from Muhammad ibn Yahya' al-Khazzaz from Musa ibn 'Isma'il from his father from Musa ibn Ja'far from his ancestors 'Alayhim al-Salam, who has said the following:

Ali *'Alayhi al-Salam* has said that the Messenger of Allah, *O Allah, please, grant compensation to Muhammad and his family worthy of their services to your cause,* once visited his daughter Fatimah, *'Alayha al-Salam,* and found her wearing a necklace and he (the Messenger of Allah) turned away from her. She then removed the necklace and threw it a side. The Messenger of Allah, *O Allah grant compensation to Muhammad and his family worthy of their services to your cause,* then said, "O Fatimah, *'Alayha al-Salam,* you are from me." Then a beggar came and she gave the necklace to the beggar. The Messenger of Allah, *O Allah grant compensation to Muhammad and his family worthy of their services to your cause,* said, "The anger of Allah and my anger become intense against those who spill my blood and trouble me by troubling my *Ahl al-Bayt* (family)."

Kashf al-Ghummah:

From Musa ibn Ja'far, *'Alayhima al-Salam,* a similar Hadith is narrated.

H 51, Ch. 3, h 16
Tafsir of Ali ibn Ibrahim:

Al-Husayn ibn Muhammad has narrated from Mu'alla' from al-Washsha' from Muhammad ibn al-Fudayl from abu Hamzah from abu Ja'far, 'Alayhi al-Salam who has said the following:

By the moon, (74:32) by the retreating night, (74:33) by the brightening dawn, (74:34) it (the army of your Lord) is certainly one of the greatest. (74:35) It is a warning for mankind (74:36) whether one steps forward to embrace the faith or one turns away from it. (74:37)

He (the Imam), *'Alayhi al-Salam,* said that this is a reference to Fatimah, *'Alayha al-Salam.*

H 52, Ch. 3, h 17
Majalis of al-Mufid: 'Amali al-Tusi:

Al-Mufid has narrated from al-Maraghi from al-Hassan ibn Ali al-Kufi from Ja'far ibn Muhammad ibn Marwan from his father from 'Abd Allah ibn al-Hassan al-Ahmasi from Khalid ibn 'Abd Allah from Yazid ibn abu Ziyad from 'Abd Allah ibn al-Harith from Sa'd ibn Malik that is ibn abu Waqqas who has said the following:

I (the narrator) heard the Messenger of Allah, *O Allah, please, grant compensation to Muhammad and his family worthy of their services to your cause,* say, "Fatimah, *'Alayha al-Salam,* is a part of me. Whoever makes her happy has made me happy and whoever troubles her has troubled me. Fatimah, *'Alayha al-Salam,* is of all people the dearest to me."

H 53, Ch. 3, h 18
'Amali al-Tusi:

Ibn al-Salt has narrated from ibn 'Uqdah from Ya'qub ibn Yusuf al-Dabi from 'Ubayd Allah ibn Musa from Ja'far al-Ahmari from al-Shaybani from Jami ' ibn 'Umayr who has said the following:

I (the narrator) heard 'A'ishah say to my aunt and I was listening when my aunt was asking her, "I swear you to Allah (to tell me) what is your opinion about Ali, *'Alayhi al-Salam.*" 'A'ishah replied, "Please leave us alone. There was no one among men more beloved to the Messenger of Allah, than Ali and there was no woman more beloved to the Messenger of Allah than Fatimah, *'Alayha al-Salam.*"

H 55, Ch. 3, h 19
'Amali al-Tusi:

Through the chain narrators to 'Ubayd Allah ibn Musa from Zakariya from Faras from Mmasruq from 'A'ishah who has said the following:

'A'ishah has said that Fatimah, *'Alayha al-Salam,* came and she walked, by Allah beside whom no one deserves worship except He, exactly like the Messenger of Allah, *O Allah, please, grant compensation to Muhammad and his family worthy of their services to your cause.* She came and when the Messenger of Allah saw her, he said, "Welcome my daughter and he (the Messenger of Allah) said it twice." Fatimah, *'Alayha al-Salam,* has said that the Messenger of Allah said to me, "Will you not be happy when on the Day of Judgment you will come as the leader of the women of the believing people or as the leader of the women of this nation?"

37

H 56, Ch. 3, h 20
'Amali of al-Saduq:

Al-Hamadani has narrated from Ali ibn Ibrahim from Ja'far ibn Salmah al-Ahawazi from Ibrahim ibn Muhammad al-Thaqafi from Ibrahim ibn Musa from abu Qatadah from 'Abd al-Rahman ibn al-'Ala' al-Hadrami from Sa'id ibn al-Musayyib from ibn 'Abbas who has said the following:

"The Messenger of Allah, *O Allah grant compensation to Muhammad and his family worthy of their services to your cause,* one day was sitting with Ali, Fatimah, *'Alayha al-Salam,* al-Hassan and al-Husayn, *'Alayhim al-Salam.* The Messenger of Allah, *O Allah grant compensation to Muhammad and his family worthy of their services to your cause,* then said, 'O Lord, You know that these are my *Ahl al-Bayt* (family), the most honorable ones to me of all people. Please love those who love them (my *Ahl al-Bayt* (family)) and hate those who hate them, be the guardian and friends of those who befriend them and who accept them as their guardians and be the enemy of those who act as their enemies, support those who support them and keep them clean from all uncleanliness, innocent of sins and support them with the holy spirit from your side."

He (the Messenger of Allah) then said, "O Ali, you are the Imam (leader) of my nation (followers) after me and my successor among them and you are the leader of the believing people to the garden (paradise). It is as if I see my daughter Fatimah, *'Alayha al-Salam,* arriving on the Day of Judgment on a noble (camel) of light in the garden (paradise) with seventy thousand angels on her right and seventy thousand angels on her left, seventy thousand angels in front of her and seventy thousand angels after her, escorting, and she will be leading the believing women of my nation (followers) to the garden (paradise).

"All the women who perform their five times *Salat* (prayer) in twenty four hours, fast during the month of Ramadan, perform al-Hajj of al-Haram House (the Sacred House of Allah), pay Zakat (obligatory charity), abide by the instructions of their husband, and accept Ali *'Alayhi al-Salam* as their beloved divine guardian after me, they will enter the garden (paradise) by the intercession of my daughter Fatimah, *'Alayha al-Salam,* because she is the leader of the women of the worlds."

It then was said, "Is she, O Messenger of Allah, the leader of the women of her world?" He (the Messenger of Allah), *O Allah, please, grant compensation to Muhammad and his family worthy of their services to your cause*, replied, "That is Maryam (Mary) daughter of 'Imran. My daughter Fatimah, *'Alayha al-Salam*, however, is the leader of the women of the worlds of the people of the past, present and future. When she stands for *Salat* (prayer) in her place of *Salat* (prayer) seventy thousand angels of the closest ones to the Lord, salute her and call her as the angels who called Maryam (Mary) in her place of *Salat* (prayer) and they say, 'O Fatimah, *'Alayha al-Salam*, Allah has chosen you, cleansed and has chosen you from among the women of the worlds.'"

He (the Messenger of Allah) then turned to Ali, *'Alayhi al-Salam* and said, "O Ali, Fatimah, *'Alayha al-Salam*, is a part of myself. She is the light of my eyes, and the fruit of my heart. Whatever troubles her troubles me and whatever makes her happy makes me happy and she will be the first one from my *Ahl al-Bayt* (family) who will join me from among the members of my *Ahl al-Bayt* (family). You must do good for her after me.

"Al-Hassan and al-Husayn, *'Alayhima al-Salam*, are my two sons and they are my two *Rayhanah* (bunches of sweet smelling flowers) and they are the two leaders of the young people of the garden (paradise). You must honor them as you honor your ears and eyes."

He (the Messenger of Allah), *O Allah, please, grant compensation to Muhammad and his family worthy of their services to your cause*, then raised his hands to the sky and said, "O Lord, I appoint You as witness that I love those who love them (Al-Hassan and al-Husayn, *'Alayhima al-Salam*) and hate those who hate them, I am at peace with those who are in peace with them and I am at war against those who are at war against them, I am an enemy of those who are their enemies and a friend of those who are their friends."

H 57, Ch. 3, h 21
'Ilal al-Shara'i':

Abu Sa'd has narrated from ibn 'Isa from Ali ibn al-Hakam from abu Jamilah from abu Ja'far, 'Alayhi al-Salam who has said the following:

"The daughters of the Prophets do not experience menses because it is a form of punishment. The first one who experienced it was Sarah."

H 58, Ch. 3, h 22
'Amali al-Tusi:

Hamawayh has narrated from abu al-Husayn from abu Khalifah from al-'Abbas ibn Fadl from 'Uthman ibn 'Umar from Israel from Maysarah ibn Habib from al-Minhal ibn 'Amr from 'A'ishah daughter of Talhah from 'A'ishah who has said the following:

"'A'ishah has said that she had never seen anyone as similar to the Messenger of Allah, in speaking and conversation, as Fatimah, *'Alayha al-Salam,* was. When she would visit him he would welcome her, kiss her hands and make her sit in his own seat and whenever he would visit her she would welcome him, and kiss his hands. Once during his illness she visited him and he spoke secretly to her and she began to weep, then he spoke to her secretly and she laughed. I (the narrator) then said, "I thought she was more excellent than other women but she weeps when she laughs and I then asked about why she wept and then laughed. She then said, 'If I tell you I will be of those who destroy the trusteeship of secrets.'

"When the Messenger of Allah, passed away I then asked her about it and she told me that when he at first spoke to me secretly, he told me about his leaving this world (his death) very soon, I wept and then he spoke to me secretly to tell me that I will be the first one from his *Ahl al-Bayt* (family) to meet him, meaning that I will die very soon and for this reason I laughed."

H 59, Ch. 3, h 23
Tafsir of Ali ibn Ibrahim:

This is about the meaning of the words of Allah, the most Majestic, the most Glorious:

"Those who annoy Allah and His messenger are condemned by Allah in this life and in the life to come. He has prepared for them a humiliating torment." (33:57)

He (the Imam) has said that this is revealed about those who usurped the rights of 'Amir al-Mu'minin, *'Alayhi al-Salam* and took away the rights of Fatimah, *'Alayha al-Salam,* disappointed and harmed her physically even though the Holy Prophet, had said, "Whoever disappoints Fatimah, *'Alayha al-Salam,* in my lifetime are just as those who disappoint and harm her after I will die and those who disappoint her after I die will be just as those who disappoint and harm her in my lifetime. Those who disappoint her have disappointed me and those who disappoint me have disappointed Allah, as He has said 'Those who disappoint Allah and His messenger are condemned by Allah in this life and in the life to come. He has prepared for them a humiliating torment.' (33:57)"

H 60, Ch. 3, h 24
Al-Khisal:

The following are certain facts that the Messenger of Allah, *O Allah, please, grant compensation to Muhammad and his family worthy of their services to your cause,* informed Ali about. "O Ali, you must bear in mind that Allah, most Majestic, most Glorious, examined the world and chose me from among all men of the worlds. He then examined it a second time then chose you from among all men of the worlds, He then examined it for a third time, then chose the *'A'immah,* (Imams) after you from among all men of the worlds and then He examined it a fourth time and He chose Fatimah, *'Alayha al-Salam,* from among all women of the worlds."

H 61, Ch. 3, h 25
Ma'ani al-Akhbar:

Al-Hamadani has narrated from Ali from his father from Muhammad ibn Sinan from al-Mufaddal who has said the following:

I (the narrator) said to 'Abu 'Abd Allah, "Please tell me about the words of the Messenger of Allah, about Fatimah, *'Alayha al-Salam,* 'Fatimah, *'Alayha al-Salam,* is the leader of the women of the worlds.' Is she the leader of the women of her world?" He (the Imam), *'Alayhi al-Salam* said, "That is about Maryam (Mary) who was the leader of the women of her world. Fatimah, *'Alayha al-Salam,* is the leader of the women of the worlds of the past, present and future."

H 62, Ch. 3, h 26
Ma'ani al-Akhbar:

Al-Qattan has narrated from Ahmad al-Hamadani from al-Mundhir ibn Muhammad from Ja'far ibn Muhammad from Ja'far ibn Sulayman from

'Isma'il ibn Mehran from 'Abayah from ibn 'Abbas who has said the following:

The Messenger of Allah, *O Allah grant compensation to Muhammad and his family worthy of their services to your cause,* has said, "Fatimah, *'Alayha al-Salam,* is a branch of me; whatever disappoints her disappoints me and whatever makes her happy makes me happy also. Allah, most Blessed, most high, becomes angry if Fatimah, *'Alayha al-Salam,* is made angry and He becomes happy if Fatimah, *'Alayha al-Salam,* is made happy."

H 63, Ch. 3, h 27
Ma'ani al-Akhbar:

Muhammad ibn Harun al-Zanjani has narrated from 'Abd al-'Aziz who has who has said the following:

He (the narrator) heard al-Qasim ibn Salam say about the meaning of the words of the Holy Prophet, *O Allah, please, grant compensation to Muhammad and his family worthy of their services to your cause,* "Al-Rahman is a *shajnah* from Allah, most Majestic, most Glorious," refers to intertwined relationships of the relatives like the veins in the body. It is like the saying of one "the story is *dhu shujun*" means that the words in it are intertwined or it is like the words of a scholar who says that one's saying "the tree that is *mushajjan*" means its branches have turned around each other." The word *shajnah* is like the branches for the tree."

H 64, Ch. 3, h 28
Sahifah al-Rida':

It is narrated from al-Rida', from his ancestors from Ali ibn al-Husayn, 'Alayhim al-Salam, who has said the following:

'Asma' daughter of 'Umays said to me, "I was with your grandmother Fatimah, *'Alayha al-Salam,* when the Messenger of Allah, *O Allah, please, grant compensation to Muhammad and his family worthy of their services to your cause,* came in and she had a necklace of gold on her neck which Ali, *'Alayhi al-Salam,* had purchased from his share of his benefits. The Messenger of Allah, *O Allah grant compensation to Muhammad and his family worthy of their services to your cause,* said, 'The people must not deceive you by saying that you are the daughter of Muhammad and you are having the garments of the tyrants on you.' She then cut it off and sold it and with its price bought a slave and then set the slave free. The Messenger of Allah, *O Allah grant compensation to Muhammad and his family worthy of their services to your cause*, became very happy for what she did."

H 65, Ch. 3, h 29
Al-Khara'ij:

It is narrated from 'Imran ibn al-Haseen who has said the following:

Once I (the narrator) was sitting with the Messenger of Allah, *O Allah, please, grant compensation to Muhammad and his family worthy of their services to your cause,* when Fatimah, *'Alayha al-Salam,* came to him, because of hunger the color of her face was changed. He (the Messenger of Allah) then asked her to come close to him. She went close. He raised his hand and placed it on her chest on the place for the necklace (she was small at that time) and said, "O Lord, who satisfies hunger and raises the falling, please do not make Fatimah, *'Alayha al-Salam,* to suffer from hunger." I (the narrator) saw blood circulation on her face just as I had seen the paleness on her face. She had said that thereafter she never experience any hunger.

H 66, Ch. 3, h 30
Al-Khara'ij:

It is narrated from Jabir ibn 'Abd Allah who has said the following:

The Messenger of Allah, *O Allah grant compensation to Muhammad and his family worthy of their services to your cause,* lived for several days without any food until it became difficult for him. He went to the chambers of his wives but did not find any food with anyone of them. He then went to Fatimah, *'Alayha al-Salam,* and said, "My dearest daughter, do you have any food; I am hungry." She replied, "By Allah, by myself and my brother, I do not have anything for food." When he left, her housemaid sent two loaves of bread and some meat with it. She took it and covered it in a basin saying, "By Allah, I will not give preference to anyone - myself or others - beside the Messenger of Allah, they all needed a morsel of food. She then sent al-Hassan or al-Husayn, to the Messenger of Allah, *O Allah, please, grant compensation to Muhammad and his family worthy of their services to your cause,* who came back to her. She then said, "Allah has given us something which I have preserved for you." He (the Messenger of Allah) said, "My dearest daughter, please bring it for me without any delays." She then uncovered the basin and found it full of bread and meat. She looked at it in surprise and noticed that it was from Allah. She thanked Allah and said, "*O Allah, please, grant compensation to Muhammad, my father and his family worthy of their services to your cause.*" She then presented it to him and when he saw it he asked, "Wherefrom have you obtained this food?" She replied, "It is from Allah who grants sustenance to whoever He wills without accounting."

He (the Messenger of Allah), *O Allah, please, grant compensation to Muhammad and his family worthy of their services to your cause,* then sent someone to call Ali, *'Alayhi al-Salam.* Ali, *'Alayhi al-Salam* was called. The Messenger of Allah, *O Allah grant compensation to Muhammad and his family worthy of their services to your cause,* Ali, Fatimah, *'Alayha al-Salam,* al-Hassan and al-Husayn, and all the wives of the Holy Prophet, ate the food and they all were satisfied. Fatimah, *'Alayha al-Salam,* has said that the basin remained full of food as it was and I extended it to all of my neighbors, because Allah had placed blessing and a great deal of good in it."

H 67, Ch. 3, h 31
Al-Khara'ij:

> It is narrated that 'Abu 'Abd Allah, 'Alayhi al-Salam has said the following:

When Khadijah *'Alayha al-Salam,* died, Fatimah, *'Alayha al-Salam,* would seek shelter with the Messenger of Allah, *O Allah, please, grant compensation to Muhammad and his family worthy of their services to your cause.* She would move around him and ask, "O Messenger of Allah, where is my mother?" The Holy Prophet, *O Allah, please, grant compensation to Muhammad and his family worthy of their services to your cause,* would not answer her. She would then move around to find someone who could asked him (the Messenger of Allah) about where her mother is but he (the Messenger of Allah) did not know what he should say about it. Jibril, came and said, "Your Lord commands you to convey His *Salam* (the phrase of offering greeting of peace) to Fatimah, *'Alayha al-Salam,* and tell her that her mother lives in a house of reeds whose joints are made of gold and its pillars are of red ruby and it is situated between 'Asiyah, the woman of the pharaoh and Maryam (Mary) daughter of 'Imran.

Fatimah, *'Alayha al-Salam,* then said, "Allah His self is *Salam* (peace), from Him is peace and to Him belongs peace.

H 68, Ch. 3, h 32
Al-Khara'ij:

It is narrated that when Fatimah, *'Alayha al-Salam,* died 'Umm 'Ayman swore not to live in al-Madinah because she could not bear to see the places where Fatimah, *'Alayha al-Salam,* would be found. She decided to go to Makkah. On the way she became very thirsty and she raised her hands saying Lord, "I am the servant of Fatimah, *'Alayha al-Salam,* please do not cause me to die of thirst." Allah then sent her a bucket from the sky from which she drank water and thereafter did not need any water or food for seven years. People would send her (for some task) during the day of intense heat but she would not experience any thirst.

H 69, Ch. 3, h 33
Al-Khara'ij:

It is narrated that Salman (Rh) has said that Fatimah, *'Alayha al-Salam,* was grinding barely to prepare barely bread. The grinding stone was in front of her with its handle stained with blood and al-Husayn, was on one side of the room, severely hungry. I (the narrator) then said, "O daughter of the Messenger of Allah, you have worked hard. It is enough. Fizzah is around she can do it." Fatimah, *'Alayha al-Salam,* said the Messenger of Allah, *O Allah, please, grant compensation to Muhammad and his family worthy of their services to your cause,* has recommended that she should serve one day which she did yesterday." Salman (Rh) has said that he then said that he is a slave whom he (the Messenger of Allah) has set free. He should either grind the barely or calm down al-Husayn, *'Alayhi al-Salam."* She then said, "I am more gentle to calm him down and you can grind the barely." I then grinded a certain amount of barely and then I heard the call for *Salat* (prayer). I then went for *Salat* (prayer) with the Messenger of Allah, *O Allah, please, grant compensation to Muhammad and his family worthy of their services to your cause,* and when I completed the *Salat* (prayer) I told Ali, *'Alayhi al-Salam* about what I had seen. He wept and went out, then he came back smiling and the Messenger of Allah, *O Allah, please, grant compensation to Muhammad and his family worthy of their services to your cause,* asked about it (the reason for his smiles). He said,

45

"I went to the room of Fatimah, *'Alayha al-Salam,* and I found her resting on her back with al-Husayn, sleeping on her chest. I found the grinding stone spinning without any hand to turn it." The Messenger of Allah, *O Allah grant compensation to Muhammad and his family worthy of their services to your cause,* smiled and said, "O Ali, did you not know that Allah has certain angels who move around on earth to serve Muhammad and *Ale* (family) Muhammad up to the coming of the Hour, the Day of Judgment."

H 70, Ch. 3, h 34
Al-Khara'ij:

It is narrated that abu Dharr has said that once the Messenger of Allah, *O Allah, please, grant compensation to Muhammad and his family worthy of their services to your cause,* sent me to call Ali, *'Alayhi al-Salam.* I then went to his house and called him but no one answered but the grinding stone was running without anyone turning it. I then called and he came out and then he (the Messenger of Allah) spoke to him something which I did not understand. I then said (to myself), "It is strange. The grinding stone runs in the house of Ali without anyone turning it." He (the Messenger of Allah) said, "Allah has filled the heart of my daughter Fatimah, *'Alayha al-Salam,* and her body with belief and certainty and Allah knows her weakness, so He helps her in her lifetime sufficiently. Did you not know that Allah has certain angels who are assigned to help *Ale* (family of) Muhammad, *O Allah, please, grant compensation to Muhammad and his family worthy of their services to your cause.*

H 71, Ch. 3, h 35
Al-Khara'ij:

It is narrated that one morning Ali, asked Fatimah, *'Alayha al-Salam,* if she had any food at home. She replied that there was no food at home. He then went out and borrowed one dinar to buy food but he met al-Miqdad suffering from hunger as well as his family. He then gave that one dinar and himself went to the Masjid. He performed al-Zuhr and al-'Asr *Salat* (prayer) with the Messenger of Allah, *O Allah, please, grant compensation to Muhammad and his family worthy of their services to your cause,* and then the Messenger of Allah took hold of the hand of Ali and they both went to the house of Fatimah,

'Alayha al-Salam. They found Fatimah, 'Alayha al-Salam, in her place for Salat (prayer) and next to her they found a basin fizzing with boiling with food.

When she heard the voice of the Messenger of Allah, she came to offer Salam (the phrase of offering greeting of peace) to him. She was the most beloved one to him. He (the Messenger of Allah) responded to her Salam (the phrase of offering greeting of peace) likewise, placing his hand over her head. He (the Messenger of Allah) then said, "Please serve us the dinner, may Allah grant you forgiveness and He has already done so. She then brought the basin and placed it in front of the Messenger of Allah, O Allah, please, grant compensation to Muhammad and his family worthy of their services to your cause. He (the Messenger of Allah) then asked, "Wherefrom have you brought this food the like of which I have never seen, I have not sensed such excellent fragrance like its fragrance and I have never tasted any food as fine as this food?" Ali, 'Alayhi al-Salam, has said, "He (the Messenger of Allah) then placed his hand between my shoulders and said, 'This is in exchange for your dinar. Allah grants sustenance to whomever He wants without accounting.'"

I ('Allamah Majlisi) like to mention that al-Zamakhshari in al-Kashshaf when speaking of the story of Zakariya and Maryam (Mary) has narrated from the Messenger of Allah, O Allah grant compensation to Muhammad and his family worthy of their services to your cause, that he became hungry during the time of famine and Fatimah, 'Alayha al-Salam, sent him two loaves of bread with some meat which she had reserved for him but he (the Messenger of Allah) came to her with the bread and meat and asked her to come. She then opened it and found it full of bread and meat. She became amazed and realized that it had come from Allah who grants sustenance to whoever He wills without accounting. He then said, "All thanks belong to Allah who has made you to be like the leader of the women of the Israelites." Thereafter, the Messenger of Allah, O Allah, please, grant compensation to Muhammad and his family worthy of their services to your cause, called Ali, al-Hassan and al-Husayn, 'Alayhim al-Salam, and all the people in the family and they all ate to their satisfaction but still the food remained as it was and Fatimah, 'Alayha al-Salam, distributed it among the neighbors.

H 72, Ch. 3, h 36
Manaqib of ibn Shahr Ashub: Al-Khara'ij:

It is narrated that Ali *'Alayhi al-Salam* borrowed a certain amount of barely from a Jewish man, leaving a certain piece of the woolen garments of Fatimah, *'Alayha al-Salam,* as a security with him. The Jewish man kept the piece of garment in a room in his house. During the night his wife went to that room for a certain house chore and to her astonishment found the room all bright with a great shining light. She then moved out to inform her husband about the astonishing great light. They both were astonished and he had forgotten that a piece of the garment of Fatimah, *'Alayha al-Salam,* was placed there. He got up quickly to see the room and found that the light of the piece of the garment has spread over the area like the light of a full moon shining from nearby. He was astonished and looked carefully at the source of the light and found it out to be coming from the piece of the garment of Fatimah, *'Alayha al-Salam.* He ran out to inform his relatives and she ran out of the house to inform her relatives about the astonishing light. They all, numbering eighty people, gathered to examine the situation and they all embraced Islam.

H 73, Ch. 3, h 37
Al-Khara'ij:

It is narrated that a Jewish family had a wedding ceremony and they came to the Messenger of Allah, *O Allah, please, grant compensation to Muhammad and his family worthy of their services to your cause,* to allow Fatimah, *'Alayha al-Salam,* to join them in their ceremony to comply with a neighborly right. They insisted to make the Messenger of Allah to agree and accept their invitation and permit Fatimah, *'Alayha al-Salam,* to come to their house. He (the Messenger of Allah) said that she is the wife of Ali ibn abu Talib; thus, he is the one to give her permission. They asked him to intercede on their behalf before Ali. The Jews gathered from all places with all kinds of ornaments and fine dresses. The Jews had thought that Fatimah, *'Alayha al-Salam,* will join them in their ceremony very poorly dressed and she will be embarrassed. Jibril then came with a dress from the garden (paradise) the like of which in fineness was not seen. Fatimah, *'Alayha al-Salam,* dressed up in that dressed. The people were amazed because of the fineness of her dress, the colors of her dress and the fine fragrance of her dress. When Fatimah, *'Alayha al-Salam,* entered the house of the Jewish person the women fell in *Sujud* (prostrations) in front of her and a large number of the Jews embraced Islam because of what they saw.

H 74, Ch. 3, h 38
Tafsir of 'Iyashi:

It is narrated from Najm from abu Ja 'far, 'Alayhi al-Salam who has said the following:

Fatimah, *'Alayha al-Salam*, promised Ali, *'Alayhi al-Salam* that she will undertake household chores like making dough, baking bread and such other household works and Ali, *'Alayhi al-Salam* promised her to do the outdoor works such as bringing firewood inside the house, and to bring in food. One day Ali, *'Alayhi al-Salam* asked, "O Fatimah, *'Alayha al-Salam*, do you have any food at home?" She replied, "I swear by the one who has made your right great that for the last three days we did not have anything to serve you." He then said, "Why did you not inform me about it?" She replied, "It is because the Messenger of Allah, *O Allah, please, grant compensation to Muhammad and his family worthy of their services to your cause,* had forbidden me to ask his cousin for anything. If he brings anything on his own that is fine, otherwise, you must not ask him."

He (the narrator) has said that he (Ali *'Alayhi al-Salam*) then went out and borrowed one dinar when coming home, when it had already become evening time, he met al-Miqdad and asked him, "What had brought you out at this hour?" He replied, "It is hunger, by the one who has made your right of a great degree, O 'Amir al-Mu'minin." He (the narrator) has said that he asked abu Ja'far, "Was the Messenger of Allah living at that time?" He (the Imam), replied, "Yes, the Messenger of Allah, *O Allah, please, grant compensation to Muhammad and his family worthy of their services to your cause,* was alive." He (Ali) then said, "The same thing has made me also to come out. I have borrowed one dinar but I prefer that you should use it". He then gave the one dinar to al-Miqdad then departed him. He found the Messenger of Allah, *O Allah, please, grant compensation to Muhammad and his family worthy of their services to your cause,* sitting and Fatimah, *'Alayha al-Salam*, performing *Salat* (prayer) and between the two of them there was something covered. When she completed her *Salat* (prayer) she pulled that thing and it was a basin of bread and meat. He then asked, "O Fatimah, *'Alayha al-Salam*, wherefrom have you obtained this?"

She replied, "It is from Allah who gives sustenance to whomever He wills without account." The Messenger of Allah, *O Allah grant compensation to Muhammad and his family worthy of their services to your cause,* said, "Should I tell you about an example which is similar to your example and her example?" He replied, "Please do so O Messenger of Allah." He (the Messenger of Allah) said, "Your case is like the case of Zakariya who visited Maryam (Mary) in her place of *Salat* (prayer) and found with her some food. He then asked, "Wherefrom have you obtained this food?" She replied, "It is from Allah. Allah gives sustenance to whomever He wills." They used that food for a whole month and that basin is the basin from which *al-Qa'im* (the one who rises with divine authority and power) will eat and the same is with us."

H 75, Ch. 3, h 39
Manaqib of ibn Shahr Ashub:

Al-Khar Kushi in both of his books: al-Lawami' and Sharaf of al-Mustafa' (the purified one) through the chain of his narrators has narrated from Salman (Rh) and abu Bakr al-Shirazi in his book from abu Salih and abu Ishaq al-Tha'labi and Ali ibn Ahmad al-Ta'i and Muhammad ibn al-Hassan ibn 'Alawayh al-Qattan in their interpretations of al-Quran have narrated from Sa'id ibn Jubayr and Sufyan al-Thawri and abu Nu' aym al-Esfahani on what is revealed of al-Quran about Ali, *'Alayhi al-Salam* from Hammad ibn Salmah from Thabit from Anas and from abu Malik from ibn 'Abbas and al-Qadi al-Natanzi from Sufyan ibn 'Uyaynah from Ja'far al-Sadiq, *'Alayhi al-Salam* in which the words are his words about the meaning of the words of Allah, most Majestic, most Glorious, "He has made the two oceans meet each other, (55:19) but has created a barrier between them so that they will not merge totally" (55:20); he has said that Ali and Fatimah, *'Alayhima al-Salam,* are two deep oceans who do not dominate each other. In a narration it is said that the "barrier between them" is the Messenger of Allah between them. "From the two oceans pearls and coral come," is a reference to al-Hassan and al-Husayn, *'Alayhima al-Salam* (55:22).

This is about the meaning of the words of Allah, the most Majestic, the most Glorious:

Their Lord answered their prayers saying, "I do not neglect anyone's labor, whether the laborer be a male or a female. You are all related to one another. Those who migrated from Makkah, those who were expelled from their homes, those who were tortured for My cause, and those who fought and were killed for My cause will find their sins expiated by Me and I will admit them into the gardens wherein streams flow. It will be their reward from Allah. Allah grants the best rewards." (3:195)

'Ammar ibn Yasar has said that the word "male" refers to Ali, and the word "female" refer to Fatimah, *'Alayhima al-Salam,* during their journey of migration to the Messenger of Allah during the night.

This is about the meaning of the words of Allah, the most Majestic, the most Glorious:

"(I swear) by . . . and by that (Power) which created the male and female," (92:3) Al-Baqir, has said that the word "male" refers to Ali, and the word "female" refers to Fatimah, *'Alayhima al-Salam,* "you strive in various ways." (92:4) (your good deeds are of various kinds) "We shall facilitate the path to bliss (92:5) for those who spend for the cause of Allah, (92:6) observe piety, and believe in receiving rewards from Allah," (92:7) by giving away their own food for the sake of Allah, fast to fulfill their vows, giving his ring in charity during his bowing position in *Salat* (prayer) and his giving preference to al-Miqdad over his own self about the dinar. He (the Imam) has said that "spend for the cause of Allah" is a reference to the garden (paradise) as good reward from Allah. "We shall facilitate the path to bliss" (is a reference to grant him the position of *Imamat* (leadership with divine authority) in goodness a good example and the father of *'A'immah,* (Imams) to make him happy in ease).

This is about the meaning of the words of Allah, the most Majestic, the most Glorious:

"We had commanded Adam (certain matters). He forgot Our commandments and We did not find in him the determination (to fulfill Our commandments)." (20:115) Al-Baqir, *'Alayhi al-Salam,* has said that the "commandment" is a reference to the instructions of Allah for Adam, *'Alayhi al-Salam,* about Muhammad, Ali, Fatimah, al-Hassan and al-Husayn, and their descendants after them, *'Alayhim al-Salam,* and this is how it was revealed to

Muhammad, *O Allah, please, grant compensation to Muhammad and his family worthy of their services to your cause.*

Al-Qadi abu Muhammad al-Karkhi in his book has narrated from al-Sadiq, 'Alayhi al-Salam who has said the following:

This is about the meaning of the words of Allah, the most Majestic, the most Glorious:

"Do not address the Messenger as you would call each other. Allah knows those who secretly walk away from you and hide themselves. Those who oppose the Messengers should beware, lest misfortune or a painful torment should befall them." (24:63)

He (al-Sadiq, *'Alayhi al-Salam*) has said that Fatimah, *'Alayha al-Salam,* has said, "After the revelation of this verse I feared to call him, (the Messenger of Allah, *O Allah, please, grant compensation to Muhammad and his family worthy of their services to your cause*), 'O dear father.' So I would call him, 'O Messenger of Allah.' He (the Messenger of Allah) turned away twice or three times (in disregard) and then he (the Messenger of Allah) said, 'O Fatimah, *'Alayha al-Salam,* this verse does not apply to you or your family and not to your descendants. You are from me and I am from you. This applies to the hardhearted and harsh mannered al-Quraysh, the people of haughtiness and arrogance. Call me, "O father." It is livelier for the heart and more pleasing to the Lord. You must also take notice that Allah has spoken of twelve women in al-Quran in a figurative manner:

We said, "O Adam, stay with your spouse (Eve) in the garden . . ." (2:35)

Allah has told the unbelievers the story of the Wives of Noah and Lot as a parable. . . . (66:10)

To the believers, as a parable, Allah has told the story of the wife of Pharaoh . . . (66:11)

About the wife of Ibrahim, *'Alayhi al-Salam* Allah has said, "His wife, who was standing nearby..." (11:71)

About the wife of Zakariya Allah has said, "We answered his prayer and granted him his son, John, by making his wife fruitful . . ." (21:90)

About Zulaykh' Allah has said, ". . .The wife of the King said, 'Now the truth has come to light. It was I who tried to seduce Joseph. He is, certainly, a truthful man." (12:51)

About the wife of Prophet Ayyub Allah has said, "We answered his prayer, relieved him from his hardships, brought his family (back to him). . ." (21:84)

About the Queen of Sheba Allah has said, "I found a woman ruling the people there and she possessed all things (almost everything) and a great throne." (27:23)

About the wife of Musa Allah has said, "He (*Shu'ayb*) said to (Moses), "I want to give one of my daughters to you in marriage . . ." (28:27)

About Hafsah and 'A'ishah Allah has said, "The Prophet told a secret to one of his wives, . . ." (66:3)

About Khadijah *'Alayha al-Salam,* Allah has said, "And did He not find you with a great deal of dependents and make you rich. . . ?" (93:8)

About Fatimah, *'Alayha al-Salam,* Allah has said, "He has made the two oceans meet each other" (55:19)

Allah then has spoken of the quality of repentance of Eve, "They replied, "Lord, we have done injustice to our souls. . . ." (7:23)

About the wishes of the wife of Pharaoh Allah has said, "Lord, establish for me a house in Paradise in your presence. Rescue me from the Pharaoh and his deeds and save me from the unjust people." (66:11)

About Sarah and her entertaining guest Allah has said, "His wife, who was standing nearby, laughed . . . ." (11:71)

About the intelligence of Queen of Sheba Allah has said, "She said, 'When Kings enter a town they do destroy it and disrespect its honorable people.' That, indeed, is what they do." (27:34)

About the bashfulness of the wife of Musa, Allah has said, "One of the women, walking bashfully, came to Moses . . ." (28:25)

About the good deeds of Khadijah *'Alayha al-Salam,* Allah has said, "And did He not find you with a great deal of dependents and make you rich (with revelation for their guidance)?" (93:8)

About good advice for Hafsah and 'A'ishah Allah has said, "Wives of the Prophet, you are not like other women. If you have fear of Allah, do not be tender in your speech lest people whose hearts are sick may lust after you. Speak to people in a normal manner. (33:32) You must stay in your homes and do not display yourselves after the manner of the (pre-Islamic) age of darkness. Be steadfast in the prayer, pay the religious tax, and obey Allah and His messenger. O People of the house, Allah wants to remove all kinds of uncleanness from you and to purify you thoroughly." (33:33)

About the infallibility of Fatimah, *'Alayha al-Salam,* Allah has said, "If anyone disputes (your prophesy) after that knowledge has come to you, say, "Allow each of us bring our children, our women, and your women. . ." (3:61)

Allah, the most High, has given ten things to ten women:

He gave repentance to Eve, the wife of Adam, *'Alayhi al-Salam,* beauty to Sarah, the wife of Ibrahim' Protection of kinship to the wife of Orophet Ayyub, Honor to the wife of the pharaoh, wisdom to Zulaykha' the wife of Yusuf, intelligence to Bilqis the wife of Sulayman, patience of Barkha' mother of Musa, purity to Maryam (Mary) mother of 'Isa, contentment to Khadijah *'Alayha al-Salam,* the wife of al-Mustafa' (the purified one) and knowledge to Fatimah, *'Alayha al-Salam,* the wife of Ali al-Murtaza' (the pleasing one).

Allah has granted acceptance to the prayers of ten people. About Noah Allah has said, "Noah called for help. How blessed was the answer which he received." (37:75)

About Yusuf Allah has said, "His Lord heard his prayers and protected him from their guile; He is All-hearing and All-knowing. (12:34)

About Musa and Harun Allah has said, "The Lord replied, "Moses, the prayer of your brother and yourself has been heard. Both of you must be steadfast (in your faith) and must not follow the ignorant ones." (10:89)

About prophet Yunus Allah has said, "We answered his prayer and saved him from his grief. Thus We save the faithful ones." (21:88)

About Ayyub Allah has said, "When Job prayed, 'O Lord, I have been afflicted with hardships. Have mercy on me; You are the Most Merciful of those who have mercy," (21:83) We answered his prayer, relieved him from his hardships, brought his family (back to him), and gave him twice as much property as that (which was destroyed). It was a mercy from Us and a reminder for the worshippers." (21:84)

About Prophet Zakariya Allah has said, "We answered his prayer and granted him his son, John, by making his wife fruitful . . ." (21:90)

About the sincere people Allah has said, "Your Lord has said, "Pray to Me for I shall answer your prayers. Those who are too proud to worship Me will soon go to hell in disgrace." (40:60)

About the people in desperation Allah has said, "(Are the idols worthier or) the One who answers the prayers of the distressed ones, removes their hardship, and makes you the successors in the land? Is there any Lord besides Allah? In fact, you take very little heed." (27:62)

About the people who pray Allah has said, "(Muhammad), if any of My servants ask you about Me, (tell them that the Lord says) "I certainly am near; I answer the prayers of those who pray." Allow My servants to ask Me for an answer to their call and believe in Me so that perhaps they may know the right direction," (2:186) about Fatimah, *'Alayha al-Salam,* and her husband *'Alayhima al-Salam*: Their Lord answered their prayers saying, "I do not neglect anyone's labor, whether the laborer be male or female. You are all related to one another. Those who migrated from Makkah, those who were expelled from their homes, those who were tortured for My cause, and those who fought and were killed for My cause will find their sins expiated by Me and I will admit them into the gardens wherein streams flow. It will be their reward from Allah. Allah grants the best rewards." (3:195).

The Messenger of Allah, *O Allah grant compensation to Muhammad and his family worthy of their services to your cause,* would worry about ten things of great importance:

1. He missed his home town, his place of birth about which Allah revealed the following verse of al-Quran, "(Muhammad), Allah, Who has commanded you to follow the guidance of the Quran, will certainly return you victoriously to your place of birth. Say, "My Lord knows best who has brought guidance and who is in plain error." (28:85)

2. He was worried about changes to take place in al-Quran after him. Allah, most High, revealed this verse of al-Quran, "We Ourselves have revealed the Quran and We are its protectors." (15:9)

3. He worried about punishment falling on his nation (followers). Allah, most High, then revealed this verse of al-Quran, "Allah would not punish them while you were among them nor while they were asking for forgiveness." (8:33)

4. He worried about the progress for his religion. Allah, most High, revealed this verse of al-Quran about it, "It is Allah Who sent His messenger with guidance and a true religion that will prevail over all other religions, even though the pagans may dislike it." (9:33)

5. He worried about the believing people after him. Allah, most High, then revealed this verse of al-Quran, "Allah strengthens the faith of the believers by the true Words in this world and in the life to come. He causes the unjust to go astray and does whatever He pleases." (14:27)

6. He worried about (the mischief of) the adversaries of his nation (followers). Allah, most High, revealed this verse of al-Quran, ". . . On the Day of Judgment, Allah will not disgrace the Prophet and those who have believed in him. Their lights will shine in front of them and to their right. They will say, "Our Lord, perfect our light for us and forgive our sins. You have power over all things." (66:8)

7. He worried about the issue of intercession. Allah, most High, revealed this verse of al-Quran, ". . . Your Lord will soon grant you sufficient favors to please you." (93:5)

8. He worried about mischief after him against the executor of his Will. Allah, most High, revealed this verse of al-Quran, "We shall exact retribution upon them either after your death (43:41) or show them to you suffering the torment with which We had threatened them. We are certainly dominant over them all." (43:42)

9. He worried about his successors from the children of Ali, 'Alayhi al-Salam. Allah, most High, then revealed this verse of al-Quran, "Allah has promised the righteously striving believers to appoint them as His deputies on earth, as He had appointed those who lived before. He will make the religion that He has chosen for them to stand supreme. He will replace their fear with peace and security so that they will worship Allah alone and consider no one equal to Him. Whoever becomes an unbeliever after this will be a sinful person." (24:55)

10. He worried about his daughter during his migration. Allah, most High, then revealed this verse of al-Quran, "It is these who speak of Allah while standing, sitting, or resting on their sides and who think about the creation of the heavens and the earth and say, 'Lord, you have not created all this without reason. Glory be to you. Lord, save us from the torment of the fire.' (3:191) Those whom You submit to the fire are certainly disgraced. There is no helper for the unjust. (3:192) 'Lord, we have heard the person calling to the faith and have accepted his call. Forgive our sins, expiate our bad deeds, and allow us die with the righteous ones. (3:193) Lord, grant us the victory that You have promised your Messenger and do not disgrace us on the Day of Judgment; You are the One who never ignores His promise.' (3:194) Their Lord answered their prayers saying, 'I do not neglect anyone's labor, whether the laborer be male or female. You are all related to one another. Those who migrated from Makkah, those who were expelled from their homes, those who were tortured for My cause, and those who fought and were killed for My cause will find their sins expiated by Me and I will admit them into the gardens wherein streams flow. It will be their reward from Allah. Allah grants the best rewards.'" (3:195)

The leaders of repenting people are four:

1. One is Adam, *'Alayhi al-Salam,* who is quoted in al-Quran to have said, "They replied, 'Lord, we have done injustice to our souls. If You will not forgive us and have mercy on us, we shall certainly have incurred a great loss.'" (7:23)

2. The second one is Prophet Yunus about whom al-Quran has said this, "*Dhan Nun* (Jonah, the companion of the Whale) went away angry (over the deeds of his people) and thought that We would never apply Our measures upon him, but in darkness he cried, 'Lord, You are the Only Lord whom I glorify. Indeed I have been of those who do wrong to themselves, (so forgive me).' (21:87) We answered his prayer and saved him from his grief. Thus We save the faithful ones." (21:88)

3. The third one is Dawud, *'Alayhi al-Salam* about whom al-Quran has said this, "David realized that it was a test from Us so he asked forgiveness from his Lord and knelt down before Him in repentance." (38:24)

4. The fourth one is Fatimah, *'Alayha al-Salam,* about whom al-Quran has said this, "It is these who speak of Allah while standing, sitting, or resting on their sides and who think about the creation of the heavens and the earth and say, 'Lord, you have not created all this without reason. Glory be to you. Lord, save us from the torment of the fire.'" (3:191)

The Four virtuous ones who experienced great fear:

1. One of them was Asiyah who was tortured with various kinds of tortures and would say, "To the believers, as a parable, Allah has told the story of the wife of Pharaoh who said, "Lord, establish for me a house in Paradise in your presence. Rescue me from the Pharaoh and his deeds and save me from the unjust people." (66:11)

2. The second one was Maryam (Mary) who for fear from people fled away. About Maryam (Mary) al-Quran has said this, "Then she heard the baby saying, 'Do not be sad. Your Lord has caused a stream to run at your feet.'" (19:24)

3. The third one was Khadijah, *'Alayha al-Salam,* whom the women of al-Quraysh had boycotted because of the Holy Prophet, *O Allah, please, grant compensation to Muhammad and his family worthy of their services to your cause.*

4. Fatimah, *'Alayha al-Salam,* in her heart breaking conditions said, "Was the Messenger of Allah, *O Allah, please, grant compensation to Muhammad and his family worthy of their services to your cause,* not my father? Why his children are not given protection? How quickly have you seized the opportunity and how quickly have you turned back!"

The leading people among the weeping people are eight: 1. Adam, *'Alayhi al-Salam,* 2. Nuh, 3. Ya'qub, 4. Yusuf, 5. Shu'ayb, 6. Dawud, 7. Fatimah, *'Alayha al-Salam,* 8. and Zayn al-'Abidin, *'Alayhi al-Salam.*

Al-Sadiq *'Alayhi al-Salam* has said that Fatimah, *'Alayha al-Salam,* wept for the Messenger of Allah, *O Allah, please, grant compensation to Muhammad and his family worthy of their services to your cause,* so much that inhabitants of al-Madinah became disturbed and they said to her, "We are disturbed very much because of your weeping. You must now weep either only during the night or during the day." She then would move to the cemetery of the martyrs and weep there.

The best of the women of the world are four:

It is said in the book of abu Bakr al-Shirazi and abu al-Huzayl has narrated from Muqatil, from Muhammad ibn al-Hanafiyah from his father who has said the following:

The Messenger of Allah, *O Allah grant compensation to Muhammad and his family worthy of their services to your cause,* reading from al-Quran "Allah has chosen and has purified you . . . to the end of the verse," then said to me, "O Ali, the best of the women of the worlds are four: They are 1. Maryam (Mary) daughter of 'Imran, 2. Khadijah *'Alayha al-Salam,* daughter Khuwaylid, 3. Fatimah, *'Alayha al-Salam,* daughter of Muhammad and 4. Asiyah daughter of Muzaham."

Abu Nu'aym in the book al-Hulyah, ibn al-Bay' in the al-Musnad, al-Khatib in the book of history, ibn Battah in the book al-Ebanah, Ahmad al-Sham'ani in the book al-Fada'il through the chain of their narrators have narrated from Mu'ammar from Qatadah from Anas and al-Tha'labi in his interpretations of al-Quran and al-Salami in the history of Khurasan, and abu Salih al-Mu'adhdhin in the book al-Arba'in through the chain of their narrators have narrated from abu Hurayrah and al-Sha'bi has narrated from Jabir ibn 'Abd Allah and Sa'id ibn al-Musayyib, and Kurayb has narrated from ibn 'Abbas, Muqatil has narrated from Sulayman from al-Dahhak from ibn 'Abbas and abu Mas'ud has narrated from 'Abd al-Razzaq and Ahmad and Ishaq all have narrated from the Holy Prophet, *O Allah, please, grant compensation to Muhammad and his family worthy of their services to your cause,* and the words are those of al-Hulyah that he, the Holy Prophet, *O Allah, please, grant compensation to Muhammad and his family worthy of their services to your cause,* said, "As examples of perfection (حسبك) in matters of excellence among the women of the worlds the following women are the best. They are Maryam (Mary) daughter of 'Imran, Khadijah *'Alayha al-Salam,* daughter of Khuwalid, Fatimah, *'Alayha al-Salam,* daughter of Muhammad and Asiyah wife of the pharaoh.

In the narration of Muqatil, al-Dahhak, and 'Ikramah from ibn 'Abbas it is said that the best among these women is Fatimah, *'Alayha al-Salam.*

In the book al-Fada'il from 'Abd al-Malik al-'Akbari and Musnad (of) Ahmad through the chain of their narrators from Kurayb from ibn 'Abbas that the Holy Prophet, *O Allah, please, grant compensation to Muhammad and his family worthy of their services to your cause,* has said that Maryam (Mary) is the leader of the women of the garden (paradise) . . . to the end the narration is the same.

In the history of Baghdad through the chain of the narrators of al-Khatib from Humayd al-Tawil from Anas who has said that the Holy Prophet, *O Allah, please, grant compensation to Muhammad and his family worthy of their services to your cause,* has said that the best of the women of the worlds are . . . to end the Hadith is the same.

Also there are narrations that the Holy Prophet, *O Allah, please, grant compensation to Muhammad and his family worthy of their services to your cause,* has said that she, Fatimah, *'Alayha al-Salam,* is more excellent than other women of the worlds in this world and in the next world.

'A'ishah has narrated so also have done others from the Holy Prophet, *'Alayhi al-Salam* who said, "O Fatimah, *'Alayha al-Salam,* there is glad news for you that Allah, most High, has chosen you from among the women of the worlds and from among the Muslim women and (Islam) is the best among the religions."

Hudhayfah has said that the Holy Prophet, *'Alayhi al-Salam* has said, "An angel came to me to tell me of the glad news that Fatimah, *'Alayha al-Salam,* is the best among the women of the garden (paradise) or the women of my nation (followers)."

Al-Bukhari and Muslim in their Sahih, abu Sa'adat in al-Fada'il of al-'Asharah, abu Bakr ibn Shaybah, in 'Amaliyah, al-Daylami in his Firdaws has narrated that the Holy Prophet, *O Allah, please, grant compensation to Muhammad and his family worthy of their services to your cause,* has said that Fatimah, *'Alayha al-Salam,* is the leader of the women of the garden (paradise).

In Hulyah abu Nu'aym has narrated from Jabir ibn Samrah from the Holy Prophet, *'Alayhi al-Salam* in a narration saying that she is the leader of the women on the Day of Judgment.

In the history of al-Biladhuri it is narrated from the Holy Prophet, *'Alayhi al-Salam* who said to Fatimah, *'Alayha al-Salam,* "You are the fastest in my family to join me." She then remained quiet. He, the Holy Prophet, *'Alayhi al-Salam* then said, "Do you not agree to be the leader of the women of the garden (paradise)." She then smiled.

H 75, Ch. 3, h 40
Manaqib of ibn Shahr Ashub:

Al-sha'bi has narrated from Masruq from 'A'ishah who has said the following:

The Holy Prophet, *O Allah, please, grant compensation to Muhammad and his family worthy of their services to your cause,* spoke to Fatimah, *'Alayha al-Salam,* secretly for which she laughed. I then asked her about its reason and she replied, He said to me, "Are you not happy that you are the leader of the women of the people of the garden (paradise) or the women of my nation (followers)?"

In the book Hulyatul Awliya' and the book of al-Shirazi 'Imran ibn Al-Haseen has narrated from Jabir ibn Samrah who has said that the Holy Prophet, visited Fatimah, *'Alayha al-Salam,* and asked, "How are you my dear daughter?" She replied, "I am in pain and it gives me more pain because I do not have any food to eat." The Holy Prophet, then said, "O my dear daughter are you not happy that you are the leader of the women of the worlds?" She then asked, "Where then does Maryam (Mary) daughter of 'Imran stand?" The Holy Prophet, replied, "She is the leader of the women of her world but you are the leader of the women of your world and your husband is the master in the world and in the next world."

It was said to al-Sadiq that the Holy Prophet, has said that Fatimah, *'Alayha al-Salam,* is the leader of the women of the garden (paradise) meaning the leader of the women of her world.

He (the Imam), *'Alayhi al-Salam* said, "That is for Maryam (Mary). Fatimah, *'Alayha al-Salam,* is the leader of the women of the garden (paradise) of the people of the past and the future."

It is narrated in a Hadith that Asiyah daughter of Muzaham, Maryam (Mary) daughter of 'Imran and Khadijah, *'Alayha al-Salam,* will walk in front of Fatimah, *'Alayha al-Salam,* as a curtain before her to the garden (paradise).

Bazl al-Harawi asked al-Husayn ibn Ruh, "How many daughters did the Holy Prophet, *'Alayhi al-Salam* have?" He replied, "They were four." He then asked, "Who among them was more excellent?" He replied, "Fatimah, *'Alayha al-Salam,* is the most excellent one." He then asked, "Why is she the most excellent one when she is the youngest among them and lived for the shortest time with the Messenger of Allah, *O Allah, please, grant compensation to Muhammad and his family worthy of their services to your cause?*" He replied, "It is for two special reasons which Allah has granted to her: She inherited from the Messenger of Allah, *O Allah, please, grant compensation to Muhammad and his family worthy of their services to your cause,* and the offspring of the Messenger of Allah continued from her and this was because of her sincere intention that Allah had found in her."

Al-Murtaza' (r.h) has said that excellence is the plenteousness of rewarding works that come into being with sincerity, certainty and pure intention. This fact, without any hindrance, may apply to her case and her sisters. The fact that she is the most excellent of the women of the worlds is a matter of consensus of Imamiyah people because of the degree of honor that the Messenger of Allah, O *Allah, please, grant compensation to Muhammad and his family worthy of their services to your cause,* maintained for Fatimah, *'Alayha al-Salam,* exclusively, before her sisters, is a fact which does not need any further argumentation.

Jami' al-Tirmizi, Ebanah of al-'Akbari, news about Fatimah, *'Alayha al-Salam,* by abu Ali al-Sawli, history of Khurasan by al-Salami through the chain of narrators all from al-Taymi who has said the following:

He (the narrator) has said that once he with his aunt visited 'A'ishah and her aunt asked 'A'ishah, "What was the reason for your rise against Ali?" 'A'ishah said, "Never mention it. No one among men was more beloved to the Messenger of Allah than Ali and from among the no women was more beloved than Fatimah, *'Alayha al-Salam.*"

Fada'il al-'Asharah by abu Sa'adat, Fada'il al-Sahabah by al-Sam'ani, in a narration from al-Sharik and A'mash, and Kathir al-Nawa, and ibn al-Hajjam all of them from Jami' ibn 'Umayr from 'A'ishah from 'Usama from the Holy Prophet, *O Allah, please, grant compensation to Muhammad and his family worthy of their services to your cause,* and it is narrated from 'Abd Allah ibn 'Ata' from 'Abd Allah ibn Buraydah from his father who has said that he asked the Messenger of Allah, *O Allah, please, grant compensation to Muhammad and his family worthy of their services to your cause,* "Who among the women is more beloved to you?" He (the Messenger of Allah) replied, "She is Fatimah, *'Alayha al-Salam.*" I (the narrator) then asked, "Who among men is more beloved to you?" He (the Messenger of Allah) replied, "He is her husband."

Jami' al-Tirmizi:

Buraydah has said that the most beloved to the Messenger of Allah, *O Allah, please, grant compensation to Muhammad and his family worthy of their services to your cause,* among the women was Fatimah, *'Alayha al-Salam,* and from among the men was Ali.

In Quwat al-Qulub it is narrated from ibn abu Talib al-Makki, in al-Arba'in from abu Salih al-Mu'dhdhin, Fada'il al-Sahabah from Ahmad through a chain of narrators from Sufyan, from al-'A'mash from abu al-Jahaf from Jami' from 'A'ishah who has said the following:

Ali, *'Alayhi al-Salam* asked the Messenger of Allah, *O Allah, please, grant compensation to Muhammad and his family worthy of their services to your cause,* when he sat between him and Fatimah, *'Alayha al-Salam,* when they were resting on their sides, which one of us is more beloved to you? Is it she or I?" He (the Messenger of Allah), *O Allah, please, grant compensation to Muhammad and his family worthy of their services to your cause,* replied, "She is more beloved (*Ahabb*) to me and you are more dear (*'A'azz*) to me than she is."

In another narration from Jabir ibn 'Abd Allah it is narrated that Ali and Fatimah, *'Alayha al-Salam,* each one of them expressed pride over the other in merit and excellence. Jibril then informed the Messenger of Allah, *O Allah, please, grant compensation to Muhammad and his family worthy of their services to your cause,* about it saying that they have lengthened their argumentation over each one's love for you, so you must settle between them.

He (the Messenger of Allah) then visited them and informed them of their words. He then turned to Fatimah, *'Alayha al-Salam,* and said, "You have the sweetness of the child and he has the dearness of man and he is more beloved to me than you." Fatimah, *'Alayha al-Salam,* then said, "I swear by the one who has chosen you, selected, has granted you guidance and has guided the nation (followers) through you that I will continue to acknowledge in his favor as long as I live.

'Amr al-Sha'bi, al-Hassan al-Basri, Sufyan al-Thawri, Mujahid, ibn Jubayr, Jabir al-Ansari, Muhammad Al-Baqir, and Ja'far al-Sadiq have narrated that the Messenger of Allah, *O Allah, please, grant compensation to Muhammad and his family worthy of their services to your cause,* has said, "Fatimah, *'Alayha al-Salam,* is but a part of myself. Whoever makes her angry makes me angry."

Al-Bukhari has extracted this Hadith from al-Musawwar ibn Makhramah.

In the narration of Jabir it is said, "One who causes her suffering has caused me to suffer and whoever causes suffering to me has caused suffering to Allah."

In Muslim and al-Hulyah it is said in the following words: "Only Fatimah, *'Alayha al-Salam,* is my daughter, and a part of myself. Whatever troubles her troubles me and whoever causes suffering to her causes me to suffer."

H 76, Ch. 3, h 41
Manaqib of ibn Shahr Ashub:

Sa'd ibn abu Waqqas has said that he heard the Messenger of Allah, *O Allah, please, grant compensation to Muhammad and his family worthy of their services to your cause,* say, "Fatimah, *'Alayha al-Salam,* is a part of myself. One who makes her happy makes me happy and one who troubles her troubles me. Fatimah, *'Alayha al-Salam,* is the dearest of all people to me."

Mustadrak of al-Hakim:

It is narrated from Sahl ibn Ziyad from 'Isma'il and in Hulyah abu Nu'aym has said that from al-Zuhri, ibn Malikah, from al-Musawwir ibn Makhramah who has said the following:

The Holy Prophet, *O Allah, please, grant compensation to Muhammad and his family worthy of their services to your cause,* has said, "Fatimah, *'Alayha al-Salam,* is my intertwined branch, whatever causes stress to her causes stress for me also and whatever brings ease for her brings ease for me also."

Suhayl ibn 'Abd Allah visited 'Umar ibn Abd al-Aziz and said, "Your people say that you give preference to the children of Fatimah, *'Alayha al-Salam,* over them." 'Umar said, "I have heard trusted companions of the Holy Prophet, who have said that the Holy Prophet, *O Allah, please, grant compensation to Muhammad and his family worthy of their services to your cause,* has said, "Fatimah, *'Alayha al-Salam,* is a part of myself. One who brings happiness to her makes me also happy and one who makes her angry makes me also angry." By Allah, I am right to seek the happiness of the Messenger of Allah because his happiness is her happiness and her happiness is achieved by making her children happy."

They knew that her happiness makes the Holy Prophet, happy very much and it makes him angry what causes her to become angry.

The above words of the Holy Prophet, show that she is infallible because (God forbid) if she was a sinner it would not make the Holy Prophet, angry because of her anger; for because of sin one becomes punishable in obedience to the Holy Prophet, *'Alayhi al-Salam.*

Abu Tha'labah al-Khushni has said that whenever the Messenger of Allah would return from a journey first he visit Fatimah, *'Alayha al-Salam.* On his arrival she would stand up for him, embrace him and kiss between his eyes.

In al-Arba'in through the chain of his narrators the author has narrated from al-Nadr ibn Shumayl from Maysarah from al-Minhal from 'A'ishah daughter of Talhah from 'A'ishah daughter of abu Bakr, and in Fada'il of al-Sam'ani through the chain of his narrators from 'Ikramah who has said that when the Holy Prophet, *O Allah, please, grant compensation to Muhammad and his family worthy of their services to your cause,* would return from his expeditions he would visit (kiss) Fatimah, *'Alayha al-Salam.*

They have narrated from 'A'ishah that whenever Fatimah, *'Alayha al-Salam,* would visit the Messenger of Allah, *O Allah, please, grant compensation to Muhammad and his family worthy of their services to your cause,* he would stand up for her from his sit, kiss her head and make her sit in his own seat. When he would meet her they would kiss each other and sit together.

Abu al-Sa'adat in Fada'il al-'Asharah, ibn al-Mu'adhdhin in al-Arba'in, through the chain of narrators of 'Ikramah from ibn 'Abbas, abu Tha'labah al-Khushni, and Nafi' from ibn 'Umar have said the following:

Whenever the Holy Prophet, *O Allah, please, grant compensation to Muhammad and his family worthy of their services to your cause,* would decide to go on a journey Fatimah, *'Alayha al-Salam,* would become the last person to say farewell and on his return from a journey the Holy Prophet would meet Fatimah, 'Alayha al-Salam, before everyone else. Had it not been because of her excellence in the sight of Allah, the Messenger of Allah, *O Allah, please, grant compensation to Muhammad and his family worthy of their services to your cause,* would not treat her as he did. It is because she was his child and Allah has commanded the children to honor their parents, thus it would not have been permissible for him to treat her as he did because of it being contrary to the command of Allah, most High.

Abu Sa'id al-Khudhari has said that Fatimah, 'Alayha al-Salam, was the dearest among the people to the Messenger of Allah, *O Allah, please, grant compensation to Muhammad and his family worthy of their services to your cause.* One day he visited her when she was performing *Salat* (prayer) and she heard the Messenger of Allah, *O Allah, please, grant compensation to Muhammad and his family worthy of their services to your cause,* from her place of *Salat* (prayer). She discontinued her *Salat* (prayer), came out of the place of her *Salat* (prayer) and offered him *Salam* (the phrase of offering greeting of peace). He (the Messenger of Allah) then placed his hand over her head and said, "My dear daughter, how is your evening, may Allah grant you blessings, please serve us dinner, may Allah forgive and He has already done so."

In reports about Fatimah, 'Alayha al-Salam, it is narrated from abu Ali al-Sawli who has said that 'Abd Allah ibn al-Hassan has said that once the Holy Prophet, *O Allah, please, grant compensation to Muhammad and his family worthy of their services to your cause,* visited Fatimah, 'Alayha al-Salam, and she brought for him pieces of dry barley bread with which he (the Messenger of Allah) discontinued his fast. Then he said, "My dearest daughter, this was the first time your father had any bread after three days." Fatimah, 'Alayha al-Salam, wept. The Messenger of Allah then wiped her face with his hand.

Abu Salih al-Mu'adhdhin in al-Arba'in through a chain of narrators from Sha'bah from 'Amr ibn Murrah from Ibrahim from Masruq from ibn Mas'ud who has said the following:

The Messenger of Allah, *O Allah grant compensation to Muhammad and his family worthy of their services to your cause,* has said that when Allah commanded me to give Fatimah, 'Alayha al-Salam, in marriage to Ali, I then did so and Jibril said to me, "Allah has made a garden of pearls in which from every reed to the reed there is a ruby decorated with nuggets of gold. The ceilings thereof are of green emerald and the arches in it are crowned with rubies. The chambers in it is made of one brick of gold, one brick of silver, one brick of pearl, one brick of ruby and one brick of aquamarine. Also there are fountains which flow in its surroundings with canals on which there are domes of pearls which are branched with chains of gold and are surrounded by trees. On every branch there is a dome under each of which there is couch of white pearl with a covering of silk brocade of thick silk woven with gold threads and its floor is covered with saffron parted with musk and ambergris. Under every dome there is *al-Hawra' al-'in* and the dome has one hundred doors in each of which there are two maidens. Under every dome there are two trees. Also in every dome there are furnishings and calligraphic writings around the domes with verse 255 of chapter two of al-Quran.

I then asked Jibril, "For whom has Allah built this garden (paradise)?" He replied, "He has built it for Ali and Fatimah, *'Alayhima al-Salam,* your daughter besides their garden (paradise) as their gift is the gift that Allah has gifted them so your eye, O Messenger of Allah, be delighted."

H 77, Ch. 3, h 42
Manaqib of ibn Shahr Ashub:

Ibn 'Abd Rabbihi al-'Undulusi in al-'iqd al-Farid has narrated from 'Abd Allah ibn al-Zubayr in a narration from Mu'awiyah ibn abu Sufyan who has said that once al-Hassan ibn Ali came to his grandfather, *O Allah, please, grant compensation to Muhammad and his family worthy of their services to your cause,* and he stumbled on the back bottom of his shirt. He whispered secretly to the Messenger of Allah, *O Allah, please, grant compensation to Muhammad and his family worthy of their services to your cause,* and saw his color changed. The Holy Prophet, *'Alayhi al-Salam* stood up and moved to the house of Fatimah, *'Alayha al-Salam.* He held her hand and pulled it to himself firmly saying, "O Fatimah, *'Alayha al-Salam,* beware of making Ali angry, because Allah becomes angry for his anger and He becomes happy for his happiness and then he (the Messenger of Allah) went to Ali then held his hand then slightly pulled to himself and said, "O abu al-Hassan, beware of the anger of Fatimah, *'Alayha al-Salam,* because the angels become angry for her anger and they become happy with her happiness."

I (the narrator) then asked, "O Messenger of Allah, how is it that you went out concerned and but you have come back happy."

He (the Messenger of Allah) replied, "O Mu'awiyah, how can I be not happy after reconciling between the two people who are the most honored ones to Allah among all creatures."

In the narration of 'Abd Allah ibn al-Harith and Habib ibn Thabit and Ali ibn Ibrahim it is said, "the most beloved two on earth to me."

Ibn Babwayh has said that this is not reliable because the two of them did not need that the Messenger of Allah, *O Allah grant compensation to Muhammad and his family worthy of their services to your cause,* reconcile them.

Al-Baqir, *'Alayhi al-Salam,* and al-Sadiq, *'Alayhima al-Salam,* have said that the Messenger of Allah, *O Allah, please, grant compensation to Muhammad and his family worthy of their services to your cause,* would not go to sleep until he (the Messenger of Allah) would kiss the whole of the face of Fatimah, *'Alayha al-Salam.* He (the Messenger of Allah) would place his face on her chest then pray for her. In another narration it is said that he (the Messenger of Allah) would kiss the width of the face of Fatimah, *'Alayha al-Salam,* and her chest.

Abu Bakr Muhammad ibn 'Abd Allah al-Shafi'i, ibn Shihab al-Zuhri and ibn al-Musayyib all from Sa'd ibn abu Waqqas, and abu Mu'adh al-Nahwi al-Marwazi, abu Qatadah al-Harrani from Sufyan al-Thawri from Hashim ibn 'Urwah from his father from 'A'ishah and al-Kharkushi in Sharaf al-Nabi, al-Ashanahi in al- 'I'tiqad, al-Sam'ani in al-Risalah, abu Salih al-Mu'adhdhin in al-Arba'in, abu al-Sa'adat in Fada'il and of our people abu 'Ubayd al-Hadhdha' and others have narrated from al-Sadiq, 'Alayhi al-Salam who has said the following:

The Messenger of Allah, *O Allah, please, grant compensation to Muhammad and his family worthy of their services to your cause,* would kiss (the face) of Fatimah, *'Alayha al-Salam,* very often but certain ones of his wives disliked it. The Messenger of Allah, *O Allah grant compensation to Muhammad and his family worthy of their services to your cause,* said, "When I was taken for the night journey to the sky, Jibril held my hand and then took me to the garden (paradise). He then gave me of the dates of the garden (paradise) and I ate it - in a narration it is said that he gave me an apple which I then ate - and it turned to a seed in my back and when I returned to earth I went to bed with Khadijah *'Alayha al-Salam,* then she conceived Fatimah, *'Alayha al-Salam.* Fatimah, *'Alayha al-Salam,* is *al-Hawra' al-Insiyah (al-Hawra' al-'in* human being). Whenever I yearn for fragrance of the garden (paradise) I sense it from my daughter."

The Holy Prophet, *O Allah, please, grant compensation to Muhammad and his family worthy of their services to your cause,* once visited Fatimah, *'Alayha al-Salam,* and found her upset. He (the Messenger of Allah) asked for the reason that had made her upset. She replied, "Al-Humayrah ('A'ishah) degrades my mother saying that she ('A'ishah) has not come to know any man before you, and you came to know my mother when she was aged." He (the Messenger of Allah) *O Allah, please, grant compensation to Muhammad and his family worthy of their services to your cause,* said, "The inside of your mother was the container of *Imamat* (leadership with divine authority)."

Ibn 'Abd Rabbihi in al-'Iqd has said that al-Mahdi saw in his dream that Sharik al-Qadi turned away his face from him. When he woke up he told al-Rabi' about his dream. He then said that Sharik is against you and that he is purely of the Fatimi people. Al-Mahdi then summoned Sharik and when he came before him he said, "I am told that you are a Fatimi man." Sharik then said, "I seek protection with Allah for being anything other than a Fatimi unless you meant thereby Fatimah daughter of Kisra' (the Persian King). He al-Mahdi said, "No, I mean thereby Fatimah daughter of Muhammad." He then said, "Do you condemn her?" He replied, "No, I do not condemn, and seek protection from Allah." He then asked, "What do you say about one who condemns her." He replied, "I say, 'May Allah condemn him.'" He then said, "If so then you must condemn this one, meaning thereby al-Rabi'." He said, "No, by Allah I do not condemn her, O 'Amir al-Mu'minin." Sharik then said, "O shameless man, how dare you mention the leader of the women of the worlds and the daughter of the leader of the messengers in the meeting place of men!" Al-Mahdi then said, "What is the meaning of the dream?" He replied, "Your dream is not the dream of Yusuf, *'Alayhi al-Salam.* Bloodshed cannot be legalized because of dreams."

A man who had insulted Fatimah, *'Alayha al-Salam,* was brought before Fadl ibn al-Rabi' and he then said to ibn Ghanim to look into his case to give his decision." He said, "Penalty is due on him." Al-Fadl then said, "She is your mother if you executed penalty on him. He then commanded to strike with a whip one hundred times and then crucified him on the roadside."

H 78, Ch. 3, h 43
Manaqib of ibn Shahr Ashub:

It is narrated that Fatimah, *'Alayha al-Salam,* wished for a *wakil* (attorney, supporter) for Ali, during his fight against the enemies. This verse of al-Quran then was revealed, ". . . and the Lord of the east and west, with due sincerity. He is the only Lord, so choose Him as your *Wakil* (Guardian, attorney)." (73:9)

In al-Sahih of al-Dar al-Qutni it is narrated that once the Messenger of Allah, *O Allah, please, grant compensation to Muhammad and his family worthy of their services to your cause,* commanded to execute the penalty on a thief who said, "O Messenger of Allah, on one hand you present the religion Islam before him and then you command to execute the penalty for a theft on him!" He (the Messenger of Allah) then said "Had it been my daughter Fatimah, *'Alayha al-Salam,* I would have executed the penalty on her." Fatimah, *'Alayha al-Salam,* heard it and she became depressed. Jibril then came with this verse of al-Quran, ". . .(even though Allah has said), 'It has been revealed to you and to those who lived before you that if you consider other things equal to Allah, your deeds will be made devoid of all virtue and you will certainly be lost?' (39:65) Upon this the Messenger of Allah, became depressed and this verse of al-Quran was revealed, "Had there been other deities in the heavens and the earth besides Allah, both the heavens and the earth would have been destroyed. Allah, the Lord of the Throne, is free of all defects of what they think He is." (21:22) The Messenger of Allah, *O Allah grant compensation to Muhammad and his family worthy of their services to your cause,* became amazed for this and Jibril then came and said, "Fatimah, *'Alayha al-Salam,* had become depressed because of your words (decision about the thief). These verses are to make her happy."

Note: These verses indicate that such conditional statements do not affect the greatness of the speaker or the one being addressed conditionally because such statements have been made by Allah, most Majestic, most Glorious, about the Holy Prophet, *'Alayhi al-Salam* and about Allah.

H 79, Ch. 3, h 44
Manaqib of ibn Shahr Ashub:

Al-Sadiq, *'Alayhi al-Salam* was asked about the meaning of "come to the best deed" A phrase in *al-Adhan* (call for *Salat* (prayer)) and he (the Imam) said, "The best deed is to be kind and supportive of Fatimah, *'Alayha al-Salam,* and her children." In another narration it is a reference to belief in guardianship of *'A'immah, 'Alayhim al-Salam* with divine authority and knowledge.

Abu Salih has narrated in al-Arba'in from abu Hamid al-Isfara'ini through the chain of his narrators from abu Hurayrah who has said the following:

The Messenger of Allah, *O Allah grant compensation to Muhammad and his family worthy of their services to your cause,* has said that the first one who will enter the garden (paradise) is Fatimah, *'Alayha al-Salam."*

It is narrated from the Holy Prophet, *O Allah, please, grant compensation to Muhammad and his family worthy of their services to your cause,* who has said that when Allah created the garden (paradise) He created it from the light of his face, then He took this light and threw it. My share was one third, one third was the share of Fatimah, *'Alayha al-Salam,* and the other third became the share of Ali and his family. Whoever found that light finds guidance to the belief in guardianship of *'A'immah* with divine authority and knowledge of *Ale* (family of) Muhammad) and those who did not fine anything of that light goes astray from the guardianship of *Ale* (family of) Muhammad with divine authority and knowledge.

Al-Husayn ibn Zayd ibn Ali has narrated from Al-Sadiq, *'Alayhi al-Salam* and Jabir al-Juhfi from Al-Baqir, *'Alayhi al-Salam,* that the Holy Prophet, *O Allah, please, grant compensation to Muhammad and his family worthy of their services to your cause,* has said that Allah becomes angry because of the anger of Fatimah, *'Alayha al-Salam,* and He becomes happy with the happiness of Fatimah, *'Alayha al-Salam.*

Ibn Shrayh through the chain of his narrators has narrated from al-Sadiq and abu Sa'id al-Wa'iz in Sharaf al-Nabi, *'Alayhi al-Salam* from 'Amir al-

Mu'minin, abu Salih al-Mu'adhdhin in Fada'il from ibn 'Abbas, abu 'Abd Allah al-'Akbari in Ibanah, Mahmud al-Isfaryini in al-Diyanah all have narrated from the Holy Prophet, who has said the following:

"O Fatimah, *'Alayha al-Salam,* Allah becomes angry when you become angry and He becomes happy when you are happy."

Abu Bakkr Mardawayh in his book through a chain of narrators has narrated from Sinan al-Awsi who has said that the Holy Prophet, has said, "Jibril has narrated to me that when Allah gave Fatimah, *'Alayha al-Salam,* in marriage to Ali, *'Alayhima al-Salam,* He commanded the keeper of the garden (paradise) to command the tree of *Tuba* (the tree in the garden (paradise)) to carry cards for the friends of *Ale* (family of) Muhammad, *O Allah, please, grant compensation to Muhammad and his family worthy of their services to your cause,* then angels of light rained down equal to the number of those cards, then the angels took those cards and when it will be the Day of Judgment and when it settles with its inhabitants Allah will send down the angels with those cards and when any of those angels will meet a man of the friends of *Ale* (family of) Muhammad, will give to him the card of freedom from the fire (of hell).

It is narrated in many books of which is Kashf of Tha'labi and Fada'il of abu 'Sa'adat about the meaning of the words of Allah, ". . . they will find neither excessive heat nor cold." (76:13) Ibn 'Abbas has said that when the people of the garden (paradise) will settle in the garden (paradise) they will see lights which will brighten the garden (paradise). The people of the garden (paradise) will say, "O Lord, you have said in your revealed book to your messenger, ". . . they will find neither excessive heat nor cold." (76:13) Then an announcer will announce, "This is not the light of the sun or that of the moon. Ali and Fatimah, *'Alayhima al-Salam,* being amused for some reason have laughed, thus the garden (paradise) has become bright because of their light."

Abu Ali al-Sawli has narrated in Akhbar of Fatimah, 'Alayha al-Salam, abu Sa'adat in Fada'il 'Asharah through a chain of narrators from abu Dharr al-Ghifari who has said the following:

Once the Holy Prophet, 'Alayhi al-Salam sent me to call Ali, 'Alayhi al-Salam. I went to his house and called him but he did not answer. I then informed the Holy Prophet, 'Alayhi al-Salam about it. He told me to go inside his house because he is home. I entered the house and saw the grinding stone is grinding but there was no one around it. I then said to Ali, "The Holy Prophet, 'Alayhi al-Salam is calling you." He came out somehow frightened until he reached in front of the Holy Prophet, 'Alayhi al-Salam. I then informed the Holy Prophet, 'Alayhi al-Salam about what I had seen. He said, "O abu Dharr do not be astonished. Allah has certain angels who move around on earth and they are assigned to help Ale (family of) Muhammad."

Al-Hassan al-Basri, and ibn Ishaq has narrated from 'Ammar and Maymunah who both have said, "We found Fatimah, 'Alayha al-Salam, sleeping and the grinding stone grinding. I (the narrator) then informed the Messenger of Allah, about it and he said, "Allah found His female servant's weakness. He then inspired the grinding stone to grind and it then begun grinding.

Abu al-Qasim al-Basti has narrated it (the above Hadith) in Manaqib of 'Amir al-Mu'minin, as well as abu Salih al-Mu'adhdhin in al-Arba'in from al-Sha'bi through a chain of narrators from Maymunah and ibn Fayyad in sharh al-Akhbar.

It is narrated that Fatimah, 'Alayha al-Salam, would remain busy in her Salat (prayer) and acts of worship and one of her children might weep and the cradle would be seen moving. The angel would move the cradle.

Muhammad ibn Ali ibn al-Husayn, 'Alayhi al-Salam, ibn Ali 'Alayhim al-Salam has said that once the Messenger of Allah, O Allah, please, grant compensation to Muhammad and his family worthy of their services to your cause, sent Salman (Rh) to the house of Fatimah, 'Alayha al-Salam, (for something). He (Salman (Rh)) has said that he stood at the door shortly and then said Salam (the phrase of offering greeting of peace). He heard Fatimah, 'Alayha al-Salam, reciting al-Quran inside the house and the grinding stone was running outside but there was no one in her company. In the end of the narration he (the narrator) has said that the Messenger of Allah, O Allah, please, grant compensation to Muhammad and his family worthy of their *services to your cause,* smiled and said, "O Salman (Rh), Allah has filled the heart of my daughter Fatimah, *'Alayha al-Salam,* as well as the members of her body with faith up to the joints of her bones, so she has devoted herself to obedience to Allah, thus Allah has sent an angel called Zuqabil –in another narration is Jibril- to make her grinding stone grind and Allah has undertaken her worldly needs as well as her needs of the next life."

H 80, Ch. 3, h 45
Manaqib of ibn Shahr Ashub:

Ali ibn Mu'ammar has said that 'Umm Ayman left for Makkah when Fatimah, *'Alayha al-Salam,* passed away, saying that she will not see al-Madinah after the death of Fatimah, *'Alayha al-Salam* During the journey in the area of al-Juhfah she faced a great degree of dehydration and thirst and she became afraid for her life. He (the narrator) has said that she then turned the corner of her eyes to the sky and said, "O Lord, will you cause me to die of thirst and I am the servant of the daughter of your Prophet?" He (the narrator) has said that a bucket of water then came down to her of the water from the garden (paradise) which she drank and thereafter for seven years she did not need any water or food.

H 81, Ch. 3, h 46
Manaqib of ibn Shahr Ashub:

Malik ibn Dinar has narrated that during al-Hajj season he saw a weak woman on a weak animal for riding and people warning her against the collapse of that animal. When we arrived in the wilderness the animal for riding became tired and she then left it alone. She then raised her head to the sky saying, "You did not allow me to remain at home and you have not taken me or to your house. I swear by your majesty and glory that if someone other than you had done this to me, I would complain about it before no one else other than you. At this time someone came to her from al-Fayfa with the reign of a camel in his hand who told her to ride the camel. She then rode and the camel then moved fast like lightening. When she arrived in the place for Tawaf I saw her performing Tawaf. I then made her to tell on oath, who she is? She said that she is Shuhrah daughter of Miskah daughter of Fizzah the servant of Fatimah, *'Alayha al-Salam,* al-Zahra', who once left a piece of her garment as security with the wife of Zayd the Jewish man in al-Madinah to borrow some barley. When Zayd came home he asked, "What is all this light in our home?" His wife replied, "It is from a piece of the garments of Fatimah, *'Alayha al-Salam.*" He became a Muslim and so also did his wife and their neighbors numbering eighty people.

Once Fatimah, *'Alayha al-Salam,* asked, the Messenger of Allah, *O Allah, please, grant compensation to Muhammad and his family worthy of their services to your cause,* for a ring who said to her, "I can tell you to do something better. When you perform your nightly optional *Salat* (prayer) *Tahajjud* (*Salat* (prayer) of eleven Rak'at during the last part of the night), you can ask Allah, the most High, for a ring and you will find your wish for a ring to have come true." He (the narrator) has said that she followed the instruction and a caller said, "O Fatimah, *'Alayha al-Salam,* what you have asked for is under your prayer rug." She then raised the prayer rug and there was a priceless ring of ruby which she happily wore on her finger. During the night she saw in her dream as if she was in the garden (paradise) where she saw three palaces the like of which was not seen in the garden (paradise). She then asked whose palaces are these." She was told, "They belong to Fatimah, *'Alayha al-Salam,* daughter of Muhammad." He (the narrator) has said that then as if she entered one of the palace s wherein she saw a bed losing balance because of one missing leg. She then asked, "Why this bed has lost balance because of one missing leg?" They replied, "It is because the owner has asked Allah for a ring. One of the legs of the bed was removed to make a ring thereof, then the bed remained on three legs instead of four."

In the morning she visited the Messenger of Allah, *O Allah, please, grant compensation to Muhammad and his family worthy of their services to your cause,* and told him about the story of her dream. The Holy Prophet, *'Alayhi al-Salam* then said, "O the community of *Ale* (family of) 'Abd al-Muttalib, the world is not for you. Instead the next life is for you and your promised place is the garden (paradise). You have nothing to do with the world because it is vanishing and deceitful." The Holy Prophet, asked her to place it back under her prayer rug. She then did as she was instructed and went to sleep on the prayer rug and she then saw in her dream as if she entered the garden (paradise), went to that palace and saw the bed standing on four legs. She then asked about its condition and they said that the owner returned the ring then the bed took its original form."

Abu Ja'far al-Tusi has narrated in Ikhtiyar al-Rijal from 'Abu 'Abd Allah, 'Alayhi al-Salam and from Salman (Rh) al-Farsi who has said the following:

When 'Amir al-Mu'minin was being taken out of his house, Fatimah, *'Alayha al-Salam,* moved out until she reached the grave (of the Holy Prophet). She then said, "You must set my cousin free, by the one who has sent Muhammad in all truth, if you did not do so I will open my hairs, then place the shirt of the Messenger of Allah over my head and scream before Allah for help. The camel of Prophet Salih is not more honorable in the sight of Allah than my children." Salman (Rh) has said that, by Allah he saw the foundations of the walls of the Masjid come off from the ground so much so that a man could pass underneath the foundation to the other side. He then moved close to her and said, "My leader, my owner, Allah, most Blessed, most high, sent your father as a mercy, so I beg you not to become a blow for them." He then saw the foundations of the wall sat back in place with rising dust underneath which filled up their nostrils."

Buraydah has said that the Messenger of Allah, *O Allah grant compensation to Muhammad and his family worthy of their services to your cause,* has said, "The angel of death gave me the choice and I asked for time until the coming of Jibril." His daughter Fatimah, *'Alayha al-Salam,* noticed the pause in his physical senses. He then said to her, "My dearest daughter, please provide me your support. You, your husband and your two sons are with me in the garden (paradise)."

Maryam (Mary) was given the glad news about her son as is said in al-Quran, "'Behold,' the angels told Mary, 'Allah has given you the glad news of the birth of a son whom He calls His Word, whose name will be Messiah, Jesus, son of Mary, who will be a man of honor in this life and the life to come, and who will be one of those nearest to Allah.'" (3:45)

Fatimah, *'Alayha al-Salam,* was given the glad news of the birth of al-Hassan and al-Husayn, *'Alayhi al-Salam.*

It is narrated in one Hadith that the Holy Prophet, *'Alayhi al-Salam* would give her the glad news of the birth of each one of the two saying, "Congratulations for the birth of an Imam who will lead the people of the garden (paradise) and may Allah, most High, complete the blessing in her offspring."

The words of Allah, "Allah made (belief in Allah) an everlasting task for his successors, so that perhaps they would return (to Him)," (43:28) is a reference to Ali, *'Alayhi al-Salam*

'Abu 'Abd Allah, *'Alayhi al-Salam* has said that the duration of her (Maryam (Mary)) pregnancy was only nine hours.

The duration between the birth of al-Hassan and al-Husayn, was six months according to one narration. Maryam (Mary) is the daughter of 'Imran and Fatimah, *'Alayha al-Salam,* is the daughter of Muhammad, *O Allah, please, grant compensation to Muhammad and his family worthy of their services to your cause.* The honor of people is because of their fathers.

The mother of Maryam (Mary) made a vow in the way of Allah to dedicate her child to be born to the place of prayer. On the other hand Muhammad, *O Allah, please, grant compensation to Muhammad and his family worthy of their services to your cause,* would seek nearness to Allah more than other creatures in other good deeds and conditions. This means that he might have offered many times more than what the mother of Maryam (Mary) had offered because his having greater degree of excellence over the other creatures. The vow in the case of Maryam (Mary) was made by a mother who is of a half size because of its being from the mother's side as compared by a vow from the side of the father.

The words of Allah say, "Zachariah took custody of her. . ." (3:37) In the case of Fatimah, *'Alayha al-Salam,* al-Zahra' her guardian was the Messenger of Allah, *O Allah, please, grant compensation to Muhammad and his family worthy of their services to your cause.* The guardianship of the Messenger of Allah is of much greater excellence than the others. To serve as a guardian of an orphan is an optional act while doing the duties of a guardian for one's own child is obligatory.

Maryam (Mary) gave birth to 'Isa during the time of ignorance. Al-Hassan and al-Husayn, on the other hand, were born from Fatimah, *'Alayha al-Salam,* with their nature of the nature of Islam.

Allah had informed Maryam (Mary) of her safety and the safety of her child, thus, it was not possible for her to be afraid of anything. Al-Zahra', *'Alayha al-Salam,* conceived with al-Hassan and al-Husayn, but she did not know what will happen to her and to her children during birth, before or after their birth in the form of safety and harmfulness. As such being the case the reward is of additional degrees and for this reason the Muslims were more excellent than the angels on the day of Badr in the fighting because they lived in the condition of fear and hope about their safety but the angels did not experience such condition.

Maryam (Mary) was told, ". . . Do not be sad..." (19:24) The Messenger of Allah, *O Allah grant compensation to Muhammad and his family worthy of their services to your cause,* said to Fatimah, *'Alayha al-Salam,* 'O Fatimah, *'Alayha al-Salam,* Allah becomes happy when you become happy.'"

About Maryam (Mary) the words of Allah say this, ". . . and into whose womb We breathed Our spirit..." (66:12)

Fatimah, *'Alayha al-Salam,* is the fifth of the five people under the cloak about whom Jibril expressed great pride saying, "Who is like the one who has become the sixth one of the five people under the cloak.

In the case of Maryam (Mary) the words of Allah say, "Shake the trunk of the palm tree, it will provide you with fresh ripe dates. (19:25) Eat, drink, and rejoice. . . ." (19:26)

It is possible that the palm tree and the stream may have been in existence from before the event because no trace of them is left as is the contrary in the case of Zamzam, the station, the place of the oven of Nuh, parting of the sea, returning of the sun. In the case of Al-Zahra', *'Alayha al-Salam,* there is the story of the al-Sayhani dates and the bowl of water.

It is narrated that 'Umm Ayman wept and said, "O Messenger of Allah, *O Allah, please, grant compensation to Muhammad and his family worthy of their services to your cause,* you gave Fatimah, *'Alayha al-Salam,* in marriage but did not shower on her any valuable gifts." The Messenger of Allah, *O Allah grant compensation to Muhammad and his family worthy of their services to your cause,* said, "O 'Umm Ayman, you should not say what is not true; when

Allah, most High, gave Fatimah, *'Alayha al-Salam,* in marriage to Ali, *'Alayhi al-Salam* He commanded the trees of the garden (paradise) to spread over them of their ornaments, and dresses, rubies, pearls, emeralds, silk brocades of thick woven silk threads and they (the audience) took so much that they could not figure out."

About Maryam (Mary) the angels said, "'Behold,' the angels told Mary, 'Allah has chosen you, purified you, and given you distinction over all women.'" (3:42) It is a reference to the women of her time; like His words addressed to the Israelites, "O children of Israel, recall My favors to you and the preference that I gave to you over all nations (of your time then)." (2:47) However, they are not more excellent than Muslims, because Allah has said that, "You are the best nation that ever existed among humanity . . ." (3:110) Moreover, the characteristics mentioned in this verse of al-Quran are found in others also. As Allah has said, "Allah chose (and gave distinction to) Adam, Noah, the family of Abraham, and 'Imrān over all the people of the world. (3:33) They were the offspring of one another. Allah is All-hearing and All-seeing." (3:34) The descendants of Fatimah, *'Alayha al-Salam,* are also of such people. The Holy Prophet, *'Alayhi al-Salam* has said that Fatimah, *'Alayha al-Salam,* is the leader of the women of the worlds of the earlier and later generations. When she stands in her place of *Salat* (prayer) seventy thousand angels who are very close to Allah, offer her Salam (greeting of peace) and they call her as Maryam (Mary) was called by the angels and they say to Fatimah, *'Alayha al-Salam,* "'Behold,' the angels say, 'Allah has chosen you, purified you, and has given you distinction over all women (of the worlds).'" (3:42)

This is about the meaning of the words of Allah, the most Majestic, the most Glorious:

"Zachariah took custody of her. Whenever he went to visit her in her place of worship, he would find with her some food. He would ask her, 'Where did this food come from?' She would reply, 'Allah has sent it.' Allah gives sustenance to whomever He wants without keeping an account." (3:37)

This verse does not say clearly that it was an invention of Allah or that the angels would bring such food for her. This verse indicates that she was a very grateful person to Allah; as one may say, "Allah has given me one dirham today" as it is said, ". . . (Muhammad). Tell them, 'Everything is from Allah. . .'" (4:78)

In the case of Al-Zahra', *'Alayha al-Salam,* there are many examples which no one among the Muslims deny such as the Hadith of al-Miqdad, the Hadith of the bird, the pomegranate, the grapes, the apple, the quince and others. This proves with certainty that she would eat of what was not available to others of all creatures, after the descending of Adam, *'Alayhi al-Salam,* and Eve.

It is narrated in a Hadith that the Holy Prophet, *O Allah, please, grant compensation to Muhammad and his family worthy of their services to your cause,* visited Fatimah, *'Alayha al-Salam,* when she was in her place of *Salat* (prayer) and on one side there a basin boiled, steaming a great deal. Fatimah, *'Alayha al-Salam,* then placed the basin in front of both of them and Ali, *'Alayhi al-Salam* asked, "Wherefrom have you obtained this?" She then replied, "This is of the extra favor of Allah and of His sustenance; He grants sustenance to whomever He wills without accounting."

Maryam (Mary) received sustenance from the garden (paradise) but Fatimah, *'Alayha al-Salam,* was created from the sustenance of the garden (paradise). It is narrated in Hadith, "Jibril gave me of its dates and I then ate it and it turned into seed in my back."

Allah, most High, has praised Maryam (Mary) in al-Quran with twenty praises.

It is authenticated in Hadith that Allah has called Fatimah, *'Alayha al-Salam,* with twenty names of which each one indicates an example of her excellence. Ibn Babwayh has written them in the book "The birth of Fatimah, *'Alayha al-Salam.*"

Allah has said in al-Quran, "He has also told, as a parable, the story of Mary, daughter of 'Imran who protected her privacy (did not look at it) and into whose womb We breathed Our spirit. She made the words of her Lord and the predictions in His Books come true. She was an obedient woman." (66:12) He thereby speaks of her chastity not of coming in contact or descendants because, if not so, He must have made her pregnancy with him, and his birth in a way other than the normal process. Since the process took place as normally does, it proves our point. There are narrations which praises becoming married and seek to have children and calls remaining without marriage undesirable.

About Al-Zahra', *'Alayha al-Salam,* Allah, most High, has said in al-Quran, ". . . O people of the house, Allah wants to remove all kinds of uncleanness from you and to purify you thoroughly." (33:33)

Hassan ibn Thabit has said, "Maryam (Mary) maintained chastity then she gave birth to 'Isa like the shining full moon.

Fatimah, *'Alayha al-Salam,* maintained chastity then she gave birth to the two grandsons of the Holy Prophet, of guidance."

H 82, Ch. 3, h 47
Fada'il: al-Rawdah:

Once the Messenger of Allah, *O Allah, please, grant compensation to Muhammad and his family worthy of their services to your cause,* visited Ali and Fatimah, *'Alayhima al-Salam,* and found them grinding a certain kind of grain called 'al-Jarush'. The Holy Prophet, then asked, "Which one of you is more tired?" Ali, *'Alayhi al-Salam* said, "Fatimah, *'Alayha al-Salam,* is more tired." He then said, "Move aside my dearest daughter." She moved aside and the Holy Prophet sat down in her place with Ali, *'Alayhi al-Salam* and helped him in grinding the grain.

H 83, Ch. 3, h 48
Kashf al-Ghummah:

From the book Ma'alim al-'Itrah by 'Abd al-Aziz ibn al-Akhdar through the chain of his narrators in a marfu' manner from Qatadah from Anas who has said the following:

The Messenger of Allah, *O Allah grant compensation to Muhammad and his family worthy of their services to your cause,* has said that the best of the women of it (the world) is Maryam (Mary) and the best of the women of it (the world) is Fatimah, *'Alayha al-Salam,* daughter of Muhammad, *'Alayhi al-Salam.*

Through the chain of his narrators (of the author) to Ahmad ibn Hanbal in a marfu' manner from Anas who has said the following:

The Holy Prophet, *'Alayhi al-Salam* has said that of the women of the worlds in excellence Maryam (Mary) daughter of 'Imran, Khadijah *'Alayha al-Salam,* daughter of Khuwaylid, Fatimah, *'Alayha al-Salam,* daughter Muhammad, *'Alayhi al-Salam* and Asiyah daughter of Muzaham wife of the pharaoh are sufficient examples.

Through the chain of his narrators from Anas who has said the following:

The Holy Prophet, *'Alayhi al-Salam* has said that of the women of the worlds in excellence Maryam (Mary) daughter of 'Imran, Khadijah *'Alayha al-Salam,* daughter of Khuwaylid, Fatimah, *'Alayha al-Salam,* daughter Muhammad, *'Alayhi al-Salam* and Asiyah daughter of Muzaham wife of the pharaoh are sufficient examples.

It is narrated from him (the narrator) that once 'A'ishah said to Fatimah, *'Alayha al-Salam,* "Should I tell you about the glad news that I have heard from the Messenger of Allah, *O Allah, please, grant compensation to Muhammad and his family worthy of their services to your cause,* who has said that the leaders of the women of the garden (paradise) are only four: They are Maryam (Mary) daughter of 'Imran, Fatimah, *'Alayha al-Salam,* daughter of Muhammad, Khadijah *'Alayha al-Salam,* daughter of Khuwaylid and Asiyah daughter of Muzaham, wife of the pharaoh.

It is narrated from Musnad of Ahmad from 'A'ishah who has said the following:

Once Fatimah, *'Alayha al-Salam,* came walking just like the Messenger of Allah, *O Allah, please, grant compensation to Muhammad and his family worthy of their services to your cause,* and he (the Messenger of Allah) said, "Welcome my dearest daughter." He (the Messenger of Allah) then made her to sit on his right or left side then secretly spoke something to her. She wept. I then said to her, "The Messenger of Allah, *O Allah grant compensation to Muhammad and his family worthy of their services to your cause,* chose you especially to talk to you but you wept then he spoke secretly certain words and you laughed." I (the narrator) then said, "I have never seen any happiness so close to sadness like what I have seen today. I (the narrator) then asked her about what he (the Messenger of Allah) had said." She said, "I am not the one to publicize the secret of the Messenger of Allah, *O Allah, please, grant compensation to Muhammad and his family worthy of their services to your cause.* When the Messenger of Allah passed away I then asked her about it and she said that first he said, "Jibril would show me al-Quran once every year but this year he has shown me twice. I only think that the time of my death has reached very near to me and you will be the first from my *Ahl al-Bayt* (family) to join me and I will be the best for you of those who have passed away. For this reason I wept. Then he said to me, "Will you not be happy to be the leader of the women of this nation (followers)?" Fatimah, *'Alayha al-Salam,* then said, "Because of his words as such I laughed."

Ibn Khaluwayh has narrated in the book of *al-Ale* (family of) from 'Abu 'Abd Allah, al-Hanbali from Muhammad ibn Ahmad ibn Quda'ah from 'Abd Allah ibn Muhammad from abu Muhammad al-'Askari, *'Alayhi al-Salam,* from his ancestors *'Alayhim al-Salam* has said that the Messenger of Allah, *O Allah, please, grant compensation to Muhammad and his family worthy of their services to your cause,* has said, "When Allah created Adam, *'Alayhi al-Salam,* and Eve they expressed pride in the garden (paradise) and Adam, *'Alayhi al-Salam,* said to Eve, "Allah has not created any creatures better than us." Allah then inspired Jibril, "Take my servant to the Firdaws al-A'la'. When the two of them entered Firdaws al-A'la', they looked at a maiden on a furnishing of the furnishing of the garden (paradise) with a crown of light on her head, two earrings of light. The garden (paradise) had become bright because of the beauty of her face. Adam, *'Alayhi al-Salam,* then asked, "My dear friend Jibril who is this maiden the beauty of whose face has brightened the garden (paradise)?" He replied, "She is Fatimah, *'Alayha al-Salam,* daughter of Muhammad, the Holy Prophet, from your descendants who will live in the end time." He then asked, "What is this crown on her head?" He replied, "It is (stands for) her husband, Ali ibn Ali ibn abu Talib, *'Alayhi al-Salam.*"

Ibn Khaluwayh has said that the word *'al-ba'l'* in Arabic stands for five things: It stands for husband, name of an idol as in "Do you worship *Ba'al* and abandon the Best Creator (37:125)" It is the name of a women and with it is named Ba'labak and al-Ba'l of the palm tree is what its roots drink without being watered and al-Ba'l is the sky and the Arabs say that the sky is the Ba'l of earth.

He then asked what for are the earrings in her ears? He replied, "They stand for her two sons, al-Hassan and al-Husayn, *'Alayhima al-Salam.*" Adam, *'Alayhi al-Salam,* then said, "My dear friend Jibril were they created before me?" He replied, "They were in existence in the deep knowledge of Allah four thousand years before you were created."

It is narrated from ibn Khaluwayh in the book *Ale* (family of) *in a marfu' manner* from Ali ibn Musa al-Rida', from his ancestors from Ali, *'Alayhi al-Salam,* who has said that the Messenger of Allah, *O Allah, please, grant compensation to Muhammad and his family worthy of their services to your cause,* has said that when it will be the Day of Judgment, a caller from beneath the Throne will call, "O the community of the creatures, you must close your eyes until Fatimah, *'Alayha al-Salam,* daughter of Muhammad, passes through. Ibn 'Urfah has added from his *rijal* (narrators) *in a marfu' manner* from abu Ayyub al-Ansari who has said that the Messenger of Allah, *O Allah, please, grant compensation to Muhammad and his family worthy of their services to your cause,* has said that when it will be the Day of Judgment a caller from beneath the Throne will call, "O people of the gathering you must bend down your heads and close your eyes until Fatimah, *'Alayha al-Salam,* passes on the bridge. She will pass with seventy thousand maidens of *al-Hawra' al-'in* and angels along with her.

It is narrated from him from Nafi' ibn abu al-Hamra' who has said the following:

I (the narrator) observed the Messenger of Allah, *O Allah, please, grant compensation to Muhammad and his family worthy of their services to your cause,* for eight months that when coming out for *Salat* (prayer) of the morning he would pass by the door of Fatimah, *'Alayha al-Salam,* and say *al-Salamu 'Alaykum Ahl al-Bayt (family of) wa rahmatu Allah wa barakatuhu al-Salat* (may peace and blessings of Allah be with you, O people of the house. It is *Salat* (prayer) time. "O People of the house, Allah wants to remove all kinds of uncleanness from you and to purify you thoroughly." (33:33)

85

It is narrated from him from al-Husayn ibn Ali from his father from the Holy Prophet, *O Allah, please, grant compensation to Muhammad and his family worthy of their services to your cause,* who had said to Fatimah, *'Alayha al-Salam,* "O Fatimah, *'Alayha al-Salam,* Allah becomes angry when you become angry and He becomes happy when you become happy.

It is in the book of abu Ishaq Tha'labi from Jami ' ibn 'Umayr from his aunt who has said that she asked 'A'ishah, "Who was more beloved to the Messenger of Allah, *O Allah, please, grant compensation to Muhammad and his family worthy of their services to your cause?*" She replied, "She was Fatimah, *'Alayha al-Salam."* She then said, "I asked you about men." 'A'ishah replied, "He was her husband whom he would not stop (from visiting him). By Allah as I know he was a fasting man, performing *Salat* (prayer) a great deal during the night and saying what is worthy of Allah and what He loves and likes."

It is narrated from Jabir who has said the following:

I (the narrator) never saw Fatimah, *'Alayha al-Salam,* walking without my remembering the Messenger of Allah, *O Allah, please, grant compensation to Muhammad and his family worthy of their services to your cause,* who when walking would slightly incline to the left, then to the right.

It is narrated from 'A'ishah who has said the following:

When Fatimah, *'Alayha al-Salam,* was mentioned 'A'ishah said, "I never found anyone more truthful than Fatimah, *'Alayha al-Salam,* except her father."

It is narrated in the book of 'The birth of Fatimah, *'Alayha al-Salam"* of ibn Babwayh that the Holy Prophet, *'Alayhi al-Salam* has said that the garden (paradise) yearns for four of the women: They are Maryam (Mary) daughter of 'Imran, Asiyah daughter of Muzaham, wife of the pharaoh, who will be wife of the Holy Prophet, in the garden (paradise), Khadijah *'Alayha al-Salam,* daughter of Khuwaylid, wife of the Holy Prophet, in the world and in the next life and Fatimah, *'Alayha al-Salam,* daughter of Muhammad, *O Allah, please, grant compensation to Muhammad and his family worthy of their services to your cause.*

It is narrated from Ali, 'Alayhi al-Salam who has said the following:

Once we were sitting in the meeting of the Messenger of Allah, *O Allah, please, grant compensation to Muhammad and his family worthy of their services to your cause,* and he said, "Tell me what the best of characteristics of the women is?" We all failed to answer until we dispersed. I then went to Fatimah, *'Alayha al-Salam,* and told to her what the Messenger of Allah, *O Allah, please, grant compensation to Muhammad and his family worthy of their services to your cause,* had asked and that no one of us knew the answer. She then said, "I know the answer. The best of the women is one who does not see men and they cannot see her."

I then returned to the Messenger of Allah, *O Allah, please, grant compensation to Muhammad and his family worthy of their services to your cause,* and said, "O Messenger of Allah, you had asked, "what the best of characteristics of the women is." The best of the women is who does not see any man and no man can see her.

He (the Messenger of Allah), asked, "Who gave this answer; you did not know it when you were with me?" I replied, "Fatimah, *'Alayha al-Salam,* gave this answer." He (the Messenger of Allah, *O Allah, please, grant compensation to Muhammad and his family worthy of their services to your cause,* was amazed and said, "Fatimah, *'Alayha al-Salam,* is a part of myself."

It is narrated from Mujahid who has said the following:

One day the Holy Prophet, *'Alayhi al-Salam* came out holding the hand of Fatimah, *'Alayha al-Salam.* He (the Messenger of Allah) said, "Those who know her they know her and those who do not know her must know that she is Fatimah, *'Alayha al-Salam,* daughter of Muhammad and she is a part of myself. She is my heart, and my spirit which is in me. Whoever causes her to suffer has caused me to suffer and whoever causes me to suffer has troubled Allah."

It is narrated from Ja'far ibn Muhammad 'Alayhima al-Salam, who has said the following:

The Messenger of Allah, *O Allah grant compensation to Muhammad and his family worthy of their services to your cause,* has said that Allah becomes angry when Fatimah, *'Alayha al-Salam,* becomes angry and He becomes happy when Fatimah, *'Alayha al-Salam,* becomes happy.

Through the same chain of narrators it is narrated from him (the Imam) *'Alayhi al-Salam* a similar Hadith and it was said to him (the Imam), "O child of the Messenger of Allah, we are told that you have stated such Hadith (as the above one)." He (the Imam), *'Alayhi al-Salam* said, "What part of it then you deny? By Allah that Allah becomes angry when His Mu'min servant becomes angry and He becomes happy when His Mu'min servant becomes happy."

It is narrated from the narrator of the previous Hadith from him (the Imam, *'Alayhi al-Salam*) who has said that the Messenger of Allah, *O Allah, please, grant compensation to Muhammad and his family worthy of their services to your cause,* has said that Fatimah, *'Alayha al-Salam,* is a branch of me, whoever causes suffering to her causes suffering to me also and whoever makes her happy he makes me also happy."

Through a chain of narrators it is narrated from him (the Imam), *'Alayhi al-Salam* a similar Hadith.

It is narrated from the book of abu Ishaq Tha'labi from Mujahid who has said the following:

One day the Messenger of Allah, *O Allah, please, grant compensation to Muhammad and his family worthy of their services to your cause,* came out holding the hand of Fatimah, *'Alayha al-Salam,* and said, "Whoever knows her it is fine but whoever does not know her must know that she is Fatimah, *'Alayha al-Salam,* daughter of Muhammad and she is a part of myself, she is my heart inside me. Whoever, troubles her has troubled me and whoever troubles me has troubled Allah."

It is narrated from Jabir ibn 'Abd Allah who has said the following:

"The Messenger of Allah has said, "Fatimah, *'Alayha al-Salam,* is a bunch of my hairs. Whoever, troubles a bunch of my hair he troubles me and whoever troubles me has troubled Allah and whoever troubles Allah, He condemns him to the fill of the skies and earth."

It is narrated from Hudhayfah who has said the following:

The Messenger of Allah, *O Allah grant compensation to Muhammad and his family worthy of their services to your cause,* would not go to sleep before kiss the whole chick of Fatimah, *'Alayha al-Salam,* or her chest.

It is narrated from Ja'far ibn Muhammad 'Alayhima al-Salam, who has said the following:

"The Holy Prophet would not go to bed before placing his face on the chest of Fatimah, *'Alayha al-Salam.*"

It is narrated that Muhammad ibn abu Bakr read this verse of al-Quran, "Satan would try to tamper with the desires of every Prophet or Messenger . . . [or a *muhaddathah*]" (22:52) I (the narrator) then said, "Is it not the case that the angels speak to the Prophets only?" He replied, "Maryam (Mary) was not a Prophet, Sarah was not a Prophet but she saw the angels who congratulated her for the birth of Ishaq and after Ishaq for Ya'qub, as is said in the following verse of al-Quran, "His wife, who was standing nearby, laughed (due to suddenly experiencing menstruation). So We gave her the glad news that she would give birth to Isaac who will have a son, Jacob." (11:71) Fatimah, *'Alayha al-Salam,* daughter of Muhammad, the Messenger of Allah, *O Allah, please, grant compensation to Muhammad and his family worthy of their services to your cause,* was a muhaddathah but she was not a Prophet.

It is narrated from 'Umm Salamah who has said the following:

Fatimah, *'Alayha al-Salam,* daughter of the Messenger of Allah, *O Allah, please, grant compensation to Muhammad and his family worthy of their services to your cause,* was the person most similar among people to the Messenger of Allah, *O Allah, please, grant compensation to Muhammad and his family worthy of their services to your cause.*"

It is narrated from Ali, 'Alayhi al-Salam who has said the following:

Fatimah, *'Alayha al-Salam,* has said that the Messenger of Allah, *O Allah, please, grant compensation to Muhammad and his family worthy of their services to your cause,* said to her, "O Fatimah, *'Alayha al-Salam,* whoever, says, *O Allah, please, grant compensation to Muhammad and his family worthy of their services to your cause,* in your favor Allah forgives such person and will join him with me in the garden (paradise) where I will be."

It is narrated from al-Zuhri from Ali ibn al-Husayn, who has said the following:

Ali ibn abu Talib, *'Alayhi al-Salam* had said to Fatimah, *'Alayha al-Salam,* "You had asked your father certain questions; did you ask him about where you will be able to meet him on the Day of Judgment?" She replied, "Yes, I did and he told me to find him around the pond of al-Kawthar." I then asked, "What will happen if I will not find you there?" He said, "Find me then under the shadow of the Throne of my Lord, when no one will be able to find such shadow." Fatimah, *'Alayha al-Salam,* then said to the Messenger of Allah, "O dear father, on the Day of Judgment everyone will be naked, will I be also as such?" He (the Messenger of Allah) replied, "Yes, that is correct, but on that day no one will pay attention to others." Fatimah, *'Alayha al-Salam,* has said that she then said to the Messenger of Allah, what a shame to be in such condition before Allah, the most High!

I had not left him yet that he said, "Jibril, the trusted spirit came and said, "O Muhammad say *Salam* (the phrase of offering greeting of peace) to Fatimah, *'Alayha al-Salam,* and tell her that He will cover her with two dresses of light." Ali *'Alayhi al-Salam* has said that he then asked her, "Did you ask him about your cousin?" She replied, "Yes, I did and he (the Messenger of Allah) said that Ali is more honorable in the sight of Allah, the most High, and will not be left without covering."

H 84, Ch. 3, h 49
Fada'il of the month of Ramadan by al-Saduq:

The author has narrated from Muhammad ibn Ibrahim ibn Ishaq from Ahmad ibn Muhammad al-Kufi from al-Mundhir ibn Muhammad from al-Hassan ibn Ali al-Khazzaz from al-Rida', 'Alayhi al-Salam who in a lengthy Hadith has said the following:

When the crescent of the month of Ramadan would rise the light of Fatimah, *'Alayha al-Salam,* would dominate its brightness but when she remained absent it then would reappear.

H 85, Ch. 3, 50
Bisharah al-Mustafa':

Through a chain of narrators from abu Ali al-Hassan ibn Muhammad al-Tusi from Muhammad ibn al-Husayn known as ibn al-Saqal from Muhammad ibn Ma'qal al-'Ijli from Muhammad ibn abu al-Sahbani from ibn Faddal from Hamzah ibn Humran from Al-Sadiq from his father, 'Alayhima al-Salam, from Jabir ibn 'Abd Allah al-Ansari who has said the following:

One day the Messenger of Allah, *O Allah, please, grant compensation to Muhammad and his family worthy of their services to your cause,* performed al-'Asr *Salat* (prayer) with us; after completing he faced the people while people were around him and in such condition a Shaykh of immigrants of Arab came to him wearing very old clothes that were about to become torn in pieces and he could hardly hold himself because of weakness. The Messenger of Allah, *O Allah grant compensation to Muhammad and his family worthy of their services to your cause,* turned to him inducing him to speak. The Shaykh said, "O Prophet of Allah, I am hungry, please feed me, and I do not have clothes please clothe me and I am poor please help me." He (the Messenger of Allah), said, "I do not have anything to help you but one who guides to goodness is like the one who does something good. Go to the house of the one whom Allah and His Messenger love who gives preference to Allah over his self. Go to the house of Fatimah, *'Alayha al-Salam.* Her house was attached to the house of the Messenger of Allah, *O Allah, please, grant compensation to Muhammad and his family worthy of their services to your cause,* where he lived away from his wives.

He (the Messenger of Allah) said to Bilal to show him the house of Fatimah, *'Alayha al-Salam.* The Arab man then left with Bilal. When he stood in front of the house of Fatimah, *'Alayha al-Salam,* he loudly said *Salam* (the phrase of offering greeting of peace) to you *Ahl al-Bayt* (family) of the Holy Prophet, the location of the coming and going of the angels, the descending place of Jibril, the trusted spirit, with revelations from the Lord of the worlds." Fatimah, *'Alayha al-Salam,* then responded to his *Salam* (the phrase of offering greeting of peace) likewise and asked, "Who are you?" He replied, "I am and old Arab man. I went to your father, the leader of mankind, as an immigrant against hardship and, I, O daughter of Muhammad am in dire need of clothes and very hungry, please help me, may Allah grant you blessings." At that time Fatimah, *'Alayha al-Salam,* Ali, and the Messenger of Allah, were living without food for three days and the Messenger of Allah knew their condition.

91

Fatimah, *'Alayha al-Salam,* then took the tanned piece of a ram on which al-Hassan and al-Husayn, would sleep and gave it to the old man saying, "Take this, O visitor, I hope Allah will give you comfort with something better." The Arab man then said, "O daughter of Muhammad, I complained before you against hunger and you have given me the skin of a ram. What do I do with it in my condition of hunger?" The old man has said that she on hearing this took her necklace which Fatimah, daughter of her uncle, Hamzah ibn 'Abd al-Muttalib had given to her as a gift and threw it to the old man saying, "Take this and sell it. I hope Allah will replace it for you for something better." The Arab man then took the necklace and went to the Masjid of the Messenger of Allah, and the Holy Prophet, *'Alayhi al-Salam* was sitting with his companions. He said, "O Messenger of Allah, Fatimah, *'Alayha al-Salam,* has given me this necklace saying that she hopes Allah will benefit me thereby." The Holy Prophet, *O Allah, please, grant compensation to Muhammad and his family worthy of their services to your cause,* then wept and said, "How will Allah not benefit you thereby when, the daughter of Muhammad, Fatimah, *'Alayha al-Salam* the leader of the daughters of Adam, *'Alayhi al-Salam,* has given it to you."

'Ammar ibn Yasir (r.h) stood up saying, "O Messenger of Allah, will you allow me to buy this necklace?" He (the Messenger of Allah) replied, "Yes, O 'Ammar, you can buy it and you should know that even if both of the two heavy communities take part in buying it Allah will not subject them to the fire." 'Ammar then asked, "For how much you like to sell it, O Arab man?" He replied, "It is for one time food to my satisfaction from bread and meat, a gown made in Yemen to cover my privacy and use it for *Salat* (prayer) to my Lord and a dinar to help me reach my family." 'Ammar had sold his share of booty which the Holy Prophet, *'Alayhi al-Salam* had given him from the assets acquired from Khaybar and nothing more was left. He then told the Arab man, "You can have twenty dinars, two hundred dirhams of Hijriyah, a Yemenite gown and my animal for riding that will take you to your family and one time food of bread and meat to your satisfaction."

The Arab man said, "How generous are you, O man!" 'Ammar then took him and delivered to him what had promised. The Arab man then returned to the Messenger of Allah, *O Allah, please, grant compensation to Muhammad and his family worthy of their services to your cause,* and the Messenger of

Allah, asked, "Did you have enough food, and clothing?" He replied, "Yes, and I am rich. I pray to Allah to keep my soul and the souls of my parents in service for your cause." He (the Messenger of Allah) then said, "You should appreciate the good deed of Fatimah, *'Alayha al-Salam,* in your favor." The Arab man then said, "O Lord, you are our Lord. We have not invented you. There is no Lord for us to worship except you. You are our provider in all respects. O Lord, grant Fatimah, *'Alayha al-Salam,* such favors which no eye has ever seen and no ears have ever heard." The Holy Prophet, *'Alayhi al-Salam* then said Amin for his prayers and turned to his companions and said, "Allah has already given Fatimah, *'Alayha al-Salam,* such things in this world. I am her father and no one in the world is like me. Ali is her husband, had he not existed there no match exist for Fatimah, *'Alayha al-Salam,* ever. He has given her al-Hassan and al-Husayn, and there is no one in the worlds like them as the leader of the youth of the grandsons of the Prophets and the leader of youths of the garden (paradise).

Nearby were al-Miqdad, 'Ammar and Salman (Rh). He said, "Should I add more for you?" They replied, "Yes, please O Messenger of Allah."

He (the Messenger of Allah), said that the spirit, meaning Jibril came to him that when she will die and will be buried the two angels ask in her grave. "Who is your Lord?" She will replied, "Allah is my Lord." They will ask, "Who is your Prophet?" She will reply, "He is my own father." They will ask, "Who is your Imam?" She will reply, "He is this one standing at the edge of my grave, Ali ibn abu Talib, *'Alayhi al-Salam.*"

He (the Messenger of Allah) then asked, "Should I add telling you more of her excellence? Take notice that Allah has assigned two groups of angels to protect her from her all sides, front, back, right and left. They are with her during her life time and near her grave, at the time of her death saying a great deal of prayers for her, her father, her husband and her sons.

Whoever visits me after my death is as he has visited me in my life ime. Whoever visits Fatimah, *'Alayha al-Salam,* is as he has visited me. Whoever visits Ali ibn abu Talib is as he has visited Fatimah, *'Alayha al-Salam,* and whoever visits al-Hassan and al-Husayn, is as he has visited Ali, and whoever visits their descendants is as he has visited the two of them."

'Ammar then turned to the necklace, treated it with fragrance of musk, wrapped it in a Yemenite gown. He had a slave called Sahm whom he had purchased with the money from his share from the booties of khaybar. He then gave the necklace to that slave saying, "Take this necklace and give it to the Messenger of Allah, *O Allah, please, grant compensation to Muhammad and his family worthy of their services to your cause,* and you also are for him."

The slave then took the necklace, gave it to the Messenger of Allah, *'Alayhi al-Salam* and informed him of what 'Ammar had said. The Holy Prophet then said, "Go to Fatimah, *'Alayha al-Salam,* and give the necklace to her and you also belong to her."

The slave then took the necklace, and then informed Fatimah, *'Alayha al-Salam,* about what the Messenger of Allah, *'Alayhi al-Salam* had said. Fatimah, *'Alayha al-Salam,* then took the necklace and set the slave free. The slave then laughed. She then asked, "What has made you laugh, O slave?" He replied, "It is the great blessings of this necklace, which has fed a hungry man, dressed him, made a poor rich, set a slave free and has returned to its Lord."

H 86, Ch. 3, h 51
Tafsir of Furat ibn Ibrahim:

'Ubayd ibn Kathir in in a Mu'an'an manner has narrated from abu Sa'id al-Khudari who has said the following:

One day Ali, *'Alayhi al-Salam* had remained hungry. He asked Fatimah, *'Alayha al-Salam,* "Do you have anything to feed me?" She replied, "No, by the one who has honored my father by making him His Prophet and has honored you by making you the Executor of the Will, this morning there is no food with me. For the last two days we did not have any food except what I would spare for you and our son al-Hassan and al-Husayn, *'Alayhima al-Salam.*" Ali then said, "O Fatimah, *'Alayha al-Salam,* you should have told me about it so that I then find some food for you." She then said, "O abu al-Hassan, I feel embarrassed before my Lord to burden you with something you cannot do." Ali, *'Alayhi al-Salam* then left Fatimah, *'Alayha al-Salam,* and went out placing his trust in Allah with optimism and borrowed one dinar. The dinar was still in the hand of Ali ibn abu Talib, *'Alayhi al-Salam* when al-Miqdad came face to face during a day of intense heat exposed to the sun from the above and troubled by the same from the ground. When Ali ibn abu Talib saw him, he did not like his condition and asked, "O al-Miqdad, what has bothered you in this hour to leave home?" He said, "O abu al-Hassan, allow me to go and do not ask what is behind me." He said, "O brother, I cannot allow you to go until I find out what you know." He then said, "O abu al-Hassan, for the sake of Allah and for your own sake allow me to go and do not discover my condition." He said, "O brother, you cannot hide your condition from me." He then said, "O abu al-Hassan, because you insist, by the One who has honored Muhammad by making him His Prophet, and has honored you by making you the Executor of the Will, nothing else has bothered me to leave home except poverty (hunger). I left my family complaining desperately of hunger. When I heard the family weeping the ground did not allow me to remain home, so I came out sad and followed my head. This is my story and condition." The eyes of Ali flooded with tears so much so that tears soaked his beard. He then told him, "I swear by the same facts up on which you swore that nothing other than what has bothered you has bothered me to leave home. I have borrowed a dinar and I gave preference to you over myself in spending this dinar." He then gave the dinar to him and returned until he entered the Masjid of the Holy Prophet, *'Alayhi al-Salam*. He performed the *Salat* (prayer) of al-Zuhr, al-'Asr and al-Maghrib *Salat* (prayers). When the Messenger of Allah, *O Allah, please, grant compensation to Muhammad and his family worthy of their services to your cause,* completed the al-Maghrib *Salat* (prayer) he passed by Ali ibn abu Talib who was in the first row. He pressed him with is foot and Ali, stood up and followed, the Messenger of Allah, *O Allah, please, grant compensation to Muhammad and his family worthy of their services to your cause,* until he reached him at the door of Masjid. He said *Salam* (the phrase of offering greeting of peace) and the Messenger of Allah, *'Alayhi al-Salam* responded likewise. He then asked, "O abu al-Hassan, do you have anything for dinner for us so we can come with you?" He paused, a little with his head bent down and unable to answer due to bashfulness, before the Messenger of Allah, *'Alayhi al-Salam,* knowing about the case of the dinar and how he got it and where he spent it. Allah, most high, had already inspired His Prophet, Muhammad, *O Allah, please, grant compensation to Muhammad and his family worthy of their services to your cause,* to have his dinner this night with Ali ibn abu Talib, *'Alayhi al-Salam.*

When the Messenger of Allah, *O Allah, please, grant compensation to Muhammad and his family worthy of their services to your cause,* observed his pause, he said, "O abu al-Hassan, why do you not answer, 'No,' so I can go away or say, 'Yes,' so I can come with you?" He then bashfully and collecting himself said, "You can come with us." The Messenger of Allah, *O Allah grant compensation to Muhammad and his family worthy of their services to your cause,* then holding the hand of Ali ibn abu Talib, moved until they arrived in the house of Fatimah, al-Zahra', *'Alayha al-Salam,* when she was in her place of *Salat* (prayer) and had just completed her *Salat* (prayer) and on one side of her room there was a basin boiling and steaming. When she heard the words of the Messenger of Allah, *O Allah, please, grant compensation to Muhammad and his family worthy of their services to your cause,* she came out of the place for her *Salat* (prayer) and offered him *Salam* (the phrase of offering greeting of peace). He was the dearest to her of all people. He responded likewise and placed his hand over her head saying, "O dearest daughter, how are you doing this evening, may Allah, most High, grant you blessings. Please serve us dinner, may Allah grant you forgiveness, which He has already done so." She then took the basin and placed it before the Holy Prophet, and Ali ibn abu Talib *'Alayhima al-Salam.* Ali ibn abu Talib, *'Alayhi al-Salam* looked at the food and sensed its fragrance. He then looked at Fatimah, *'Alayha al-Salam,* sharply and curiously. Fatimah, *'Alayha al-Salam,* said, "Allah is free of all defects, how critical and intense is your look! Have I done anything wrong between me and you to deserve it?" He then said, "What sin can be bigger than what you have done. Did you not say the day before, swearing by Allah, that you are facing difficulty because of not having any food for two days?" She then looked to the sky and said, "My Lord knows in His sky and earth that I did not say anything but the truth." He then asked, "O Fatimah, *'Alayha al-Salam,* how then did you get this food the like of which in color or aroma and fineness I have not seen?"

He (the narrator) has said that the Messenger of Allah, *O Allah, please, grant compensation to Muhammad and his family worthy of their services to your cause,* then placed his holy palm on the shoulder of Ali ibn abu Talib and tapped saying, "O Ali, this is the replacement for your dinar and the reward for it to you from Allah. ". . . 'Allah has sent it.' Allah gives sustenance to whomever He wants without keeping an account." (3:37)

The Messenger of Allah, *O Allah grant compensation to Muhammad and his family worthy of their services to your cause,* then felt like weeping saying,

All praise belongs to Allah who has refused to allow you both leave this world without receiving your rewards, and treats you, O Ali, like He treated Zakariya and treats Fatimah, *'Alayha al-Salam,* like He treated Maryam (Mary) daughter of 'Imran like when Zakariya visited her in her place for *Salat* (prayer) and found sustenance with her as the al-Quran says, ". . . took custody of her. Whenever he (Zachariah) went to visit her in her place of worship, he would find with her some food. He would ask her, 'Where did this food come from?' She would reply, 'Allah has sent it.' Allah gives sustenance to whomever He wants without keeping an account." (3:37)

Kashf al-Ghummah:

Abu Sa'id has narrated a similar Hadith.

'Amali al-Tusi:

A group has narrated from abu al-Mufaddal from Muhammad ibn Ja'far ibn Muskan from 'Abd Allah ibn al-Husayn from Yahya' ibn 'Abd al-Hamid al-Hammani from Qays ibn al- Rabi' from abu Harun al-'Abdi from abu Sa'id a similar Hadith.

H 87, Ch. 3, h 52
Al-Kafi: [H 3742, Ch. 24, h 6, from al-Kafi]

Ali ibn Ibrahim has narrated from his father from ibn abu 'Umayr from Ishaq ibn 'Ammar ibn 'Abd al-'Aziz from Zurara from abu 'Abd Allah, 'Alayhi al-Salam, who has said the following:

"Once Fatimah, *'Alayha al-Salam,* came to the Messenger of Allah and complained about certain matters. The Messenger of Allah gave her a tablet to read. It was written on the tablet: 'Whoever believes in Allah and the Day of Judgment must not cause suffering to his neighbor. Whoever believes in Allah and the Day of Judgment must treat his guest with honor. Whoever believes in Allah and the Day of Judgment must speak of good or remain silent.'"

H 88, Ch. 3, h 53
Al-Kafi: [H 10088, Ch. 168, h 5, from al-Kafi]

A number of our people have narrated from Ahmad ibn abu 'Abd Allah from 'Isma'il ibn Mehran from 'Ubayd ibn Mu'awiyah ibn Shurayh from Sayf ibn 'Amirah from 'Amr ibn Shamir from Jabir from abu Ja'far, 'Alayhi al-Salam, from Jabir ibn 'Abd Allah al-Ansariy who has said the following:

"One day the Messenger of Allah, *O Allah, grant compensation to Muhammad and his family worthy of their services to Your cause,* came out to visit Fatimah, *'Alayha al-Salam,* and I was with him (the Messenger of Allah). When I reached the door, he (the Messenger of Allah) placed his hand on it and pushed then said, '*Al-Salamu 'Alaykum.*' Fatimah, *'Alayha al-Salam,* responded saying, 'Alay*kum al-Salam,* O Messenger of Allah.' He (the Messenger of Allah) asked, 'Can I come in?' She said, 'Please come in, O Messenger of Allah.' He (the Messenger of Allah) then asked, 'Can I come in with the person who is with me?' She said, 'O Messenger of Allah, I do not have a veil on me.' He (the Messenger of Allah) said, 'O Fatimah, take the extra of your bed sheet and use it as veil to cover your head.' She did accordingly and he (the Messenger of Allah) then said, *'Al-Salamu Alaykum.*' Fatimah, responded saying, 'Alay*ka al-Salam,* O Messenger of Allah.' He (the Messenger of Allah) asked, 'Can I come in?' She replied, 'Yes, O Messenger of Allah.' He (the Messenger of Allah) then asked, 'Can I come in with the person with me?' She replied, 'Yes, you may come with the person with you.' Jabir has said that the Messenger of Allah entered and I also entered and I saw the face of Fatimah looked yellow like the belly of a locust. The Messenger of Allah, *O Allah, grant compensation to Muhammad and his family worthy of their services to Your cause,* asked, 'What has happened, O Fatimah that your face looks yellow?' She replied, 'O Messenger of Allah, it is hunger.' He (the Messenger of Allah) prayed saying, 'O Lord, who satisfies hunger, repels the cause of loss, satisfy Fatimah daughter of Muhammad.' Jabir has said, 'I then saw blood flow through its course and her face turned to its normal color and thereafter she did not experience any more hunger.'"

H 89, Ch. 3, h 54
Tafsir of Furat ibn Ibrahim:

Al-Husayn ibn Sa'id in in a Mu'an'an manner has narrated from Ja'far from his father who has said the following:

The Messenger of Allah, *O Allah, grant compensation to Muhammad and his family worthy of their services to Your cause,* has said the following: "When it will be the Day of Judgment a caller will announce from underneath the Throne saying, "O the community of creatures, you must close your eyes until the daughter of the most beloved to Allah passes to her palace." Fatimah, *'Alayha al-Salam,* then will pass by on her way to her palace dressed in two special green sheets of the fine fabrics of the garden (paradise) and seventy thousand *al-Hawra' al-'in* around her. When she will arrive at the gate of her palace she will find al-Hassan standing and al-Husayn, sleeping with his head cut off. She will ask al-Hassan, "Who is this?" He will replied, "This is my brother. The nation (followers) of your father had murdered him and they cutoff his head also." A call then from Allah will say, "O daughter of the one most beloved to Me, I just have shown you what the nation (followers) of your father has done to him. I have preserved it (the condition), to offer you solace for your suffering in his case and I offer you solace today in the form of not looking in the account matters of my creatures before you and your descendants enter the garden (paradise) as well as your (*Shi'a,* followers of *Ahl al-Bayt*) and those who have offered you appreciable assistance of non-*Shi'a,* before I commence looking in to the account of the creatures."

Fatimah, *'Alayha al-Salam,* my daughter will then enter the garden (paradise) along with her descendants and her *Shi'a,* followers of *Ahl al-Bayt* and those who had offered her appreciable assistance of the non-*Shi'a* people and this is from the words of Allah, most Majestic, most Glorious, "They will not even hear the slightest sound from it while enjoying the best that they can wish for in their everlasting life. (21:102) They will not be affected by the great horror. The angels will come to them with this glad news: 'This is your day which was promised to you.'" (21:103)

They will consist of Fatimah, *'Alayha al-Salam,* her descendants, her (*Shi'a,* followers of *Ahl al-Bayt*) and those who had offered them assistance who were not (*Shi'a,* followers of *Ahl al-Bayt*).

H 90, Ch. 3, h 55
Al-Kafi: [H 1240, Ch. 114, h 7, from al-Kafi]

Through the same chain of narrators it is narrated from Salih ibn 'Aqaba from 'Amr ibn Shimr from Jabir from abu Ja'far, 'Alayhi al-Salam, who has said the following:

"Abu Ja'far, *'Alayhi al-Salam,* has said, 'Once, the Holy Prophet, *'Alayhi al-Salam,* said to Fatimah, *'Alayha al-Salam,* "Rise and bring that tray." She went and took out the tray with fresh bread and steaming meat on it. The Holy

Prophet, Ali, Fatimah, al-Hassan and al-Husayn, *'Alayhim al-Salam,* continued to have their meals from it for thirteen days. Then 'Umm Ayman saw al-Husayn, *'Alayhi al-Salam,* with certain things with him. She asked, "Where did you get it from?" He replied, "We have been having this for our meal for the past thirteen days." 'Umm Ayman came to Fatimah, *'Alayha al-Salam,* and said, "O Fatimah, if 'Umm Ayman finds anything it is all for Fatimah, *'Alayha al-Salam,* and her sons but if Fatimah, *'Alayha al-Salam,* finds something then there is nothing in it for 'Umm Ayman." She (Fatimah) then took out food for her from the tray and 'Umm Ayman ate but the food from the tray vanished. The Holy Prophet, *'Alayhi al-Salam,* said to Fatimah, *'Alayha al-Salam,* "Were you not to feed her (a non-infallible) from it, you and your descendants could have found food in it up to the Day of Judgment.""

"Abu Ja'far, *'Alayhi al-Salam,* then said, 'The tray is with us and our *al-Qa'im* (the one who will rise with Divine Authority and power) will take it out at his time.'"

H 91, Ch. 3, h 56
Al-Kafi: [H 5100, Ch. 33, h 14, from al-Kafi]

Through the same chain of narrators as the previous Hadith it is narrated from Salih ibn 'Uqbah from 'Uqbah who has said the following:

"Abu Ja'far, *'Alayhi al-Salam,* has said, 'In worshipping Allah in the form of praises no other thing is better than Tasbih of Fatimah al-Zahra', *'Alayha al-Salam.* If anything other than this could make a better gift the Messenger of Allah would have instead given to Fatimah al-Zahra', *'Alayha al-Salam.*'"

H 92, Ch. 3, h 57
Tafsir of Furat ibn Ibrahim:

Sahl ibn Ahmad al-Daynuri has narrated in in a Mu'an'an manner from 'Abu 'Abd Allah, Ja'far ibn Muhammad 'Alayhima al-Salam, who has said the following:

Jabir once said to abu Ja'far, *'Alayhi al-Salam* I pray to Allah to keep my soul in service for your cause, please narrate for me a Hadith on the excellence of your grandmother, Fatimah, *'Alayha al-Salam,* that if I will narrate to (*Shi'a,* followers of *Ahl al-Bayt*) they become happy."

Abu Ja'far, *'Alayhi al-Salam* then said, "My father has narrated from my grandfather from the Messenger of Allah, *O Allah, please, grant compensation to Muhammad and his family worthy of their services to your cause,* who has said that when it will become the Day of Judgment, pulpits of light will be set for the Prophets and Messengers. My pulpit will be the highest pulpit on the Day of Judgment. Allah will then say, 'O Muhammad, give a speech.' I will then give a speech which no one of the Prophets had ever heard and so also will be the case of the Messengers. Thereafter pulpits of light will be set for the Executors of the Wills and the pulpit of Ali ibn abu Talib will be in the middle of the pulpits and his pulpit will be higher than the others. Allah will then say, 'O Ali, give a speech.' He will give a speech the like of which no one of the Executors of the Wills had ever heard. Thereafter pulpits of light will be set for the descendants of the Prophets and the Messengers. For my grandsons, the delights of my eyes in my lifetime there will be pulpits of light and then they will be asked to give a speech and they will give a speech which no one of the children of the Prophets and Messengers had ever heard.

"The announcer, who is Jibril, *'Alayhi al-Salam* then will call, 'Where is Fatimah, *'Alayha al-Salam,* daughter of Muhammad? Where is Khadijah *'Alayha al-Salam,* daughter of Khuwaylid? Where is Maryam (Mary) daughter of 'Imran? Where is Asiyah daughter of Muzaham? Where is Kulthum mother of Yahya' ibn Zakariya?' They will then rise and Allah, most High, will say, 'O the people of the gathering of resurrection, to who does generosity belong today?' Muhammad, Ali, al-Hassan, and al-Husayn, *'Alayhim al-Salam,* will say, 'It belongs to Allah, who is one and dominant.' Allah will then say, 'O people of the gathering of resurrection, I have made kindness and generosity to remain in the hands of Muhammad, Ali, al-Hassan, al-Husayn and Fatimah, *'Alayhim al-Salam.* O people of the gathering of resurrection bend down your heads and close your eyes, because Fatimah, *'Alayha al-Salam,* is coming to the garden (paradise).' Jibril, *'Alayhi al-Salam* will bring her on a camel of the camels of the garden (paradise) decorated on both sides with its reign made of pearls, just bedecked, with a seat of emerald on it and the camel will be made to sit down before her and she will ride and one hundred thousand angels will move escorting on the right side and another one hundred thousand angels move on the left and one hundred thousand angels will carry her on their wings until they arrive at the gate of the garden (paradise). When they arrive at the gate of the garden (paradise) she will turn around and pause. Allah will say, 'O

101

daughter of my beloved one, why have you paused and turned around, when I have already commanded to escort you to my garden (paradise)?'

"She will replied, 'I wanted to find out how much my importance in such a today is.' Allah will say, 'O daughter of my beloved one, you may turn back and find those who has any affection in their heart for you or any of your descendants you can admit them in the garden (paradise).'

"Abu Ja'far, *'Alayhi al-Salam* has said, 'By Allah, O Jabir, on that day she will pick up her (*Shi'a*, followers of *Ahl al-Bayt*) just as birds pick up fine grains from among the useless ones. When her (*Shi'a*, followers of *Ahl al-Bayt*) are found with her at the gate of the garden (paradise) Allah then will drop in their hearts to pause and turn around and when they do so Allah, most Majestic, most Glorious, will ask, "O my beloved ones, why have you paused and turned around, when Fatimah, *'Alayha al-Salam,* daughter of my most beloved one has already interceded on your behalf?" They will replied, "O Lord, we liked to make our importance become known on such a day."

'Allah will say, "O my beloved ones, you can find out those who loved you because of your honoring and respecting Fatimah, *'Alayha al-Salam,* and find those who fed you because of your honoring and respecting Fatimah, *'Alayha al-Salam,* and those who clothed you because of your honoring and respecting Fatimah, *'Alayha al-Salam,* find those who served you drinks for your honoring and respecting Fatimah, *'Alayha al-Salam,* find those who defended you against backbiting because of your honoring and respecting Fatimah, *'Alayha al-Salam,* then hold their hands and admit them in the garden (paradise)."'

Abu Ja'far, *'Alayhi al-Salam* has said that no one will remain among people except the doubting, or unbelievers, or hypocrites.

When they are found in the levels (of hell) they will cry as Allah, most High, has said, "We neither have anyone to intercede for us before Allah (26:100) nor a loving friend." (26:101) They will cry, "Would that we could have a chance to live again so that we might become believers." (26:102)

Abu Ja'far, *'Alayhi al-Salam,* has said that, never, ever will their wish come true. They will be barred from that which they wish, as al-Quran has said,

"Whatever they had concealed will be revealed to them. If they were to return to (the worldly life), they would again worship idols, for they are liars." (6:28)

H 93, Ch. 3, h 58
Tafsir of Furat ibn Ibrahim:

Muhammad ibn al-Qasim ibn 'Ubayd in in a Mu'an'an manner has narrated from' abu 'Abd Allah, 'Alayhi al-Salam who has said the following:

This is about the meaning of the words of Allah, the most Majestic, the most Glorious:

"In the Name of Allah, the Beneficent, the Merciful. We revealed the Quran on the Night of Destiny (power). (97:1) . . ." He (the Imam), *'Alayhi al-Salam* has said that "night" stands for Fatimah, *'Alayha al-Salam,* and "power" stands for Allah. Whoever recognizes Fatimah, *'Alayha al-Salam,* properly such person finds the night of destiny (power). She is named 'Fatimah' because creatures are separated from knowing her.

H 94, Ch. 3, h 59
Muhaj al-Da'awat:

It is narrated from Shaykh Ali ibn Muhammad ibn Ali ibn 'Abd al-Samad from his grandfather from al-Faqih abu al-Hassan from abu al-Barakat Ali ibn al-Husayn al-Jawzi, from al-Saduq from al-Hassan ibn Muhammad ibn Sa'id from Forat ibn Ibrahim from Ja'far ibn Muhammad ibn Bishrwayh from Muhammad ibn Idris ibn Sa'id al-Ansari from Dawud ibn Rashid, and al-Walid ibn Shuja' ibn Marwan from 'Asem from 'Abd Allah ibn Salman (Rh) al-Farsi from his father who has said the following:

Once ten days after the passing away of the Holy Prophet, *O Allah, please, grant compensation to Muhammad and his family worthy of their services to your cause,* I came out of my house and Ali ibn abu Talib, the cousin of the Messenger of Allah, *O Allah, please, grant compensation to Muhammad and his family worthy of their services to your cause,* met me and said to me, "You have been unfair to us after the Messenger of Allah, *'Alayhi al-Salam.*" I said, "My dearest one, abu al-Hassan, people like you cannot be treated unfairly. However, my sadness because of the Messenger of Allah is prolonging and it has prevented me from visiting you." He then said, "You should come to the house of Fatimah, *'Alayha al-Salam,* daughter of the Messenger of Allah, *'Alayhi al-Salam,* because she misses you and she wants to give a gift because you have a gift from the garden (paradise)." I then asked, "Does Fatimah, *'Alayha al-Salam,* have a gift for me from the garden (paradise)?" He (the Imam) replied, "Yes, she received it yesterday." I (Salman (Rh)) moved fast to the house of Fatimah, *'Alayha al-Salam,* daughter of the Messenger of Allah, *O Allah, please, grant compensation to Muhammad and his family worthy of their services to your cause,* and found her siting with a gown on her head which fell short from covering her head or feet. If she covered her head the other end of it fell short from covering her feet (pedicel). When she saw me, she covered her head and said, "O Salman, *you* have not been fair to me after the passing away of my father, the Holy Prophet, *'Alayhi al-Salam."*

I then said, "My dearest one, have I been unfair to you?" She then said, "What else can it be? Sit down and think about what I say to you. Yesterday, I was sitting here and the door of the house was closed and I was thinking about the discontinuation of the coming of the divine revelation to us and turning away of the angels from our house. At that time the door opened without anyone opening it, then three very beautiful maidens, the like of whom, in beauty, shape, youthfulness of their faces, and their increasing fragrance, no one has ever seen, came in. When I saw them I stood up and moved to them not knowing who they were, and asked, 'For the sake of my father, tell me; are you people from the inhabitants of Makkah or al-Madinah?'

"They replied, 'O daughter of Muhammad, we are not of inhabitants of Makkah or al-Madinah and we are not of the inhabitants of any part of the earth. We are *al-Hawra' al-'in* from *dar al-Salam,* (the house of peace). Allah the Lord of majesty has sent us, O daughter of Muhammad, we are yearning to be with you.' I then turned to the one whom I thought was bigger in age and asked, 'What is your name?' She replied, 'My name is Maqdudah.' I then asked, 'Why your name is Maqdudah?' She replied, 'I am created for al-Miqdad ibn Aswad al-Kindy, the companion of the Messenger of Allah, *O Allah, please, grant compensation to Muhammad and his family worthy of their services to your cause.'* I then asked the second one, 'What is your name?' She replied, 'My name is Dharrah.' I then asked, 'Why are you named Dharrah, and you are very noble in my eyes?' She replied, 'I am created for abu Dharr al-Ghifari, the companion of the Messenger of Allah, *O Allah, please, grant compensation to Muhammad and his family worthy of their services to your cause.'* I then asked the third one, 'What is your name?' She replied, 'My name is Salma'.' I then asked, 'Why are you named Salama'?' She replied, 'It is because I am for Salman al-Farsi, the Mawla of your father, the Messenger of Allah, *O Allah, please, grant compensation to Muhammad and his family worthy of their services to your cause.*' Fatimah, *'Alayha al-Salam,* then said, 'They took out for me bluish looking fresh date like *khushknanij* (sweet dry bread), large and whiter than snow of increasing fragrance like al-Adhfar musk."

She then brought it forward and said, "O Salman, use this for your dinner to break your fast. In the morning bring for me its date stones" or that she said, "its *'Ajmah.*"

Salman (Rh) has said that he then took the date and everyone that he passed of the companions of the Messenger of Allah, asked me, "O Salman (Rh) do you carry musk." At the time of breaking the fast I broke my fast with it but I did not find any date stone in it. I then went to the daughter of the Messenger of Allah, *O Allah grant compensation to Muhammad and his family worthy of their services to your cause,* during the second day and said to her that I used her gift for breakfast but did not find any date stone in them. She then said, "It was not to have any date stone in it because they were from a palm tree that Allah has planted in Dar al-Salam with the word that my father, Muhammad, *O Allah, please, grant compensation to Muhammad and his family worthy of their services to your cause,* had taught me and I would say them in the morning and the evenings."

Salman (Rh) has said that he then asked her to teach those words to him. She then said, "If you like not to be troubled by fever in your life then read these words very often." Salman (Rh) has said that she then taught him the following words (the prayers of light):

Bismillah, (in the name of Allah, most Beneficent, most Merciful)

In the name of Allah, the light, in the name of Allah, the light of the light, in the name of Allah, the light over light, in the name of Allah, who is He who manages all affairs.

In the name of Allah who created light from light. Praise be to Allah who created light from light, and sent down light on the mountain (Tur), in the

105

inscribed book, in the parchment unrolled, by a measure, well-determined, on the (Holy) Prophet, the giver of glad tidings. All Praise belongs to Allah; it is He who is spoken of with majesty, of the highest of the high attributes, known to be the most glorious. In joy and happiness, in sorrow and distress, He (alone) is thankfully praised. Blessings of Allah be on our master, Muhammad, and on his pure descendants.

Salman (Rh) has said that he then taught it (to others) and by Allah they numbered more than a thousand souls of people of al-Madinah and Makkah who suffered from fever and they all found cure thereby by the permission of Allah, most High.

H 95, Ch. 3, h 60
From some books on virtues:

The author through the chain of his narrators has narrated from 'Usamah who has said the following:

I (the narrator) once passed by Ali and 'Abbas who were sitting in the Masjid. They said, please ask the Messenger of Allah, to grant us permission for a meeting with him. I (the narrator) then said to the Messenger of Allah, *O Allah, please, grant compensation to Muhammad and his family worthy of their services to your cause,* that Ali and 'Abbas wanted permission for a meeting with him. He (the Messenger of Allah) then asked, "Do you know for what reason they want to meet?" I replied, "I do not know." He (the Messenger of Allah) said, "But I know for what they want to meet me." He (the Messenger of Allah) granted them permission and they came in and sat down then they asked, "O Messenger of Allah, who in your family is more beloved to you?" He (the Messenger of Allah) replied, "She is Fatimah, *'Alayha al-Salam.*"

Through the chain of his narrators from 'Abd Allah ibn al-Zubayr from his father from 'A'ishah who has said the following:

Whenever she would speak of Fatimah, *'Alayha al-Salam,* daughter of the Messenger of Allah, *O Allah, please, grant compensation to Muhammad and his family worthy of their services to your cause,* she would say, "I never saw anyone more truthful than her except the ones born from her."

Through the chain of his narrators the author has narrated from Ahmad ibn Muhammad al-Tha'labi from 'Abd Allah ibn Hamid from abu Muhammad al-Muzni from abu Ya 'li al-Musali from Sahl ibn Zanjalah al-Razi from 'Abd Allah ibn Salih from ibn Luhay 'ah , from Muhammad ibn al-Munkadir from Jabir ibn 'Abd Allah who has said the following:

The Messenger of Allah, *O Allah grant compensation to Muhammad and his family worthy of their services to your cause,* remained without food for several days until it became difficult for him. He (the Messenger of Allah), then went to the houses of his wives but did not find anything with anyone of them. He then went to the house of Fatimah, *'Alayha al-Salam,* and said, "My dearest daughter, do you have any food to eat? I am hungry." She replied, "No, by Allah, I pray to Allah to keep my soul and the souls of my parents in service for your cause." When he left her house, a neighbor sent her a loaf of bread and a piece of meat. She took it and then placed it in a basin then covered it, saying, "I must preserve it for the Messenger of Allah, *O Allah, please, grant compensation to Muhammad and his family worthy of their services to your cause,* myself and those who are with me" and they all needed food. She then sent al-Hassan or al-Husayn, *'Alayhima al-Salam,* to the Messenger of Allah, *'Alayhi al-Salam.* When he came back she said, "Allah has given us something which I have preserved secretly." He (the Messenger of Allah) then said, "Bring it then, please." She then brought it and uncovered the basin and found it full of bread and meat. When she looked at it she became amazed and realized that it was due to kindness of Allah, most Majestic, most Glorious. She then thanked Allah and said, *"O Allah, please, grant compensation to Muhammad and his family worthy of their services to your cause."* He (the Messenger of Allah) then asked, "Wherefrom have you got it, O my dearest daughter?" She replied, "It is from Allah who gives sustenance to whomever He wills without accounting." He then thanked Allah, most Majestic, most Glorious, saying, "All praise belongs to Allah who has made you similar to the leader of the worlds of the Israelites in their time because when she would receive food from Allah and then she was asked about it she would say, 'It is from Allah who gives sustenance to whoever He wills without accounting.'" The Messenger of Allah, *O Allah grant compensation to Muhammad and his family worthy of their services to your cause,* then sent someone to call Ali, *'Alayhi al-Salam,* then the Messenger of Allah, Ali, Fatimah, al-Hassan and al-Husayn, *'Alayhim al-Salam,* ate to their satisfaction as well as all the wives of the Holy Prophet, but the basin still remained full as it was before. Fatimah, *'Alayha al-Salam,* has said, "I then extended from it to all of my neighbors and

Allah placed blessing and goodness in it as He had done for Maryam (Mary) *'Alayha al-Salam.'*

Manaqib of ibn Shahr Ashub:

Tha'labi in his interpretations of al-Quran and ibn al-Muzni in al-Arba'in through the chain of their narrators from Muhammad ibn al- Munkadir from Jabir have narrated a similar Hadith.

H 96, Ch. 3, h 61
From the book of virtues mentioned above it is narrated from abu al-Faraj Muhammad ibn Ahmad al-Makki from al-Muzaffar ibn Ahmad ibn Muhammad al-Mawazi and narrated to me also Qadi al-Qudat Muhammad ibn al-Hassan al-Baghdadi from al-Husayn ibn Muhammad ibn Ali al-Zaynabi from al-Karimah Fatimah daughter of Ahmad ibn Muhammad al-Marwaziyah in Makkah (may Allah, most High, keep her safe) from abu Ali Zahir ibn Ahmad from Mu'adh ibn Yusuf al-Jurjani from Ahmad ibn Muhammad ibn Ghalib from 'Uthman ibn abu Shaybah from (ibn) Namir from Mujalid from ibn 'Abbas who has said the following:

An Arab man from banu Salim went out in the wilderness (perhaps hunting) and he saw a lizard fleeing away from him. He chased it until he hunted the lizard and he then placed it in his sleeve. He then moved toward the Holy Prophet, *O Allah, please, grant compensation to Muhammad and his family worthy of their services to your cause,* and when he stood in front of him, he called, O Muhammad, O Muhammad. It was of the manner of the Messenger of Allah, *O Allah, please, grant compensation to Muhammad and his family worthy of their services to your cause,* upon being called as, O Muhammad! He would respond, O Muhammad! If he would have been called as, O Ahmad! He would respond, O Ahmad! If he were called, O abu al-Qasim! He would respond, O abu al-Qasim! If he were called, O Messenger of Allah! He would respond, *Labbayka wa Sa'dayka* (here I am ready at your disposal to happily respond to your call) and his face would become cheerful. When the Arab man called him, O Muhammad! O Muhammad! The Holy Prophet, *'Alayhi al-Salam* responded, O Muhammad! O Muhammad! He then said, "Are you the liar magician who has exceeded, in speaking lies, everyone who can speak under the green sky and over the soil. Are you the one who thinks in the green sky there is a Lord who has sent you to the black and white people and to al-Lat and al-'Uzza' (two idols), were I not afraid being called hasty by my people

I would strike you with my sword, this one, with a strike that killed you to make you an example for the people of the past and future."

'Umar ibn al-Khattab then jumped toward him to intimidate him but the Holy Prophet, said, "Sit down O abu Hafs; a forbearing one can almost become a Prophet." The Holy Prophet, *O Allah, please, grant compensation to Muhammad and his family worthy of their services to your cause,* then turned to Arab man and said, "O brother from banu Salim, is this the way Arabs behave, attack us in our meetings and face us with harsh words. O Arab man, by the one who has sent me as a Prophet in all truth that whoever, hits me in this world, tomorrow, in the next life, will be placed in the blazing fire. O Arab man, by the one who has sent me as a Prophet, that the inhabitants of seventh sky call me Ahmad the truthful one. O Arab man, you must become a Muslim, then you will remain safe from the fire. You will enjoy what we do and you will become responsible for whatever we are responsible and you will be one of our brothers in Islam."

He (the narrator) has said that the Arab man became angry and said, "By al-Lat and al-'Uzza', I will not believe in you, O Muhammad, unless this lizard believes in you." He then dropped the lizard from his sleeve. When the lizard fell on the ground it fled in fright. The Holy Prophet, *O Allah, please, grant compensation to Muhammad and his family worthy of their services to your cause,* called it saying, "O lizard come back to me." It then came back to him (the Messenger of Allah) and started looking to the Holy Prophet, *'Alayhi al-Salam.*

He (the narrator) has said that the Holy Prophet, *O Allah, please, grant compensation to Muhammad and his family worthy of their services to your cause,* then asked, "O lizard, Who am I?" The lizard began to speak in an eloquent fluent language without any pause. It said, "You are Muhammad ibn 'Abd Allah ibn 'Abd al-Muttalib ibn Hashim ibn 'Abd Manaf."

The Holy Prophet, *'Alayhi al-Salam* then asked, "Who do you worship?" It replied, "I worship Allah, most Majestic, most Glorious, who splits the grain to grow and forms the seed (of human beings), who has taken Ibrahim as His close friend and has chosen you as His beloved one." It then began to recite these lines of poems:

It is certain that you, O Messenger of Allah are truthful.

Blessings are with you as a well guided one and as a guide,

You have begun preaching for us an easy religion to follow;

After a time when we worshiped donkeys and tyrants.

O the best one called and the best messenger,

Sent to al-Jinn after that the human beings said *'Labbayk'* (we are at your disposal) for your call,

We are a people from banu Salim,

And we have come to you in the hope to gain heights.

You have come with clear proofs from Allah; you have lived with us as a person of increasing true words.

You are a blessing, living are dead,

You were born as a blessing as well as grown to manhood.

He (the narrator) has said that then the mouth of the lizard became closed and it could not answer anything. When the Arab man saw this he said, "Amazing, I hunted a lizard from the wilderness then brought it in my sleeve and it did not think or speak and did not understand but it spoke to Muhammad, *O Allah, please, grant compensation to Muhammad and his family worthy of their services to your cause,* all these words, testified with this testimony. I do not want to search for traces after finding the very substance I am searching for. Extend you hand; I testify that only Allah deserves worship, He is one and has no partners and I testify that you, Muhammad, are His servant and Messenger." The Arab man became a Muslim and made it good.

The Holy Prophet, *'Alayhi al-Salam* then turned to his companions to teach him chapters of al-Quran. The Holy Prophet, then asked, "Do you have any belongings?" He replied, "We are four thousand souls in banu Salim and there is no one poorer than me. The Holy Prophet, *O Allah, please, grant compensation to Muhammad and his family worthy of their services to your cause,* then turned to his companions and said, "Who can give this Arab man a camel, so that I can guarantee him from Allah to give him a camel of light of the garden (paradise)?" Sa'd ibn 'Ubadah sprang up saying, "I pray to Allah to keep my soul and the souls of my parents in service for your cause, I have a red camel which is about to give birth to its young and I can give it to the Arab man." The Holy Prophet, *'Alayhi al-Salam* said, "O Sa'd you have expressed boastfulness before because of your camel. Should I tell you about the camel that I will give you to replace the camel that you have given to the Arab man?" He replied, "Yes, 'I pray to Allah to keep my soul and the souls of my parents in service for your cause, please do so." He (the Messenger of Allah) then said, "O Sa'd, the camel is of red gold, its legs are of ambergris, its fur is of saffron, its eyes are of red ruby, its neck is of green emerald, its hump is of yellow camphor, its chin is of pearls, its nose is of fresh pearls. On the back of it there is a canopy of transparent white pearls and it will fly within the garden (paradise)."

The Holy Prophet, *O Allah, please, grant compensation to Muhammad and his family worthy of their services to your cause,* then turned to his companions and said, "Who among you can crown this Arab man so that I guarantee for him a crown of protection, and piety?" Ali ibn abu Talib, *'Alayhi al-Salam* then sprang up saying, "'I pray to Allah to keep my soul and the souls of my parents in service for your cause, what is the crown of protection, piety? Please describe some of its qualities."

He (the narrator) has said that Ali, *'Alayhi al-Salam* then removed his turban and placed on the head of the Arab man.

The Holy Prophet, *O Allah, please, grant compensation to Muhammad and his family worthy of their services to your cause,* then asked, "Who among you can provide him provisions so that I will provide him with the provision of protection, piety?"

Salman (Rh) al-Farsi then sprang up and asked saying, "I pray to Allah to keep my soul and the souls of my parents in service for your cause, what is the provision of protection, piety?" He (the Messenger of Allah) replied, "O Salman, on your last day of this world, Allah will dictate you the testimony: I testify that only Allah deserves worship, He is one and has no partners and I testify that Muhammad is His servant and Messenger. When you say it you will meet me and I will meet you and if you will not say it you will not be able to meet me and I will never meet you."

He (the narrator) has said that Salman (Rh) then went to all of the nine homes of the Messenger of Allah, *'Alayhi al-Salam* but he could not find anything with them. When he turned back his eyes fell on the chamber of Fatimah, *'Alayha al-Salam,* and he said to himself, "If there is goodness it must be in the house of Fatimah, *'Alayha al-Salam,* daughter of Muhammad, *O Allah, please, grant compensation to Muhammad and his family worthy of their services to your cause.* He knocked at the door and from behind the door she responded asking, "Who is there?" He then replied, "I am Salman (Rh) al-Farsi." She then asked, "What do you ask?" He then explained the whole story of the Arab man and the lizard with the Holy Prophet, *'Alayhi al-Salam* and she said to Salman (Rh), "O Salman (Rh) by the one who has sent Muhammad, *O Allah, please, grant compensation to Muhammad and his family worthy of their services to your cause,* as a Prophet in all truth that since three days we did not have any food. Al-Hassan, and al-Husayn, *'Alayhima al-Salam,* have become restless because of hunger. They then went to sleep like baby birds stripped off of their feathers, but I do not want to turn away goodness when it comes to my door. O Salman (Rh) take my Dar' (a certain kind of garment) to Sham'un, the Jewish man and tell him that Fatimah, *'Alayha al-Salam,* daughter of Muhammad says loan us one Sa' of dates and barley and keep this garment as security until we return your dates and barley, by the will of Allah, most High."

Salman (Rh) then took the piece of garment to the Jewish man and said to him O Sham'un, this garment belongs to Fatimah, *'Alayha al-Salam,* daughter of Muhammad, *O Allah, please, grant compensation to Muhammad and his family worthy of their services to your cause.* She asks you to loan her for it one Sa' of dates and barley until she returns to you the same amount by the will of Allah."

He (the narrator) has said that Sham'un then took the garment in his hand and turned side to side with his eyes flooded with tears. He said to Salman, "O Salman (Rh), this is the example of restricting one's self from the worldly matters about which Musa *'Alayhi al-Salam,* ibn 'Imran has informed us in the

Torah. I testify that only Allah deserves worship, He is one and has no partners and I testify that Muhammad is His servant and Messenger. He became a Muslim, and made himself a true one."

He then gave to Salman (Rh) one Sa' of dates and barley which Salman (Rh) brought to Fatimah, *'Alayha al-Salam,* who grinded it to flour and baked bread, then brought it to Salman (Rh) saying to him, "Take it to the Holy Prophet, *'Alayhi al-Salam.''*

He (the narrator) has said that Salman (Rh) said, "O Fatimah, *'Alayha al-Salam,* keep some bread to treat al-Hassan and al-Husayn, *'Alayhima al-Salam,*" but she said, "This is what we have dedicated for Allah, most Majestic, most Glorious, and we do not take anything from it."

He (the narrator) has said that Salman (Rh) then took the bread and dates to the Holy Prophet, *O Allah, please, grant compensation to Muhammad and his family worthy of their services to your cause,* and when he saw Salman (Rh) he asked, "Wherefrom have you got it?" Salman (Rh) replied, "It is from the house of your daughter, Fatimah, *'Alayha al-Salam.''*

He (the narrator) has said that the Holy Prophet, *'Alayhi al-Salam* did not have any food for three days. He (the narrator) has said that the Holy Prophet, *'Alayhi al-Salam* then sprang up until he reached the house of Fatimah, *'Alayha al-Salam,* and knocked the door. Whenever, the Holy Prophet, would knock the door only Fatimah, *'Alayha al-Salam,* would open the door. When Fatimah, *'Alayha al-Salam,* opened the door for him, the Holy Prophet, *'Alayhi al-Salam* looked at her face which had turned pale and her eyes that seemed as changed and he asked, "My dearest daughter, daughter what is it that I see has happened to your face that has turned pale and your eyes are changed?" She replied, "My dear father we have not been finding any food for three days now. Al-Hassan and al-Husayn, *'Alayhima al-Salam,* had become restless because of hunger and then they went to sleep like baby birds stripped off of their feathers."

He (the narrator) has said that the Holy Prophet, *'Alayhi al-Salam* then woke them up. He placed one on his one thigh and the other on his other thigh and asked Fatimah, *'Alayha al-Salam,* to sit in front of him and then embraced her. Ali ibn abu Talib, *'Alayhi al-Salam* came in and he embraced the Holy

113

Prophet, from behind him. Thereafter the Holy Prophet, *'Alayhi al-Salam* raised his eyes to the sky and said, "My Lord, my master, these are my *Ahl al-Bayt* (family). O Lord, please keep all uncleanliness away from them and keep them pure and clean as it can be." He (the narrator) has said that then Fatimah, *'Alayha al-Salam,* daughter of Muhammad, *O Allah, please, grant compensation to Muhammad and his family worthy of their services to your cause,* sprang up to her place of *Salat* (prayer). She performed two *Rak'at Salat* (prayer) then raised the palm of her hand to the sky and said, "O my Lord, my master, this is your Prophet, Muhammad, this is Ali, the cousin of your Prophet, and these are al-Hassan and al-Husayn, *'Alayhima al-Salam,* the two grandsons of your Prophet, O Lord, please send for them a table from the sky as you had done for the Israelites who ate from it but rejected it. O Lord, please send a table for us; we believe in it."

Ibn 'Abbas has said that, by Allah her appeal was not yet finished that a tray steaming with food was placed nearby to her with fragrance increasing more than yellow saffron. She then picked it up then brought it to the Holy Prophet, Ali, al-Hassan and al-Husayn, *'Alayhim al-Salam.* When Ali ibn abu Talib, *'Alayhi al-Salam* saw it he asked, "O Fatimah, *'Alayha al-Salam,* wherefrom have you got it?"

He did not know of any food available with Fatimah, *'Alayha al-Salam.* The Holy Prophet, *'Alayhi al-Salam* said, "O abu al-Hassan, do not ask, praise Allah who has not caused me to die before granting me a child like her who is like Maryam (Mary) daughter of 'Imran about whom al-Quran says, "Whenever he went to visit her in her place of worship, he would find with her some food. He would ask her, 'Where did this food come from?' She would reply, 'Allah has sent it. Allah gives sustenance to whomever He wants without keeping an account.' (3:37)"

He (the narrator) has said that the Holy Prophet, Ali, Fatimah, *'Alayha al-Salam,* and al-Hassan and al-Husayn, ate their food and then the Holy Prophet, came out and the Arab man then, on his animal for riding, went to banu Salim. They were four thousand men at that time. He stood in their middle and called them at the peak of his voice to say, "We testify that only Allah deserves worship, He is one and has no partners and we testify that Muhammad is His servant and Messenger."

He (the narrator) has said that when they heard his words they rushed toward him with their swords and unsheathed them and then they said to him, "You have been affected by the religion of Muhammad, the liar magician." He said to them, "He is not a magician and he is not a liar." He then said, "O the community of banu Salim, the Lord of Muhammad, *O Allah, please, grant compensation to Muhammad and his family worthy of their services to your cause,* is the best Lord. Muhammad, *O Allah, please, grant compensation to Muhammad and his family worthy of their services to your cause,* is the best Prophet. I went to him hungry, he fed me, without clothes he dressed me, and without any animal for riding and he gave one. He then explained for them the story of the lizard with the Holy Prophet, then recited the lines of poems of the lizard which it had recited about the Holy Prophet, *'Alayhi al-Salam.* He then said, "O the community of banu Salim if you become Muslims, you will remain safe from the fire." On that day four thousand men became Muslims. They carried green banners when surrounding the Messenger of Allah, *O Allah, please, grant compensation to Muhammad and his family worthy of their services to your cause.*

I ('Allamah Majlisi) I found this Hadith in an old book of 'Ammah (non-Shi'a Muslims) with the following chains of narrators:

Narrated to us abu Bakr Ahmad ibn Ali, al-Tarshishi, in Baghdad, in the year 484 who said that narrated to us Karimah daughter of Ahmad ibn Muhammad ibn Hatim al-Marwazi in Makkah, may Allah keep her safe, by reading it to us in Masjid al-Haram (the Sacred Masjid) in the month of Dhul Hajjah in the year 431 (A.H) who said that narrated to us abu Ali, Zahir, ibn Ahmad ibn Muhammad ibn Ghalib from 'Uthman ibn abu Shaybah from ibn Numayr from Mujalid from ibn 'Abd Allah a similar Hadith.

H 97, Ch. 3, h 62
From the same book mentioned above:

It is narrated in a Mursal Ahadith that al-Hassan and al-Husayn, *'Alayhima al-Salam,* had only old clothes to wear when very little time was left to the day of 'Id. They said to their mother, Fatimah, *'Alayha al-Salam,* that for the children of so and so family new dresses are tailored with which one can really feel proud. Why we do not have any such dresses, O beloved mother?" She replied, "I by the will of Allah will tailor for you also. "When it was the 'Id day Jibril, *'Alayhi al-Salam* came with two shirts of the garments of the garden (paradise) to the Messenger of Allah, *O Allah grant compensation to Muhammad and his family worthy of their services to your cause,* who asked, "What is this, O brother Jibril?" He then informed him about the words of al-Hassan and al-Husayn, to Fatimah, *'Alayha al-Salam,* and that Fatimah, *'Alayha al-Salam,* had said that she will tailor for them new dresses by the will of Allah. Jibril then said, that Allah, most High, on listening their words did not like to make the words of Fatimah, *'Alayha al-Salam,* "I will tailor for you new clothes by the will of Allah" become untrue.

It is narrated from Sa'id al-Huffaz al-Daylami through the chain of his narrators from Anas who has said the following:

The Messenger of Allah, *O Allah grant compensation to Muhammad and his family worthy of their services to your cause,* has said that when the people of the garden (paradise) will settle in the garden (paradise) and enjoy and the people of the fire will settle in the fire, a light will shine for the people of the garden (paradise) and they ask each other about what that light is all about and perhaps it is a manifestation of our Lord, the Lord of majesty who is looking to us. Ridwan (the keeper of the garden (paradise), will say to them, "No, it is not what you think it is. In fact, Ali, *'Alayhi al-Salam,* entertaining Fatimah, *'Alayha al-Salam,* has made her to smile and this light is because of her smiling.

Through a chain of narrators it is narrated from ibn 'Abbas who has said the following:

The Holy Prophet, *O Allah, please, grant compensation to Muhammad and his family worthy of their services to your cause,* has said, "I was taken for the night journey and I entered the garden (paradise). I then reached the palace of Fatimah, *'Alayha al-Salam,* then I saw seventy palaces made of red coral decorated with pearl, their gates, walls and furnishings all of one vein (quality, structure, streak, color).

Al-Hassan has said that there was no one worshipping as much as Fatimah, *'Alayha al-Salam,* did; whose feet had swelled because of standing for lengthy periods of time.

H 98, Ch. 3, h 63
Tanbih al-Khatir:

Once the Holy Prophet, *O Allah, please, grant compensation to Muhammad and his family worthy of their services to your cause,* was in the Masjid and people were around him. He was waiting for Bilal to come and say the *Adhan* for *Salat* (prayer). He then arrived and the Holy Prophet, *O Allah, please, grant compensation to Muhammad and his family worthy of their services to your cause,* asked, "What has delayed you, O Bilal?" He replied, "I passed by Fatimah, *'Alayha al-Salam,* and found her grinding grains to make flour. She had placed her son al-Hassan next to the grinding stone who was weeping. I then said to her, "I can help you either with grinding or entertain your son." She said, "I am gentler in entertaining my son." I worked the grinding stone and this delayed me." The Holy Prophet, *O Allah, please, grant compensation to Muhammad and his family worthy of their services to your cause,* said, "You have been kind to her, may Allah be kind to you."

I ('Allamah Majlisi) say that ibn Shiruwayh in al-Firdaws has narrated from ibn 'Abbas and abu Sa'id from the Holy Prophet, O Allah, please, grant compensation to Muhammad and his family worthy of their services to your cause, who has said the following:

Fatimah, *'Alayha al-Salam,* is the leader of the women of the worlds except Maryam (Mary) daughter of 'Imran."

It is narrated from al-Miswar ibn Makhramah from the Holy Prophet, O Allah, please, grant compensation to Muhammad and his family worthy of their services to your cause, who has said the following:

Fatimah, *'Alayha al-Salam,* is a part of myself. Whoever makes her angry has made me angry and whoever troubles her has troubled me.

It is narrated from 'Umar ibn al-Khattab from the Holy Prophet, O Allah, please, grant compensation to Muhammad and his family worthy of their services to your cause, who has said the following:

I must say that Fatimah, *'Alayha al-Salam,* Ali, al-Hassan and al-Husayn, are in a community of holiness in a white palace which has the Throne of the beneficent Allah, most Majestic, most Glorious, for its ceiling.

I ('Allamah Majlisi) say that al-Sayyid ibn Tawus (r.h) in the book Sa'd and al-Sa'ud has said that he has read in the book "facts revealed in al-Quran al-Hakim about the Holy Prophet, *O Allah, please, grant compensation to Muhammad and his family worthy of their services to your cause,* and his *Ahl al-Bayt* (family), *'Alayhim al-Salam* compiled by Muhammad ibn al-'Abbas, ibn Ali, ibn Marwan al-Marwah has said that narrated to us Muhammad ibn al-Qasim ibn 'Ubayd al-Bukhari from Ja'far ibn 'Abd Allah al-'Alawi from Yahya' ibn Hashim from Ja'far ibn Sulayman from abu Harun al-'Abdi from abu Sa'id al-Khudari who has said the following: A special *amaranth* (a special art work) was given as a present to the Messenger of Allah, *O Allah, please; grant compensation to Muhammad and his family worthy of their services to your cause,* by the King of Utopia (Habashah) which was woven with gold. The Messenger of Allah, *O Allah, please, grant compensation to Muhammad and his family worthy of their services to your cause,* said, "I want to give this to a man who loves Allah and His messenger and Allah and His messenger love him. The companions of the Holy Prophet then raised their necks for the gift but the Messenger of Allah, *O Allah, please, grant compensation to Muhammad and his family worthy of their services to your cause,* asked, "Where is Ali?" 'Ammar ibn Yasar has said that when I heard it I sprang up to find out Ali, *'Alayhi al-Salam* and I informed him about it. He came and the Messenger of Allah, *O Allah, please, grant compensation to Muhammad and his family worthy of their services to your cause,* gave the amaranth to him saying, "This is for you." He then went to the *suq* (market place) during the night then sold every thread of it, then distributed the money among the people of Muhajir (immigrants) and al-Ansar (people of al-Madinah). He then returned home and not one dinar had remained with him of the money. The next day when the Messenger of Allah, *O Allah, please, grant compensation to Muhammad and his family worthy of their services to your cause,* met him he said, " O abu al-Hassan yesterday you received three thousand Mithqal of gold, so I and the people of Muhajir (immigrants) and al-Ansar (people of al-Madinah) will have lunch with you tomorrow." Ali, *'Alayhi al-Salam* said, 'Yes, O Messenger of Allah." The next day the Messenger of Allah, *O Allah, please, grant compensation to Muhammad and his family worthy of their services to your cause,* along with the people of Muhajir (immigrants) and al-Ansar (people of al-Madinah) arrived at the door of the house of Ali, *'Alayhi al-Salam* and knocked it. He came out and because of shyness he had perspired; there was nothing of small or large quantity at home to serve them. The Messenger of Allah, *O Allah grant compensation to Muhammad and his family worthy of their services to your cause,* entered the house as well as the people of Muhajir (immigrants) and al-Ansar (people of al-Madinah) and they all sat down. Ali and Fatimah, *'Alayha al-Salam,* also came in with a large basin full of *Tharid* (a special Arabic dish, bread broken in the broth from meat) steaming with the fragrance of al-Azfar musk. Ali, tried to lift it but he could not pick it up and then Fatimah, *'Alayha al-Salam,* helped him to left it until they placed it before the Messenger of Allah, *O Allah, please, grant compensation to Muhammad and his family worthy of their services to your cause,* who then came to Fatimah, *'Alayha al-Salam,* and asked, "My dearest daughter wherefrom have you got it?" She replied, "O father, it is from Allah, who grants sustenance to whomever He wills without accounting." The Messenger of Allah, *O Allah grant compensation to Muhammad and his family worthy of their services to your cause,* then said, "All praise belongs to Allah who has not taken me out of the world before seeing with my daughter what Zakariya saw with Maryam (Mary) daughter of 'Imran."

Fatimah, *'Alayha al-Salam,* then asked, "O dear father, am I more excellent or Maryam (Mary)?" The Messenger of Allah, *O Allah grant compensation to Muhammad and his family worthy of their services to your cause,* replied, "You are in your nation (followers) and Maryam (Mary) was in her nation (followers)."

H 99, Ch. 3, h 64
Al-Misbah al-Anwar:

It is narrated from abu Ja'far, 'Alayhi al-Salam who has said the following:

Once Fatimah, *'Alayha al-Salam,* came to the Messenger of Allah, *O Allah, please, grant compensation to Muhammad and his family worthy of their services to your cause,* who found signs of hunger on her face and he then asked her to sit on his right thigh. She then said, "O dear father I am hungry." He then raised his hands to the sky and said, "O Lord, the one who lifts up the one going down and satisfies the hungry ones, please satisfy the hunger of Fatimah, *'Alayha al-Salam,* the daughter of your Prophet." Abu Ja'far has said that thereafter she never felt hungry up to the time she left this world."

It is narrated from 'Amir al-Mu'minin, *'Alayhi al-Salam* that Fatimah, *'Alayha al-Salam,* daughter of Muhammad once felt ill. The Messenger of Allah, *O Allah grant compensation to Muhammad and his family worthy of their services to your cause,* came to visit her. He sat next to her and asked about how she was feeling. She said, "I desire some fine food." The Holy Prophet, *O Allah, please, grant compensation to Muhammad and his family worthy of their services to your cause,* then stood up to go to the niche in the room and brought back a tray full of raisins, cake, sour cream and a bunch of grapes. He (the Messenger of Allah) placed it before Fatimah, *'Alayha al-Salam.* He then reciting *Bismillah,* (in the name of Allah, most Beneficent, most Merciful) extended his hand to the tray and asked them to eat. Fatimah, *'Alayha al-Salam,* the Messenger of Allah, Ali, al-Hassan and al-Husayn, *'Alayhim al-Salam,* then had begun to eat that a beggar stood at the door said *Salam* (the phrase of offering greeting of peace) and asked, "Please give us from the sustenance that Allah has given to you."

The Messenger of Allah, *O Allah grant compensation to Muhammad and his family worthy of their services to your cause,* said, "Go away!" Fatimah, *'Alayha al-Salam,* said, "O Messenger of Allah, a destitute person is not turned away in such a way!" "The Holy Prophet, *O Allah, please, grant compensation to Muhammad and his family worthy of their services to your cause,* said, "That is Satan. Jibril brought you this food from the garden (paradise) and Satan wanted to eat thereof but he does not deserve it."

It is narrated from Hudhayfah who has said the following:

The Holy Prophet, *O Allah, please, grant compensation to Muhammad and his family worthy of their services to your cause,* would not go to sleep before kissing the side of the face of Fatimah, *'Alayha al-Salam,* or her chest.

It is narrated from Ja'far ibn Muhammad 'Alayhima al-Salam, who has said the following:

The Messenger of Allah, *O Allah grant compensation to Muhammad and his family worthy of their services to your cause,* would not go to sleep before placing his face over the chest of Fatimah, *'Alayha al-Salam.*

H 100, Ch. 3, h 65
'Ilal al-Shara'i':

Al-Qattan has narrated from al-Sukkary from al-Jawhari from al-Shu'ayb ibn Waqid from Ishaq ibn Ja'far ibn Muhammad ibn 'Isa ibn Zayd ibn Ali who has said the following:

I (the narrator) heard 'Abu 'Abd Allah, *'Alayhi al-Salam* say, "Fatimah, *'Alayha al-Salam,* is called Muhaddathah because the angels would come down from the sky and call her as they would call Maryam (Mary) daughter 'Imran. They would say, "[O Fatimah, *'Alayha al-Salam*] Behold, Allah has chosen you, purified you, and given you distinction over all women. (3:42) Mary, [O Fatimah] pray devotedly to your Lord, prostrate yourself before Him and bow down with those who bow down before Him." (3:43) Fatimah, *'Alayha al-Salam,* would speak to them and the angels would speak to her. One night she asked them, "Is Maryam (Mary) daughter 'Imran not the preferred woman in excellence over the women of the worlds?" They replied, "Maryam (Mary) was the leader of the women of her world. Allah, most Majestic, most Glorious, has made you the leader of the women of your world, the leader of the women of her world and the women of the past and future generations."

Dala'il al-Imamah of al-Tabari:

From abu Muhammad Harun ibn Musa al-Talakbari from al-Saduq a similar Hadith is narrated.

H 101, Ch. 3, h 66
'Ilal al-Shara'i':

My father has narrated from 'Abd Allah ibn al-Hassan al-Mu'addab from Ahmad ibn Ali al-Asbahani from Ibrahim ibn Muhammad al-Thaqafi from 'Isma'il ibn Bashshar who has said that narrated to us Ali ibn Ja'far al-Hadrami in Misr thirty years ago who has said that narrated to us Sulayman, who has said that narrated Muhammad ibn abu Bakr about the meaning of the words of Allah, most Majestic, most Glorious:

"Satan would try to tamper with the desires of every Prophet or Messenger [or muhaddith] that We sent. Then Allah would remove Satan's temptations and strengthen His revelations. Allah is All-knowing and All-wise." (22:52) I (the narrator) then asked, "Do the angels speak to anyone else other than the Prophets?" He then said, "Maryam (Mary) was not a female prophet but she was a Muhaddathah. The mother of Musa ibn 'Imran was a Muhaddathah but she was not a female prophet. Sarah, wife of Ibrahim observed the angels who congratulated her for the birth of Ishaq and after him Ya'qub and she was not a female prophet. Fatimah, *'Alayha al-Salam*, daughter of the Messenger of Allah, *O Allah, please, grant compensation to Muhammad and his family worthy of their services to your cause,* was a Muhaddathah and not a female prophet."

Al-Saduq (r.h) has said that about Allah in His words: "The messengers that We had sent before you were only men to whom We had given revelation. Ask the people of *al-Dhikr* (family of the Holy Prophet) if you do not know." (21:7) Allah has said, in His book, that He has sent men not women prophets to the people. The Muhaddah ones are not messengers or prophets.

H 101, Ch. 3, h 67
Basa'ir al-Darajat: [Al-Kafi:] [H 633, Ch. 40, h 5, from al-Kafi]

Muhammad ibn Yahya has narrated from Ahmad ibn Muhammad from ibn Mahbub from ibn Ri'ab from abu 'Ubayda who has said the following:

"People from our group asked abu 'Abd Allah, *'Alayhi al-Salam*, about *Jafr* and the Imam said, 'It is the skin of a bull which is full of knowledge.' They then asked the Imam about *al-Jami'ah*. The Imam replied, 'It is a parchment that is seventy yards long with the width of a hide like that of the leg of a huge camel. It contains all that people may need. There is no case for which there is not a rule in it. In it there is the law even to settle the compensation for a scratch caused to a person.'

"I (the narrator) then asked the Imam, 'What is the Mushaf of Fatimah?' The Imam waited for quite a while. Then he said, 'You ask about what you really mean and what you do not mean. *Fatimah, 'Alayha al-Salam*, lived after the Messenger of Allah for seventy-five days. She was severely depressed because of the death of her father. Jibril (peace be upon him) would come to provide her solace and condolence due to the death of her father. Jibril would comfort her soul; inform her about her father, his place, of the future events and about what would happen to her children. At the same time Ali, *'Alayhi al-Salam*, would write all of them down and this has come to be the Mushaf of Fatimah, *'Alayha al-Salam*.'"

H 102, Ch. 3, h 68
Basa'ir al-Darajat:

Ahmad ibn Muhammad has narrated from 'Umar ibn Abd al-Aziz from Hammad ibn 'Uthman who has said the following:

I (the narrator) heard 'Abu 'Abd Allah, *'Alayhi al-Salam* say, "In the year one hundred twenty-eight atheists will appear because I have read it in Mushaf of Fatimah, *'Alayha al-Salam.* He (the narrator) has said that he then asked, "What is Mushaf of Fatimah, *'Alayha al-Salam?*" He (the Imam), *'Alayhi al-Salam* replied, "When Allah, most High, took the Holy Prophet, *O Allah, please, grant compensation to Muhammad and his family worthy of their services to your cause,* from this world, Fatimah, *'Alayha al-Salam,* became very depressed so much so that only Allah, most Majestic, most Glorious, knows the degree of her sadness. He then sent an angel to offer her solace in her sadness and he would speak to her. She then informed Ali, *'Alayhi al-Salam* about it and he asked her to inform him when the angels comes and you hear his voice. She then would informed him and he would write down whatever he heard until it became a Mushaf, a large book." He (the narrator) has said that he (the Imam) *'Alayhi al-Salam* then said, "In this Mushaf there is nothing about the lawful and unlawful issue. It has the knowledge about what will happen."

H 103, Ch. 3, h 69
Al-Kafi: al-'Uddah from Ahmad ibn Muhammad a similar Hadith is narrated.

I ('Allamah Majlisi) say that we have recorded many facts of the excellence of Fatimah, *'Alayha al-Salam,* and her virtues and history in the chapter on usurpation of Fidak and in the chapter on the excellence of the people of the cloak, *'Alayhim al-Salam.*

Al-Hassan ibn Sulayman has narrated in the book al-Muhtadar of interpretations of Tha'labi through the chain of his narrators from Mujahid who has said the following:

The Messenger of Allah, *O Allah grant compensation to Muhammad and his family worthy of their services to your cause,* one day came out holding the hand of Fatimah, *'Alayha al-Salam,* said, "Whoever knows this lady, then it is fine, and whoever does not know her they must know that she is Fatimah, *'Alayha al-Salam,* daughter of Muhammad and she is a part of myself. She is my heart between my sides. Whoever, troubles her troubles me and whoever troubles me troubles Allah."

The book of Dala'il of al-Tabari from abu al-Faraj al-Mu'afa' from Ishaq ibn Muhammad from Ahmad ibn al-Hassan from Muhammad ibn 'Isma'il ibn Ibrahim ibn Ja'far ibn Muhammad from his father from his uncle Zayd ibn Ali who has said the following:

Fatimah, *'Alayha al-Salam,* daughter of The Messenger of Allah, *O Allah grant compensation to Muhammad and his family worthy of their services to your cause,* narrated to me that the Messenger of Allah, *'Alayhi al-Salam* said to her, "I like to give you the glad news that when Allah wills to gift the wife of His friend in the garden (paradise) He will send to you to send her one dress from your wardrobe."

Chapter 4 - The Manners of Fatimah, *'Alayha al-Salam,* her Moral behaviors and the Manners of some of her housemaids

H 104, Ch. 4, h 1
Qurb al-Asnad:

Al-Sindy ibn Muhammad has narrated from abu al-Bakhtari from 'Abu 'Abd Allah, from his father 'Alayhima al-Salam, who has said the following:

Ali and Fatimah, *'Alayhima al-Salam,* asked the Messenger of Allah, *O Allah grant compensation to Muhammad and his family worthy of their services to your cause,* about how much of the household routine tasks each one of them should do. He (the Messenger of Allah) required Fatimah, *'Alayha al-Salam,* to do the indoor household routine tasks and he required Ali, *'Alayhi al-Salam* to do the outdoor routine tasks. He (the narrator) has said that Fatimah, *'Alayha al-Salam,* then said, "One does not know how happy I became for his decision of making my task to do the easier part and placing the load on the neck of the men."

H 105, Ch. 4, h 2
'Yun Akhbar al-Rida':

Through the three chains of narrators it is narrated from al-Rida', from his ancestors from Ali ibn al-Husayn, 'Alayhima al-Salam, who has said the following:

He (the narrator) has said that 'Asma' daughter of 'Umays has said, "I was with Fatimah, *'Alayha al-Salam,* when the Messenger of Allah, *O Allah grant compensation to Muhammad and his family worthy of their services to your cause,* visited and she was wearing a necklace of gold which Ali ibn abu Talib, *'Alayhi al-Salam* had bought from the spoils of war. The Messenger of Allah, *O Allah grant compensation to Muhammad and his family worthy of their services to your cause,* said, 'O Fatimah, *'Alayha al-Salam,* the people must not say that the daughter of Muhammad wears the garments of the tyrants.' She then removed it and sold it, then bought a slave and then set the slave free. The Messenger of Allah, *O Allah grant compensation to Muhammad and his family worthy of their services to your cause,* became happy for what she did.

125

H 106, Ch. 4, h 3
'Ilal al-Shara'i':

Ibn Maqbarah has narrated from Muhammad ibn 'Abd Allah al-Hadrami from Jandal ibn Waliq from Muhammad ibn 'Umar al-Mazini from 'Ubadah al-Kalbi from Ja'far ibn Muhammad from his father from Ali ibn al-Husayn, from Fatimah al-Sughra' from al-Husayn ibn Ali from his brother al-Hassan ibn Ali ibn abu Talib, 'Alayhim al-Salam, who has said the following:

He (the narrator) has said that he saw his mother Fatimah, *'Alayha al-Salam,* stand up in her place for *Salat* (prayer) in her Friday night and continued *Ruku'* (bowing down on one's knees) and *Sujud* (prostrations) until the streak of dawn appeared and I heard her pray for believing people, male and female pronouncing their names and pray for them a great deal but did not pray for herself for anything. I then asked her, "O dear mother, why did you not pray for yourself as you did for others?" She replied, "My dear child, neighbors first, then is the household."

H 107, Ch. 4, h 4
'Ilal al-Shara'i':

Ahmad ibn Muhammad ibn 'Abd al-Rahman al-Marwazi has narrated from Ja'far al-Muqri from Muhammad ibn al-Hassan al-Musuli from Muhammad ibn 'Asem ibn Hamid from abu Zayd al-Kahhal from his father from Musa ibn Ja'far from his father from his ancestors 'Alayhim al-Salam who has said the following:

When Fatimah, *'Alayha al-Salam,* prayed she would pray for believing people, male and female but not for herself. It was said to her, "O daughter of the Messenger of Allah, why is it that you pray for people but not for yourself?" She replied, "Neighbors first, then is the household."

H 108, Ch. 4, h 5
'Ilal al-Shara'i':

Al-Qattan has narrated from al-Sukkari from al-Hakam ibn Aslam from ibn 'Alyah from al-Hariri from abu al-Ward ibn Thamamah from Ali, 'Alayhi al-Salam who once said to a man of banu Sa'd:

I must tell you about me and Fatimah, *'Alayha al-Salam.* She was with me as the most beloved one to me in my family. To maintain the water supply for the house she carried so much water with the water-skin that the load had caused injuries on her chest. She worked with the grinding stone so much that calluses had formed in her hands. Sweeping the house had made dust settle on her clothes. Working with firewood for cooking had darkened the color of her clothes and it had caused her great harms. I then said to her that if she can go to her father and ask him to find a housemaid to help her in the house routine tasks it will make it easier for her. She then went to the Holy Prophet, *O Allah grant compensation to Muhammad and his family worthy of their services to your cause,* and found him busy with events. She felt shy to say anything, so she returned home. He (the narrator) has said that the Holy Prophet, *'Alayhi al-Salam* found out that she had come for something that she needed. The Messenger of Allah, *O Allah grant compensation to Muhammad and his family worthy of their services to your cause,* came to us and our heads were covered under the comforter, the bedsheet. He said, "*Salam* (the phrase of offering greeting of peace) but we felt shy because of the condition so we remained quiet and he then said *Salam* (the phrase of offering greeting of peace) again. We felt afraid that if we did not respond he will return back. He would do so three times then turn away if he did receive any response. I then said, "Greeting of peace to you, O Messenger of Allah, please come in. It did not take a long time that we found him sitting near our heads and he asked, "O Fatimah, *'Alayha al-Salam,* what did you need for which you had come to Muhammad yesterday?" I felt afraid that if I did not answer him he will go back. I then uncovered my head and said, "By Allah, I can inform you, O Messenger of Allah about what she needed. To maintain the water supply for the house she carried so much water with the water-skin that the load had caused injuries on her chest. She worked with the grinding stone so much that calluses had formed in her hands, sweeping the house had made dust settle on her clothes, working with firewood for cooking had darkened the color of her clothes and it had caused her great harms. I then said to her that if she can go to her father and ask him to find a housemaid to help her in the house routine tasks it will make it easier for her."

He (the Messenger of Allah), said, "May I teach both of you something that will be better for you then the service of a house maid?" When you are about to go to sleep say thirty three time *Tasbih* (Allah is free of all defects), thirty three times *Tahmid,* (all praise belongs to Allah) and thirty four time *Takbir* (Allah is great beyond description). He (the narrator) has said that she then uncovered her head and said, "I accept it from Allah and His messenger." She said it three times.

H 109, Ch. 4, h 6
Al-Kafi: Makarim al-Akhlaq:

It is narrated from Zurarah from abu Ja'far, 'Alayhi al-Salam who has said the following:

When the Messenger of Allah, would go for a journey he would say farewell to whomever he wanted of his family, then the last one to whom he would say farewell was Fatimah, *'Alayha al-Salam,* and then he would commence his journey from her house. On his return from a journey he would visit Fatimah, *'Alayha al-Salam,* first. One time he went on a journey and Ali, *'Alayhi al-Salam* had received something from the spoils of war. He gave it to Fatimah, *'Alayha al-Salam.* She went out and bought two silver bracelets and a covering for the door of her house. When the Messenger of Allah, *O Allah grant compensation to Muhammad and his family worthy of their services to your cause,* came back he entered the Masjid then went to the house of Fatimah, *'Alayha al-Salam,* as he would do so. She stood up in happiness to receive her father and he looked at her hand to the two silver bracelets and the curtain at the door. The Messenger of Allah, *O Allah grant compensation to Muhammad and his family worthy of their services to your cause,* sat down looking at her.

She wept sadly and said, "He would not do this to me before." She then called her two sons, gave the bracelet to one of them and the curtain to the other one and told them to go to her father, convey her *Salam* (the phrase of offering greeting of peace) to him and tell him that we have not done anything after you went on your journey except this. You can do with it whatever you like. They went to the Messenger of Allah, and conveyed to him what their mother had told to do. The Messenger of Allah, *O Allah grant compensation to Muhammad and his family worthy of their services to your cause,* kissed them, held them (against his chest) then made each one sit on one of his thighs. He then divided the bracelets among the people of the *suffah* (the platform) in front of the Masjid who were a group of *Muhajir* (immigrants) people who did not have any homes and belongings. He then called those who did not have any covering to replace their covering which could cover only the top or the bottom parts of their body with pieces of that curtain which Fatimah, 'Alayha al-Salam, had bought for the door of her house. It was long but with very little width. He divided it among the men to use as a loin cloth. He then commanded the women not to raise their heads from *Ruku'* (bowing down on one's knees) or *Sujud* (prostrations) before men did. It was because of the small width of their loin cloth that when they made *Ruku'* (bowing down on one's knees) or *Sujud* (prostrations) their private parts became visible from behind them and this became a tradition that women should raise their heads from *Ruku'* (bowing down on one's knees) or *Sujud* (prostrations) after the men did so.

The Messenger of Allah, *O Allah grant compensation to Muhammad and his family worthy of their services to your cause,* then said, "May Allah grant blessings to Fatimah, 'Alayha al-Salam, and may He dress her for this from the dresses of the garden (paradise) and grant her ornaments for these bracelets from the ornaments of the garden (paradise).

It is narrated from al-Kazim *'Alayhi al-Salam* that the Messenger of Allah, *O Allah grant compensation to Muhammad and his family worthy of their services to your cause,* visited his daughter Fatimah, *'Alayha al-Salam,* and he found a necklace around her neck. He turned away from her. She then removed it away. The Messenger of Allah, *O Allah grant compensation to Muhammad and his family worthy of their services to your cause,* said to her, "You are a part of me. Please give it to me, O Fatimah, *'Alayha al-Salam.*" Then a beggar came and he (the Messenger of Allah) gave him the necklace.

H 110, Ch. 4, h 7
Manaqib of ibn Shahr Ashub:

It is narrated in Hulyah of abu Nu'aym and Musnad of abu Ya'li that *'A'ishah has said the following:*

I never found anyone more truthful than Fatimah, 'Alayha al-Salam, except her father.

It is narrated that once there was a conflicting issue between the two of them and 'A'ishah said, "O Messenger of Allah, you can ask her; she does not speak lies."

The above two Hadith are narrated by 'Ata' and 'Amr ibn Dinar.

Al-Hassan al-Basri have narrated saying that in this nation (Muslims) there was no one more devoted in worshipping than Fatimah, *'Alayha al-Salam*. She would stand for *Salat* (prayer) so much that her feet had swelled.

The Holy Prophet, *O Allah grant compensation to Muhammad and his family worthy of their services to your cause,* asked her, "What is the best for a woman?" She replied, "The best for a women is that she does not see any man and no man sees her."

He then held her to his self, saying, "Descendants who are one from another."

Al-Hulyah:

Al-Awza'i has narrated from al-Zuhri who has said the following:

Fatimah, *'Alayha al-Salam,* daughter of the Messenger of Allah, *O Allah grant compensation to Muhammad and his family worthy of their services to your cause,* would work with the grinding stone so much that calluses had formed in her hands and the grinding stones had affected them.

H 111, Ch. 4, h 8
Manaqib of ibn Shahr Ashub:

It is narrated in Sahihayn that Ali, once said, "I am troubled by the weight of the water skin." Fatimah, *'Alayha al-Salam,* said, "My hands are troubled by spinning the grinding stones." With the Holy Prophet, there were resources from the spoils of war, so he said, "Ask your father to provide for you a housemaid." She then went to the Holy Prophet, *O Allah grant compensation to Muhammad and his family worthy of their services to your cause,* offered *Salam* (the phrase of offering greeting of peace) but she came back. 'Amir al-Mu'minin, *'Alayhi al-Salam* asked if she has received any assistance. She replied, "I, by Allah, could not speak to the Messenger of Allah, *O Allah grant compensation to Muhammad and his family worthy of their services to your cause,* because of his prestigious status." Ali, *'Alayhi al-Salam* then accompanied her to meet the Holy Prophet, *'Alayhi al-Salam.* The Holy Prophet, *'Alayhi al-Salam* asked, "What has brought the two of you here?" Ali, *'Alayhi al-Salam* then explained their story of the hardships both of them were facing. He (the Messenger of Allah) said, "But I sell them (the resources) to meet the expenses of the people of *al-Suffah* (the poor ones who lived on the platform in front of the Masjid). He (the Messenger of Allah) then taught her *Tasbih* of al-Zahra' *'Alayha al-Salam.*

The book of al-Shirazi:

The two of them explained their story of facing hardship and asked for a housemaid. The Messenger of Allah, *O Allah grant compensation to Muhammad and his family worthy of their services to your cause,* wept and said, "O Fatimah, *'Alayha al-Salam,* by the one who has sent me in all truth that in the Masjid there are four hundred men who have no food and clothes, were I not afraid of hunger I would give you what you have asked for. O Fatimah, *'Alayha al-Salam,* I do not want to negate your reward because of a housemaid. I fear that Ali ibn abu Talib, may complain against you on the Day of Judgment before Allah, most Majestic, most Glorious, and demand his rights from you." He then taught her *Salat* (prayer) of *Tasbih* which is also called *Salat* (prayer) of Ja'far al-Tayyar (r.h).

'Amir al-Mu'minin *'Alayhi al-Salam* then said, "You went to the Messenger of Allah, asking for the worldly things but he (the Messenger of Allah) gave us rewards of the next life."

He (the author) has said that abu Hurayrah has said that when the Messenger of Allah, *O Allah grant compensation to Muhammad and his family worthy of their services to your cause,* left the house of Fatimah, *'Alayha al-Salam,* Allah then sent this verse to His messenger. "If you are not able to assist them, [your relatives, your daughter Fatimah, *'Alayha al-Salam,* because you seek the happiness of Allah, His blessings, that is sustenance] at least speak to them in a kind manner." (17:28)

When this verse was revealed, he (the Messenger of Allah) sent for her a housemaid and called her Fiddah.

Interpretations of al-Tha'labi:

It is narrated from Ja'far ibn Muhammad, 'Alayhima al-Salam: interpretations of al-Qushayri:

It is narrated from Jabir al-Ansari who has said the following:

The Holy Prophet, *O Allah grant compensation to Muhammad and his family worthy of their services to your cause,* saw Fatimah, *'Alayha al-Salam,* wearing a garment of *Ajlah al-'ibil* (camel wool), working the grinding stone with her hand while breastfeeding her child. The eyes of the Messenger of Allah, *O Allah grant compensation to Muhammad and his family worthy of their services to your cause,* flooded with tears. He then said, "O my dearest daughter, you have hurried to experience the bitterness of the world in exchange for the sweetness of the next life." She then said, "O Messenger of Allah, I thank Allah for His bounties and appreciated His favors to me. Allah then sent this verse of al-Quran: "Your Lord will soon grant you sufficient favor to please you." (93:5)

Ibn Shahin has narrated in Virtues of Fatimah, 'Alayha al-Salam, and Ahmad in Musnad al-Ansari through the chain of their narrators have narrated from abu Hurayrah and Thawban who both have said the following:

The Holy Prophet, *O Allah grant compensation to Muhammad and his family worthy of their services to your cause,* whenever he would want to travel, would commence his journey from the house of Fatimah, *'Alayha al-Salam,* and on his return end it at the house of Fatimah, *'Alayha al-Salam.* One time during the period of his journey she made a curtain of al-Khaybari fabric before the coming of her father and husband. When the Holy Prophet, *O Allah grant compensation to Muhammad and his family worthy of their services to your cause,* saw it he just passed by and did not look to her and anger showed at his face until he sat near the pulpit. She then removed the necklace, the earrings, both their grips and the curtain then sent them to her father saying, "You can use them whatever cause you like in the way of Allah." When it reached to him he said, "She has done it, may her father be made a ransom for her." He said it three times. "What *Ale* (family of) Muhammad has to do with the world; they are created for the next life and the world is created for them."

In the narration of Ahmad it is said, "These are my *Ahl al-Bayt* (family) and I do not like for them to consume their resources of goodness in their worldly lives."

Abu Salih al-Mu'adhdhin in his book through a chain of narrators from Ali, 'Alayhi al-Salam has narrated the following:

Once the Holy Prophet, *O Allah grant compensation to Muhammad and his family worthy of their services to your cause,* visited his daughter Fatimah, *'Alayha al-Salam,* and found her wearing a necklace. He turned away from her. She removed and placed it away. The Messenger of Allah, *O Allah grant compensation to Muhammad and his family worthy of their services to your cause,* said, "O Fatimah, *'Alayha al-Salam,* you are a part of myself." Then a beggar came and she then gave the necklace to the beggar.

Abu al-Qasim al-Qushayri in his book has said that certain ones of them remained behind the caravan in the wilderness and he found a woman. He asked her, "Who are you?" She said, "We have told him, '. . . say to them "with peace." They will soon know . . .' (43:89)"

He then said *Salam* (the phrase of offering greeting of peace) and asked her, "What are you doing here?" She then read, "Who can mislead one whom Allah has guided? Is Allah not Majestic and capable to exact recompense?" (39:37) He then asked her, "Are you from Jinn or from man?" She then recited, "Children of Adam, dress well when attending the mosques, eat and drink but do not be excessive for Allah does not love those who are excessive (in what they do)." (7:31) He then asked, "From where have you come?" She recited, "It is as though they had been called from a distant place." (41:44) He then asked her, "Where do you want to go?" She recited, "Those who have the means and ability have a duty to Allah to visit the House and perform the *Hajj* (pilgrimage) rituals. . . ." (3:97) He then asked her, "Since when she remained away from the caravan?" She then recited, "We created the heavens, the earth, and all that is between them in six days . . ." (50:38) He then asked her, "Do you need any food?" She then recited, "We had not made them such bodies that would not eat any food nor were they immortal." (21:8)

He then gave her food then told her to walk briskly but do not rush. She then recited, "Allah does not impose on any soul a responsibility beyond its ability. . ." (2:286)

He then asked her, "Should I make you ride behind me?" She then recited, "Had there been other deities in the heavens and the earth besides Allah, both the heavens and the earth would have been destroyed. . ." (21:22) He then dismounted and made her to ride. She then recited, ""Glory belongs to Him who has made it subservient to us when we would not have been able to do so ourselves." (43:13) When we approached the caravan I asked her, "Do you have anyone in the caravan?" She then recited, ""avid, We have appointed you as Our deputy on earth . . ." (38:26) Muhammad is only a Messenger. . ." (3:144), We commanded John, Zachariah's son, to follow the guidance . . ." (19:12) "Moses, (20:11) I am your Lord. . . ." (20:12) I then called the people of these names and four young men turned up to her. I asked, "What is your relationship with them?" She recited, "Children and property are the ornaments of the worldly life, . . ." (18:46) When they came to her she recited, "Father, hire him; the best whom you may hire is a strong and trustworthy one." (28:26) They then compensated me with something and she recited, "Allah gives in multiples to those whom He wants. . ." (2:261) They then increased the compensation for me and I asked about who she was. They said that she was their mother the housemaid of Fatimah, al-Zahra' *'Alayha al-Salam.* She has not spoken for twenty years from anything except al-Quran.

H 112, Ch. 4, h 9
Al-Duru' of the book about the abstaining of the Holy Prophet, O Allah grant compensation to Muhammad and his family worthy of their services to your cause, from worldly matters by abu Ja'far Ahmad al-Qumi.

This is about the meaning of the words of Allah, the most Majestic, the most Glorious:

"Hell is the promised place for them all. (15:43) It has seven gates and each gate is assigned for a certain group of people." (15:44)

He (the narrator) has said that when the above verse of al-Quran was revealed to the Holy Prophet, *O Allah grant compensation to Muhammad and his family worthy of their services to your cause,* he wept intensely. The companions also wept because of his weeping and they did not know what Jibril has brought to him and no one of the companions were able to speak to him. The Holy Prophet, *O Allah grant compensation to Muhammad and his family worthy of their services to your cause,* upon seeing Fatimah, *'Alayha al-Salam,* would become happy. A certain one of his companions went to her house. He found some barley in front of her which she was grinding and reciting, ". . . but the means for enjoyment (which you will receive from Allah) in the life to come will be better and everlasting. Will you then not take heed?" (28:60) He then said *Salam* (the phrase of offering greeting of peace) to her and informed her about the condition of the Holy Prophet, and about his weeping. She covered herself wither an old covering sheet which was patched at twelve spots with palm tree fibers. When Salman (Rh) looked at her covering he wept and said, "Daughters of Kisra' and Qaysar dress up in silk and pure silk but the daughter of Muhammad, *O Allah grant compensation to Muhammad and his family worthy of their services to your cause,* has a covering which is patched at its twelve spots."

When she arrived, she said, "O Messenger of Allah, *O Allah grant compensation to Muhammad and his family worthy of their services to your cause,* Salman (Rh) is astonished because of the condition of my clothes. I swear by the one who has sent you in truth that Ali and I for the last five years did not have anything except the skin of a ram on which during the day we feed our camel and during the night we use it as our mattress and our pillow is made of a piece of hide (skin) and for its filling palm tree fibers are used."

The Holy Prophet, *O Allah grant compensation to Muhammad and his family worthy of their services to your cause,* said, "Salman (Rh) my daughter is of the group of the race winners."

She then asked saying, "O my father, may I become ransom for you, what has made you to weep?" He (the Messenger of Allah) then explained for her the two verses of al-Quran that Jibril had brought. He (the narrator) has said that Fatimah, *'Alayha al-Salam,* then fell on her face, saying, "*Wayl,* (woe, wretchedness) is on those who are thrown in the fire." When Salman (Rh) heard it he said, "I wish I was a sheep of my family who would consume my flesh and tear my skin into pieces so I would not hear any explanation about the fire (of hell)."

Abu Dharr then said, "I wish my mother was barren and did not give birth to me so I would not hear any explanation about the fire (of hell)."

Miqdad then said, "I wish I was a bird in the wilderness, not responsible for any accounting and punishment so I would not hear any explanation about the fire (of hell)."

Ali, *'Alayhi al-Salam* said, "I wish the beasts had torn my flesh in pieces. I wish my mother had not given birth to me so I would not hear any explanation about the fire (of hell)." Ali, *'Alayhi al-Salam* then placed his hand on his head and began to weep and say, "Oh! How lengthy is the journey. How little is the provision for the journey to the Day of Judgment, they go to hell and they are kidnaped, they are sick from which they never recover, their sick ones are not visited, their injured do not receive any medicine, the captives are never released from the fire from which they eat and drink and in its levels they turn upside down. After dressing in cotton they dress in cutting garments of the fire and after embracing their spouses they are joined with Satans (the devils).

H 113, Ch. 4, h 10
Kashf al-Ghummah:

It is narrated from Musnad of ibn Hanbal from Thawban Mawla of the Messenger of Allah who has said the following:

When the Messenger of Allah, would leave for a journey the last person to whom he would say farewell was Fatimah, *'Alayha al-Salam,* and the first one to see after his return from the journey was also Fatimah, *'Alayha al-Salam.*

One time he returned from an armed expedition and he then went to see Fatimah, *'Alayha al-Salam.* He found a curtain on her door and saw al-Hassan and al-Husayn, wearing pendants of silver. He (the Messenger of Allah) returned back without visiting Fatimah, *'Alayha al-Salam.* When she noticed it she realized that it is because of what he had seen. She then removed the curtain and the pendants from the children. They cried. She then divided it for them. They both went to the Messenger of Allah, *O Allah grant compensation to Muhammad and his family worthy of their services to your cause,* weeping. The Messenger of Allah, *O Allah grant compensation to Muhammad and his family worthy of their services to your cause,* took it from them and said, "O Thawban, go to so and so people in al-Madinah then buy from them for Fatimah, *'Alayha al-Salam,* a pendants made of the bones of certain sea animals and two bracelets of ivory because I do not like for my *Ahl al-Bayt* (family) to enjoy fine things in the worldly life."

H 113, Ch. 4, h 11
Al-Kafi: [H 11754, Ch. 19b, h 1, from al-Kafi]

Muhammad ibn Yahya has narrated from Ahmad ibn Muhammad, from 'Uthman ibn 'Isa, from Furat ibn Ahnaf who has said the following:

"I once heard abu 'Abd Allah, *'Alayhi al-Salam*, saying, 'On the face of earth there is no herb more beneficial and graceful than *al-Farfakh* (purslane) and it is the herb of Fatimah, *'Alayha al-Salam*.' He (the Imam) then said, 'May Allah condemn banu Umayyah who named it foolish herb due to their animosity toward Fatimah, *'Alayhi al-Salam*.'"

H 114, Ch. 4, h 12
Al-Kafi: [H 11738, Ch. 15, h 10, from al-Kafi]

Muhammad ibn Yahya has narrated from Ahmad ibn Muhammad from abu Yahya al-Wasitiy from certain persons of our people who has said the following:

"Abu 'Abd Allah, *'Alayhi al-Salam*, has said, 'The endive is the herb of the Messenger of Allah, *O Allah, grant compensation to Muhammad and his family worthy of their services to Your cause.* The herb of `Amir al-Mu'minin, *'Alayhi al-Salam*, is al-Badharuj (sweet basil) and the herb of Fatimah, *'Alayha al-Salam*, is al-*Farfakh* (purslane).

H 115, Ch. 4, h 13
Al-Tahdhib:

Muhammad ibn Ali ibn Mahbub has narrated from Muhammad ibn al-Husayn from Muhsin ibn Ahmad ibn Janab from Yunus from 'Abu 'Abd Allah, 'Alayhi al-Salam who has said the following:

Fatimah, *'Alayha al-Salam*, would visit the graves of the martyrs every Saturday. She then would go to the grave of Hamzah (r.h) and ask Allah to grant him blessings and forgiveness.

H 116, Ch. 4, h 14
Tafsir of Ali ibn Ibrahim:

This is about the meaning of the words of Allah, the most Majestic, the most Glorious:

"Holding secret counsels for (evil purposes) is a work of Satan to cause grief to the believers, but he can do no harm to them except by the will of Allah. Believers must trust Allah." (58:10)

The author has said that narrated to me my father from Muhammad ibn abu 'Umayr from abu Basir from 'Abd Allah, 'Alayhi al-Salam who has said the following:

The reason for the coming of this verse was Fatimah, *'Alayha al-Salam.* She had seen in her dream that the Messenger of Allah, *O Allah grant compensation to Muhammad and his family worthy of their services to your cause,* decided to go out of al-Madinah, along with Fatimah, *'Alayha al-Salam,* Ali, al-Hassan and al-Husayn, *'Alayhim al-Salam.* They left the city until they crossed the walls around the city. The path then forked but the Messenger of Allah, *'Alayhi al-Salam* took to his right until they reached a place where there were palm trees and water. The Messenger of Allah, *O Allah grant compensation to Muhammad and his family worthy of their services to your cause,* then bought a *kubara'* (large sheep) or that which has a white spot on one of its ears, he then ordered to slaughter it and when they ate they all died in their places. Fatimah, *'Alayha al-Salam,* woke weeping and frightened but she did not inform the Messenger of Allah, *O Allah grant compensation to Muhammad and his family worthy of their services to your cause,* about it.

In the morning the Messenger of Allah, *O Allah grant compensation to Muhammad and his family worthy of their services to your cause,* brought a donkey for the conveyance of Fatimah, *'Alayha al-Salam,* and ordered Ali, al-Hassan and al-Husayn, to come for an outing beyond the walls of the city as Fatimah, *'Alayha al-Salam,* had seen in her dream. When the crossed the boundary walls around the city of al-Madinah the path became divided in two different directions and the Messenger of Allah, *O Allah grant compensation to Muhammad and his family worthy of their services to your cause,* took the path to the right side as Fatimah, *'Alayha al-Salam,* had seen in her dream, until they arrived in a place that had palm trees and water. The Messenger of Allah, *O Allah grant compensation to Muhammad and his family worthy of their services to your cause,* then bought a sheep as Fatimah, *'Alayha al-Salam,* had seen in her dream and ordered to slaughter it. It was slaughtered and roasted. When they wanted to eat Fatimah, *'Alayha al-Salam,* stood up and then moved to the side away from them weeping for her fear from their dying. The Messenger of Allah, *O Allah grant compensation to Muhammad and his family worthy of their services to your cause,* looked around for her and found her weeping. He asked, "My dearest daughter why are you weeping?"

She replied, "O Messenger of Allah, last night I saw such and such dream and you have done exactly what I had seen in my dream. I moved away from you so that I will not see you all die."

The Messenger of Allah, *O Allah grant compensation to Muhammad and his family worthy of their services to your cause,* then stood up to perform two Rak'at *Salat* (prayer) and prayed to Allah. Jibril then came to him and said, "O Muhammad, there is a Satan called al-Dahar. He is the one who showed Fatimah, *'Alayha al-Salam,* this dream. This Satan troubles believing people in their dreams to make them feel sad and depressed. He then commanded Jibril who brought him in front of the Messenger of Allah, *O Allah grant compensation to Muhammad and his family worthy of their services to your cause.* He asked him if he was the one who frightened Fatimah, *'Alayha al-Salam,* in her dream?" He replied, "Yes, O Muhammad, I did it." He (the Messenger of Allah), then spat on him three times, and made three places of his body to hurt.

Jibril then said to Muhammad, O Muhammad say, when you see in your dream what you do not like, or if any believing person sees such a dream he or she should say, "I seek refuge with the one with whom the angels close to Allah, the Prophet messengers and the virtuous servants of Allah seek protection against the evil of what I have seen in my dream." Then recite, chapters, 1, 113, 114 and 112 of al-Quran, and then spit three times to his left. What he has seen will not harm him. Allah then sent the above verse of al-Quran about it.

I ('Allamah Majlisi) say that he has not found in the available dictionaries the word *Kubara'* meaning as such.

H 117, Ch. 4, h 15
Tafsir of 'Iyashi:

It is narrated from abu Basir from 'Abu 'Abd Allah, 'Alayhi al-Salam who has said the following:

Once Fatimah, *'Alayha al-Salam,* saw in her dream that al-Hassan ibn Ali and al-Husayn, *'Alayhima al-Salam,* were slaughtered. It made her very sad and she told the Messenger of Allah, *O Allah grant compensation to Muhammad and his family worthy of their services to your cause,* about it. He (the Messenger of Allah) then asked, "O dream!" It (the dream) then appeared before him in the form of a person." He (the Messenger of Allah) asked, "Did you show her this affliction?" It replied, "No, I did not do it." He (the Messenger of Allah) then called, "O *Adgh'ath* (confusing dream), did you show the affliction to Fatimah, *'Alayha al-Salam?*" It replied, "Yes, O Messenger of Allah, I did so." He (the Messenger of Allah) then asked, "Why did you do so?" It replied, "I wanted to make her sad." He (the Messenger of Allah) then said to Fatimah, *'Alayha al-Salam*, "Did you hear it?" It in actuality is nothing."

H 118, Ch. 4, h 16
Nawadir by al-Rawandi:

Through the chain of his narrators he has narrated from Musa ibn Ja'far from his ancestors, *'Alayhim al-Salam*, who have said the following:

Once a blind man asked permission to come in and Fatimah, *'Alayha al-Salam*, wore her complete *Hijab* (modest dress for women). The Messenger of Allah, *O Allah grant compensation to Muhammad and his family worthy of their services to your cause*, asked her, "Why did you wear complete *Hijab* when he cannot see you (he is blind)?" She replied, "He cannot see me but I can see him and he can sense the scent."

The Messenger of Allah, *O Allah grant compensation to Muhammad and his family worthy of their services to your cause*, then said, "I testify that you are a part of myself."

Through the same chain of narrators as that of the previous Hadith the following is narrated:

He (the narrator) has said that the Messenger of Allah, *O Allah grant compensation to Muhammad and his family worthy of their services to your cause*, asked his companions about the woman and what she is. They replied, "She is a privacy." He then asked, "When is she nearest to her Lord?" They could not answer. When Fatimah, *'Alayha al-Salam*, heard this question, she said, "A woman is closest to her Lord when she is in the deepest private place of her house."

The Messenger of Allah, *O Allah grant compensation to Muhammad and his family worthy of their services to your cause,* then said, "Fatimah, *'Alayha al-Salam,* is a part of myself."

Chapter 5 - About the Marriage of Fatimah, *'Alayha al-Salam*

H 119, Ch. 5, h 1
Iqbal al-'A'mal:

Through the chain of his narrators from Shaykh al-Mufid in the book Hada'iq al-Riyad has narrated the following:

The marriage of Fatimah, *'Alayha al-Salam,* daughter of the Messenger of Allah took place in the twenty first of the month of Muharram. It was a Thursday night in the year 3 (A.H), in the house of 'Amir al-Mu'minin, *'Alayhi al-Salam.* It is preferable to fast that day to express thanks before Allah, most High, for His joining the one who possessed authority from Him in marriage to the one who was His al-Mustafa' (the one who He had purified).

It is in the history of Baghdad through the chain of his narrators from ibn 'Abbas who has said the following:

When Fatimah, *'Alayha al-Salam,* was married to Ali, in her wedding procession the Holy Prophet, was in front of her, Jibril on her right, Michael on her left and seventy thousand angels after her who did *Tasbih* (Allah is free of all defects) and spoke of the Holiness of the name of Allah, until daybreak.

H 120, Ch. 5, h 2
Misbah:

The marriage of Fatimah, *'Alayha al-Salam,* took place on the first day of the month of Dhul Hajjah. The Messenger of Allah, *O Allah grant compensation to Muhammad and his family worthy of their services to your cause,* gave Fatimah, *'Alayha al-Salam,* in marriage to 'Amir al-Mu'minin, *'Alayhi al-Salam.*

It is narrated that it was on the sixth of the month of Dhul Hajjah.

H 121, Ch. 5, h 3
'Yun Akhbar al-Rida':

Ja'far ibn Nu'aym al-Shadhani has narrated from Ahmad ibn Idris from Hashim from Ali ibn Ma'bad from al-Husayn ibn Khalid from abu al-Hassan

Ali ibn Musa al-Rida', from his father from his ancestors from Ali, who has said the following:

The Messenger of Allah, *O Allah grant compensation to Muhammad and his family worthy of their services to your cause,* once said to me, "O Ali certain men from al-Quraysh are critical of me about the issue of Fatimah, *'Alayha al-Salam.* They say, 'We proposed to give her in marriage to us but you refused, yet you gave her in marriage to Ali." I told them, "By Allah, I did not refuse to give her in marriage to you and then gave her in marriage to Ali. In fact Allah refused to give her in marriage to you. He gave her in marriage to Ali." Jibril then descended to me saying "O Muhammad Allah, most Majestic, most Glorious, says, 'Had I not created Ali, there would have been no match for Fatimah, *'Alayha al-Salam,* your daughter on the face of the earth from Adam, *'Alayhi al-Salam,* and thereafter.'"

'Yun Akhbar al-Rida':

Al-Hamadani has narrated from Ali and from his father from Ali ibn Ma'bad a similar Hadith.

H 122, Ch. 5, h 4
'Amali al-Tusi:

Al-Mufid has narrated from Muhammad ibn al-Husayn from al-Husayn, ibn Muhammad al-Asadi from Ja'far ibn 'Abd Allah al-'Alawi from Yahya' ibn Hashim al-Ghassani from Muhammad ibn Marwan from Juwayr ibn Sa'd from al-Dahhak ibn Muzaham who has said the following:

I (the narrator) heard Ali ibn abu Talib, *'Alayhi al-Salam* say, "Abu Bakr and 'Umar came to me and said, "Would that you go to the Messenger of Allah, and speak to him about Fatimah, *'Alayha al-Salam.*" He has said that he then went to the Messenger of Allah, *O Allah grant compensation to Muhammad and his family worthy of their services to your cause,* and when he saw me, he smiled and asked, "What brings you here, O abu al-Hassan? What do you need?" He has said that he then spoke of his relationship, his being the first to accept Islam, helping him, and working hard for him." He (the Messenger of Allah) said, "You have spoken the truth. You are more excellent than what you said you are." I then said, "O Messenger of Allah, will you give Fatimah, *'Alayha al-Salam,* in marriage to me?" He (the Messenger of Allah) said, "O Ali, several people have spoken to me about her and I informed her about their marriage proposal but I noticed dislike in her face, however, you should wait until I come back." He (the Messenger of Allah) went inside. She stood up for him, took his gown, removed his shoes, and brought water for washing. She washed him with her own hands, then sat on one side. He then said, "O Fatimah!" She replied, "I am at your disposal. How can I help you, O Messenger of Allah?" He (the Messenger of Allah) said, "You know about relationship of Ali ibn abu Talib with us, about his excellence and about his (being the first to accept) Islam. I have asked my Lord to give you in marriage to best one among His creatures and the most beloved one to Him from among them. He (Ali, *'Alayhi al-Salam*) has spoken to me something about you. So what do you say about it?" She remained quiet. She did not turn her face away and the Messenger of Allah, *O Allah grant compensation to Muhammad and his family worthy of their services to your cause,* did not observe any sign of dislike on her face. He (the Messenger of Allah) stood up saying, *"Takbir* (Allah is great beyond description), her remaining quiet is the sign of her accepting the proposal of marriage to Ali, *'Alayhi al-Salam."*

Jibril, *'Alayhi al-Salam* then came to him saying, "O Muhammad, give her in marriage to Ali, *'Alayhi al-Salam,* because Allah has accepted this marriage proposal on behalf of both of them; Ali, *'Alayhi al-Salam* and Fatimah, *'Alayha al-Salam."*

Ali, *'Alayhi al-Salam* has said that the Messenger of Allah, *O Allah grant compensation to Muhammad and his family worthy of their services to your cause,* gave her in marriage to me. He (the Messenger of Allah) came to me, held my hand and said, "Stand up in the name of Allah and say, 'With the blessing of Allah, as Allah has wished, there is no power without Allah, I place my trust in Allah.'" He (the Messenger of Allah) then took me until he made me sit near Fatimah, *'Alayha al-Salam,* and he said, "O Lord, they are the most beloved ones to me from among your creatures. Please love them and grant them blessings in their descendants, assign for them protectors from your side and I seek your protection for them and for their descendants against the Satan the condemned one by stoning."

H 123, Ch. 5, h 5
'Amali al-Tusi:

145

A group has narrated from abu Ghalib Ahmad ibn Muhammad al-Razi from his maternal uncle from al-ASh'ari from al-Barqiy from ibn Asbat from Dawud from Ya'qub ibn Shu'ayb from 'Abu 'Abd Allah, 'Alayhi al-Salam who has said the following:

He (the Imam) has said that when the Messenger of Allah, *O Allah grant compensation to Muhammad and his family worthy of their services to your cause,* gave Fatimah, *'Alayha al-Salam,* in marriage to Ali, he (the Messenger of Allah) went in her chamber and found her weeping. He then asked, "Why do you weep? By Allah had there been anyone in my *Ahl al-Bayt* (family) better than him I would have given you in marriage to the one better than him. I have not given you in marriage to him but it is Allah who has given you in marriage to him and for your dowry He has assigned the one fifth for the length of the life of the skies and the earth."

Ali, *'Alayhi al-Salam* has said that the Messenger of Allah, *O Allah grant compensation to Muhammad and his family worthy of their services to your cause,* told me to sell my coat of arms and I then stood up to sell it. I received the price then went to the Messenger of Allah, *'Alayhi al-Salam.* I placed the dirhams in his lap. He did not ask how many they were nor did I inform him about the amount of dirhams. He picked up a hand full and called Bilal and told him to buy perfumes for Fatimah, *'Alayha al-Salam.* The Messenger of Allah, *O Allah grant compensation to Muhammad and his family worthy of their services to your cause,* then picked from the dirhams with both his hands. He then gave it to abu Bakr to buy for Fatimah, *'Alayha al-Salam,* what is proper of dresses and household items, joining with him 'Ammar ibn Yasar along with a number of his companions. They went to the market to look for proper items. They would not buy anything before showing it to abu Bakr. If he agreed then they would buy that item. Of the items they bought was a shirt for seven dirhams, a veil for four dirhams, a black garment made in Khaybar, a woven bed, two sackcloth mattresses, one filled with palm tree fibers and the other one filled with sheep's wool, four amenities (pillows) of hide from Taef filled with *Adhkhar* (certain kind of plant fibers) with its cover made of wool, a mat made in Hajari in Yemen, a hand-run grinding stone, a dyer made of copper, a water sack made of hide, a milk container cup, a water jug, a sanitizer treated with pitch, a green sweeper, and two earthenware mugs.

When shopping was complete abu Bakr carried some of the purchased items and other companions of the Holy Prophet carried the rest of the items.

When the items were shown to the Messenger of Allah, *O Allah grant compensation to Muhammad and his family worthy of their services to your cause,* he began to examine them by turning them side to side saying, "May Allah, make them blessings for *Ahl al-Bayt* (family)."

Ali, *'Alayhi al-Salam* has said, "I passed the time for one month. I would perform my *Salat* (prayer) with the Messenger of Allah, *O Allah grant compensation to Muhammad and his family worthy of their services to your cause,* and then go to my home and would not mention anything about Fatimah, *'Alayha al-Salam.* Thereafter the wives of the Holy Prophet, said, 'Why should we not ask the Messenger of Allah, to grant permission to Fatimah, *'Alayha al-Salam,* to come to you?' I then said, 'You should then do so.' They went to the Messenger of Allah, and 'Umm Ayman said, 'O Messenger of Allah, had Khadijah *'Alayha al-Salam,* been living she would enjoy to prepare Fatimah, *'Alayha al-Salam,* as a bride. Ali wants his bride. Please allow Fatimah, *'Alayha al-Salam,* to join her bridegroom. Bring them together and make it a delight for our eyes.' He (the Messenger of Allah) then said, 'Why does he not ask me for his wife and I expected him to do so.'" Ali, *'Alayhi al-Salam* has said that he said, "Shyness prevented, me, O Messenger of Allah."

He then turned to the women, asking, "Who is here?" 'Umm Salamah then said, "I am 'Umm Salamah, this is Zaynab, this is so and so and so and so." The Messenger of Allah, *O Allah grant compensation to Muhammad and his family worthy of their services to your cause,* said, "Prepare for my daughter and my cousin a chamber." 'Umm Salamah asked, "In which one of the homes, O Messenger of Allah?" He (the Messenger of Allah) said, "Prepare in your home." He (the Messenger of Allah) then commanded the women to decorate and make the preparations for her.

'Umm Salamah has said that she asked Fatimah, *'Alayha al-Salam,* "Do you have any perfumes that you may have preserved for yourself?" She replied, "Yes, I do have perfumes." She then brought a bottle and poured some perfumes on my palms and I then smelled it and I found the fragrance to be as

147

such which I had never sensed before. I asked, "What is this?" She replied, "Dihyah al-Kalbi would visit the Messenger of Allah, *O Allah grant compensation to Muhammad and his family worthy of their services to your cause,* and he would ask me to bring for him the pillow and place it on the ground for my uncle. I would place the pillow in place for him on which he would sit and when he would leave certain things would fall from his clothes and he would command me to collect them."

Ali, *'Alayhi al-Salam* asked the Messenger of Allah about it and he said that it is ambergris which falls from the wings of Jibril.

Ali, *'Alayhi al-Salam* has said that the Messenger of Allah, *O Allah grant compensation to Muhammad and his family worthy of their services to your cause,* told me to prepare extra food for my family." He (the Messenger of Allah) then said, "From our side is meat and bread and you should bring dates and oil." I then bought dates and oil. The Messenger of Allah, *O Allah grant compensation to Muhammad and his family worthy of their services to your cause,* pulled up his sleeves to his elbows and began to mix the dates in oil until it became consistent with oil. He sent for us a fat ram which was slaughtered and a large amount of bread.

The Messenger of Allah, *O Allah grant compensation to Muhammad and his family worthy of their services to your cause,* then said to me, "Invite whomever you like and then I went to the Masjid which was full of the companions of the Holy Prophet, and I felt shy to invite a certain group and not others. I then climbed on a higher ground and called, "Please join us for a banquet of wedding celebration of Fatimah, *'Alayha al-Salam.*" People then came freely and I felt shy because of the large number of the people and the small amount of food. The Messenger of Allah, *O Allah grant compensation to Muhammad and his family worthy of their services to your cause,* noticed my feelings and said, "O Ali, I pray to Allah for increased blessings."

Ali, *'Alayhi al-Salam* has said that all the people ate, to the last one of them, our food and drank our drinks and prayed for blessing for us and they then left. They were more than four thousand people but nothing was reduced from the food.

The Messenger of Allah, *O Allah grant compensation to Muhammad and his family worthy of their services to your cause,* then asked for trays which were filled to be sent to the houses of his wives. He then asked for a tray which he filled saying, "This is for Fatimah, *'Alayha al-Salam,* and her husband." It became almost sunset. The Messenger of Allah, *O Allah grant compensation to Muhammad and his family worthy of their services to your cause,* said, "O 'Umm Salamah, bring Fatimah, *'Alayha al-Salam,* to me." She then left and brought her and the train of her dress dragged on the ground. She was drenched in perspiration due to feeling shy before the Messenger of Allah. She then stumbled, about to fall and the Messenger of Allah said, "May Allah hold you firm in this world and the next life."

When she stood in front of him he removed the gown from her face until Ali, *'Alayhi al-Salam* saw her. He (the Messenger of Allah) then took her hand and then gave her hand in the hand of Ali, *'Alayhi al-Salam* saying, "May Allah grant you blessings in your marriage to the daughter of the messenger of Allah. O Ali, *'Alayhi al-Salam* Fatimah, *'Alayha al-Salam,* is a good wife. O Fatimah, *'Alayha al-Salam,* Ali, is a good husband. You can go to your home and wait (do not do anything) until I come."

Ali, *'Alayhi al-Salam* has said, "I then held the hand of Fatimah, *'Alayha al-Salam,* and left until I sat on the side of the platform and she sat next to it with her head bent down to the ground because of shyness from me and I also had bent down my head to the ground because of shyness from her. Then the Messenger of Allah, *O Allah grant compensation to Muhammad and his family worthy of their services to your cause,* came and said, "Who is there?" We then said, "Please, come in, O Messenger of Allah, you are welcome as a visitor coming in." He then came inside. He made Fatimah, *'Alayha al-Salam,* to sit on one side of him and told her to bring some water." She then went to bring the cup of water, filled it up with water and then brought it to him and then he took a sip, rinsed his mouth then poured it in the cup then poured some of it on her head and then he called her to come forward. When she came forward he poured some over her chest. He then asked her to turn around and when she did so he pour some of it between her shoulders and then he said, "O Lord, this is my daughter, the most beloved among the creatures to me. O Lord, this is my brother, the most beloved among the creatures to me. O Lord, make him a friend of yourself and most gracious, grant him blessing in his family." He then said, "O Ali, you can join your wife and may Allah grant you blessings and kindness, and more blessings on both of you; He is praise worthy and glorious."

H 124, Ch. 5, h 6
'Amali al-Tusi:

A group has narrated from abu Ghalib al-Razi from al-Kulayni from a number of his people from Ahmad ibn Muhammad from al-Washsha from al-Khaybari from Yunus ibn Zabayan who has said the following:

I (the narrator) heard 'Abu 'Abd Allah, *'Alayhi al-Salam* say, "If Allah would not create Ali, *'Alayhi al-Salam,* no match could ever be found for Fatimah, *'Alayha al-Salam,* on earth."

H 125, Ch. 5, h 7
'Amali al-Tusi:

It is narrated that the wedding of Ali and Fatimah, *'Alayhima al-Salam,* took place after the death of her sister Ruqayah, wife of 'Uthman. This happened after his return from Badr, which was after a few days had passed from the month of Shawwal. It is also narrated that this happened on a Tuesday on the sixth of the month of Dhul Hajjah. Allah knows best.

H 126, Ch. 5, h 8
Al-Khisal:

Al-Taliqani has narrated from al-Hassan ibn Ali al-'Adwi from 'Amr ibn al-Mukhtar from Yahya' al-Hamani from Qays ibn al-Rabi' from al-'A'mash from 'Abayah ibn Rib'i from abu Ayyub al-Ansari who has said the following:

Once the Messenger of Allah, *O Allah grant compensation to Muhammad and his family worthy of their services to your cause,* became ill and Fatimah, *'Alayha al-Salam,* went to visit him when he had become weak because of his illness. When she found the Messenger of Allah, *O Allah grant compensation to Muhammad and his family worthy of their services to your cause,* in such condition of weakness and suffering, emotional feelings choked her with tears which flowed on her cheeks. The Holy Prophet, *'Alayhi al-Salam* then said to her, "O Fatimah, *'Alayha al-Salam,* Allah, most Majestic, most Glorious, examined the earth for information and then He chose your husband therefrom. He then sent inspiration to me and then I give you in marriage to him. Did you,

O Fatimah, *'Alayha al-Salam,* know that it is of Allah's honoring you that your husband is the first Muslim, a man of the greatest degree of forbearance and knowledge among the people."

He (the narrator) has said that Fatimah, *'Alayha al-Salam,* became happy because of the good news but the Messenger of Allah, *O Allah grant compensation to Muhammad and his family worthy of their services to your cause,* wanted to give her more of such good news of goodness that Allah has made the share of Muhammad and his family. He then said, "O Fatimah, *'Alayha al-Salam,* Ali, *'Alayhi al-Salam* has eight special attributes. Belief in Allah and in His messenger, his knowledge, wisdom, his wife, the two grandsons, al-Hassan and al-Husayn, *'Alayhima al-Salam,* his making others do good and stopping what is unlawful and his issuing judgment according to the book of Allah.

O Fatimah, *'Alayha al-Salam,* we are a family who are given seven qualities which are not given to any of the people of the past and no one will ever have them in future after us.

Our Prophet is the best of the Prophets and he is your father, our executor of the will is the best among the Executors of the Wills and he is your husband, from us is the one who has two wings with which he will fly in the garden (paradise) and he is Ja'far and from us are the two grandsons of this nation (Muslims) and they are your sons.

H 127, Ch. 5, h 9
'Amali of al-Saduq:

My father and al-'Attar have narrated from Muhammad al-'Attar from Muhammad ibn 'Abd al-Jabbar from abu Ahmad al-Azdi from Aban ibn 'Uthman from Aban ibn Taghlib from 'Ikramah from ibn 'Abbas who has said the following:

The Messenger of Allah, *O Allah grant compensation to Muhammad and his family worthy of their services to your cause,* has said that Allah, most High, established brotherhood between me and Ali ibn abu Talib, *'Alayhi al-Salam* and gave my daughter to him in marriage over the seven skies and assigned the angels close to Him as witnesses. He made him the Executor of my Will, and my successor. Ali is from me and I am from him. Those who love him are beloved to me and those who hate him I hate them.

H 128, Ch. 5, h 10
'Amali of al-Saduq:

Ibn al-Walid has narrated from Sa'd from ibn 'Isa from Ali ibn al-Hakam from al-Husayn ibn al-'Ala' from al-Sadiq from his ancestors 'Alayhim al-Salam who has said the following:

'Amir al-Mu'minin, 'Alayhi al-Salam has said that once 'Umm 'Ayman came to the Messenger of Allah with something inside her bed sheet. The Messenger of Allah, *'Alayhi al-Salam* asked, "What are the things with you O 'Umm 'Ayman?" She then said, "O Messenger of Allah, *O Allah, please, grant compensation to Muhammad and his family worthy of their services to your cause,* so and so was given in marriage and they spread valuable things on her and I picked up from them. She then wept saying, "O Messenger of Allah, you gave Fatimah, *'Alayha al-Salam,* in marriage but did not shower on her any valuable gifts." The Messenger of Allah, *O Allah grant compensation to Muhammad and his family worthy of their services to your cause,* said, "O 'Umm Ayman, you should not say what is not true; when Allah, most High, gave Fatimah, *'Alayha al-Salam,* in marriage to Ali, *'Alayhi al-Salam* He commanded the trees of the garden (paradise) to spread over them of their ornaments, and dresses, rubies, pearls, emeralds, silk brocades of thick woven silk threads and they (the audience) took so much that they could not figure out. Allah gave *al-Tuba* (the tree in the garden (paradise) for the dowry of Fatimah, *'Alayha al-Salam,* and has placed it in the house of Ali, *'Alayhi al-Salam.*"

Tafsir of 'Iyashi:

It is narrated from 'Amr ibn Shimr from Jabir from abu Ja'far, *'Alayhi al-Salam* a similar Hadith.

H 129, Ch. 5, h 11
Tafsir of Ali ibn Ibrahim:

My father has narrated in in a marfu' manner from his people the following:

Whoever would speak to the Messenger of Allah, *O Allah grant compensation to Muhammad and his family worthy of their services to your cause,* about the marriage of Fatimah, *'Alayha al-Salam,* he would turn away and it happened so often that people lost all hope in their success for their proposal. When he (the Messenger of Allah) decided to give Fatimah, *'Alayha al-Salam,* in marriage to Ali, *'Alayhi al-Salam* he spoke to her privately and she said, "O Messenger of Allah. You have the priority to make the decision. However, woman of al-Quraysh speak to me and say that he is a man of a big belly, long hands, large joint bones, receding hairs of his forehead, large eyes, with his head close to his body, his joint bones look like those of camels; of a big smile and he has no belongings."

The Messenger of Allah, *O Allah grant compensation to Muhammad and his family worthy of their services to your cause,* then said: O Fatimah, *'Alayha al-Salam,* did you know that Allah examined the world and he then chose me from among all men of the worlds, then He examined the world and chose Ali from among all the men of the worlds. He then examined the world and chose you from among all the women of the worlds. O Fatimah, *'Alayha al-Salam,* when I was taken for the night journey to the sky I found a writing on a rock in Bayt al-Maqdis that said, "Only Allah deserves worship, He is one and has no partners and that Muhammad is His servant whom I have supported with him (the Imam) as his vizier, and I grant him victory through his vizier." I then asked Jibril, "Who is my vizier?" He replied, "He is Ali ibn abu Talib."

When I arrived at the last lotus tree I found a writing on it that said, "I am Allah, only who deserves worship, Muhammad is my chosen one from among my creatures whom I have supported with his vizier, granted victory through his vizier." I asked Jibril, "Who is my vizier?" He replied, "He is Ali ibn abu Talib, *'Alayhima al-Salam.* I then passed the lotus tree to the Throne of the Lord of the worlds and on one of its pillar I found a writing that said, "I am Allah, only I deserve worship, Muhammad is my beloved one whom I have supported with his vizier, and have granted victory through his vizier."

When I entered the garden (paradise) in the garden (paradise) I saw the *Tuba* (the tree in the garden (paradise) with its root in the house of Ali with one branch of it in every palace and house of the garden (paradise). On such branches there were containers of ornaments of silk and silk of very thickly woven threads. A believing person will have a million of such containers of ornaments and in every container there were one hundred thousand packages and no one of which was similar to the others in colors and they are the dresses of the people of the garden (paradise) in the center of which is the extended shadow. The width of the garden (paradise) is like the width of the sky and earth, which is prepared for those who believe in Allah and His messenger. A rider will not be able to cross that shadow in one hundred years as it is spoken of in al-Quran, " . . . and amid the extended shade." (56:31) Below this are the fruits of the inhabitants of the garden (paradise) and their food ready in their homes. In one of the stems there are fruits of hundreds of colors, which you see in the lower world, and they are such fruits which you have not seen or heard of and you will not hear of the like of them. Whenever anything is picked up another one grows in its place. They cannot be finished and prohibited. A canal flows from the roots of this tree from which four canals, the canal of water, the canals of milk the taste of which does not change, the canals of wine which gives pleasure to those who drink from it, and the canal of pure honey.

O Fatimah, *'Alayha al-Salam,* Allah has given me in Ali seven attributes. He will be the first for whom the grave will split open with me, the first one with me to stand on the bridge then he will say to the fire, "Take this and that one," the first one to dress up when I dress up, the first one to stand with me on the right side of the Throne, the first one with me to knock at the door of the garden (paradise), the first one to reside with me in *'Illiyin,* and the first one to drink with me from the sealed container of drinks which end with the fragrance of musk for which contestants must contest.

O Fatimah, *'Alayha al-Salam,* this is what Allah has granted to Ali in the next life and has prepared for him in the garden (paradise) because he has no belongings in the world.

You have said that his belly is large, it is because it is full of knowledge. Allah has specially favored him and has honored him from among the people of my nation (followers).

You have said that his forehead hairs are receding and he has large eyes, it is because Allah has created him with the qualities of Adam, *'Alayhi al-Salam.* His hands are long because Allah, most Majestic, most Glorious, through their length will kill his enemies and the enemies of His Messenger and through them Allah will make the religion dominant even though the pagans dislike it and through them Allah will grant victory and he will fight the pagans on the issue of the coming of the divine revelation as well as the hypocrites, the rebels, the apostates and the criminal ones on the issue of the interpretations of divine revelations.

From his seed Allah will bring out the leaders of the youth of the garden (paradise) and beautify His Throne with them.

O Fatimah, *'Alayha al-Salam,* Allah has not sent any Prophet without placing his descendants in his back. He has placed my descendants in the back of Ali. Had Ali not come in existence I could have no descendants.

Fatimah, *'Alayha al-Salam,* then said, "O Messenger of Allah, I will not chose anyone, of the inhabitants of the earth, other than him." The Messenger of Allah, *O Allah grant compensation to Muhammad and his family worthy of their services to your cause,* then gave her in marriage to Ali, *'Alayhi al-Salam.*

Ibn 'Abbas at that time said, "By Allah there was no match for Fatimah, *'Alayha al-Salam,* except Ali, *'Alayhi al-Salam.*

H 130, Ch. 5, h 12
'Amali of al-Saduq:

Ibn al-Walid has narrated from al-Saffar from Salmah ibn al-Khattab from Ibrahim ibn Muqatil from Hamid ibn Muhammad from 'Umar ibn Harun from Al-Sadiq from his ancestors 'Alayhim al-Salam from Ali, 'Alayhi al-Salam who has said the following:

"I wanted to marry Fatimah, *'Alayha al-Salam,* daughter of Muhammad, *O Allah grant compensation to Muhammad and his family worthy of their services to your cause,* but could not dare to speak about it to the Holy Prophet, still the idea pricked in my chest day and night until one day I visited the Messenger of Allah, *O Allah grant compensation to Muhammad and his family worthy of their services to your cause,* he said, "O Ali!" I replied, "Here I am at your disposal." He then asked, "Do you want to get married?" I replied, "The Messenger of Allah, *O Allah grant compensation to Muhammad and his family worthy of their services to your cause,* knows best, if he likes that I marry one of the women of al-Quraysh but I am afraid about (of missing) Fatimah, *'Alayha al-Salam.*" Then I did not sense anything but suddenly the Messenger of Allah sent someone for me who said, "You must come to see the Holy Prophet, and must do so quickly." We have not seen the Messenger of Allah, *O Allah grant compensation to Muhammad and his family worthy of their services to your cause,* as intensely happy as we have seen him today." Ali, *'Alayhi al-Salam,* has said, "I went quickly and found him in the chamber of 'Umm Salamah. When he saw me his face turned bright with happiness and smiled until the whiteness of his teeth became visible and shining. He said, "I have glad news for you, O Ali; Allah, most Majestic, most Glorious, has made my wish to come true about the issue of your marriage." I then asked, "How has that happened, O Messenger of Allah?" He replied, "Jibril came to me with an ear of carnation, (cloves) of the garden (paradise). He gave it to me and I smelled its fragrance and asked him the reason for bringing the ear of carnation, (cloves). He said, "Allah, most blessed, most high, has commanded the inhabitants of the garden (paradise) and the angels and all those in it to decorate the garden (paradise) all of it with its plantations, trees, fruits, and palaces. He has commanded its winds to blow with all kinds of perfumes, and fragrances. He has commanded *al-Hawra' al-'in* in it to recite in the garden (paradise) the chapters of al-Quran like *Ta, Ha, Tawasin, Yasin, Ha, Mim 'Ayn, Sin Qaf.*

"An announcer then from under the Throne made an announcement that said, 'Today is the day of the wedding ceremony of Ali, and Fatimah, *'Alayhima al-Salam.* I assign you as witness that I have given Fatimah, *'Alayha al-Salam,* daughter of Muhammad in marriage to Ali ibn abu Talib, *'Alayhima al-Salam.* I am happy that they are from each other.'

"Then Allah, most blessed, most high, sent a white cloud which rained on them pearls, emeralds and rubies of the garden (paradise) and the angels stood up to spread the ears of carnation, and cloves of the garden (paradise) and this is of what the angels spread because of the happy occasion. Allah, most blessed, most high, commanded an angel of the angels of the garden (paradise) called Rahil, the like of whom in eloquence there is no other angel. He delivered a speech which no one of the inhabitants of the skies and the earth had ever heard. An announcer then announced: O my angels and the inhabitants of my garden (paradise) you must congratulate Ali ibn abu Talib, the beloved one to Muhammad and Fatimah, *'Alayha al-Salam,* the daughter of Muhammad because I have congratulated them. You must take notice that I have given in marriage the woman most beloved to me among all women to the man most beloved to me among all men after the prophets and messengers.

"Rahil, the angel then asked, 'O Lord, what is your congratulation and blessings for them above what we have seen in your home and the gardens (paradise)?' He, Allah, most Majestic, most Glorious, said, 'O Rahil, of my blessing for them is that I have joined them (in marriage) on the basis of my love, that I have made them my authority among my creatures, by my majesty and glory that I will create from them such creatures, establish from them such descendants whom I will make the treasurers on my earth, the mines of my knowledge, preachers for my religion and with them I will establish my argumentation among creatures after my prophets and the messengers.'

"Thus, this is the glad news for you, O Ali, that Allah, most Majestic, most Glorious, has honored you with such honors which no one have ever received the like of it and I have given my daughter Fatimah, *'Alayha al-Salam,* to you in marriage as the Beneficent has done so and I have accepted what Allah has accepted and agreed with. You can receive your family because you are more rightful than me and Jibril has informed me that the garden (paradise) is yearning for both of you. Had Allah, most Majestic, most Glorious, not determined to bring up from you the divine authorities to establish His argumentations against the creatures He would answer the plea of the garden (paradise) and its inhabitants to receive you.

"You are the best brother and the best son-in-law, the best companion and it is sufficient appreciation in your favor that Allah is happy with you."

Ali, *'Alayhi al-Salam* has said that he then asked, "O Messenger of Allah, has my position reached a state that I am spoken of in the garden (paradise), that Allah has given –celebrated my marriage among the angels?"

He (the Messenger of Allah), said, "When Allah, most Majestic, most Glorious, honors and loves His beloved one He honors him in such manner that no eye has ever seen and no ear has ever heard. Allah has given her to you as a gift, O Ali, *'Alayhi al-Salam.*"

Ali, *'Alayhi al-Salam* then said, ". . . Lord, inspire me to thank you for Your favors to me and my parents and to act righteously so as to please you. Admit me, by Your mercy into the company of Your righteous servants." (27:19) The Messenger of Allah, *O Allah grant compensation to Muhammad and his family worthy of their services to your cause,* then said Amin.

'Yun Akhbar al-Rida':

Muhammad ibn Ali ibn al-Shat has narrated from Ahmad ibn al-Muzaffar from Muhammad ibn Zakariya from Mahadi ibn Sabiq from al-Rida', from his ancestors from Ali, *'Alayhi al-Salam* a similar Hadith.

'Yun Akhbar al-Rida':

Al-Daqaq has narrated from ibn Zakariya Al-Qattan from ibn Habib from Ahmad ibn al-Harith from abu Mu'awiyah from al-'A'mash from Al-Sadiq, *'Alayhi al-Salam* from his ancestors from Ali, *'Alayhi al-Salam* a similar Hadith.

H 130, Ch. 5, h 13
Tafsir of Furat ibn Ibrahim:

'Uqbah ibn Mukram al-Dabi has narrated from Muhammad ibn Ali, ibn 'Amr from 'Amr ibn 'Abd Allah ibn Harun al-Tusi from Ahmad ibn 'Abd Allah al-Shaybani from Muhammad ibn Ja'far ibn Muhammad ibn Ali ibn al-Husayn from his father from his ancestors from Ali, *'Alayhi al-Salam* a similar Hadith and at the end has said, "In the garden (paradise) Allah has given you such gifts which no eyes have ever seen, no ears have ever heard." He (the narrator) has said that Ali ibn abu Talib, *'Alayhima al-Salam,* then said, "(Solomon) smiled at the ant's remarks and said, 'Lord, inspire me to thank you for Your favors to me and my parents and to act righteously so as to please you.' (27:19) Lord, make my offspring virtuous. . . ." (46:15) The Messenger of Allah, *O Allah grant compensation to Muhammad and his family worthy of their services to your cause,* then said, Amin, O Lord, of the worlds, O the best helper."

H 131, Ch. 5, h 14
Qurb al-Asnad:

Ibn Tarif has narrated from ibn 'Ulwan from Ja'far from his father 'Alayhima al-Salam, who has said the following:

The house furnishings of Ali, and Fatimah, *'Alayhima al-Salam*, when they got married consisted of a treated skin of a ram which they would turn upside down when they wanted to sleep so as to sleep on its furry side. He (the Imam) has said that their pillow was a piece of hide filled with palm tree fibers. Her dowry was one coat of arms made of iron.

H 132, Ch. 5, h 15
'Amali al-Tusi:

Abu 'Amr has narrated ibn 'Uqdah from Muhammad ibn Ahmad ibn al-Hassan from Musa ibn Ibrahim al-Marwazi from Musa ibn Ja'far from his father from his grandfather 'Alayhim al-Salam from Jabir ibn 'Abd Allah who has said the following:

When the Messenger of Allah, *O Allah grant compensation to Muhammad and his family worthy of their services to your cause*, gave Fatimah, *'Alayha al-Salam*, in marriage to Ali, *'Alayhi al-Salam*, certain persons from Quraysh came to the Messenger of Allah to say that he has given Fatimah, *'Alayha al-Salam*, in marriage to Ali, for a very insignificant dowry. He (the Messenger of Allah), *O Allah grant compensation to Muhammad and his family worthy of their services to your cause*, then said to them, "I have not given her in marriage to Ali. It is Allah, most Majestic, most Glorious, who gave her in marriage to Ali, in the night in which he (the Messenger of Allah) was taken for the night journey, near the lotus tree. Allah then inspired the lotus tree to shower what it has on it of pearls, jewels, and coral. *Al-Hawra' al-'in* then hurried to pick up the jewels expressing pride and saying that what they have picked up is of the valuables showered down on the occasion of the wedding of the daughter of Muhammad, *O Allah grant compensation to Muhammad and his family worthy of their services to your cause*. On the night of the wedding the Holy Prophet, brought the *shahba'* mule with a sheet of fabric folded on it and then he told Fatimah, *'Alayha al-Salam*, to ride. He commanded Salman (Rh) to lead the mule and the Messenger of Allah drove. On the way the Holy Prophet, heard the sound of a movement and he found it to be because of the coming of Jibril along with seventy thousand angels, as well as Michael with seventy thousand angels. The Holy Prophet, *O Allah grant compensation to Muhammad and his family worthy of their services to your cause,* asked, "What brings you to earth?" They replied, "We have come to take part in the wedding ceremony of Fatimah, and Ali ibn abu Talib, *'Alayhima al-Salam.* Jibril then said *Takbir* (Allah is great beyond description), Michael said *Takbir* (Allah is great beyond description) and so also did the angels. The Holy Prophet, *O Allah grant compensation to Muhammad and his family worthy of their services to your cause,* said *Takbir* (Allah is great beyond description) and from that time on *Takbir* (Allah is great beyond description) is said during the celebration of a wedding ceremony."

H 133, Ch. 5, h 16
'Yun Akhbar al-Rida':

Through the chain of narrators of al-Tamimi it is narrated from al-Rida', from his ancestors who have said the following:

The Messenger of Allah, *O Allah grant compensation to Muhammad and his family worthy of their services to your cause,* has said that he did not give Fatimah, *'Alayha al-Salam,* in marriage except until after Allah, most Majestic, most Glorious, commanded him to do so.

H 134, Ch. 5, h 17
'Yun Akhbar al-Rida':

Through the three chains of narrators it is narrated from al-Rida', from his ancestors 'Alayhim al-Salam, who have said the following:

The Messenger of Allah, *O Allah grant compensation to Muhammad and his family worthy of their services to your cause,* has said that Jibril came to him and said, "O Muhammad, Allah sends you *Salam* (the phrase of offering greeting of peace) and says that He has given Fatimah, *'Alayha al-Salam,* in marriage to Ali, *'Alayhi al-Salam* so you also must give her in marriage to him. I have commanded the *Tuba* (the tree in the garden (paradise)) to carry pearls, rubies and corals emeralds and the inhabitants of sky have become happy for it. Two boys who will be the leaders of the youth of the garden (paradise) will be born to her and with them the inhabitants of the garden (paradise) will be beautified. O Muhammad, you can enjoy this glad news because you are the best of the past and future generations of people.

In Sahifah of al-Rida', *'Alayhi al-Salam,* a similar Hadith is narrated.

H 135, Ch. 5, h 18
'Amali al-Tusi:

Al-Haffar has narrated from al-Ja'abi' from Ali ibn Ahmad 'from al-'Ijli from 'Abbad ibn Ya'qub from 'Isa ibn 'Abd Allah al-'Alawi from his father from his father from his grandfather from Ali, 'Alayhi al-Salam who has said the following:

He (the narrator) has said that the Messenger of Allah, *O Allah grant compensation to Muhammad and his family worthy of their services to your cause,* came looking for me and he asked, "Where is my brother, O 'Umm 'Ayman?" She then asked, "Who is your brother (cousin)?" He replied, "He is Ali, *'Alayhi al-Salam.*" She then said, "O Messenger of Allah, if Ali is your brother then why do you give your daughter in marriage to him?" He (the Messenger of Allah), replied, "Yes, I swear by Allah that I have given her in marriage to a very respectable match who is honorable in the world and in the next life and is of the close ones to Allah.

H 136, Ch. 5, h 19
'Amali al-Tusi:

Al-Husayn ibn Ibrahim al-Qazwini has narrated from Muhammad ibn Wahban from Ali ibn Hubaysh from 'Abbas ibn Muhammad ibn al-Husayn from his father from Safwan from al-Husayn ibn abu Ghundur from Ishaq ibn 'Ammar and abu Basir from 'Abu 'Abd Allah, 'Alayhi al-Salam who has said the following:

He (the narrator), *'Alayhi al-Salam* has said that Allah, most High, assigned one fourth of the world as dowry of Fatimah, *'Alayha al-Salam,* thus, one fourth of it belongs to her. He also has given the garden (paradise) and the fire to her. She can send her enemies to the fire. She can send to the garden (paradise) those who honor and respect her. She is the great truthful one and on the basis of the acknowledgement of this fact the previous centuries functioned.

H 137, Ch. 5, h 20
Qurb al-Asnad:

Muhammad ibn al-Walid has narrated from ibn Bukayr who has said the following:

I (the narrator) heard 'Abu 'Abd Allah, *'Alayhi al-Salam* say, "The Messenger of Allah, *O Allah grant compensation to Muhammad and his family worthy of their services to your cause,* gave Fatimah, *'Alayha al-Salam,* in marriage to Ali, *'Alayhi al-Salam* and for the expenses of the marriage ceremony there was one (Hatmiyah) coat of arms, valued at thirty dirhams."

I ('Allamah Majlisi) say that in the section on the marriage of abu Ja'far al-Thani, *'Alayhi al-Salam* it will be mentioned that he (the narrator) has said that Muhammad ibn Ali ibn Musa proposed marriage to 'Umm al-Fadl the daughter of 'Abd Allah al-Ma'mun with an amount of dowry equal to the amount of the dowry of his grandmother, Fatimah, *'Alayha al-Salam,* which was five hundred dirhams of excellent quality.

H 138, Ch. 5, h 21
Al-Khara'ij:

It is narrated that for the wedding of Fatimah, *'Alayha al-Salam,* the Messenger of Allah, *O Allah grant compensation to Muhammad and his family worthy of their services to your cause,* prepared sweet meat and asked Ali, *'Alayhi al-Salam* to invite the people for food. Ali, *'Alayhi al-Salam* has said that he went to the people and invited them for the wedding banquet. They came and the Holy Prophet, *'Alayhi al-Salam* said, "Bring in ten of them at a time. They came and were served food in the form of al-Tharid (bread mashed in broth). They ate the food and then were served with dates in oil. The food would become more blissful and increasing. When men were served he then examined the remaining food. He prayed on it for blessing and mixed in it his saliva then sent from it to his wives and said to tell them to eat from it and serve those who may come to them.

The Messenger of Allah, *O Allah grant compensation to Muhammad and his family worthy of their services to your cause,* then asked for a tray on which he put aside a share of food and said, "This is for you and your family."

Jibril then came with a group of the angels with a gift. He then said to 'Umm Salamah, fill up the cup with water. He then said to me, "O Ali, drink one half of it." He then said to Fatimah, *'Alayha al-Salam,* "You must drink some and then leave the remaining." He then took the remaining and poured it on her face and neck. He then opened the basket in which there were cakes, bananas, and raisins. He then said, "This is the gift of Jibril." He then turned, with his hand, a piece of quince and made it in to two pieces then he gave one piece to Ali saying, "This is a gift from the garden (paradise) to both of you." He gave one half to Ali and one half to Fatimah, *'Alayha al-Salam.*"

H 139, Ch. 5, h 22
Manaqib of ibn Shahr Ashub:

This is about the meaning of the words of Allah, the most Majestic, the most Glorious:

"It is He who has created the human being from water to have relationships of both lineage and wedlock. Your Lord has all the power." (25:54)

Ibn 'Abbas, ibn Mas'ud, Jabir, al-Bara', Anas, 'Umm Salamah, al-Sadi, ibn Sirin, and al-Baqir, have said that this is a reference to Muhammad, Ali, al-Hassan, and al-Husayn, *'Alayhim al-Salam,* and "Your Lord has all the power" is a reference to *al-Qa'im* (the one who rises with divine authority and power) in the end times. This is because in no one of the companions and relatives both kinds of relationship because of "lineage and wedlock" comes together except in him and for this reason he deserves the legacy because of both kinds of relationships. According to one narration "human being" is a reference to the messenger and "lineage" is a reference to Fatimah, *'Alayha al-Salam,* and the relationship because of "wedlock" is a reference to Ali, *'Alayhi al-Salam.*

Tafsir of Tha'labi:

Ibn Sirin has said that the above verse of al-Quran was revealed about the Holy Prophet, and Ali, *'Alayhima al-Salam.* The Holy Prophet gave Fatimah, *'Alayha al-Salam,* in marriage to Ali, *'Alayhi al-Salam* who is his cousin then their relationship took shape in the form of both "lineage and wedlock".

Ibn al-Hajjaj has said: "By al-Mustafa' (the purified one) and his son-in-law and his Executor of the Will on the day of al-Ghadir." (This seems to be part of the lines of his poems on the occasion of Ghadir.)

Ka'b ibn Zuhayr has said: "son-in-law of the Holy Prophet, and the best of all people."

Al-Sadiq, *'Alayhi al-Salam* has said that Allah, most High, sent revelation to His Messenger, *O Allah grant compensation to Muhammad and his family worthy of their services to your cause,* to say to Fatimah, *'Alayha al-Salam,* "You must not disobey Ali, *'Alayhi al-Salam* because if he becomes angry I become angry because of it."

The Holy Prophet, *'Alayhi al-Salam* was blamed for about the marriage of Fatimah, *'Alayha al-Salam,* (to Ali, *'Alayhi al-Salam*). The Holy Prophet, *'Alayhi al-Salam* said, "If Allah had not created Ali, no match for Fatimah, *'Alayha al-Salam,* existed on earth."

Al-Mufaddal has narrated from 'Abu 'Abd Allah, 'Alayhi al-Salam who has said the following:

If Allah, most High, had not created 'Amir al-Mu'minin, Ali, *'Alayhi al-Salam,* no match existed on the face of the earth from Adam, *'Alayhi al-Salam,* and thereafter ever."

If they say that the Holy Prophet, married the daughters of the two Shaykhs and gave two of his daughters in marriage to 'Uthman, we say marriage does not establish excellence. Marriage becomes lawful on the basis of the two testaments of faith. Moreover, the Holy Prophet, married to a whole group. About the marriage of 'Uthman there are great differences. They were married as unbelievers before him. The case of Fatimah, *'Alayha al-Salam,* is different; she was born Muslim, she is one of the people of the cloak, of al-Mubahalah, (verse 3:61 of al-Quran) of the Muhajir (immigrants) during the most difficult times, one of the people to whom verse 33 of chapter 33 of al-Quran applies, and Jibril had expressed pride for being one of them, that Allah testified to prove their truthfulness, that she is the mother of the 'Imams up to the Day of Judgment, and that from her al-Hassan and al-Husayn, *'Alayhima al-Salam,* were born. She is the only surviving child of the Messenger of Allah, *O Allah grant compensation to Muhammad and his family worthy of their services to your cause,* she is the leader of the women of the worlds that her husband is from her own lineage and not a stranger.

The two Shaykhs begged before the Messenger of Allah, *O Allah grant compensation to Muhammad and his family worthy of their services to your cause,* for such relationship but in the case of Ali, the Messenger of Allah, *O*

Allah grant compensation to Muhammad and his family worthy of their services to your cause, proposed to give Fatimah, 'Alayha al-Salam, in marriage to Ali, after rejecting the marriage proposals from both Shaykhs. The solemnizing authority in the marriage of Fatimah, 'Alayha al-Salam, and Ali, 'Alayhi al-Salam was Allah, most High, the accepting party of the marriage proposal was Jibril, the speaker about the marriage ceremony was Rahil, the angel, the witnesses were the carrier of the Throne, the spreader of the valuable gifts for the ceremony was Ridwan (the manager of the garden (paradise), the containers of gifts were from the tree of *Tuba* (the tree in the garden (paradise) that carried, pearls, rubies, and coral, the Messenger of Allah, *O Allah grant compensation to Muhammad and his family worthy of their services to your cause,* was the comber, and 'Asma' was the manager of the wedding chamber. The children from this marriage were the Imams, 'Alayhim al-Salam.

Ibn Shahin al-Marwazi in the book merits of Fatimah, 'Alayha al-Salam, through the chain of his narrators has narrated from al-Husayn ibn Waqid from abu Baridah from his father and al-Beladhuri in the history through the chain of his narrators has said that abu Bakr proposed marriage before the Holy Prophet, with Fatimah, 'Alayha al-Salam, and he responded saying, "I am waiting for *al-Qada'* (divine determination) about her marriage." Then 'Umar proposed marriage with Fatimah, 'Alayha al-Salam, before the Holy Prophet, and he responded saying, "I am waiting for *al-Qada'* (divine determination) about her marriage..." to the end of the narration.

Musnad of Ahmad, his book on excellence, Sunan of abu Dawud, 'Ibanah of ibn Battah, Tarikh of al-Khatib, the book of ibn Shahin in which the words are his words about the meaning of the words of Allah, most Majestic, most Glorious, through the chain of his narrators from Khalid al-Hadhdha', abu Ayyub, 'Ikramah, ibn Sulayman, abu Najih, and 'Ubaydah ibn Sulayman all of them from ibn 'Abbas have narrated that when the Holy Prophet, *O Allah grant compensation to Muhammad and his family worthy of their services to your cause,* gave Fatimah, 'Alayha al-Salam, in marriage to Ali, he said to him to give something to her. Ali, 'Alayhi al-Salam said, "I do not have anything to give to her." He (the Messenger of Allah) then asked, "Where is your al-Hatmiyah coat of arms?"

In the narration of others it is narrated that Ali, *'Alayhi al-Salam* said, "It is with me." The Holy Prophet, then said, "You can give it to her."

In the History of al-Khatib, al-Beladhuri, Hulyah of abu Nu'aym, 'Ibanah al-'Akbari, Sufyan al-Thawri from al-'A'mash from al-Thawri from 'Alqamah, from ibn Mas'ud who has said that in the morning of the wedding Fatimah, *'Alayha al-Salam,* felt *Ra'dah* (fear, concern). The Holy Prophet, *'Alayhi al-Salam* then said to her, "O Fatimah, *'Alayha al-Salam,* I have given you in marriage to a leader in the world and in the next life he will be among the virtuous ones. O Fatimah, *'Alayha al-Salam,* when Allah, most High, decided that I must give you in marriage to Ali, Allah, most High, commanded Jibril to stand in the fourth sky. The angels then formed rows and rows and he gave a speech. He (Allah) then gave you in marriage to Ali, *'Alayhi al-Salam.* Then Allah, most Blessed, most high, commanded the tree in the garden (paradise) and it carried ornaments and dresses and then He commanded it to spread them for the angels. Whoever of them collected a larger amount than the others, they keep expressing pride about it up to the Day of Judgment.

'Umm Salamah has said that Fatimah, *'Alayha al-Salam,* would express pride before the women for the fact that Jibril, was the one who gave the speech for her wedding.

It is popularly known according to the *Sihah* (authentic books) through the chain of narrators from 'Amir al-Mu'minin, ibn 'Abbas, ibn Mas'ud, Jabir al-Ansari, Anas ibn Malik, al-Bara' ibn 'Azib and 'Umm Salamah in different wordings but the same meaning that abu Bakr and 'Umar proposed marriage to the Holy Prophet, to give Fatimah, *'Alayha al-Salam,* in marriage to them time after time but he turned down their proposal.

Ahmad has narrated in al-Fada'il from Baridah that abu Bakr and 'Umar proposed marriage to the Holy Prophet, to give Fatimah, *'Alayha al-Salam,* in marriage to them. The Holy Prophet said to them that she is very young (small).

Ibn Battah has narrated in Ibanah that 'Abd al-Rahman proposed to the Holy Prophet, to give Fatimah, *'Alayha al-Salam,* in marriage to him but he did not respond to his proposal. In the narration of others it is said that he said, "For such and such amount of dowry." The Holy Prophet, *'Alayhi al-Salam* became angry. He extended his hand to the pebbles and picked up from them, it began to say *Tasbih* (Allah is free of all defects) in his hands; he then found all of them to have turned into pearls and coral in response to nullify his offering a dowry.

When Ali, *'Alayhi al-Salam* proposed marriage. He said, "O Messenger of Allah, I have heard you saying that all relationships because of lineage or marriage will become cut off except the relationship with me because of lineage or marriage."

The Holy Prophet, said, 'The issue of marriage is arranged by Allah and the lineage is made close (a reference to their being cousins) by Allah. He looked happy and celebrative by his face and he asked, "Do you have anything so I can give her in marriage to you?" He then replied, "My condition is not unknown before you. I have one horse, one mule, one sword and one coat of arms."

The Holy Prophet, then said, "You can sell your coat of arms."

It is narrated that Salman (Rh) came to him and said, "You must answer the call of the Messenger of Allah, *O Allah grant compensation to Muhammad and his family worthy of their services to your cause.*" When he came to the Messenger of Allah, he said, "I have a glad news for you, O Ali, *'Alayhi al-Salam;* Allah has given her in marriage to you in the sky before I give her in marriage to you on earth. An angel came to me and said, 'I have glad news for you, O Muhammad, of a settlement of affairs and purification of offspring.' I then asked, 'What is your name?' He replied, 'It is Nasta'il, one of the angels assigned to guard the pillars of the Throne. I asked Allah to allow me to convey this glad news to you and Jibril is just behind me with the same glad news.'"

Abu Baridah has narrated from his father who has said that Ali, *'Alayhi al-Salam* proposed to the Holy Prophet, to give Fatimah, *'Alayha al-Salam,* in marriage to him. The Holy Prophet said, "*Marhaban* and *Ahlan*" (you are well received and welcomed).

It then was said to Ali, *'Alayhi al-Salam,* "Only one was enough for you. He gave you *Ahl* (family) and *Rahb* (open heartedness to receive you)."

Ibn Battah, ibn al-Mu'adhdhin, al-Sam'ani in their books through the chain of their narrators have narrated from ibn 'Abbas and Anas ibn Malik that the two have said the following:

Once, when the Messenger of Allah was sitting that Ali, *'Alayhi al-Salam* came. He (the Messenger of Allah) asked, "What brings you here, O Ali?" He replied, "I came to say *Salam* (the phrase of offering greeting of peace) to you." The Messenger of Allah, *O Allah grant compensation to Muhammad and his family worthy of their services to your cause,* then said, "This is Jibril who informs me that Allah, most Majestic, most Glorious, has given Fatimah, *'Alayha al-Salam,* in marriage to you and He has appointed forty thousand angels as witnesses to this fact. Allah has inspired *Tuba* (the tree in the garden (paradise) to spread on them pearls and rubies and it has spread pearls and rubies on them and *al-Hawra' al-'in* have rushed to collect them in the trays made of pearls and rubies and they present to each other as gifts up to the Day of Judgment. They have been giving gifts to each other saying that it is the gift from the best one among the women."

In the narration of ibn Battah from 'Abd Allah it is said, "Those of them who collected more or of better quality than the others, they express pride for it over the others up to the Day of Judgment."

Ibn Mardwayh has narrated in his book through the chain of his narrators from 'Alqamah who has said the following:

When Ali, *'Alayhi al-Salam* and Fatimah, *'Alayha al-Salam,* were married, fruits of the garden (paradise) were spread over the angels.

'Abd al-Razzaq has narrated through the chain of his narrators from 'Umm 'Ayman in a lengthy narration from the Holy Prophet, *'Alayhi al-Salam:* Jibril and Michael in the sky solemnized the marriage of Ali, and Fatimah, *'Alayhima al-Salam.* Jibril was the speaker from the side of Ali, *'Alayhi al-Salam* and Michael was the one to respond to his assertions.

In the Hadith of Khubab ibn al-Arth it is said that Allah, most High, revealed to Jibril to give in marriage the light to the light. The guardian was Allah, Jibril solemnized the marriage, the announcer was Michael, the caller was Israfil, and the spreader of gifts was 'Izrael, the witnesses were the angels of the skies and earths.

Allah then sent inspiration to *Tuba* (the tree in the garden (paradise) to spread what it has on it. It then spread white pearls, red ruby and green emeralds, and fresh pearls. *Al-Hawra' al-'in* then rushed to collect them and give each other as gifts.

Al-Sadiq, *'Alayhi al-Salam* has said in a Hadith that the Messenger of Allah called him and said, "O Ali, I have glad news for you that Allah has granted to me what was important to me about your marriage." Ibn Shahr Ashub has narrated a shorter version of what was mentioned earlier according to the narration of al-Saduq (r.h). He then has said that it is narrated in certain books that Rahil solemnized the marriage in Bayt al-Ma'mur in a gathering of inhabitants of the seven skies and he said, "All praise belongs to Allah, the first before the first-ness of the first ones, and the eternal after the annihilation of the worlds. We praise Him for His making us, the angels, and spiritual ones and in His Lordship we believe and we appreciate all that He has granted to us. He has curtained us against sins and covered us against defects, settled us in the skies, has kept us close to the pavilion. He has kept away from us lust and craving for food, which He has replaced with our yearning for speaking of the Holiness of the name of Allah, and *Tasbih* (Allah is free of all defects). His blessings are widespread, His bounties are granted. He is glorious and away from the deviations of the inhabitants of the earth and the pagans. He most high because of His greatness is clear from the heresies of the deviant ones.

Thereafter, he said, "The all dominant King has chosen His selected and honored one, the servant of His greatness for his nation (followers) the leader of the women, the daughter of the best of the Prophets, the leader of the messengers, the leader of the pious ones, and He has connected his rope to the rope of a man from his family and his truthful companion who has acknowledged his mission, who quickly accepted his words to join him with Fatimah, *'Alayha al-Salam*, al-Batul (the virgin) the daughter of the Messenger of Allah, *O Allah grant compensation to Muhammad and his family worthy of their services to your cause."*

It is narrated that Jibril has narrated from Allah, most High, following it by the words of Allah, most Majestic, most Glorious, "All praise is my gown, Greatness is my pride, all creatures are my slaves and female slaves. I have given Fatimah, *'Alayha al-Salam,* my female servant, in marriage to my chosen one, so, O my angels, bear witness to this matter."

The time between the marriage ceremony of Ali and Fatimah, *'Alayha al-Salam,* in the sky and their marriage ceremony on earth was forty days. The Messenger of Allah, *O Allah grant compensation to Muhammad and his family worthy of their services to your cause,* solemnized their marriage on the first day of the month of Dhul Hajjah. It is narrated that it was on the sixth of this month.

H 140, Ch. 5, h 23
Ma'ani al-Akhbar: Al-Khisal: 'Amali of al-Saduq:

Masrur has narrated from ibn 'Amir from Mu'alla' from al-Bazanti from Ali ibn Ja'far who has said the following:

I (the narrator) heard abu al-Hassan Musa ibn Ja'far, *'Alayhima al-Salam,* say, "Once when the Messenger of Allah was sitting that an angel came in and he had twenty four faces. The Messenger of Allah, *O Allah grant compensation to Muhammad and his family worthy of their services to your cause,* asked, "O my beloved one, Jibril I have not seen you in this form before." The angel said, "I am not Jibril. I am Mahmud. Allah, most Majestic, most Glorious, has sent me to solemnized the marriage of the light to the light." He (the Messenger of Allah) then asked, "Marriage of whom to whom?" He replied, "It is the marriage of Fatimah, *'Alayha al-Salam,* to Ali, *'Alayhi al-Salam.*" He (the narrator) has said that when the angel turned to go; between his shoulders there was a writing that said, "Muhammad is the Messenger of Allah and Ali is the Executor of his Will." The Messenger of Allah, *O Allah grant compensation to Muhammad and his family worthy of their services to your cause,* then asked, "Since when did you have this writing between your shoulders?" He replied, "It was there twelve thousand years before Allah, most Majestic, most Glorious, created Adam, *'Alayhi al-Salam.*"

H 141, Ch. 5, h 24
Manaqib of ibn Shahr Ashub:

From Ali ibn Ja'far a similar Hadith is narrated. He then has said that according to one Hadith it was fourteen thousand years before the creation of Adam, *'Alayhi al-Salam.*

'Abd Allah ibn Maymun has narrated from abu Hurayrah from ibn al-Zubayr from Jabir al-Ansari in a *Mahmud* (admired) Hadith and abu Ya'li al-'Attar and abu al-Mu'ayyidd al-Khatib informed me of a similar Hadith except that they have narrated: "Ali ibn Ibrahim has narrated from his father from al-Nawfaliy from al-Sakuniy who has narrated the following: "The angel who had twenty heads with a thousand tongues in each head." The name of the angel was Sarsael.

Abu Bakr Mardway in Fada'il of 'Amir al-Mu'minin through a chain of narrators has narrated from Anas ibn Malik, the book of abu al-Qasim Sulayman al-Tabari through the chain of his narrators from Sha'bah from 'Amr ibn Murrah from Ibrahim from Masruq from ibn Mas'ud both from the Holy Prophet, O Allah grant compensation to Muhammad and his family worthy of their services to your cause, who has said the following:

"Allah, most High, commanded me to give Fatimah, *'Alayha al-Salam,* in marriage to Ali, *'Alayhi al-Salam.*"

The Book of ibn Mardwayh:

He the author has said that ibn Sirin has said that 'Ubayd has said that 'Umar ibn al-Khattab spoke of Ali, *'Alayhi al-Salam* and that he is the son-in-law of the Messenger of Allah, *O Allah grant compensation to Muhammad and his family worthy of their services to your cause.* Jibril came to the Messenger of Allah and said that Allah commands you to give Fatimah, *'Alayha al-Salam,* in marriage to Ali, *'Alayhi al-Salam.*

Ibn Shahin through a chain of narrators from abu Ayyub has narrated the following:

The Messenger of Allah, *O Allah grant compensation to Muhammad and his family worthy of their services to your cause,* has said, "I was commanded to give you in marriage *al-Bayda'.* In a narration it is said, "from the sky".

Al-Dahhak has said that the Holy Prophet, *'Alayhi al-Salam* said to Fatimah, *'Alayha al-Salam,* "Ali ibn abu Talib is one of those whose relationship with us is known to you as well his excellent merits in Islam and I have asked my Lord to give you in marriage to the best among His creatures and the most beloved one to Him. He has spoken about you something, so what do you say about it?" She remained quiet and the Messenger of Allah, *O Allah grant compensation to Muhammad and his family worthy of their services to your cause,* came out saying *Takbir* (Allah is great beyond description). Her silence is proof that she has agreed."

Ibn Mardawayh has narrated that the Messenger of Allah, *O Allah grant compensation to Muhammad and his family worthy of their services to your cause,* said to Ali, *'Alayhi al-Salam,* "Speak up in your own behalf to propose marriage." He then said, "All praise belongs to Allah who is near to those who praise Him and close to those who ask Him for help, who has promised the garden (paradise) to those who remain pious before Him, has warned about the fire those who disobey Him. We praise Him for His eternal kindness and for His bounties like the one who knows that He is his creator, his Lord, the one who causes his death and gives life, whom, he asks for help in his bad times. We seek assistance from Him as well as guidance and protection and we testify that only Allah deserves worship, He is one and has no partners. We testify with a testimony, which reaches Him and makes Him happy. We testify that Muhammad is His servant and Messenger, *O Allah grant compensation to Muhammad and his family worthy of their services to your cause,* a compensation which can make him happy and satisfied, raises his ranks as the purified one.

"Marriage is of the issues, which Allah has commanded to have and He is happy with it. Our coming together is what Allah has determined and has granted permission. This is the Messenger of Allah, *O Allah grant compensation to Muhammad and his family worthy of their services to your cause,* who gives his daughter Fatimah, *'Alayha al-Salam,* in marriage to me. Her dowry is five hundred dirhams which I agree to pay, you can ask him about it and bear witness."

In a narration it is said that he said, "I have given my daughter Fatimah, *'Alayha al-Salam,* to you in marriage as the Beneficent has given her to you in marriage and I agree with whatever Allah has agreed for her. You must now look after your family; you have greater priority in this task than I do."

In a narration it is said that he said, "You are the best brother, the best son-in-law and the best companion. The fact that Allah is happy with you makes you free of all needs." Ali, *'Alayhi al-Salam* then fell in *Sujud* (prostrations) for thanksgiving reciting the verse of al-Quran, ". . . Lord, inspire me to thank you for Your favors to me and my parents and to act righteously so as to please you. Admit me, by Your mercy into the company of Your righteous servants." (27:19) (the Holy Prophet, *'Alayhi al-Salam* then said, "Amin." When he raised his head from Sajdah (prostration) the Holy Prophet, congratulated both, of them saying, "May Allah place blessing on and with you make your efforts a success, bring you together, and grant you fine offspring." The Holy Prophet, *O Allah grant compensation to Muhammad and his family worthy of their services to your cause,* then asked for a tray filled with unripe dates and commanded (those present) to grab a piece. He then entered the room of the women and commanded them to play *al-daf* (a kind of drum).

Al-Husayn, ibn Ali, *'Alayhima al-Salam,* in a Hadith has said that the Holy Prophet, *'Alayhi al-Salam* gave Fatimah, *'Alayha al-Salam,* in marriage to Ali, *'Alayhi al-Salam* and her dowry was four hundred and eighty dirhams. It also is narrated that it was four hundred Mithqal of silver and it is narrated also that it was five hundred dirhams and this is the correct answer.

The reason for the discrepancy is what 'Amr ibn Miqdam has narrated as well as Jabir al-Juhfi from 'Abu 'Abd Allah, 'Alayhi al-Salam who has said the following:

The amount of dowry of Fatimah, *'Alayha al-Salam,* was one gown made in Hibra and the hide of a sheep (filled) with herbs of fine fragrance.

It is narrated from al-Sadiq, *'Alayhi al-Salam* who has said that the amount of dowry of Fatimah, *'Alayha al-Salam,* was a Hatmiyah coat of arms and the hide of a ram or a goat. This is narrated by abu Ya'li in al-Musnad from Mujahid.

Al-Kulayni in Al-Kafi has said that the Holy Prophet, *O Allah grant compensation to Muhammad and his family worthy of their services to your cause,* gave Fatimah, *'Alayha al-Salam,* in marriage to Ali, *'Alayhi al-Salam* for a dowry of a worn gown.

It was said to the Holy Prophet, "We know about the dowry of Fatimah, *'Alayha al-Salam,* on earth what it was, but what is it in the sky?" The Holy Prophet, replied, "Ask about what concerns you. Do not ask about what does not concern you." It was said, "This concerns us, O Messenger of Allah." He

173

said, "Her dowry in the sky was one fifth of the earth. Whoever walks on it with hatred and (anger) toward her and her children has walked on it in an unlawful manner until the Day of Judgment."

In al-Jala' and al-Shifa' in a lengthy narration it is narrated from al-Baqir, 'Alayhi al-Salam, who has said the following:

I have assigned for her from Ali, one fifth of the world and one third of the garden (paradise). On the earth I have assigned for her four rivers: al-Forat, Nile in Egypt, Nahrawan, and Nahr (river) of Balkh. You, O Muhammad, give her in marriage to Ali, for a dowry of five hundred dirhams to set a tradition in your nation (followers).

In the Hadith of Khubab ibn Art it is said that the Messenger of Allah then said, "I have given in marriage to you my daughter Fatimah, 'Alayha al-Salam, because Allah, most High, has commanded me to do for an amount of dowry of one fifth of the earth and four hundred and eighty dirhams of which one fifth of the earth is on demand and four hundred and eighty dirhams is payable immediately."

The Hadith about the one fifth of the earth as the dowry of Fatimah, 'Alayha al-Salam, is narrated from al-Sadiq, 'Alayhi al-Salam by Ya'qub ibn 'Shu'ayb, Ishaq ibn 'Ammar and abu Basir who has said the following:

Al-Sadiq, 'Alayhi al-Salam has said that Allah, most High, has assigned one fourth of the worlds as dowry of Fatimah, 'Alayha al-Salam, so one fourth of it belongs to her. Of her dowry are the garden (paradise) and the fire. She will admit those who honor and respect her in the garden (paradise) and will send her enemies in the fire.

'Amali of abu Ja'far al-Tusi:

Al-Sadiq, 'Alayhi al-Salam in a Hadith has said that he (Ali, 'Alayhi al-Salam) dropped the dirhams in the lap of the Messenger of Allah who then gave from it to 'Umm 'Ayman a handful which was sixty three dirhams or sixty six dirhams to buy household items therewith and one handful thereof to 'Asma' daughter of 'Umays to buy therewith perfumes and one handful thereof to 'Umm Salamah to prepare food. He (the Messenger of Allah) then sent 'Ammar, abu Bakr and Bilal to buy other items needed for the house.

I ('Allamah Majlisi) say that he then has mentioned similar matters which have narrated from 'Amali of Shaykh to his words, "one green pitcher, two pottery mugs" then he has said that in a narration, "one piece of *Nat'* (floor covering) made of hide, one gown made in Qatwan, and one water sack."

Wahab ibn Wahab al-Qarashi has said that of the items to prepare his house was soft sand spread (on the floor), fixing of a piece of wood from one wall to the other wall for hanging clothes, one piece of hide of a ram as floor covering, a pillow filled with palm tree fibers.

Abu Bakr Mardwayh in a Hadith has said that he (Ali, *'Alayhi al-Salam*) waited twenty nine days. Ja'far and 'Aqil then said, "You should ask him (the Messenger of Allah) to allow your family to come to your own home. 'Umm 'Ayman then learned about it and she said that this was the task of women. 'Umm Salamah then went to him (the Messenger of Allah) and asked him for the completion of the task. The Holy Prophet, then called him and said, "This is a matter of love and honor." The companions brought gifts and he (the Messenger of Allah) ordered to grind wheat for bread and ordered Ali, *'Alayhi al-Salam* to slaughter the cow and the sheep. The Holy Prophet separated the meat in pieces but no traces of blood were seen on his hands. When cooking was done the Holy Prophet, ordered to invite from the rooftop, "People, you must answer the call of the Messenger of Allah. It was similar to the following verse of al-Quran, "(We commanded Abraham), 'Call people for Hajj - an act of worship accomplished by visiting the sacred sites in Mecca.' They will come on foot and on lean camels from all the distant quarters." (22:27) People then came from among the palm trees, and plantations. Floor coverings were spread in the Masjid and people numbering about four thousand men and other women of al-Madinah all gathered. They served themselves with the food as much as they wanted and nothing was reduced from the food. The next day also they came and ate and on the third day they ate what abu Ayyub had sent.

The Messenger of Allah, *O Allah grant compensation to Muhammad and his family worthy of their services to your cause,* then asked for trays to be filled up with food to be sent to his wives and he then took one tray and said, "This is for Fatimah, *'Alayha al-Salam,* and her husband. He (the Messenger of Allah) called Fatimah, *'Alayha al-Salam,* held her hand and placed her hand in the hand of Ali, *'Alayhi al-Salam* saying, "May Allah grant you blessings in your marriage with the daughter of the Messenger of Allah. O Ali, Fatimah, *'Alayha al-Salam,* is the best wife. O Fatimah, *'Alayha al-Salam,* Ali is the best husband."

The Holy Prophet, *O Allah grant compensation to Muhammad and his family worthy of their services to your cause,* had ordered his wives to prepare her for the wedding in the house of 'Umm Salamah. They asked Fatimah, *'Alayha al-Salam,* if she had any perfumes. She then brought a bottle and they asked her about it. She said that Dihyah al-Kalbi would visit the Messenger of Allah and he would tell me, "O Fatimah, *'Alayha al-Salam,* bring the pillow and place it (properly) on the floor for your uncle." When he would leave something would fall from his garments and the Messenger of Allah would command me to collect them. The Messenger of Allah, *O Allah grant compensation to Muhammad and his family worthy of their services to your cause,* was asked about it and he replied, "It is ambergris that falls from the wings of Jibril." She then brought rose water and 'Umm Salamah asked about it. She said that it is of the perspiration of the Messenger of Allah, *O Allah grant compensation to Muhammad and his family worthy of their services to your cause,* which I would take from him during his *Qaylulah* (siesta) in my chamber."

It is narrated that Jibril brought a dress with a value equal to the whole world. When she wore it the women of al-Quraysh were amazed and asked, "Wherefrom have you got it?" She replied, "This is from Allah."

History of al-Khatib, the book of ibn Mardwayh, ibn al-Mu'adhdhin, Shirwayh, al-Daylami through the chain of their narrators from Ali ibn al-Ju'd from ibn Bastam from Sha'bah ibn al-Hajjaj, from 'Ulwan from Shu'bah from abu Hamzah al-Dab'i from ibn 'Abbas and Jabir who has said the following:

In the night of the wedding of Fatimah, *'Alayha al-Salam,* and Ali, *'Alayhi al-Salam* the Holy Prophet walked in front of her, Jibril on her right side, Michael on her left side and seventy thousand angel after her escorting and saying *Tasbih* (Allah is free of all defects), and speaking of the Holiness of the name of Allah, until dawn.

The book about the birth of Fatimah, 'Alayha al-Salam, by ibn Babwayh in a Hadith the following is stated:

The Holy Prophet, *O Allah grant compensation to Muhammad and his family worthy of their services to your cause,* commanded the daughters of 'Abd al-Muttalib, women of Muhajir (immigrants) and al-Ansar (people of al-Madinah) to accompany Fatimah, *'Alayha al-Salam,* and express happiness, recite praising rhymes, *Takbir* (Allah is great beyond description) *Tahmid,* (all praise belongs to Allah) but they must not say anything with which Allah does not agree.

Jabir has said that she was placed on the back of his camel. According to one Hadith, she was placed on al-Shahba' mule. Salman (Rh) held the reign with seventy thousand *al-Hawra' al-'in* around her. The Holy Prophet, Hamzah, 'Aqil, Ja'far and members of his family walked after her with their swords drawn. The wives of the Holy Prophet, walked in front of her reciting lines of praises and 'Umm Salamah recited the following lines:

My neighbors walk with the help of Allah,

And you must thank Him in all conditions.

You must remember the bounties the Lord the most high has granted,

And how many of hardships and afflictions has He removed,

He has guided us after being unbelievers,

The Lord of skies has revived us,

You can walk along with the best women among all creatures,

Whose paternal and maternal aunts are ransom for her,

O daughter of the one whom the most high has granted excellence,

By means of divine revelations and messages.

Thereafter 'A'ishah recited:

O women you must wear head scarves,

And say what is good in public to say,

Speak of the Lord of the people,

Who has granted us His religion, along with every appreciating person,

All praise belongs to Allah for His extra favors, and thanks belong to Allah, Most Majestic, most Glorious, the Powerful one,

You should walk along with her because Allah has spoken of her and has Done special favor to her with the much purified one.

Thereafter Hafsah recited:

Fatimah, *'Alayha al-Salam,* is the best of among the women of human beings,

The one who is for her has a face like the face of the moon,

Allah has granted you excellence above all people,

With the excellence of the one who has received special favors by the verses of al-Zumr,

Allah has given you in marriage to the youth of excellence,

Who is Ali, the best of all people present,

You must walk along my neighbors with her,

She is the most graceful, daughter of the great personality.

Thereafter Mu'adhah Mother of Sa'd ibn Mu'adh recited:

I say the words in which there is what there is,

I speak of good and I begin,

Muhammad is the best of the children of Adam, *'Alayhi al-Salam,*

He is not arrogant and lost,

Through his favor we have learned guidance,

May Allah grant him good compensations,

We are with the daughter of guidance,

Who possesses honor, who has taken her place in it,

At the peak whose roots are very firm,

And I do not see anything that can be come close to him (in excellence).

The women would repeat the first line of each recital. They then would say *Takbir* (Allah is great beyond description).

Thereafter the Messenger of Allah called Ali, *'Alayhi al-Salam* to the Masjid then called Fatimah, *'Alayha al-Salam,* and held her hand then placed her hand in his hand and said, "May Allah grant you blessing in your marriage with the daughter of the Messenger of Allah."

The book of ibn Mardwayh:

It is narrated that the Holy Prophet, *'Alayhi al-Salam* asked for water then took a sip, rinsed his mouth, then poured it in the cup then poured it on her head. He then asked her to come closer, when she came closer he then poured it over her chest, he asked her to turn around. When she did so he poured it between her shoulders and then he prayed for both of them.

The book of ibn Mardwayh:

O Lord, place blessings in both of them and on them and grant blessings with their two *shibl* (sons).

It is narrated that he said, "O Lord, these two are the most beloved ones to me from among your creatures, please love them and grant blessings in their descendants, assign for them protectors from your side and I seek your protection for them and their descendants against Satan, condemned by stoning.

It is narrated that he prayed for them and said, "O Lord, please keep all forms of filth away from them and purify them thoroughly."

It is narrated that he said, "The two joining oceans are most welcome, the two stars getting closer to each other."

He (the Messenger of Allah) then moved to the door saying, "Allah has purified you as well as your offspring. I am at peace with those who are at peace with you and I am at war against those who are at war against you. I leave you in the trust of Allah and in His protection on my behalf. 'Asma' the daughter of 'Umays spent the nights for a week with her because of the will of Khadijah 'Alayha al-Salam. The Holy Prophet, 'Alayhi al-Salam prayed to Allah for her wellbeing in this world and in the next life.

In the morning he came to them, said *Salam* (the phrase of offering greeting of peace) and asked, "Can I come in?" 'Asma' then opened the door. They were sleeping under the gown. He said, "(You do not have to get up), you may remain as you are." He (sat down) stretched his legs (under the gown) between the two of them then Allah informed of their private worship, "Their sides give up rest in beds in order to pray before their Lord in fear and hope. They spend for the cause of Allah out of what we have given them" (32:16)

He (the Messenger of Allah), then asked, "What kind of wife you have found her to be?" Ali, 'Alayhi al-Salam replied, "She is the best helper in worshipping Allah." He then asked Fatimah, 'Alayha al-Salam, and she replied, "He is a good husband." He (the Messenger of Allah) then said, "Lord please place together what they need to be placed in order, tie their hearts together and make them and their descendants the heirs of the bountiful garden (paradise). Grant them, pure, fine and blessed descendants, place blessings in their descendants and make them the Imams who will guide by your command to obedience to you and command for what will make you happy."

He then asked 'Asma' to leave saying, "May Allah reward you goodness." He then remained in privacy with her by a hint from the Messenger of Allah.

Sharahbil through the chain of his narrators has narrated that in the morning of the wedding of Fatimah, 'Alayha al-Salam, the Holy Prophet, 'Alayhi al-Salam brought a pot full of milk. He said to Fatimah, 'Alayha al-Salam, "Drink, may your father be a ransom for you. He then said to Ali, "Drink, may your cousin be ransom for you."

H 142, Ch. 5, h 25
Makarim al-Akhlaq:

Jabir has narrated from abu Ja'far, 'Alayhi al-Salam who has said the following:

When Ali, 'Alayhi al-Salam married Fatimah, 'Alayha al-Salam, he leveled the floor of his house with soft sand. Their bedding consisted of a (tanned) hide of a ram and their pillow was filled with palm tree fibers. They fixed a piece of wood on which they placed their water container and covered it with a gown.

Al-Husayn ibn Nu'aym has narrated from 'Abu 'Abd Allah, 'Alayhi al-Salam who has said the following:

The Messenger of Allah, *O Allah grant compensation to Muhammad and his family worthy of their services to your cause,* admitted Fatimah, 'Alayha al-Salam, in the house of Ali, 'Alayhi al-Salam. Her covering was a gown, her floor covering was the hide of a ram and her pillow was a piece of skin filled with palm tree fibers.

H 143, Ch. 5, h 26
Kashf al-Ghummah:

Al-Hafiz Muhammad ibn Mahmud al-Bukhari has narrated from men whom he has mentioned, the following:

He (the narrator) has said that he heard 'Asma' the daughter of 'Umays say that she heard Sayyidah Fatimah, 'Alayha al-Salam, say, "In the night of our wedding in our bed, I was shocked because of Ali ibn abu Talib, 'Alayhima al-Salam."

I then asked, "Were you, O leader of all women, shocked!"

She replied, "It is because I heard the earth speak to him and he spoke to the earth, thus, I was shocked and I told my father, about it. He fell in *Sajdah* (prostration) for a long time then raised his head and said, "O Fatimah, 'Alayha al-Salam, you have the glad news about the purity and fineness of offspring, because Allah has granted extra favors to your husband over His creatures and has commanded the earth to speak to him and inform him about her news and about whatever goes on it from her east to her west."

H 144, Ch. 5, h 27
Kamil al-Ziyarat: Iqbal al-'A'mal:

Muhammad ibn al-Najjar has narrated to me along with the Ahadith for which he has granted me permission to narrate from the book as an addendum to the history of al-Khatib in the Tarjumah of Ahmad ibn Muhammad al-Dallal who has narrated from Ahmad ibn Muhammad al-Atrush and abu Bakr Muhammad ibn al-Hassan ibn Durayd al-Azdi from whom abu al-Hassan Ali ibn Muhammad ibn Muhammad ibn Yusuf al-Bazzaz and abu Muhammad al-Hassan ibn Muhammad ibn Yahya' al-Fahham both from Samarra' narrated to us abu Ali Diya' ibn Ahmad ibn abu Ali and abu Hamid 'Abd Allah ibn Muslim ibn Thabit and Yusuf ibn al-Mayyal ibn Kamil who have said that narrated to us abu Bakr Muhammad ibn 'Abd al-Baqi al-Bazzaz who has said that narrated to us abu al-Husayn Muhammad ibn Ahmad al-Bursi who has said that narrated to him al-Qadi Ahmad ibn Muhammad ibn Yusuf al-Samiri who has said that narrated to us abu al-Tayb Ahmad ibn Muhammad al-Shahid al-Ma'ruf al-Dallal, narrated to us Muhammad ibn Ahmad known as al-Atrush and narrated to us abu 'Amr Sulayman ibn abu Mi'shar from Sulayman ibn 'Abd al-Rahman from Muhammad ibn 'Abd al-Rahman from 'Asma' the daughter of Wathilah ibn al-Asqa' from 'Asma' the daughter of 'Umays a similar Hadith.

H 145, Ch. 5, h 28
Kashf al-Ghummah: from Manaqib of al-Kharazmi from Ali, 'Alayhi al-Salam who has said the following:

It was proposed to the Messenger of Allah to give Fatimah, *'Alayha al-Salam,* in marriage. Then a Mawlat (house maid) said to me, "Are you aware that marriage to Fatimah, *'Alayha al-Salam,* is proposed before the Messenger of Allah, *O Allah grant compensation to Muhammad and his family worthy of their services to your cause?*" I replied, "No, I am not aware." She then said, "Marriage is proposed. What prevents you from going to the Messenger of Allah, so he can give Fatimah, *'Alayha al-Salam,* in marriage to you?" I then said, "Do I have anything belonging to me with which I can propose marriage?" She said, "If you go to the Messenger of Allah, *'Alayhi al-Salam,* he will give Fatimah, *'Alayha al-Salam,* in marriage to you." By Allah she kept persuading me until I then went to the Messenger of Allah, *O Allah grant compensation to Muhammad and his family worthy of their services to your cause,* who had a personal glory and awesomeness. When I sat down in front of him I remained tongue-tied and could not speak.

The Messenger of Allah, *O Allah grant compensation to Muhammad and his family worthy of their services to your cause,* asked, "What brings you here today, do you need anything?" I remained quiet. He (the Messenger of Allah) then said, "Perhaps you have come to propose marriage to Fatimah, *'Alayha al-Salam.*" I then said, "That is correct." He then asked, "Do you have anything to make her marriage with you lawful?" I replied, "No, I do not have anything." He then asked, "What have you done with the coat of arms with which you would arm yourself?" I replied, "It is with me and I swear by the one in whose hands is the soul of Ali that it is a Hatmiyah coat of arms and its value is less than four hundred dirhams." He (the Messenger of Allah), *O Allah grant compensation to Muhammad and his family worthy of their services to your cause,* then said, "I accept your marriage proposal with Fatimah, *'Alayha al-Salam,* and you now can send the coat of arms to her to make your marriage with her lawful and this will be the dowry for Fatimah, *'Alayha al-Salam,* the daughter of the Messenger of Allah, *O Allah grant compensation to Muhammad and his family worthy of their services to your cause.*

H 146, Ch. 5, h 29
Kashf al-Ghummah:

It is narrated from the narrator of the previous Hadith from Anas who has said the following:

I (the narrator) once was with the Messenger of Allah, *O Allah grant compensation to Muhammad and his family worthy of their services to your cause,* when divine revelations overwhelmed him. When his condition became normal he said to me, "Do you know, O Anas what Jibril had brought to me from the owner of the Throne?" I replied, "Allah and His messenger know best." He then said, "He has commanded me to give Fatimah, *'Alayha al-Salam,* in marriage to Ali, *'Alayhi al-Salam.* You must now go call for abu Bakr, 'Umar, 'Uthman, Ali, Talhah, al-Zubayr and equal to their number from al-Ansar (people of al-Madinah)." He (the narrator) has said that I then left and called them. When they took their seats the Messenger of Allah, *O Allah grant compensation to Muhammad and his family worthy of their services to your cause,* said:

"All praise belongs to Allah who is praiseworthy because of His bounties, is worshipped because of power, obeyed because of authority, feared because of His punishment, who is liked because of the good things with Him, whose command is executed in His earth and sky, who has created the creatures with His power, and has distinguished them by His laws, honored them with His religion, dignified them with His Prophet, Muhammad. Thereafter, Allah has made wedlock relationships attached to lineage and an obligation and has interlaced thereby relatives and has made it binding on people. Allah, most blessed, most high, has said, 'It is He who has created the human being from water to have relationships of both lineage and wedlock. Your Lord has all the power.' (25:54) The command of Allah takes place according to His approval, His approval follows His determination. For every instance of His approval there is determination and for every instance of His determination is a time and every instance of time has a book in which Allah records whatever He wills and deletes whatever He wills; with Him is the mother book. 'For every event Allah has ordained His decree. Allah establishes or effaces whatever He wants and with Him is the original Book.' (13:39)

"I now assign you as witness that I have given Fatimah, *'Alayha al-Salam*, in marriage to Ali for a dowry of four hundred Mithqal of silver if Ali agrees" – he was not present at that time. The Messenger of Allah, *O Allah grant compensation to Muhammad and his family worthy of their services to your cause,* had sent him for a certain task. He (the Messenger of Allah) then ordered to spread a tray of unripen dates in front of us and then said, "You can *grab* some." At that time Ali, *'Alayhi al-Salam* arrived. The Messenger of Allah smiled at him and then said, "O Ali, Allah has commanded me to give Fatimah, *'Alayha al-Salam,* in marriage to you and the amount of dowry is four hundred mithqal of silver. Do you accept the offer and agree?" He said, "I accept and agree, O Messenger of Allah." He then stood up and fell in *Sajdah* (prostration) before Allah. The Holy Prophet, *'Alayhi al-Salam* said, "Allah has placed good in you a great deal of good and fine and has blessed it for you."

Anas have said, "By Allah a great deal of goodness and fineness came out of this marriage."

Manaqib of ibn Shahr Ashub:

The Messenger of Allah, *O Allah grant compensation to Muhammad and his family worthy of their services to your cause,* delivered a speech from the pulpit on the occasion of the marriage of Fatimah, *'Alayha al-Salam.*

Yahya' ibn Mu'in has narrated it in his Amali (book of dictations) and ibn Battah in Ibanah through the chain of the narrators of the two of them from Anas ibn Malik *in a marfu' manner* and we have narrated it from al-Rida', who has said a similar Hadith.

H 147, Ch. 5, h 30
Kashf al-Ghummah:

It is narrated from al-Manaqib from 'Abd Allah ibn Mas'ud who has said the following:

The Holy Prophet, *'Alayhi al-Salam* then said to Fatimah, *'Alayha al-Salam,* "O Fatimah, *'Alayha al-Salam,* I have given you in marriage to a leader in the world and in the next life he will be among the virtuous ones. O Fatimah, *'Alayha al-Salam,* when Allah, most High, decided that I must give you in marriage to Ali, *Allah,* most High, commanded Jibril to stand in the fourth sky. The angels then formed rows and rows and he gave a speech. He (Allah) then gave you in marriage to Ali, *'Alayhi al-Salam.* Then Allah, most Blessed, most high, commanded the tree in the garden (paradise) and it carried ornaments and dresses and then He commanded it to spread them for the angels. Whoever of them collected a larger amount than the others keep expressing pride about it up to the Day of Judgment.

From the same source it is narrated from ibn 'Abbas who has said the following:

People would speak (propose marriage of Fatimah, *'Alayha al-Salam*) to the Messenger of Allah, *O Allah grant compensation to Muhammad and his family worthy of their services to your cause.* Whoever would speak to him he would turn down his proposal until they all lost hope for their success in their marriage proposal. Sa'd ibn Mu'adh one day met Ali, *'Alayhi al-Salam* and said, "I by Allah, see no other reason for his turning down marriage proposals except that he has her for you." Ali, *'Alayhi al-Salam* then asked, "What makes you to think so? By Allah I am not one of the two men nor am I the owner of the world so people seek the world from me and he knows that I do not own any yellow (gold) or white (silver)."

Sa'd then said, "I swear you to provide me relief about her because for me in this there is relief." He (Ali, 'Alayhi al-Salam) then asked, "What should I say then?" Sa'd said, "You should say, 'I have come to propose marriage, before Allah and His messenger, with Fatimah, 'Alayha al-Salam, the daughter of Muhammad, *O Allah grant compensation to Muhammad and his family worthy of their services to your cause.*'"

He (the narrator) has said that Ali, 'Alayhi al-Salam left to see the Holy Prophet, and he was heavy and restricted."

The Holy Prophet, 'Alayhi al-Salam said, "It seems as if you need something O Ali." He replied, "Yes, I have come to you to propose marriage, before Allah and His messenger, with Fatimah, 'Alayha al-Salam, daughter of Muhammad." The Holy Prophet, 'Alayhi al-Salam said, "(To say) you are welcome, is a weak statement (in response to you)." Ali, 'Alayhi al-Salam then returned to Sa'd and informed him about whatever had transpired. Sa'd then said, "I swear by the one who has sent Muhammad in all truth that he has given her in marriage to you. Now there is no disregard of what he has said or lies from his side. I swear you that you must come tomorrow and ask Him, "When will you explain the statement to me?" Ali, 'Alayhi al-Salam then said, "This is more difficult for me than what you asked before this to do." Why should I not say instead, "O Messenger of Allah, what about my appeal for help" Sa'd said, "You must say what I told you to say." Ali, 'Alayhi al-Salam then left to see the Messenger of Allah and asked him, "When will you explain the statement to me?" He (the Messenger of Allah) *replied*, "I will do so, tonight by the will of Allah."

He then called Bilal and said to him, "O Bilal, I have given my daughter in marriage to my cousin and I like to make the wedding banquet a tradition for my nation (followers). Go to the sheep and get one ewe and four *mod* of (grain). Place then in a bowl so that perhaps Muhajir (immigrants) and al-Ansar (people of al-Madinah) gather for a banquet and when you are done then inform me about it."

Bilal then left and he then did as he was told to do and he then brought the bowl. He placed it in front of him. The Messenger of Allah, *O Allah grant compensation to Muhammad and his family worthy of their services to your cause,* then tapped on his head saying, "You can now call them to come group by group. People then came in one group after the other group before it had left until the last group also had left the house. The Holy Prophet then turned to the remaining food. He dropped his saliva in it and asked Allah to grant blessings and then told Bilal, "Take this to your mothers (wives of the Holy Prophet) and tell them to eat and feed those who may come to you."

The Holy Prophet, *'Alayhi al-Salam* then stood up to visit the women. He said, to them, "I have given in marriage my daughter to my cousin. You know her status with me. I am about to give her to him. Thus, here is your daughter."

The women then rose and they covered her with their perfumes, and ornaments. They arranged furnishing in her house, which had palm tree fibers as their fillings, like a pillow, a gown made in Khaybar, and makeup container. They assigned 'Umm 'Ayman as the door guard.

The Holy Prophet, *'Alayhi al-Salam* then came in and the women sprang up. There was a curtain between them and the Holy Prophet, *O Allah grant compensation to Muhammad and his family worthy of their services to your cause,* 'Asma' the daughter of 'Umays remained behind. The Holy Prophet asked saying stay where you are but who are you?" She replied, "I am guarding your daughter. Young women must not be left alone in the first night of her wedding. Some women should be nearby, accessible to her in case she needed something so she can reach her for help." He (the Messenger of Allah) said, "I ask Allah to guard you from front, back, right and left against Satan condemned to be stoned. He called Fatimah, *'Alayha al-Salam,* loudly. She came but when she saw Ali, *'Alayhi al-Salam* sitting on one side of the Messenger of Allah, *O Allah grant compensation to Muhammad and his family worthy of their services to your cause,* she became restricted and wept. The Messenger of Allah, *O Allah grant compensation to Muhammad and his family worthy of their services to your cause,* felt concerned about her weeping because Ali did not have any belongings. The Holy Prophet, asked, "Why do you weep, by my soul that I have found for you the best of my family, I swear by the one in whose hand is my soul that I have given you in marriage to the leader in the world and in the next life he will be of the virtuous." It then relieved her and made it possible for her to stop weeping.

The Holy Prophet, *'Alayhi al-Salam* then said, "O 'Asma', bring for me the dye container." He filled it with water and then sprinkled in it, then with it washed his feet and face, then he called Fatimah, *'Alayha al-Salam*, then took a handful of water and poured it on her head, one handful in front of her then sprinkled on his skin and on her's then held her to himself saying, "O Lord, she is from me and I am from her. O Lord, as you have kept me away from all uncleanliness and has purified me thoroughly please purify her thoroughly also." He then asked for another dye container then called Ali, *'Alayhi al-Salam* and he then did to him what he had done with Fatimah, *'Alayha al-Salam*, and he prayed for him as he had prayed for Fatimah, *'Alayha al-Salam*, then he said, "You both can now go to your house. May Allah bring you together and place blessings in your offspring, settle your affairs."

He (the narrator) has said that then he closed the door on them.

Ibn 'Abbas has said that 'Asma' the daughter of 'Umays informed me that she looked at the Messenger of Allah and found him still praying for them specially and did not include anyone else in prayer for the both of them until he went inside his room.

Al-Jazari:

Al-Jazari has said in a Hadith about the marriage of Fatimah, *'Alayha al-Salam*, it is said that he prepared food and told Bilal to bring people in for food of the wedding (*ziffa*) group by group, meaning, one pack of them after the other, one party after the other party. For this reason is *ziffa* (grouping) because of their walking and proceeding in a hurry, but this interpretation is not free from being remote.

In al-Nihayah in a Hadith about the marriage of Fatimah, 'Alayha al-Salam, the following is stated:

When she saw Ali, sitting on one side of the Holy Prophet, she became restricted and wept meaning she felt shy and became cut off (from saying anything); the matter pressured her just as confinement confines the confined.

He (the narrator) has said that the Holy Prophet, *'Alayhi al-Salam*, asked Fatimah, *'Alayha al-Salam*, "What has made you to weep? I swear that I have not disregarded anything in this matter except that I have found for you the best from among my relatives, Ali as your husband.

H 148, Ch. 5, h 31
Kashf al-Ghummah:

Al-Khawarazmi has said that abu al-'Ala' al-Hafiz al-Hamadani informed me in a marfu' manner from al-Husayn, ibn Ali, 'Alayhima al-Salam, who has said the following:

Once the Holy Prophet, *O Allah grant compensation to Muhammad and his family worthy of their services to your cause,* was in the house of 'Umm Salamah that an angel descended to him and he had twenty heads with a thousand tongues in each head saying *Tasbih* (Allah is free of all defects) and to speak of the Holiness of the name of Allah, with each tongue in a distinctly different language. His palm was wider than the seven skies and seven earths. The Holy Prophet, *'Alayhi al-Salam* thought he was Jibril so he said, "O Jibril you had never come to me in this form before." He then said, "I am not Jibril. I am Sarsael. Allah has sent me to you so you must give light in marriage to light." The Holy Prophet, *O Allah grant compensation to Muhammad and his family worthy of their services to your cause,* then asked, "Who must I give in marriage to whom?" He replied, "They are your daughter Fatimah, *'Alayha al-Salam,* and Ali ibn abu Talib, *'Alayhima al-Salam.*" Then the Holy Prophet gave Fatimah, *'Alayha al-Salam,* in marriage to Ali, *'Alayhi al-Salam* in the presence of Jibril, Michael and Sarsael as witnesses.

He (the narrator) has said that then the Holy Prophet, *'Alayhi al-Salam* looked and found a writing between the shoulders of Sarsael that said, "I testify that only Allah deserves worship, He is one and has no partners and I testify that Muhammad is His servant and Messenger and Ali ibn abu Talib possesses divine authority." The Holy Prophet, *'Alayhi al-Salam* then asked, "Since when did you have this writing between your shoulders, O Sarsael?"

He replied, "It was twelve thousand years before Allah create the world."

From the book of Manaqib from Bilal ibn Hamamah who has said the following:

The Messenger of Allah, *O Allah grant compensation to Muhammad and his family worthy of their services to your cause,* one day came to us and his face was bright like the full moon. 'Abd al-Rahman ibn 'Awf stood before him and asked, "O Messenger of Allah, what is this light (on your face)?" He (the Messenger of Allah) replied, "It is because of the glad news that has come to me from my Lord about my brother and cousin and my daughter. Allah has given Fatimah, *'Alayha al-Salam,* in marriage to Ali, *'Alayhi al-Salam.* He has commanded Rizwan the keeper of the garden (paradise) to shake *Tuba* (the tree in the garden (paradise). It then carried cards that are certificates equal to the number of the people who love my *Ahl al-Bayt* (family) and invented beneath it angels of light and gave one certificate to each angel. When it will be the Day of Judgment the angels will announce among the creatures and then no one of those who love my *Ahl al-Bayt* (family) will remain without receiving one of those certificates, which proves their freedom from the fire. Because of my brother and cousin and my daughter is the freedom of the necks of the men and women of my nation (followers) from the fire.

In al-Khara'ij from the Holy Prophet, there is a similar Hadith.

Manaqib of ibn Shahr Ashub:

History of Baghdad through a chain of narrators from Bilal ibn Hamamah a similar Hadith is narrated in which the author then has said that in a narration the certificate will say, "This is a certificate of freedom from the fire given by the most high the all dominant one for the (*Shi'a,* followers) of Ali, and Fatimah, *'Alayhima al-Salam.*

H 149, Ch. 5, h 32
Kashf al-Ghummah: and from al-Manaqib from ibn 'Abbas:

In the night of the wedding of Fatimah, *'Alayha al-Salam,* with Ali ibn abu Talib, *'Alayhima al-Salam,* the Holy Prophet, *'Alayhi al-Salam* was in front of her, Jibril on her right, Michael on her left and seventy thousand angels after her saying *Tasbih* (Allah is free of all defects) and *Taqdis,* to speak of the Holiness of the name of Allah, until dawn.

It is from al-Manaqib from Ali, 'Alayhi al-Salam who has said the following:

He (the narrator) has said that the Messenger of Allah, *O Allah grant compensation to Muhammad and his family worthy of their services to your cause,* has said, "An angel came to me and said, 'O Muhammad, Allah, most Majestic, most Glorious, sends you *Salam* (the phrase of offering greeting of peace) and says that He has given Fatimah, *'Alayha al-Salam,* in marriage to Ali, *'Alayhi al-Salam* so you must also give her in marriage to him. I have commanded *Tuba* (the tree in the garden (paradise) to carry pearls, rubies and corals. The inhabitants of the sky are happy for it. From them two of the leaders of the youth of the garden (paradise), will be born and with them the garden (paradise) will beautify. This glad news is for you, O Muhammad; you are the best of the past and future generations.'"

From al-Manaqib narrated from 'Umm Salamah, Salman (Rh) al-Farsi and Ali ibn abu Talib, 'Alayhi al-Salam, who all have said the following:

When Fatimah, the daughter of the Messenger of Allah, *O Allah grant compensation to Muhammad and his family worthy of their services to your cause,* became of age as women do, the elders of al-Quraysh, people of excellence, and background in Islam, social prestige and wealth all proposed marriage with her before the Messenger of Allah, but the Messenger of Allah would turn his face away from those proposing marriage. His turning away his face was as such that one would think that he is angry with him or that divine revelation has come about him from the sky. Abu Bakr proposed marriage with her before the Messenger of Allah who said that her affairs are in the hands of her Lord. After abu Bakr 'Umar ibn al-Khattab proposed. The Messenger of Allah, *O Allah grant compensation to Muhammad and his family worthy of their services to your cause,* gave him the same response as the one to abu Bakr.

He (the narrator) has said that one day abu Bakr and 'Umar were sitting in the Masjid of the Messenger of Allah, *'Alayhi al-Salam* and with them was Sa'd ibn Mu'adh al-Ansari, then al-Awsi. They spoke about Fatimah, *'Alayha al-Salam,* daughter the Messenger of Allah, *O Allah grant compensation to Muhammad and his family worthy of their services to your cause.* Abu Bakr then said, "The prestigious people have proposed marriage with her before the Messenger of Allah and he has said that her affairs are in the hands of her Lord who if wills will give her in marriage. However, Ali ibn abu Talib has not proposed marriage before the Messenger of Allah with her and has not spoken to him about her. I do not think that if he proposes marriage he will refuse his proposal, except because of his poverty, and I think that Allah and His messenger have reserved her for him.

He (the narrator) has said that abu Bakr then turned to 'Umar ibn al-Khattab and Sa'd ibn Mu'adh and said, "Will you come to see Ali ibn abu Talib and speak to him about it and if his poverty has kept him away from proposing marriage we will help. Sa'd ibn Mu'adh then said, "O abu Bakr may Allah grant you good fortune and you continue to have good fortunes, allow us to go by the blessings of Allah and His pouring favors."

Salman al-Farsi (Rh) has said that they left the Masjid to see Ali, *'Alayhi al-Salam* in his home but they did not find him there because he was supplying water on his camel to the palm trees of a man of al-Ansar (people of al-Madinah) on hire. When Ali, *'Alayhi al-Salam* saw them, he asked what brings you here and what is happing behind you (in the town)?" Abu Bakr said, "O abu al-Hassan, there no good trait of the good traits is left without you being the foremost in it in excellence. Your position with the Messenger of Allah, *'Alayhi al-Salam* is very close as you already know as a relative and as in companionship with its history. The nobles of al-Quraysh have proposed marriage before the Messenger of Allah with his daughter Fatimah, *'Alayha al-Salam,* but he has turned their proposal down saying that her affairs are in the hands of her Lord. What prevents you from proposing marriage before the Messenger of Allah, *O Allah grant compensation to Muhammad and his family worthy of their services to your cause,* with her? I hope that Allah and His messenger have reserved her just for you."

He (the narrator) has said that the eyes of Ali, became flooded with tears and said, "O abu Bakr, you just have agitated in me what was calm and quiet and have awakened me about an issue of which I am unaware. Fatimah, *'Alayha al-Salam,* is someone to wish for and a person like me does not just sit without the wish for the one like her. Only poverty prevents me. Abu Bakr then said, "Do not say this, O abu al-Hassan; the world and all that is in it in the sight of Allah and His messenger is like scattered dust."

He (the narrator) has said that Ali ibn abu Talib then released his watering camel and began to lead toward his home. He then tied down the camel, wore his shoes, then left to meet the Messenger of Allah, *O Allah grant compensation to Muhammad and his family worthy of their services to your cause,* who at that time was in the house of his wife 'Umm Salamah, the daughter of abu 'Umayyah ibn al-Mughirah al-Makhzumi. He (Ali) knocked at the door and 'Umm Salamah asked, "Who is there?" The Messenger of Allah, *O Allah grant compensation to Muhammad and his family worthy of their services to your cause,* said to her, before Ali, had said, "This is Ali. Get up O 'Umm Salamah and open the door for him and ask him to come in; this is the man whom Allah and His messenger love and he loves them both." 'Umm Salamah then said, "I pray to Allah to keep my soul and the souls of my parents in service for your cause, who is he about whom you have said all of such things that you just said without seeing him?" The Messenger of Allah, *O Allah grant compensation to Muhammad and his family worthy of their services to your cause,* said, "O 'Umm Salamah why must I not say so; he is not a transgressing rattle-brained man. He is my brother, my cousin and the most beloved to me from among all creatures." 'Umm Salamah has said, "I then quickly got up to open the door and I was about to fall over my gown. I opened the door and I found Ali ibn abu Talib, *'Alayhima al-Salam,* in front of me. By Allah he did not enter when I opened the door until knowing that I had gone back to my private chamber. He then entered the room of the Messenger of Allah, saying *al-Salamu 'Alaykum,* O Messenger of Allah, His kindness and blessing be upon you." He (the Messenger of Allah) then said, "*'Alayka al-Salam,* O abu al-Hassan on you is *Salam* (peace), please sit down."

'Umm Salamah has said that Ali ibn abu Talib, *'Alayhima al-Salam,* then sat in front of the Messenger of Allah and kept looking down on the ground due to his feeling shy in the presence of the Messenger of Allah, *O Allah grant compensation to Muhammad and his family worthy of their services to your cause.*

'Umm Salamah has said that it seemed as if the Messenger of Allah, *O Allah grant compensation to Muhammad and his family worthy of their services to your cause,* knew what was in the soul of Ali, *'Alayhi al-Salam* and he said to him, "O abu al-Hassan I know you have come for a certain task. What do you want? Say what is in your soul because whatever you ask I will meet your needs."

Ali, *'Alayhi al-Salam* has said, "I then said, 'I pray to Allah to keep my soul and the souls of my parents in service for your cause, you know that you took me from your uncle abu Talib and Fatimah, daughter of Asad, when I as a child did not have understanding (of the conditions then). You fed me from your own food and trained me with your own manners. You were better for me than my father abu Talib and Fatimah, daughter of Asad, in virtue and compassion Allah, most High, granted me guidance through you and at your hand and rescued me from the condition in which my ancestors and uncles lived, from confusion and doubts. You, O Messenger of Allah, by Allah are everything for me in the world and in the next life. O Messenger of Allah, despite the fact that Allah through you has given me strength, I like to have a home and a wife to live in comfort. I have come before you with great interest, to propose marriage with your daughter Fatimah, *'Alayha al-Salam.* Will you, O Messenger of Allah, give Fatimah, *'Alayha al-Salam,* in marriage to me?'"

'Umm Salamah has said, "I saw the face of the Messenger of Allah, turned bright with joy and happiness smiling at the face of Ali, *'Alayhi al-Salam* and said, 'O abu al-Hassan, do you have anything with which I can arrange wedding and marriage for you?"

Ali, *'Alayhi al-Salam* replied, "I pray to Allah to keep my soul and the souls of my parents in service for your cause, my belongings are not unknown to you. I own my sword, my coat of arms, my water carrier and I do not own anything other than these items."

The Messenger of Allah, *O Allah grant compensation to Muhammad and his family worthy of their services to your cause,* said, "O Ali, you need your sword to work hard with it in the way of Allah and fight the enemies of Allah, your water carrier is what you need to supply water for your family and palm trees and to transport your belongings on a journey. However, your coat of arms can be used to pay for the expenses of your wedding and I accept your proposing marriage with Fatimah, *'Alayha al-Salam,* on the account of the coat of arms. O abu al-Hassan I congratulate you."

Ali, *'Alayhi al-Salam* has said, "I then said, yes, 'I pray to Allah to keep my soul and the souls of my parents in service for your cause, please grant me congratulations; you have always been the source of good fortune, blessed omens, brilliant in settling the affairs, *May Allah, grant compensation to you and your family worthy of their services to His cause.'"*

The Messenger of Allah, *O Allah grant compensation to Muhammad and his family worthy of their services to your cause,* then said to me there is glad news for you that Allah has given her in marriage to you in the sky before I give her in marriage to you on earth. Right in this place just before your coming an angel from the sky came to me and he had various faces and wings, the like of whom I had not seen before. He said to me, *"Salam* (the phrase of offering greeting of peace), with kindness and blessings, congratulations to you, O Muhammad, for the orderly settlement of the affairs and the purity of the offspring." I then asked, "What does that mean, O angel?" He then said, "O Muhammad, I am Sitatael, the angel assigned to guard one of the pillars of the Throne. I asked my Lord to grant me permission to congratulate you and this is Jibril behind me who will inform you from your Lord, most Majestic, most Glorious, about the graciousness of Allah, most Majestic, most Glorious."

The Holy Prophet then said that his words were not yet complete that Jibril came to me and said, *"Salam* (the phrase of offering greeting of peace), kindness and blessings of Allah. O Prophet of Allah. He then placed a white piece of silk of the garden (paradise) in my hand on which there two lines were written with light.

I then asked, my beloved friend Jibril, about the piece of silk and about the lines of writing on it.

Jibril said, "O Muhammad, Allah, most Majestic, most Glorious, examined the earth in an examination. He then chose you from among His creatures, and then He sent you as His messenger. He then examined the earth for a second time and then He chose for you a brother and vizier, as a companion and son-in-law. He then gave Fatimah, *'Alayha al-Salam,* in marriage to him." I then asked, "O Jibril who is this man?" Jibril then said to me, "O Muhammad, he is your brother in the world and your cousin in lineage, he is 'Amir al-Mu'minin Ali ibn abu Talib, *'Alayhima al-Salam.* Allah has inspired the garden (paradise) to beautify and it did so and *Tuba* (the tree in the garden (paradise)) to carry ornaments and dresses and *al-Hawra' al-'in* have beautified themselves. Allah has commanded the angel to come together in the fourth sky near al-Bayt al-Ma'mur. They then descended down from the above and climbed up from below to it and Allah, most Majestic, most Glorious, command Rizwan (the keeper of the garden (paradise) and he placed the pulpit of grace at the gate of al-Bayt al-Ma'mur and it is the one from which Adam, *'Alayhi al-Salam,* delivered a speech when telling about the names to the angels and it is the pulpit of light.

"Allah then sent divine revelation to one of the angels of His curtains who is called Rahil to climb on that pulpit to praise Allah with His praises and glorify Him with His glory and adore Him with that which is proper for Him. There is no angel among the angels more eloquent and of beautiful speech than him and of sweeter language then Rahil. He climbed on the pulpit, praised his Lord, spoke of His glory and of the Holiness of the name of Allah, and adorned Him in the manner, which is proper about Him. The skies then shook with joy and happiness."

Jibril said, "Allah then sent divine revelation to me to solemnize the marriage because He has already given His female servant Fatimah, *'Alayha al-Salam,* the daughter of His beloved one, Muhammad, His servant to Ali ibn abu Talib. I have solemnized the marriage and have appointed all angels as witness and it is recorded on this piece of silk and my Lord has commanded me to present it before you and seal it with the seal of musk and give it to Rizwan.

"When Allah, most Majestic, most Glorious, assigned the angels as witness to the marriage of Ali and Fatimah, *'Alayha al-Salam,* He commanded *Tuba* (the tree in the garden (paradise) to spread what it carries of ornaments and dresses. It then spread what it carried then the angels and *al-Hawra' al-'in* collected them and they present their collection to each other and express pride for it up to the Day of Judgment.

"O Muhammad, Allah, most Majestic, most Glorious, has commanded me to command you to solemnize on earth the marriage of Ali and Fatimah, *'Alayhima al-Salam,* and congratulate them with the birth of two intelligent, noble, pure, fine virtuous and excellent sons in the world and in the next life."

"O abu al-Hassan, by Allah the angel had not yet left that you knocked at the door. Now I must execute the command of my Lord, Allah, most Majestic, most Glorious. O abu al-Hassan walk in front of me, because I must go to the Masjid to solemnize your marriage in public and speak of your excellence which will make your eyes delightful as well as the eyes of those who love you in the world and in the next life."

Ali, *'Alayhi al-Salam* has said, "I then left the meeting of the Messenger of Allah, *O Allah grant compensation to Muhammad and his family worthy of their services to your cause,* in a hurry and I was not able to figure out things because of joy and happiness. Abu Bakr and 'Umar came face to face with me and asked about what has happened. I then said to them, "The Messenger of Allah, *O Allah grant compensation to Muhammad and his family worthy of their services to your cause,* has given his daughter Fatimah, *'Alayha al-Salam,* in marriage to me and has informed me that Allah, most Majestic, most Glorious, has given her in marriage to me in the sky and this is the Messenger of Allah, *O Allah grant compensation to Muhammad and his family worthy of their services to your cause,* coming behind me to make this public in the gathering of the people." The two of them became very happy and returned back with me to the Masjid.

We had not reached the Masjid that the Messenger of Allah, *'Alayhi al-Salam* joined us and his face showed brightness because of joy and happiness. He said, "O Bilal! He answered saying, "Here I am at your disposal, O Messenger of Allah." He (the Messenger of Allah) said, "Call for me Muhajir (immigrants) and al-Ansar (people of al-Madinah). He gathered them. He (the Messenger of Allah) then climbed one step on the pulpit, praised Allah and adorned Him and said, "O the community of the Muslims, Jibril came to me a while ago and informed me from my Lord Allah, most Majestic, most Glorious, that He had gathered the angels near al-Bayt al-Ma'mur and had assigned them as witnesses to His giving His female servant Fatimah, *'Alayha al-Salam,* the daughter of His messenger in marriage to His male servant Ali ibn abu Talib and has commanded me to solemnize their marriage on earth and assign you as witness thereof."

He (the Messenger of Allah) then sat down and commanded Ali, *'Alayhi al-Salam* saying, "Stand up, O abu al-Hassan, give a speech (to address your marriage)."

He (the narrator) has said that he then stood up, praised Allah, adorned Him and said, "*O Allah grant compensation to Muhammad and his family worthy of their services to your cause.*" He then said, "I praise Allah in thanksgiving for His bounties, and favors. No one deserves worship except Allah, is the testimony to reach Him and gain His happiness. May Allah, grant compensation to Muhammad and his family worthy of their services to His cause to make him happy and fortunate. Marriage is of the issues that Allah, most Majestic, most Glorious, has commanded to be fulfilled and He is happy with it. Our gathering is of the matters that Allah has determined and has granted permission. The Messenger of Allah, *O Allah grant compensation to Muhammad and his family worthy of their services to your cause,* has given his daughter Fatimah, *'Alayha al-Salam,* in marriage to me and has made my coat of arms her dowry. I have agreed to it. You can ask him about it and bear witness."

The Muslims then asked the Messenger of Allah, *'Alayhi al-Salam* about it and he (the Messenger of Allah) replied, "Yes, what he has said is true and correct." They then congratulated both of them praying for their happiness and wellbeing.

The Messenger of Allah, *O Allah grant compensation to Muhammad and his family worthy of their services to your cause,* then returned to his wives and commanded them to play *al-daf* (a kind of drum) for the occasion.

Ali, *'Alayhi al-Salam* has said that the Messenger of Allah, turned to me and said, "Now you must go and sell your coat of arms and bring to me its price so I can prepare for you and for my daughter Fatimah, *'Alayha al-Salam,* what is proper for you."

Ali, *'Alayhi al-Salam* has said, "I then left and sold it for four hundred black Hijri dirhams to 'Uthman ibn 'Affan. When I received the price and he took the delivery of the coat of arms from me he said, "O abu al-Hassan, I do not deserve the coat of arms more than you do but you deserve the dirhams more than me." I said, "Yes, that is correct." He then said, "The coat of arms is a gift from me to you." I then took both the dirhams and the coat of arms. I then went to the Messenger of Allah, *O Allah grant compensation to Muhammad and his family worthy of their services to your cause.* I placed both the coat of arms and the dirhams before him and informed him about the story of 'Uthman. He prayed for him for good things.

The Messenger of Allah, *O Allah grant compensation to Muhammad and his family worthy of their services to your cause,* then took a handful from the dirhams, then called abu Bakr, gave the dirhams to him and asked him to buy household needs for his daughter. He sent Salman (Rh) and Bilal to help him in carrying the items, which will be purchased.

Abu Bakr has said, "The dirhams that he gave were sixty three. I then bought a mattress of Egyptian Khish (name of a place) with its filling made of wool, a floor covering made of hide, pillows made of hide with fillings of palm tree fibers, a gown made in Khaybar, a water sack, two jugs, a pitcher, a sterilizer for water, and a curtain made of fine wool. We then brought them and placed them before the Messenger of Allah, *'Alayhi al-Salam.* When he looked at those items his tears flowed down (his face). He raised his head to the sky and said, "O Lord, make it a blessing for a people whose utensils are mostly made of earthenware."

Ali, *'Alayhi al-Salam* has said that the Messenger of Allah, *'Alayhi al-Salam* gave the remaining dirhams to 'Umm Salamah to keep them. I then remained after this time for a month without mentioning anything to the Messenger of Allah, *'Alayhi al-Salam* about Fatimah, *'Alayha al-Salam,* due to shyness except that whenever I would get a chance to be with the Messenger of Allah privately he would say, "O abu al-Hassan, how good and beautiful is your wife. Congratulations, O abu al-Hassan I have given to you in marriage the leader of the women of the worlds."

Ali, *'Alayhi al-Salam* has said that after one month my brother 'Aqil ibn abu Talib came to me saying, "O my brother I have never become so happy as I have become happy with your marriage with Fatimah, *'Alayha al-Salam,* daughter of Muhammad, *O Allah grant compensation to Muhammad and his family worthy of their services to your cause.* O brother why do you not ask the Messenger of Allah, *'Alayhi al-Salam* to send her to your home so that then we see you settle in your family and our eyes will be delighted?"

Ali, *'Alayhi al-Salam* then said, "O dear brother I love what you just said but shyness prevents me from speaking to him about it. He then said, "I swear you to (Allah), to come with me." We then went to the Messenger of Allah, *'Alayhi al-Salam* but we met 'Umm 'Ayman, *Mawlat* (female servant) of the Messenger of Allah, *'Alayhi al-Salam,* on the way. We mentioned our story to her and she said, "Do not do this. Instead allow us to speak to him because the words of women in this matter are better and more effective on the hearts of men." She then turned back then entered in the house of 'Umm Salamah and informed her as well as other wives of the Holy Prophet, *'Alayhi al-Salam* of the story. They all gathered before the Messenger of Allah, *'Alayhi al-Salam* when he was in the house of 'A'ishah. They circled around him and said, "We pray to Allah to keep our souls and the souls of our parents in service for your cause, O Messenger of Allah we have gathered for a matter that if Khadijah *'Alayha al-Salam* were alive it would have been a delight for her eyes."

'Umm Salamah has said that when we spoke of Khadijah *'Alayha al-Salam* the Messenger of Allah, *'Alayhi al-Salam* wept and he then said, "Khadijah *'Alayha al-Salam!"* Where is someone like Khadijah *'Alayha al-Salam,* who testified to my truthfulness when people called me a liar; she supported me in the matters of the religion of Allah and helped me with her wealth. Allah, most Majestic, most Glorious, has commanded me to congratulate Khadijah, *'Alayha al-Salam* for her house in the garden (paradise) which is made of reeds (of emeralds) where there is no tension or fatigue."

'Umm Salamah has said, "We then said, 'We pray to Allah to keep our souls and the souls of our parents in service for your cause, whatever you say about Khadijah *'Alayha al-Salam* were all just as you said they were, however, she has gone to her Lord. May Allah congratulate her for it and bring us together in the levels of His happiness, and blessings. O Messenger of Allah, this is your brother in the world and your cousin in lineage, Ali ibn abu Talib, *'Alayhima al-Salam,* and he wants to have his wife, Fatimah, *'Alayha al-Salam,* in his own home to settle with her their affairs.'"

He (the Messenger of Allah), said, "O 'Umm Salamah, what is the matter with Ali. Why does he not ask me about it?" I said, "It is because of his shyness, O Messenger of Allah."

'Umm 'Ayman has said that the Messenger of Allah said to me, "Go and call Ali, *'Alayhi al-Salam* for me." I then left from the meeting of the

Messenger of Allah and found Ali, 'Alayhi al-Salam waiting for me to ask me about the response from the Messenger of Allah, 'Alayhi al-Salam. When he saw me he asked, "What is the news behind you O 'Umm 'Ayman?" I said, "The Messenger of Allah, *O Allah grant compensation to Muhammad and his family worthy of their services to your cause,* is calling you and you must answer his call."

He (the Imam) has said that he entered his chamber and his wives all left his meeting. I sat in front of him looking down on the ground due to shyness before him. He asked, "Do you like me to send your wife to your home?" I then replied, "Yes, please I pray to Allah to keep my soul and the souls of my parents in service for your cause." He then said, "Yes, it is a graceful honor, O abu al-Hassan; I will send her to your home tonight or tomorrow night by the will of Allah." I then left joyfully and happy. The Messenger of Allah, *O Allah grant compensation to Muhammad and his family worthy of their services to your cause,* then commanded his wives to prepare Fatimah, 'Alayha al-Salam, for her wedding, her dress and a furnished chamber for the bride and bridegroom.

The Messenger of Allah, *O Allah grant compensation to Muhammad and his family worthy of their services to your cause,* then took ten dirhams from the dirhams that he had told 'Umm Salamah to keep. He gave them to me to buy oil and dates and *iqt* (a milk derivative). I then purchased those items and brought them to the Messenger of Allah, 'Alayhi al-Salam. He then pulled his sleeves up to his elbows, asked for a table spread of hide then mixed the dates and oil with *iqt* (a milk derivative) until it turned in to *Hays* (a sweet preparation). He then said, "O Ali, you can invite whoever you like to invite."

I then went to the Masjid where the companions of the Messenger of Allah were present and said, "The Messenger of Allah, *O Allah grant compensation to Muhammad and his family worthy of their services to your cause,* has invited you, please respond to his invitation. They all stood up to come to the Messenger of Allah, *O Allah grant compensation to Muhammad and his family worthy of their services to your cause.* I then informed him about their large number. He then shined the table spread with a towel and told me to bring in ten of them at a time. I then did as he had instructed. They would eat, then leave but the food would not reduce until seven hundred men and women ate from that *Hays* because of the blessing of the Holy Prophet, *'Alayhi al-Salam.*

'Umm Salamah has said that he then called his daughter Fatimah, *'Alayha al-Salam,* and Ali, *'Alayhi al-Salam.* Ali, *'Alayhi al-Salam* sat on his right side and Fatimah, *'Alayha al-Salam,* sat on his left side. He then held both of them against his chest and kissed between their eyes.

He then handed over Fatimah, *'Alayha al-Salam,* to Ali, *'Alayhi al-Salam* saying, "Your wife is the best wife," then he turned to Fatimah, *'Alayha al-Salam,* saying, "O Fatimah, *'Alayha al-Salam,* your husband is the best husband." He then stood up and walked between the two of them until he lead them in their home which was prepared for them then he came out from their room, then held the two sides of the door jam and said, "Allah has cleansed you and your offspring. I am at peace with those who are at peace with you and I am at war against those who are at war against you. I leave you in the trust of Allah and assign Him to replace me in looking after you."

Ali, *'Alayhi al-Salam* has said that the Messenger of Allah, *'Alayhi al-Salam* did not visit us for three days after that time. In the morning of the fourth day he came to see us and at that time 'Asma' the daughter of 'Umays al-Khath'amiyah was in our room. He said to her, "What makes you to be here when there is a man in the room?" She said, "I pray to Allah to keep my soul and the souls of my parents in service for your cause, a young female at the time of her wedding needs the presence of a women to serve her in case she may need something, thus I remained here to look after the needs of Fatimah, *'Alayha al-Salam."* He, *'Alayhi al-Salam* said, "O 'Asma' may Allah fulfill your needs in this world and in the next life."

Ali, *'Alayhi al-Salam* has said that it was a cold morning, Fatimah, *'Alayha al-Salam,* and I were under one gown and when we heard the Messenger of Allah, *'Alayhi al-Salam* speaking to 'Asma' we wanted to get up but he said, "I swear you to my rights that you must not leave your place until I join you." We then remained in our place and the Holy Prophet, *'Alayhi al-Salam* came in, then sat near our heads then stretched his legs between the two of us. I then held his right leg against my chest and Fatimah, *'Alayha al-Salam,* held his left leg against her chest and we began to warm up his legs from cold until they became warm.

He then said, "O Ali, bring for me a jug of water. When I brought the jug of water he dropped his saliva in it three times and recited several verses of the book of Allah, most High, then he said, "O Ali, *'Alayhi al-Salam*, drink from it but leave some water in it." I then did as he had said to do. He then sprinkled the remaining on my head and on my chest saying, "Allah has kept all filth away from you, O abu al-Hassan and has cleansed you thoroughly."

He then said, "Bring for me new water." I then did as I was told to do and he did as he had done then gave the rest to his daughter, *'Alayha al-Salam,* and told her to drink but leave a little which she did and then he sprinkled the remaining on her head and on her chest saying, "Allah has kept all filth away from you and has cleansed you thoroughly. He then asked me to leave the room. He remained with his daughter in the room and asked, "How you are my child, and how is your husband?" She replied, "He is a good husband except that women from al-Quraysh came to me and said that the Messenger of Allah, *'Alayhi al-Salam,* has given you in marriage to a poor man who does not have any belongings." He then said to her, "My dear daughter, your father is not poor and your husband is not poor. The treasures of the earth were offered to me, all gold and silver but I chose what is with my Lord Allah, most Majestic, most Glorious. My dear child, if you had known what your father knows the world would seem distasteful in your eyes. By Allah, O my dear child, I have not twisted good advice from you. Your husband is the first one among them to become a Muslim, of the greater degree of knowledge among them and of greater forbearance among them.

"My dear daughter, Allah, most Majestic, most Glorious, examined the earth in an examination then He chose from among its inhabitants two men. He made one of them to be your father and the other to be your husband. O my dearest child, your husband is the best husband and you must not disobey his orders."

He (the Messenger of Allah), *O Allah grant compensation to Muhammad and his family worthy of their services to your cause,* then called me saying, "O Ali!" I then said, "Here I am at your disposal O Messenger of Allah." He said, "Please come in your home, be kind to your wife, be gentle with her; Fatimah, 'Alayha al-Salam, is a part of myself. Whatever troubles her troubles me and whatever makes her happy makes me happy. I leave you in the trust of Allah and assign Him to replace me in looking after you."

Ali, 'Alayhi al-Salam has said that "I never troubled her or caused her to dislike any of the affairs until Allah, most Majestic, most Glorious, took her away and she never made me angry or disobey me. I would look at her to remove and cast away all of my concerns and sadness."

Ali, 'Alayhi al-Salam has said that the Messenger of Allah, *O Allah grant compensation to Muhammad and his family worthy of their services to your cause,* stood up to leave but Fatimah, 'Alayha al-Salam, said, "O dear father, I am not strong enough to do all the household chores. Please find a servant for me to help me in doing the house hold chores." He (the Messenger of Allah) then said, "O Fatimah, 'Alayha al-Salam, would you like to have something better than a servant?" Ali, 'Alayhi al-Salam said, "Say yes." She then said, "Something better than a servant." He then said, "You should say *Tasbih* (Allah is free of all defects) thirty three times, *Tahmid,* (all praise belongs to Allah) thirty three times and *Takbir* (Allah is great beyond description) thirty four times. This is one hundred times by the tongue and one thousand good deeds in the balance. O Fatimah, 'Alayha al-Salam, if you say this every morning Allah will replace it with that which you need in the world and in the next life.

I ('Allamah Majlisi) say that a similar Hadith is narrated in the book 'Kifayatu al-Talib' compiled by Muhammad ibn Yusuf al-Kanji al-Shafi'i from ibn 'Abbas in brief and with changes which we have chosen not to repeat its contents.

Muhammad ibn Yusuf then has said that this is how ibn Battah has narrated and it is *Hasan* (good) and *'Al* (high).

He has said that the mention of 'Asma' the daughter of 'Umays in this Hadith is not correct; this 'Asma' was the wife of Ja'far ibn abu Talib who got married with abu Bakr after Ja'far and gave birth to Muhammad ibn abu Bakr. When abu Bakr died, Ali ibn abu Talib married her. The 'Asma' who attended the wedding of Fatimah, 'Alayha al-Salam, was 'Asma' daughter of Yazid ibn al-Sakan al-Ansari. 'Asma' the daughter of 'Umays was with her husband in Ethiopia who returned on the day of the conquest of Khaybar in the year seven (A.H.). The wedding of Fatimah, *'Alayha al-Salam,* took place a few days after the event of Badr. It is correct to say that 'Asma' mentioned in this Hadith was 'Asma' the daughter of Yazid from whom there are Ahadith from the Holy Prophet, *'Alayhi al-Salam.*

H 150, Ch. 5, h 33
Kashf al-Ghummah:

I ('Allamah Majlisi) have narrated from the book 'al-Dhurriyah al-Tahirah' compiled by abu Bishr Muhammad ibn Ahmad ibn Hammad al-Ansari known as al-Dulabi from a manuscript with the handwriting of Shaykh ibn Waddah al-Hanbali al-Shahr bani who has given me permission to narrate from him as he narrates from his Shaykhs and he narrates a great deal. Also Al-Sayyid has said that Jalal al-Din ibn 'Abd al-Hamid ibn Fakhkhar al-Musawi al-Hayiri, may Allah continue to grant him prestige, has given me permission to narrate from him from Shaykh Abd al-Aziz ibn al-Akhdar al-Muhaddith who has given permission in the month of Muharram in the year six hundred and ten and from Shaykh Burhan al-Din abu al-Husayn Ahmad ibn Ali al-Ghaznawi, who gave permission in the month of Al-Rabi' al-Awwal in the year six hundred fourteen who both from Shaykh al-Hafiz abu ibn Fadl Muhammad ibn Nasir al-Salami through the chain of his narrators and Al-Sayyid has said that granted me permission in the past to narrate all that he narrates and with this book in the month of Dhul Hajjah in the year six hundred seventy six from Ali, *'Alayhi al-Salam* who has said the following:

Abu Bakr and 'Umar proposed marriage before the Messenger of Allah, *'Alayhi al-Salam* with Fatimah, *'Alayha al-Salam.* The Messenger of Allah, *O Allah grant compensation to Muhammad and his family worthy of their services to your cause,* did not accept their proposal.

'Umar then said to Ali, to propose marriage before the Messenger of Allah, *'Alayhi al-Salam* with Fatimah, *'Alayha al-Salam.* Ali, *'Alayhi al-Salam* said, "I do not own anything except a coat of arms which I can leave as security." The Messenger of Allah, *O Allah grant compensation to Muhammad and his family worthy of their services to your cause,* gave Fatimah, *'Alayha al-Salam,* in marriage to Ali, *'Alayhi al-Salam*. When Fatimah, *'Alayha al-Salam*, learned about it she wept.

He (the narrator) has said that the Messenger of Allah, *'Alayhi al-Salam* then went to her home and asked her, "What has made you weep, O Fatimah? By Allah I have given you in marriage to the one who is more knowledgeable than all of them, more forbearing than all of them and the first one among all of them in accepting Islam."

It is narrated from Ja'far ibn Muhammad, 'Alayhima al-Salam, who has said the following:

Ali, *'Alayhi al-Salam* married Fatimah, *'Alayha al-Salam,* in the month of Ramadan and his wedding took place in the month of Dhul Hajjah in the year 2 of (A.H).

It is narrated from Mujahid from Ali, 'Alayhi al-Salam who has said the following:

Marriage with Fatimah, *'Alayha al-Salam,* was proposed before the Messenger of Allah, *'Alayhi al-Salam*. A *Mawlat* (female servant) of the Messenger of Allah, *'Alayhi al-Salam* said to me, "Do you know that people propose marriage to the Messenger of Allah, with Fatimah, *'Alayha al-Salam?*" I replied, "No, I do not know about it." She said, "Yes, marriage with her is proposed. What prevents you from going to the Messenger of Allah, *'Alayhi al-Salam* to propose marriage with Fatimah, *'Alayha al-Salam.*" I said, "Do I have anything belonging to me so I can propose marriage?" She said, "If you go to the Messenger of Allah, *'Alayhi al-Salam,* he will give her in marriage to you." By Allah she continued to shake me until I decided to go to the Messenger of Allah, *'Alayhi al-Salam* who had his glorious and awesome personality. When I sat down, I by Allah could not say a word. He then asked, "What brings you here today, what do you need?" I remained quiet. He then said, "Perhaps you have come to propose marriage with Fatimah, *'Alayha al-Salam.*" I then replied, "Yes, I do propose marriage with her." He then asked, "Do you have any belongings with which you can make the marriage with her lawful?" I replied, "No, by Allah, O Messenger of Allah." He then asked, "What have you done with the coat of arms with which I had armed you?" I replied, "I still have it, by the one in whose hands is my soul that it is Hatmiyah (made by Hatmiyah people) and its value is only four hundred dirhams." He then said, "I have accepted your marriage proposal. You must send the coat of arms to me for the dowry of the daughter of the Messenger of Allah, *'Alayhi al-Salam*."

H 151, Ch. 5, h 34
Kashf al-Ghummah:

It is narrated from 'Ata' ibn abu Rabah who has said the following:

When Ali, *'Alayhi al-Salam* proposed marriage with Fatimah, *'Alayha al-Salam,* the Messenger of Allah, *'Alayhi al-Salam* went to her and said, "Ali has proposed marriage with you. She remained quiet. He (the Messenger of Allah) then came out and give her in marriage to Ali, *'Alayhi al-Salam*.

It is narrated from ibn Buraydah from his father who has said the following:

A few people from al-Ansar (people of al-Madinah) said to Ali, that he should propose marriage before the Messenger of Allah, *O Allah grant compensation to Muhammad and his family worthy of their services to your cause,* with Fatimah, *'Alayha al-Salam.* He came to the Messenger of Allah, offered him *Salam* (the phrase of offering greeting of peace) and he asked, "What does Ali ibn abu Talib need?" He replied, "I have remembered (proposed marriage with) Fatimah, *'Alayha al-Salam,* the daughter of the Messenger of Allah, *O Allah grant compensation to Muhammad and his family worthy of their services to your cause.*" He said, "*Marhaban* and *Ahlan*" (you are welcome and well received) and he did not say any more words than this much. Ali then came out to the group of the al-Ansar (people of al-Madinah) who were waiting. They asked, "What is behind you" meaning the story behind him? He replied, "I do not know except that he (the Messenger of Allah) said, "*Marhaban* and *Ahlan*" (you are welcome and well received)." They said, "Only one of these is sufficient for you. The Messenger of Allah, *O Allah grant compensation to Muhammad and his family worthy of their services to your cause,* has given you *Ahlan* (family) and being well received. Afterwards he (the Messenger of Allah) said, "O Ali, for a wedding a banquet is necessary."

Sa'd then said, "I have a ram (for this purpose). A group of al-Ansar (people of al-Madinah) arranged for several kilos of corn. In the night of the wedding the Messenger of Allah said, "You must not invent (speak) anything until I meet you." The Messenger of Allah, *O Allah grant compensation to*

Muhammad and his family worthy of their services to your cause, asked for water with which he made *wudu* then poured water on Ali, *'Alayhi al-Salam* saying, "O Lord, make this marriage a blessing for them and send blessings on them for their two children (young lions). Ibn Nasir has said, "make it a blessing in their offspring."

'Asma' the daughter of 'Umays has said that she was there during the wedding of the Fatimah, *'Alayha al-Salam,* the daughter of the Messenger of Allah, *'Alayhi al-Salam.* In the morning the Holy Prophet, *'Alayhi al-Salam* came to the door and said, "O 'Umm 'Ayman call for me my brother (cousin)." Is he your brother and you have given your daughter in marriage to him?" He (the Messenger of Allah) replied, "Yes, O 'Umm 'Ayman. "She has said that the women heard his voice and they went in hiding and I also hid in a corner."

Ali, *'Alayhi al-Salam* came, then he (the Messenger of Allah) poured water on him and prayed for him. He then said, "Call Fatimah, *'Alayha al-Salam,* for me." She came severely stressed by her shyness. The Messenger of Allah, *'Alayhi al-Salam* said to her, "Calm down; I have given you in marriage to the most beloved one to me in my family. Then he poured water on her and prayed for her."

She has said that he (the Messenger of Allah, *'Alayhi al-Salam*) went back and saw a black figure in front of him. He then asked, "Who is it?" I then said, "I am 'Asma' the daughter of 'Umays." He then asked, "Have you come for the wedding of Fatimah, *'Alayha al-Salam,* to honor her?" I replied, "Yes, that is correct." She has said that he prayed for her."

Ali ibn 'Isa has said the following:

Narrated to me Al-Sayyid Jalal al-Din 'Abd al-Hamid ibn Fakhkhar al-Musawi something meaning as follows:

'Asma' the daughter of 'Umays has said that at the time of her death, Khadijah *'Alayha al-Salam,* wept. I then said, "Why do you weep? You are the leader of the women of the worlds. You are the wife of the Holy Prophet, *'Alayhi al-Salam,* you are congratulated with the garden (paradise) by his tongue. She said, "I do not weep for this reason. During the night of the wedding a female person needs help in her private matters. Fatimah, *'Alayha al-Salam,* is a child. I am afraid that she many not find that kind of help at such time." I then said, "My leader, I promise before Allah if I will be alive at such time I will be the one on your behalf in the matter. When it was the night of the wedding the Messenger of Allah, *'Alayhi al-Salam* came and he commanded the women to leave but I remained. When he wanted to leave he saw the blackness of my figure and asked, "Who are you?" I replied, "This is 'Asma' the daughter of 'Umays." He then said, "Did I not command you to leave?" I then said, "O Messenger of Allah, that is correct, I pray to Allah to keep my soul and the souls of my parents in service for your cause. I did not mean to oppose you, however, I had promised Khadijah *'Alayha al-Salam*. I told him the story. He wept and asked, "I swear you to Allah, have you remained behind for this reason?" I replied, "Yes, by Allah, that is the reason." He then prayed for me.

Now back to the narration of al-Dulabi:

'Asma' the daughter of 'Umays has said that she prepared Fatimah, *'Alayha al-Salam,* the daughter of the Messenger of Allah, *'Alayhi al-Salam* for her wedding with Ali ibn abu Talib, *'Alayhima al-Salam.* Their bed and pillows for filling did not have anything but palm tree fibers. The wedding banquet of Fatimah, *'Alayha al-Salam,* at that time was the best banquet. He left his coat of arms for security with a Jewish man. The banquet items consisted of several kilos of barley, dates and *Hays* (the confectionary made of dates, oil and sour cream).

H 152, Ch. 5, h 35
Kashf al-Ghummah:

It is narrated from the book 'Kifayat al-Talib fi Manaqib Ali ibn abu Talib, 'Alayhima al-Salam, compiled by Muhammad Yusuf al-Kanji al-Shafi'i from abu Hurayrah who has said the following:

Fatimah, *'Alayha al-Salam,* said, "O Messenger of Allah, you have given me in marriage to Ali ibn abu Talib who is poor and has no belongings." He said, "O Fatimah, will you not become happy to know that Allah examined the earth in an examination then He chose from it two men of whom one is your father and the other one is your husband?"

It is narrated from Jabir ibn Samrah who has said the following:

The Messenger of Allah, *O Allah grant compensation to Muhammad and his family worthy of their services to your cause,* once said, "O people, this is Ali ibn abu Talib. You think that I have given in marriage to him my daughter Fatimah, *'Alayha al-Salam,* but the prestigious people from al-Quraysh had proposed marriage and their proposals were turned down. This is because I expected to receive news from the sky until Jibril came to me in the twenty fourth night of the month of Ramadan and said, "O Muhammad, *al-'Ali al-'Ala'* sends you *Salam* (the phrase of offering greeting of peace). He has gathered *al-Ruhaniyin* (the spiritual beings) and *al-Karrubin* in the valley called al-Afyah under *Tuba* (the tree in the garden (paradise). He has given Fatimah, *'Alayha al-Salam,* in marriage to Ali. He commanded me to give the marriage proposing speech, Allah, most High, is the guardian and He commanded *Tuba* (the tree in the garden (paradise) to carry ornaments and dresses, pearls, and rubies to spread over them and commanded *al-Hawra' al-'in* to collect them and they present their collection as gifts and express pride over it until the Day of Judgment saying, "This is of what was spread during the wedding of Fatimah, *'Alayha al-Salam.*"

It is narrated from 'Alqamah from 'Abd Allah who has said that in the morning of the wedding Fatimah, *'Alayha al-Salam,* felt *Ra'dah* (fear, concern). The Holy Prophet, *'Alayhi al-Salam* then said to her, "O Fatimah, *'Alayha al-Salam,* I have given you in marriage to a leader in the world and in the next life he will be among the virtuous ones. O Fatimah, *'Alayha al-Salam,* when Allah, most High, decided that I must give you in marriage to Ali, Allah, most High, commanded Jibril to stand in the fourth sky. The angels then formed rows and rows and he gave a speech. He (Allah) then gave you in marriage to Ali, *'Alayhi al-Salam.* Then Allah, most blessed, most high, commanded the tree in the garden (paradise) and it carried ornaments and dresses and then He commanded it to spread them for the angels. Whoever of them collected a larger amount than the others keep expressing pride about it up to the Day of Judgment.

'Umm Salamah has said that Fatimah, *'Alayha al-Salam,* would express pride before the women for the fact that Jibril, was the one who gave the speech for her wedding.

It is narrated that the Messenger of Allah, in the night of the wedding came to Fatimah, *'Alayha al-Salam,* with a bowl of milk and said, "Drink this, may your father be ransom for you." He then said to Ali, "Drink, may your cousin be ransom for you."

It is narrated that when Fatimah, *'Alayha al-Salam,* and Ali, *'Alayhi al-Salam* were wedded, Jibril, Michael and Israfil came along with seventy thousand angels. The mule, Dul dul, was lead with Fatimah, *'Alayha al-Salam,* on his back, who was covered with a gown.

He (the narrator) has said that Jibril held the reign; Israfil held the stirrup and Michael held the back part of the saddle. The angels said *Takbir* (Allah is great beyond description), thus, saying *Takbir* (Allah is great beyond description) became a tradition during a wedding up to the Day of Judgment.

H 153, Ch. 5, h 36
Kashf al-Ghummah:

It is narrated from Ja'far ibn Muhammad from his ancestors, who has said the following:

Abu Bakr came to the Messenger of Allah, *'Alayhi al-Salam* to propose marriage with Fatimah, *'Alayha al-Salam,* but his proposal was turned down, then 'Umar came to him with the same proposal and his proposal was also not accepted. They both then went to 'Abd al-Rahman ibn 'Awf saying to him that he was wealthier among the people of al-Quraysh and if you go to the Messenger of Allah to propose marriage to him with Fatimah, *'Alayha al-Salam,* Allah will increase your nobility. He went to the Messenger of Allah, *'Alayhi al-Salam,* then presented his proposal for marriage but the Messenger of Allah, *'Alayhi al-Salam* turned away from him. He then came back to the two of them saying, "What had happened to you happened with me also."

The two of them then went to Ali ibn abu Talib *'Alayhima al-Salam,* who was watering his palm trees. They said to him, "We know you are a relative of the Messenger of Allah, *'Alayhi al-Salam* and you are the first one who accepted Islam. We like that you go to the Messenger of Allah, *'Alayhi al-Salam* to propose marriage before him with Fatimah, *'Alayha al-Salam,* Allah will increase your excellence and honor."

He said, "It is good that you reminded me. He left to take wudu and a bath and to put on a gown made in Qatar then performed two *Rak'at Salat* (prayer) then went to the Holy Prophet, *'Alayhi al-Salam* and said, O Messenger of Allah, please give Fatimah, *'Alayha al-Salam,* in marriage to me." He (the Messenger of Allah), asked, "If I give her in marriage to you, what you will give for her dowry?" He replied, "I can give as dowry my sword, horse, coat of arms and water carrier camel."

He said, "Your water carrier, your sword, and your horse are such things without which you cannot do anything against your enemies. However, your coat of arms is something that you can use."

Ali, *'Alayhi al-Salam* then left, sold his coat of arms for four hundred Qatari dirhams which he them placed before the Messenger of Allah, *'Alayhi al-Salam*. He (the Messenger of Allah) did not count them and Ali, *'Alayhi al-Salam* did not inform him of how much they were. The Messenger of Allah, *O Allah grant compensation to Muhammad and his family worthy of their services to your cause,* then took a handful from it and gave it to al-Miqdad ibn al-Aswad and told him to buy such items for the wedding of Fatimah, *'Alayha al-Salam,* which she needs, but buy for her more perfumes.

Al-Miqdad then left for the market. He bought a grinding stone, a water sack, pillows of hide, and a mat made in Qatar. He brought them to show to the Messenger of Allah, *'Alayhi al-Salam* and 'Asma' the daughter of 'Umays was with him. She said, "O Messenger of Allah, *'Alayhi al-Salam* people of age and wealth from al-Quraysh proposed marriage but you turned them down and now you give her in marriage to this boy?" The Messenger of Allah, *O Allah grant compensation to Muhammad and his family worthy of their services to your cause,* said, "O 'Asma' you will also marry this boy and give birth for him to a boy."

Note: This and the narration that she was in Ethiopia is strange. She married 'Amir al-Mu'minin and gave birth as the Messenger of Allah, had said.

At the night of the wedding he told Salman (Rh) to bring for him al-Shahba' mule which he then brought to be used as conveyance for Fatimah, *'Alayha al-Salam.* Salman (Rh) drove the mule and the Messenger of Allah, stood with it and at such time he sensed a movement and then he found out that Jibril,

Michael, Israfil and a great number of angels had arrived. He (the Messenger of Allah) then asked Jibril, "What brings you here?" He replied, "We are attending the wedding of Fatimah, *'Alayha al-Salam,* with her husband. Jibril then said *Takbir* (Allah is great beyond description), Michael said *Takbir* (Allah is great beyond description), Israfil said *Takbir* (Allah is great beyond description) then the angels said Takbir (Allah is great beyond description) then the Holy Prophet said *Takbir* (Allah is great beyond description) then Salman (Rh) said *Takbir* (Allah is great beyond description) then saying *Takbir* (Allah is great beyond description) became a tradition during the wedding after that night.

She was brought to the house of Ali, *'Alayhi al-Salam* and seated on one side of Ali, *'Alayhi al-Salam* on a mat made in Qatar.

He (the Messenger of Allah) then said, "O Ali, this is my daughter, whoever honors her has honored me, and whoever, insults her has insulted me."

He (the Messenger of Allah) then said, "O Lord, grant the two of them congratulations and blessings. Grant them fine offspring; you listen and hear the prayers. He (the Messenger of Allah) then sprang and she hugged him and wept. He (the Messenger of Allah) then asked her, "What had made you to weep? I have given you to the one who is the greatest among them in forbearance and is the one with the largest degree of knowledge."

H 154, Ch. 5, h 37
Kashf al-Ghummah:

The author of the book al-Firdaws has narrated from the Holy Prophet, *'Alayhi al-Salam,* who has said, "If Ali, *'Alayhi al-Salam* did not exist no match could ever be found for Fatimah, *'Alayha al-Salam.*"

The author of the book al-Firdaws has also narrated from ibn 'Abbas from the Holy Prophet who has said the following:

O Ali, Allah has given Fatimah, *'Alayha al-Salam,* in marriage to you. He has assigned the earth and all that walks on it as her dowry, thus, whoever walks on it with his condition of dislike and hate toward you, he has walked in an unlawful way.

Ibn Babwayh has narrated in a lengthy narration about the marriage of 'Amir al-Mu'minin and Fatimah, *'Alayhima al-Salam,* that he took some water in his mouth then called Fatimah, *'Alayha al-Salam,* and made her sit in front of him then poured that water in a basin. He then washed his feet and face then called Fatimah, *'Alayha al-Salam,* picked up a hand full of water then poured it on her head, one handful on her front side then sprinkled on her skin. He then asked for another basin then called Ali, *'Alayhi al-Salam* and did what he had done with Fatimah, *'Alayha al-Salam.* He then held both of them against himself and said, "O Lord, they are from me and I am from them. Lord as you have kept all filth away from me, please keep it away from them also and cleanse them thoroughly. He then said, "Now you can go to your room. May Allah place harmony between the two of you, blessings in your manners, and settle your affairs." He then left and closed the door with his hand.

Ibn 'Abbas has said that 'Asma' informed me that she glanced at the Messenger of Allah, *'Alayhi al-Salam* who continued praying for both of them especially without including anyone else in his prayer until he entered in his room.

In a narration it is said that he said, "May Allah place blessings in your manners, settle your affairs, place harmony through belief in your hearts. Be mindful about your family. Peace be with you both."

It is narrated from Jabir ibn 'Abd Allah who has said that when the Messenger of Allah, *O Allah grant compensation to Muhammad and his family worthy of their services to your cause,* gave Fatimah, *'Alayha al-Salam,* in marriage to Ali, Allah, most High, was the solemnizer of their marriage from on top of His Throne, Jibril gave the proposal speech, Michael and Israfil along with seventy thousand angels were witnesses to the marriage and Allah sent divine revelation to *Tuba* (the tree in the garden (paradise) to spread what it carried of ornaments of large pearls, rubies and pearls. Allah inspired *al-Hawra' al-'in* to collect the valuable gems and they then gave them as gifts to each other until the Day of Judgment to express happiness for the marriage of Fatimah, and Ali, *'Alayhima al-Salam.*

It is narrated from Sharahbil ibn Sa'id who has said the following:

The Messenger of Allah, *O Allah grant compensation to Muhammad and his family worthy of their services to your cause,* in the morning of the wedding of Fatimah, *'Alayha al-Salam,* visited her with a bowl of milk. He then said, "Drink it, may your father be a ransom for you." He then said to Ali, *'Alayhi al-Salam,* "Drink it, may your cousin be a ransom for you."

It is narrated from Sharahbil that in the morning of her wedding Fatimah, *'Alayha al-Salam,* was found feeling *Ra'dah* (fear, concern). The Messenger of Allah, *O Allah grant compensation to Muhammad and his family worthy of their services to your cause,* said, "I have given you in marriage to the leader in the world and in the next life he will be of the virtuous ones."

It is narrated from abu Ja'far, who has said the following:

Fatimah, *'Alayha al-Salam,* complained before the Messenger of Allah, *'Alayhi al-Salam* against Ali, *'Alayhi al-Salam* saying that he does not leave anything of his sustenance without giving them to the destitute people. He said, "O Fatimah, *'Alayha al-Salam,* are you making me angry at my brother and cousin? Making him angry is making me angry and making me angry is making Allah angry.

She then said, "I seek protection with Allah against His anger and the anger of His messenger."

It is narrated from Asbagh ibn Nabatah who has said the following:

I (the narrator) heard 'Amir al-Mu'minin, *'Alayhi al-Salam* say, "I want to say something which no one other than me can speak except a liar. I have inherited from the Holy Prophet of kindness, my wife is the best of the women of the nation (followers) and I am the best of the Executors of the Wills."

H 154, Ch. 5, h 38
Al-Kafi: [H 9577, Ch. 46, h 1, from al-Kafi]

Mahr of the Marriage of Amir Al-Mu'minin, 'Alayhi al-Salam

A number of our people have narrated from Sahl ibn Ziyad from Ahmad ibn Muhammad from ibn abu Nasr from 'Abd al-Karim ibn 'Amr al-Khath'amiy from ibn abu Ya'fur who has said the following:

"I once heard abu 'Abd Allah, *'Alayhi al-Salam*, saying that Ali, *'Alayhi al-Salam*, married Fatimah, *'Alayha al-Salam*, for a *mahr* (dower) from the price of a single gown, a shield and a bed which was made of the hide of a ram.'"

H 155, Ch. 5, h 39
Al-Kafi:[H 9578, Ch. 46, h 2, from al-Kafi]

Muhammad ibn Yahya has narrated from Ahmad ibn 'Isa from ibn Faddal from ibn Bukayr who has said the following:

"I once heard abu 'Abd Allah, *'Alayhi al-Salam*, saying, 'The Messenger of Allah, *O Allah, grant compensation to Muhammad and his family worthy of their services to Your cause*, arranged the marriage of Fatimah and Ali, *'Alayhim al-Salam*, for a *mahr* (dower) from one shield made by Hatmiyah (a certain people) valued at thirty dirham.'"

H 156, Ch. 5, h 40
Al-Kafi: [H 9579, Ch. 46, h 3, from al-Kafi]

Ahmad ibn Muhammad has narrated from Ali ibn al-Hakam from Mu'awiyah ibn Wahab who has said the following:

"Abu 'Abd Allah, *'Alayhi al-Salam*, has said, 'The Messenger of Allah, *O Allah, grant compensation to Muhammad and his family worthy of their services to Your cause*, arranged marriage of Ali and Fatimah, *'Alayhim al-Salam*, with a *mahr* (dower) from a shield made by Hatmiyah and their bed was made of the hide of ram and when sleeping they would turn its fury face under their side.'"

H 157, Ch. 5, h 41
Al-Kafi: [H 9580, Ch. 46, h 4, from al-Kafi]

Certain persons of our people have narrated from Ali ibn al-Husayn from al-'Abbas ibn 'Amir 'Abd Allah ibn Bukayr who has said the following:

"Abu 'Abd Allah, *'Alayhi al-Salam*, has said, 'The Messenger of Allah, *O Allah, grant compensation to Muhammad and his family worthy of their services to Your cause*, arranged the marriage of Fatimah and Ali, *'Alayhim al-Salam*, for a *mahr* (dower) from one shield made by Hatmiyah (a certain people) valued at thirty dirham.'"

H 158, Ch. 5, h 42
Al-Kafi: [H 9581, Ch. 46, h 5, from al-Kafi]

A number of our people have narrated from Sahl ibn Ziyad from Muhammad ibn walid al-Khazzaz from Yunus ibn Ya'qub from abu Maryam al-Ansariy who has said the following:

"Abu Ja'far, *'Alayhi al-Salam*, has said that *mahr* (dower) of Fatimah, *'Alayha al-Salam*, was from a gown which was patched, a shield of Hatmiyah and her bed was of hide of a ram which the wife and husband used as floor covering and bed on which they would sleep.'"

H 159, Ch. 5, h 43
Al-Kafi: [H 9582, Ch. 46, h 6, from al-Kafi]

A number of our people have narrated from Ahmad ibn Muhammad ibn Khalid from Ali ibn Asbat from Dawud from Ya'qub ibn Shu'ayb who has said the following:

"He (the Imam), *'Alayhi al-Salam*, has said, 'When the Messenger of Allah, *O Allah, grant compensation to Muhammad and his family worthy of their services to Your cause*, arranged the marriage of Ali and Fatimah, *'Alayhim al-Salam*, he went to see her but found her weeping. He (the Messenger of Allah) asked her, 'What has made you weep, by Allah, had there been anyone better in my family than him I would not have given you in marriage to him, and I have not given you in marriage to him but it is Allah who has given you in marriage to him with a *mahr* (dower) of al-Khums (one-fifth), for as long as there are the skies and earth.'"

H 160, Ch. 5, h 44
Al-Kafi: [H 9583, Ch. 46, h 7, from al-Kafi]

Ali ibn Muhammad has narrated from 'Abd Allah ibn Ishaq from al-Hassan ibn Ali ibn Sulayman from those who narrated to him who has said the following:

"Abu 'Abd Allah, *'Alayhi al-Salam*, has said, 'Fatimah, *'Alayha al-Salam*, said to the Messenger of Allah, *O Allah, grant compensation to Muhammad and his family worthy of their services to Your cause*, 'You have given me in marriage for a very little *mahr* (dower).' The Messenger of Allah said, 'I have not given you in marriage but it is Allah who has given you in marriage from the heaven and has assigned one-fifth of the world as your *mahr* (dower) for as long as there are the skies and the earth.'"

H 161, Ch. 5, h 45
Al-Kafi: [H 10121, Ch. 178, h 1, from al-Kafi]

Ali ibn Ibrahim has narrated from his father from ibn abu 'Umayr from Jamil ibn Darraj who has said the following:

"Abu 'Abd Allah, *'Alayhi al-Salam*, has said, 'Vigilance and protectionism is not needed against lawful matters, in the light of the words of the Messenger of Allah, *O Allah, grant compensation to Muhammad and his family worthy of their services to Your cause*, "The two of you (Ali and Fatimah, *'Alayhim al-Salam*,) you must not do anything until I come back to you" and when he (the Messenger of Allah) came back he stretched his legs between them in the furnishing.'"

H 162, Ch. 5, h 46
Al-Kafi: [H 10232, Ch. 190, h 52, from al-Kafi]

Ali ibn Ibrahim has narrated from his father from abu 'Abd Allah, al-Barqiy in a marfu' manner has said the following:

"When the Messenger of Allah, *O Allah, grant compensation to Muhammad and his family worthy of their services to Your cause*, gave Fatimah, *'Alayha al-Salam*, in marriage and people said, 'We wish her prosperity and sons, but he (the Messenger of Allah) said, 'No, we wish for her goodness and blessings.'"

H 163, Ch. 5, h 47
Al-Kafi: [H 10234, Ch. 190, h 54, from al-Kafi]

Muhammad ibn Yahya has narrated from Ahmad ibn Muhammad from al-'Abbas ibn Ma'ruf from Ali ibn Mahziyar from al-Mukhallad ibn Musa from Ibrahim ibn Ali from Ali ibn Yahya al-Yarbu'iy from Aban ibn Taghlib who has said the following:

"Abu Ja'far, *'Alayhi al-Salam*, has said that the Messenger of Allah, *O Allah, grant compensation to Muhammad and his family worthy of their services to Your cause*, has said, 'I am a human being like you. I marry from you and give in marriage to you except Fatimah, *'Alayha al-Salam*, because her marriage came from the heaven.'"

H 164, Ch. 5, h 48

Tafsir of Furat ibn Ibrahim:

Ali ibn Muhammad ibn Mukhallad al-Juhfi has narrated in a Mu'an'an manner from ibn 'Abbas who has said the following:

This is about the meaning of the words of Allah, the most Majestic, the most Glorious:

"It is He who has created the human being from water to have relationships of both lineage and wedlock. Your Lord has all the power." (25:54)

Allah created a white sperm, then placed it in the back of Adam, *'Alayhi al-Salam,* then transferred it from the back of Adam, *'Alayhi al-Salam,* to the back of Shith, then to the back of Anwash, then to the back of Qaynan until the backs of noble ones inherited it as well as the clean wombs until Allah placed it in the back of 'Abd al-Muttalib then divided it into two halves, one half went to 'Abd Allah and the other half went to abu Talib and this is the offspring who was born from 'Abd Allah as Muhammad and from abu Talib as Ali, *'Alayhima al-Salam,* and this is to which the words of Allah, most Majestic, most Glorious, refer, "It is He who has created the human being from water to have relationships of both lineage and wedlock. Your Lord has all the power." (25:54) Fatimah, *'Alayha al-Salam,* the daughter of Muhammad, married Ali, thus, Ali is from Muhammad and Muhammad is from Ali, al-Hassan, al-Husayn and Fatimah, *'Alayhim al-Salam,* form the lineage and the wedlock relationship.

H 165, Ch. 5, h 49

Al-Misbah al-Anwar:

The brief book of al-Hassan ibn Sulayman quoting from Kitab al-Firdaws from the Holy Prophet who has said the following:

"If Ali, *'Alayhi al-Salam* did not exist a match for Fatimah, *'Alayha al-Salam,* could have never been found."

It is narrated from the narrator of the previous Hadith in a marfu' manner through the chain of his narrators from ibn 'Abbas from the Holy Prophet, who has said the following:

The Holy Prophet, *O Allah grant compensation to Muhammad and his family worthy of their services to your cause,* said to Ali, "O Ali, Allah, most Majestic, most Glorious, has given Fatimah, *'Alayha al-Salam,* to you in marriage and He has assigned the earth and all that walks on it for her dowry. Those who walk on it with dislike and hatred in their hearts against her, they walk on it in unlawful manner."

Chapter 6 - The manners of Fatimah, *'Alayha al-Salam,* in her living with Ali, *'Alayhi al-Salam*

H 166, Ch. 6, h 1
'Ilal al-Shara'i':

Al-Qattan has narrated from al-Sukkari from al-Husayn ibn Ali al-'Abdi from Abd al-Aziz ibn Muslim from Yahya' ibn 'Abd Allah from his father from abu Hurayrah who has said the following:

One day we performed the morning *Salat* (prayer) with the Messenger of Allah, *O Allah grant compensation to Muhammad and his family worthy of their services to your cause.* He then stood up with a depressed looking face and we also stood up with him when he moved toward the house of Fatimah, *'Alayha al-Salam.* He then saw Ali sleeping in front of the door on the soil. The Holy Prophet, *'Alayhi al-Salam* sat down, then began to clean dust from his back, saying I pray to Allah to keep my soul and the souls of my parents in service for your cause, O abu Turab. He then held his hand and they both entered the house. We waited a little then we heard a loud laughing, then the Messenger of Allah, *O Allah grant compensation to Muhammad and his family worthy of their services to your cause,* came out to us with a bright face. We then asked, "O Messenger of Allah, how is it that you entered the house with a depressed face but now come out differently?" He then said, "How can I not be happy when I have established reconciliation between the most beloved ones of the inhabitants of the earth to the inhabitants of the sky."

Note: This is an indication of the existence of some kind of differences between Ali, and Fatimah, *'Alayha al-Salam,* which the Holy Prophet, settled and reconciled them. However, the reason and any details are not mentioned. Perhaps it was to bring to light their excellence that was not known to people, which still has remained unknown to us.

H 167, Ch. 6, h 2
'Ilal al-Shara'i':

Al-Qattan has narrated from al-Sukkari from 'Uthman ibn 'Imran from 'Ubayd Allah ibn Musa from Abd al-Aziz from Habib ibn abu Thabit who has said the following:

There was an issue between Fatimah, and Ali, *'Alayhima al-Salam*. The Messenger of Allah, *O Allah grant compensation to Muhammad and his family worthy of their services to your cause,* came to their home and a floor covering was spread for him, he lied down on it. Then Fatimah, *'Alayha al-Salam,* came and lied down on one side then Ali, *'Alayhi al-Salam,* came and lied down on the other side.

He (the narrator) has said that the Messenger of Allah took the hand of Ali then placed it on his bellybutton and then he took the hand of Fatimah, *'Alayha al-Salam,* and placed it on his bellybutton. This condition continued until he established reconciliation between them, then he came out and it was said to him, "O Messenger of Allah, you went inside in a condition and now that you have come out we see joy on your face." "What can prevent me from being happy when I have established reconciliation between the most beloved ones on the face of the earth to me?"

Al-Saduq (r.h) has said that this narration is not reliable to him and it is not part of his belief also because Ali and Fatimah, *'Alayhima al-Salam,* were not as such that differences could take place between them to require the Messenger of Allah, *'Alayhi al-Salam* to come and establish reconciliation between them. One of them is the leader of the executors of the wills and the other one is the leader of the women of the worlds.

Note: This (disputes between Ali, and Fatimah, *'Alayhima al-Salam)* is against the obvious. We just learned in the Hadith 17 of Ch. 3 above that the Messenger of Allah, *O Allah grant compensation to Muhammad and his family worthy of their services to your cause,* said "Fatimah, *'Alayha al-Salam,* is a part of me. Whoever makes her happy has made me happy and whoever troubles her has troubled me. Fatimah, *'Alayha al-Salam,* is of all people the dearest to me."

H 168, Ch. 6, h 3
'Ilal al-Shara'i':

My father has narrated from Sa'd from al-Hassan ibn 'Urfah from Waki' from Muhammad ibn Israel from abu Salih from abu Dharr (r.h) who has said the following:

Ja'far ibn abu Talib and I were of the immigrants to Ethiopia. A slave girl valued at four thousand dirham was given to Ja'far as a gift. When we arrived in al-Madinah he gave that salve girl to Ali, *'Alayhi al-Salam* as a housemaid. Ali, *'Alayhi al-Salam* kept her in the house of Fatimah, *'Alayha al-Salam*. One day Fatimah, *'Alayha al-Salam,* came home and found Ali, *'Alayhi al-Salam,* with his head placed in the lap of the slave girl. She then said, "O abu al-Hassan, have you done her?" He replied, "No, by Allah, O daughter of Muhammad, I have not done anything. What do you want?" She said, "Allow me to go to the house of the Messenger of Allah, *O Allah grant compensation to Muhammad and his family worthy of their services to your cause.*" He said, "You are allowed." She then dressed up and wore her veil intending to go to the Holy Prophet, *'Alayhi al-Salam."* Jibril, *'Alayhi al-Salam* came and said, "O Muhammad, Allah sends you *Salam* (the phrase of offering greeting of peace) and says, "This is Fatimah, *'Alayha al-Salam,* is coming to complain before you against Ali, *'Alayhi al-Salam*. You must not accept from her anything against Ali."

Fatimah, *'Alayha al-Salam,* came and the Messenger of Allah, *'Alayhi al-Salam* said, "Have you come to complain against Ali?" She replied, "Yes, by the Lord of al-Ka'bah." He (the Messenger of Allah) then told her to go back and say, "It (my coming back) is against what I felt just to make you happy." She then returned to Ali, *'Alayhi al-Salam* and said, "O abu al-Hassan, "It (my coming back) is against what I felt just to make you happy." She said it three times. Ali, *'Alayhi al-Salam* said, "Have you complained against me before my beloved one the Messenger of Allah, *'Alayhi al-Salam*. It is awful, O Fatimah, *'Alayha al-Salam*. Allah is my witness O Fatimah, *'Alayha al-Salam,* that the slave girl is free for the sake of Allah, and the four hundred dirham that was left of my share of benefits is charity for the poor ones in al-Madinah. He then dressed up and wore his shoes to see the Holy Prophet, *'Alayhi al-Salam*. Jibril then came and said, "O Muhammad, Allah sends you *Salam* (the phrase of offering greeting of peace) and says, "Tell to Ali, *'Alayhi al-Salam,* that I have given to you the garden (paradise) for your setting free the slave girl to make Fatimah, *'Alayha al-Salam,* happy. The fire is for the four hundred dirhams, which you have given in charity. You can now admit in the garden (paradise) whomever you like through my mercy and take out of the fire whomever you like through my pardoning. At such time Ali, *'Alayhi al-Salam* said, "I am the distributer of the garden (paradise) and the fire."

Note: No migration by abu Dharr to Ethiopia is known to have taken place.

Manaqib of ibn Shahr Ashub and abu Mansur al-Katib in the book al-Ruh and al-Rayhan has narrated a similar Hadith.

Bisharat al-Mustafa:

My father abu al-Qasim and 'Ammar ibn Yasar and his son Sa'd all of them from Ibrahim ibn Nasr al-Jurjani from Muhammad ibn Hamzah al-Mar'ashi from Muhammad ibn al-Hassan from Muhammad ibn Ja'far from Hamzah ibn 'Isma'il from Ahmad ibn Khalil from Yahya' ibn 'Abd al-Hamid from Sharik from Layth ibn abu Salim from Mujahid and ibn 'Abbas has narrated a similar Hadith with a very few changes and we have recorded it in the chapter "He is the distributor of the garden (paradise) and the fire"

H 169, Ch. 6, h 4
Manaqib of ibn Shahr Ashub:

The author has said that when Fatimah, *'Alayha al-Salam,* returned from the court of abu Bakr she turned to Ali, *'Amir al-Mu'minin, 'Alayhi al-Salam* and said, "O ibn abu Talib you have adopted the manner of the baby (fetus), and you have stayed in the room like a suspect, you have been crushing your opponent armed to the teeth but now the unarmed opponent has tricked you. Ibn abu Quhafah has snatched away the gift that I had received and it was for the sustenance of my children. He has been very loud against me and I found him persistently opposing me. People of the tribe of Qaylah (al-Ansar (people of al-Madinah), people of al-Madinah) held back their support from me and Muhajir (immigrants) showed themselves as his (abu Bakr's) relatives, people in the gathering kept looking down instead of supporting me, there was no defender for me to prevent injustice (from affecting me). I left home with intense anger but I have returned defeated and there is no choice for me. I wish I had died before being insulted and before being (wrongfully) made to fall. O Allah grant me pardon for crossing my limits. From you is support. Woe is me in every morning and woe is me, the support I once had is dead, and the shoulder is weakened. I take my complaint before my father and my Lord. O Lord, you are the strongest power."

'Amir al-Mu'minin, *'Alayhi al-Salam* then said, "Woe is not on you. Woe is on those who are against you. Restrain your emotions, O daughter of the chosen one, the surviving child of the Prophet-hood. I have not neglected my religion and I have not miscalculated my abilities. You wanted sustenance, rest assured it is guaranteed for you and your guardian is trusted. What he has prepared for you is better than what is cut off from you. You must count it on Allah."

She then said, "Allah is enough support for me and the best attorney."

H 170, Ch. 6, h 5
Manaqib of ibn Shahr Ashub:

Ma'qal ibn Yasar, abu Qubayl, ibn Ishaq, Habib ibn Thabit, 'Imran ibn al-Haseen, ibn Ghassan and al-Baqir, *'Alayhi al-Salam* with variations in words but of the same meaning have said that the women said to Fatimah, *'Alayha al-Salam,* "O daughter of the Messenger of Allah, *O Allah grant compensation to Muhammad and his family worthy of their services to your cause,* so and so and so had proposed to your father to give you in marriage but he has refused and instead he has given you in marriage to an extremely poor man." The Messenger of Allah, *O Allah grant compensation to Muhammad and his family worthy of their services to your cause,* came to her and she said, "O Messenger of Allah, you have given me in marriage to an extremely poor man." He (the Messenger of Allah) held her by her wrist and nudged saying, "No, O Fatimah, in fact I have given you in marriage to the one who accepted Islam before every one of them, more knowledgeable than every one of them, of greater degree of forbearance than every one of them. O Fatimah, he is my brother (cousin) in the world and in the next life." She then laughed and said, "I accept, O Messenger of Allah."

In the narration of abu Qubayl it is narrated that he said, "I did not give you in marriage until Jibril commanded me to do so."

In the narration of 'Imran ibn al-Haseen and Habib ibn abu Thabit it is narrated that he (the Messenger of Allah) said, "I however have given you in marriage to the best of whom I know."

In the narration of ibn Ghassan it is said, "I have given you in marriage to the best of them."

In the book of ibn Shahin 'Abd Razaq from Mu'ammar from Ayyub from 'Ikramah who has said the following:

The Holy Prophet, *O Allah grant compensation to Muhammad and his family worthy of their services to your cause,* said, "I have given you in marriage to the one most beloved to me in the family."

H 171, Ch. 6, h 6
Al-Rawdah, al-Fada'il:

It is narrated from ibn 'Abbas who in a marfu' manner has narrated from Salman (Rh) who has said the following:

I was standing in front of the Messenger of Allah, *O Allah grant compensation to Muhammad and his family worthy of their services to your cause,* pouring water on his hands when Fatimah, *'Alayha al-Salam,* came weeping. The Holy Prophet placed his hand over her head and asked, "What has made you to weep, may Allah not make your eyes weep, O Huwriah?" She said, "I passed by a group of women of al-Quraysh who all had their make-ups. When they looked at me they then began speaking about me and my cousin maliciously." He (the Messenger of Allah) then asked, "What did you hear from them?" She replied, "They said that Muhammad needs solace for his giving his daughter in marriage to the extremely poor man of al-Quraysh."

He (the Messenger of Allah), *O Allah grant compensation to Muhammad and his family worthy of their services to your cause,* then said, "O my dearest daughter, I did not give you in marriage. It was Allah who gave you in marriage to Ali, *'Alayhi al-Salam,* so He was the one who initiated.

"It is because so and so and so proposed marriage at that time I left your affairs in the hands of Allah, most High, and held back from the people. In such conditions, one day after the morning *Salat* (prayer) on a Friday when I heard movements of the angels and there was my beloved one Jibril along with seventy thousand rows of angels all wearing crowns, earrings, and bracelets. I asked, "What are all these cracklings from the sky O my brother Jibril?"

He replied, "O Muhammad, Allah, most Majestic, most Glorious, examined the earth to find out something. From the earth Allah then chose Ali from men and Fatimah, *'Alayha al-Salam,* from among the women then He gave Fatimah, *'Alayha al-Salam,* in marriage to Ali, *'Alayhi al-Salam.*"

She then raised her head and smiled after weeping and said, "I accept what is accepted by Allah and His Messenger."

The Messenger of Allah, *O Allah grant compensation to Muhammad and his family worthy of their services to your cause,* said, "Would you like it, O Fatimah, if I inform you more of such facts of your interest?" She replied, "Yes, please do so." He (the Messenger of Allah) said, "No one is more honorable than the four of us who will arrive before Allah while riding, my brother Salih on his camel, my uncle Hamzah on my camel al-Ghadba', I on Buraq, your husband on a camel of light of the camels of the garden (paradise)." She said, "Please explain for me out of what substance the camels are made?" He (the Messenger of Allah) replied, "The camel is made out of the light of Allah, most Majestic, most Glorious, with its both sides decorated with special kind of silk called Dibaj, of a yellow color, of a red head, of black eye balls, his legs are made of gold, his belly is made of emerald and on his back there is a dome of white pearls which is transparent and it is created from the forgiveness of Allah, most Majestic, most Glorious. That camel of the camels of Allah has seventy thousand corners and between each two corners there seventy thousand angels will do *Tasbih* (Allah is free of all defects) of Allah, most Majestic, most Glorious, in various kinds of *Tasbih* (Allah is free of all defects). By each group of angels that he will pass they will asked, 'Who is this servant of Allah, how honorable is he in the sight of Allah, most Majestic, most Glorious. It seems he is a Messenger Prophet, or a close angel, or is the carrier of the Throne or the Chair.' An announcer then will announce from inside the Throne and say, 'O people, take notice that he is not a messenger or a close angel. This is Ali ibn abu Talib, *'Alayhima al-Salam.'* The people then group after group express regret saying *'istirja'* (to Allah we belong and to Him we all return), they told us about him but we did not accept, they advised us about him but we did not acknowledge. Those who love him, they have grabbed the strong ring and in this way they find salvation in the next life.'

"O Fatimah, *'Alayha al-Salam,* would you like me to inform you of more of such informations to increase your interest in Ali?" She said, "Yes, O dear father please do so."

He (the Messenger of Allah), *'Alayhi al-Salam* said, "Ali in the sight of Allah is more honorable than Harun because Harum made Musa angry but Ali has never made me angry. I swear by the one who has sent your father in all truth as the Prophet I never have become angry with him and whenever I look at his face my anger vanishes.

"O Fatimah, *'Alayha al-Salam,* would you like me to increase your interest in Ali, *'Alayhi al-Salam?*" She replied, "Yes, please do so O the Holy Prophet of Allah."

He (the Messenger of Allah) then said, "Jibril came to me and said, 'O Muhammad convey to Ali, *'Alayhi al-Salam, Salam* (the phrase of offering greeting of peace) from peace (one of the names of Allah).'"

Fatimah, *'Alayha al-Salam,* then stood up and said, "I accept Allah as my Lord, I accept you, O dear, father as the Holy Prophet of Allah and my cousin as my husband and *Waliy* (the guardian with divine authority and knowledge)."

H 172, Ch. 6, h 7
Al-Kafi: [H 8384, Ch. 11, h 1, from al-Kafi]

Ali ibn Ibrahim has narrated from his father from ibn abu 'Umayr from Hisham ibn Salim abu 'Abd Allah, 'Alayhi al-Salam, who has said the following:

"Amir al-Mu'minin, *'Alayhi al-Salam*, would bring firewood, water and sweep the house. Fatimah al-Zahra', *'Alayha al-Salam*, would grind wheat, make dough and bake."

'Amali al-Tusi:

Al-Husayn ibn Ibrahim al-Qazwini has narrated from Muhammad ibn Wahban from Ahmad ibn Ibrahim from al-Hassan ibn Ali, al-Za'farani from al-Barqiy from his father from ibn abu 'Umayr a similar Hadith.

H 173, Ch. 6, h 8
'Amali al-Tusi:

Al-Husayn has narrated from ibn Wahban from Ali ibn Hubaysh from al-ibn Muhammad ibn al-Husayn from his father from Safwan from al-Husayn ibn abu Ghundur from ibn abu Ya'fur from 'Abu 'Abd Allah, 'Alayhi al-Salam who has said the following:

He (the Imam), *'Alayhi al-Salam,* has said that Allah, most High, sent divine revelation to His Messenger to say to Fatimah, *'Alayha al-Salam,* "You must not disobey Ali because if he becomes angry I become angry because of his becoming angry."

H 174, Ch. 6, h 9

In the book of poems ascribed to 'Amir al-Mu'minin, *'Alayhi al-Salam,* during his illness addressing Fatimah, *'Alayha al-Salam,* he has said, as narrated by abu al-'Ala' al-Hassan ibn al-'Attar from al-Hassan al-Muqri from 'Abu 'Abd Allah, al- Hafiz from Ali ibn Ahmad al-Muqri from Zayd ibn Muskan from 'Ubayd Allah ibn Muhammad al-Balwi that he composed these poems when he had fever and he eulogized Fatimah, *'Alayha al-Salam.*

During my living with you O daughter of Ahmad,

I would firmly hide my suffering from you,

However, before the command of Allah our necks remain weak,

There is no show of strength against the command of Allah,

Could fever fight me in your presence and make me complain, before you when there were no men as strong as me?

I insist to bear patience and overpower longings because with patience it become far from men to show weakness,

In this fever there is the sign that it is the harbinger of death of all people and a lead.

H 175, Ch. 6, h 10
Da'wat al-Rawandi:

It is narrated from Suwayd ibn Ghafalh who has said the following:

Ali, *'Alayhi al-Salam* suffered hardships and Fatimah, *'Alayha al-Salam,* went to the Messenger of Allah, *O Allah grant compensation to Muhammad and his family worthy of their services to your cause,* and knocked the door.

He (the Messenger of Allah) said, "I sense the presence of the beloved one at the door. O 'Umm 'Ayman get up and look." She then opened the door for her and she came in. He (the Messenger of Allah), *'Alayhi al-Salam* said, "You have come to us at a time in which you would not come before." Fatimah, *'Alayha al-Salam,* asked, "O Messenger of Allah, what is the food of the angels with our Lord?" He (the Messenger of Allah), replied, "It is *Tahmid,* (all praise belongs to Allah) "She then asked, "What is our food?"

The Messenger of Allah, *O Allah grant compensation to Muhammad and his family worthy of their services to your cause,* replied, "I swear by the one in whose hands is my soul that for a whole month no fire has been lit in the house of *Ale* (family) Muhammad. I like to teach you the five expressions that Jibril, had taught me." She then asked, "What are those expressions O Messenger of Allah?" He (the Messenger of Allah) said, "O Lord of the first and the last generations, O the owner of firm power, O merciful to the destitute, the most merciful of the merciful ones." She then returned. When Ali, *'Alayhi al-Salam* saw her he asked saying, "I pray to Allah to keep my soul and the souls of my parents in service for your cause, what is there outside, O Fatimah, *'Alayha al-Salam?*" She replied, "I went for the world but I have come back with the next life." Ali, *'Alayhi al-Salam* said, "There is goodness before you, there is goodness ahead of you indeed."

H 176, Ch. 6, h 11
Misbah al-Anwar:

It is narrated from Ja'far ibn Muhammad *'Alayhima al-Salam,* who has said the following:

Fatimah, *'Alayha al-Salam,* complained before the Messenger of Allah, *'Alayhi al-Salam* against Ali, *'Alayhi al-Salam* saying, "O Messenger of Allah he leaves nothing from his sustenance without giving them all to the destitute people." He (the Messenger of Allah), said to her, "O Fatimah, *'Alayha al-Salam,* are you making me angry against my brother and cousin? His anger is my anger and my anger is the anger of Allah, most Majestic, most Glorious."

H 177, Ch. 6, h 12
'Amali al-Tusi:

A group has narrated from abu Ghalib al-Razi from his maternal uncle from al-Ash'ariy from 'Abu 'Abd Allah, (Muhammad ibn Khalid al-Barqiy) from Mansur ibn al-'Abbas from 'Isma'il ibn Sahl al-Katib from abu Talib al-Ghanawi from Ali ibn abu Hamzah from abu Basir from 'Abu 'Abd Allah, 'Alayhi al-Salam who has said the following:

Allah made it unlawful for Ali, 'Alayhi al-Salam to marry other women during the lifetime of Fatimah, 'Alayha al-Salam. I (the narrator) then asked, "What was the reason?" He (the Imam) said, "Because she was purified and free from experiencing menses."

H 178, Ch. 6, h 13
Manaqib of ibn Shahr Ashub:

The scholar was asked the following:

"Why is it that Allah, most High, has revealed chapter 76 of al-Quran in which all the bounties of the garden (paradise) is mentioned except *al-Hawra' al-'in*?"

He (the Imam), 'Alayhi al-Salam said, "It is because of the greatness of the honor of Fatimah, 'Alayha al-Salam."

This is about the meaning of the words of Allah, the most Majestic, the most Glorious:

". . . souls are reunited with their bodies" (81:7)

Sufyan al-Thawri has narrated from 'A'mash from abu Salih who has said that every believing person on the Day of Judgment after crossing the bridge will join four women of the women of the world and seventy thousand *al-Hawra' al-'in* of the *al-Hawra' al-'in* of the garden (paradise) except Ali, 'Alayhi al-Salam because he was the husband of al-Batul in the world and he will be her husband in the next life in the garden (paradise). He will not have any other wife other than her in the garden (paradise) of the women of the world; however, he will have seventy thousand *al-Hawra' al-'in* who each will have seventy thousand maidens.

I ('Allamah Majlisi) say that some of the Ahadith of this chapter will be mentioned in the chapter on her funeral and burial conditions.

Chapter 7 - The injustice to which she was subjected, her weeping, sadness and her complaints (During her illness to the time of her martyrdom), her *Ghusl*, (washing of a dead person), burial and the reason for burying her secretly and the condemnation of Allah on those who did injustice to her

H 179, Ch. 7, h 1
Al-Khisal:

    Ibn al-Walid has narrated from al-Saffar from ibn Ma'ruf from Muhammad ibn Suhayl al-Bahrani in a marfu' *manner from 'Abu 'Abd Allah, 'Alayhi al-Salam who has said the following:*

The people who wept more than all others are five:

They are Adam, *'Alayhi al-Salam,* Ya'qub, Yusuf, Fatimah, *'Alayha al-Salam,* daughter of Muhammad and Ali ibn al-Husayn, *'Alayhima al-Salam.*

Adam, *'Alayhi al-Salam,* wept because of the garden (paradise). He wept so much that it made his both cheeks look like a valley. Ya'qub wept for Yusuf so much that he lost his eyesight and it was said to him, "They said, 'You are always remembering Joseph. By Allah, it will either make you sick or you will die.'" (12:85)

Yusuf wept for Ya'qub. His weeping had disturbed other prisoners, and they told him to weep only during the day and reaming quiet during the night or weep during the night then remain quiet during the day. He then settled it for one of them.

Fatimah, *'Alayha al-Salam,* wept for the Messenger of Allah, *O Allah grant compensation to Muhammad and his family worthy of their services to your cause.* She wept so much that it had disturbed the inhabitants of al-Madinah and they said to her that her excessive weeping has disturbed them. She then would go out to the graves of the martyrs and weep to find relief, then return home.

Ali ibn al-Husayn, wept for twenty or forty years. Whenever food or drink was brought before him he would weep. His weeping was so much that one of his servants said to him, "O child of the Messenger of Allah, I am afraid for your life. It is because you weep so much." He (the Imam) replied, "I complain of my sorrow and grief only to Allah. 'I know about Allah what you do not know.' (12:86) Whenever, I remember the fall of the children of Fatimah, *'Alayha al-Salam,* weeping impulses and tears strangulates me."

Al-'Amali:

Al-Husayn ibn Ahmad ibn Idris has narrated from his father from ibn 'Isa from ibn Ma'ruf a similar Hadith.

H 179, Ch. 7, h 2
'Amali al-Tusi:

Al-Mufid has narrated from al-Saduq from his father from Ahmad ibn Idris from Muhammad ibn 'Abd al-Jabbar from ibn abu 'Umayr from Aban ibn 'Uthman from Aban ibn Taghlib from 'Ikramah from 'Abd Allah ibn 'Abbas who has said the following:

At the time when the Messenger of Allah, *O Allah grant compensation to Muhammad and his family worthy of their services to your cause,* was about to pass away he wept so much that his tears soaked his beard. He was asked about the reason for his weeping. He said, "I weep because of what the evil ones of my nation will do to my descendants after me. It is as if I see my daughter Fatimah, *'Alayha al-Salam,* is subjected to injustice after me and she laments saying, "Oh father!" No one from my nation (followers) helps her." Fatimah, *'Alayha al-Salam,* heard his words and she wept."

The Messenger of Allah, *O Allah grant compensation to Muhammad and his family worthy of their services to your cause,* said, "My dearest daughter please do not weep." She said, "I do not weep because of what (kinds of injustice) they will do to me. I weep because I will miss you." He (the Messenger of Allah) then said to her, "O daughter of Muhammad, I can give you the glad news of your joining me very soon as the first one from my family."

H 180, Ch. 7, h 3
Qasas al-'Anbiya':

Al-Saduq has narrated from al-Sinani from al-Asadi from al-Barmaki from Ja'far ibn Sulayman from 'Abd Allah ibn Yahya' from al-'A'mash from 'Abayah from ibn 'Abbas who has said the following:

During the illness of the Messenger of Allah, *'Alayhi al-Salam* from which he passed away Fatimah, *'Alayha al-Salam,* came to see him. The Messenger of Allah, *O Allah grant compensation to Muhammad and his family worthy of their services to your cause,* said, "I am informed of my death very soon." Fatimah, *'Alayha al-Salam,* then wept. He (the Messenger of Allah) said, "Do not weep because you will not live after me more than seventy-two and a half days after my death. You will join me and you will not join me before receiving gifts of the fruits of the garden (paradise)." Fatimah, *'Alayha al-Salam,* then laughed.

H 181, Ch. 7, h 4
Al-Khara'ij:

'Abu 'Abd Allah, *'Alayhi al-Salam* has said that Fatimah, *'Alayha al-Salam,* lived only seventy-five days after the death of the Holy Prophet, *'Alayhi al-Salam.* She suffered from extreme sadness and grief because of the death of her father. Jibril would come to give her solace, inform her about her father and of his place in the garden (paradise) and would inform her about what will happen to her descendants and Ali, *'Alayhi al-Salam* would write down those informations.

H 181, Ch. 7, h 5
Manaqib of ibn Shahr Ashub:

Once 'Umm Salamah visited Fatimah, *'Alayha al-Salam,* and asked how was your last night, O daughter of the Messenger of Allah?" She replied, "I passed it in the condition of being aggravated and distressed, because of the loss of the Holy Prophet and the wrong doing against the executor of his will. By Allah his rights are violated. One wakes in the morning and finds out that his right of leadership with divine authority is usurped in disregard of the rules sanctioned by Allah through divine revelation, as well as being established by the Holy Prophet from the interpretations of divine revelation. However, due to malevolent intentions formed because of Badr, and 'Uhud on which the hearts of the hypocrites had settled, as well as the emergence of the condition favorable to the opportunists, when the issue (of successor-ship) was targeted, its consequence in the form of shooting flames from an imaginative basis of illusion, and fantasized discord, descended on us, as a result, the chord, the string of the bow of faith broke, awfully, at its center, despite the fact that Allah has promised to protect the mission and suffice the believing people, they reserved their success in the form of the worldly deception after their misuse of being supported by the one who eradicated their ancestors in the stressful condition and confusing environments."

I ('Allamah Majlisi) say the above narration was found with printing mistakes and distortions but we did not find it in other places being edited. I then have quoted it as is.

H 182, Ch. 7, h 6
From certain books of Manaqib:

It is narrated from Sa'd ibn 'Abd Allah al-Hamadani from Ahmad ibn Musa ibn Mardwayh from Ja'far ibn Muhammad ibn Marwan from his father from Sa'id ibn Muhammad al-Jurmi from 'Amr ibn Thabit from his father from Habbah from Ali, 'Alayhi al-Salam, who has said the following:

I (the narrator) washed the body of the Messenger of Allah, *O Allah grant compensation to Muhammad and his family worthy of their services to your cause,* in his shirt. Fatimah, *'Alayha al-Salam,* would ask me to show her his shirt. Upon smelling the shirt she would become unconscious. I noticed it and I then hid the shirt from her.

H 183, Ch. 7, h 7
Man la' yahduruhu al-Faqih:

It is narrated that when the Holy Prophet, *'Alayhi al-Salam* passed away Bilal stopped saying *'Adhan* saying, "I will not say *'Adhan* for anyone after the Messenger of Allah, *O Allah grant compensation to Muhammad and his family worthy of their services to your cause."* One day Fatimah, *'Alayha al-Salam,* said, "I like to hear the *'Adhan* from the one who would say it for my father, *'Alayhi al-Salam."* This reached Bilal and he began to say *'Adhan* (call for *Salat* (prayer)). He said *Takbir* (Allah is great beyond description). *Takbir* (Allah is great beyond description). It reminded Fatimah, *'Alayha al-Salam,* of the days when her father was living. She could not control her weeping and when he said "I testify that Muhammad is His servant and Messenger." Fatimah, *'Alayha al-Salam,* sobbed severely and fell on her face unconscious.

People then said to Bilal, "O Bilal, you must stop. The daughter of the Messenger of Allah has just died." They thought that she has died. He stopped saying *'Adhan* before completing but Fatimah, *'Alayha al-Salam,* regained consciousness and asked him to complete the *'Adhan* but he refused saying, "O leader of all women, I fear for your strong feelings when you hear my voice saying *'Adhan.* She then excused him.

H 184, Ch. 7, h 8
Ma'ani al-Akhbar:

Narrated to us Ahmad ibn al-Hassan al-Qattan saying that narrated to us 'Abd al-Rahman ibn Muhammad al-Husayni who has said that narrated to us abu al-Tabib Muhammad ibn al-Husayn ibn Humayd al-Lakhmi who has said that narrated to us abu 'Abd Allah Muhammad ibn Zakariya who has said that narrated to us Muhammad ibn 'Abd al-Rahman al-Muhallabi who has said that narrated to us 'Abd Allah ibn Muhammad ibn Sulayman from his father from 'Abd Allah ibn al-Hassan from His mother Fatimah, daughter of al-Husayn, who has said the following:

She has said that when the illness of Fatimah, *'Alayha al-Salam,* the daughter of the Messenger of Allah, became serious and it overpowered her, the women of Muhajir (immigrants) and al-Ansar (people of al-Madinah) gather around her and they asked, "How are you feeling this morning, O daughter of the Messenger of Allah?" She replied, "I have entered upon morning, in dislike to your world with anger at your men whom I have discarded after observing their manners and examining their faith and intentions. It is a shame and ugly to find out that the sword has turned blunt and the spear has become weak, and thoughts have become fallacious (addressed to companions of the Holy Prophet). '. . . Vile is what their souls have achieved! They have invoked the wrath of Allah upon themselves and they will live forever in torment.' (5:80) This being their condition, I, therefore, (finding no help) left them on their own (like throwing the camels reign on his neck, free of the control of the rider). I have shunned their being jealous about it (leadership after the Holy Prophet). Therefore it is a dishonor (like a cutoff nose and legs). May the unjust ones be crushed and destroyed.

"Woe on them! Why do they try to displace it (leadership after the Holy Prophet) from the firmly established pillars and foundations (house) of messenger-ship and Prophet–hood and the location of the descent of divine

237

revelation, which is trusted and is the healer of the worldly ills and religion? Is this not the most manifest loss? It certainly is. Their attitudes are hostile toward abu al-Hassan only because of their dislike toward his sword (against the enemies of the religion of Allah), his firm feet, dislike of his status and position, his bullying (the enemy) just for the sake of Allah, most Majestic, most Glorious.

"By Allah, had they left the reign (the post of leadership) where the Messenger of Allah had left, he would shoulder it lovingly then lead them smoothly. Its (the reign of the government) load would not make it to sustain any injuries and its rider would not feel any jolts. He would lead and show them the waterhole, for a pleasant drink, with great openness on both sides of the pathway to the waterhole and would lead them out with their bellies full due to the abundance of the water to a degree of being more than the needed amount unless its use is reduced just to calm down the blaze of hunger. 'Had the people of the towns believed (in Our revelations) and maintained piety, We would have certainly showered on them Our blessings from the sky and the earth...' (7:96) Allah holds them responsible for what they have done.

"You must take notice that if you live longer, time will show you strange and astonishing things. If this remark is astonishing, then what has happened must make you more astonished.

"On what basis they have based what they have done and to what kind of protective ring do they hold for support. They have turned the tail, by Allah, to where the head is and the rear to where the withers is (ridge between shoulder bones of a horse). Despite their failure (to follow the instructions of the Holy Prophet) they think that they have done a good deed, in reality, they have done something evil but do not realize it.

"'...Say, "Only Allah guides to the Truth." Is the one who guides to the Truth a proper guide or one who himself cannot find guidance unless he is guided (by others)? What is wrong with you that you judge (so unjustly)?'" (10:35)

"May Allah grant you long life, you just wait; only inception has taken place, until it gives birth then they will fill the bowl with fresh blood instead of milk and with bitter poison, then the followers of the falsehood will suffer a great loss. The future generations will find what the previous ones have done.

"You then can become certain to prepare yourselves for the emergence of mischief and the rise of the cutting sword, complete chaos and the tyranny which will reduce your windfall profits to very little and your plantations harvested (totally lost).

"How sad I feel for you! Woe is on you. 'Noah replied, "My people, do you think that - if my Lord has sent me a miracle and granted me mercy but your ignorance has obscured them from your sight - we can force you to believe when you do not want to?'" (11:28)"

Then he (the narrator of the previous hadith) narrated to us this hadith: [abu al-Hassan] Ali ibn Muhammad ibn al-Hassan known as ibn Maqbarah al-Qazwini who has said that narrated to us 'Abu 'Abd Allah, Ja'far ibn Muhammad ibn al-Hassan ibn Ja'far ibn al-Hassan ibn al-Hassan ibn 'Amir al-Mu'minin Ali ibn abu Talib, 'Alayhima al-Salam, who has said that narrated to us Muhammad ibn Ali al-Hashimi who has said that narrated to us 'Isa ibn 'Abd Allah ibn Muhammad ibn 'Umar ibn Ali ibn abu Talib, 'Alayhima al-Salam, who has said that narrated to me my father from his father from his grandfather from Ali ibn abu Talib, 'Alayhima al-Salam, who has said the following:

When Fatimah, 'Alayha al-Salam, was about to pass away she called me and asked if I will execute her will. I replied, "Yes, I will do so." She then made her will and said, "When I will die, you must bury me during the night and you must not allow the two men to attend my funeral."

He (the narrator) has said that when her illness became serious the women of Muhajir (immigrants) and al-Ansar (people of al-Madinah) gathered to visit her and ask how she was doing with her illness. They asked, "How are you this morning O daughter of the Messenger of Allah, 'Alayhi al-Salam?" She then said, "I have entered up on this morning in dislike to your world with anger at your men. . ." to the end of the above Hadith.

Al-Saduq (r.h) has said, "I asked Ahmad ibn al-Husayn ibn 'Abd Allah ibn Sa'id al-'Askari about the meaning of this Hadith and he said that the meaning of her words, "in dislike to your world with anger at your men. . ." We will deal with the additional parts of it with certain variations as follows.

H 185, Ch. 7, h 9
Al-Ihtijaj:

Suwayd ibn Ghafalh has said that when Fatimah, *'Alayha al-Salam,* became ill with the illness because of which she died, the women of Muhajir (immigrants) and al-Ansar (people of al-Madinah) gathered to visit her and asked, "How are you doing O daughter of the Messenger of Allah, *'Alayhi al-Salam?*" She praised Allah and said, *"O Allah grant compensation to Muhammad and his family worthy of their services to your cause."* Thereafter she said, "I have entered upon this morning in dislike to your world and with anger at your men. Similar to the dates (the particular fruit) after exposing its stones I found it to have become spoiled, I have discarded them. I have dismissed them after my examining them. It is hideously ugly indeed when the cutting-edge turns dull, seriousness (of religion) turns into gimmicks and it (the cutting edge) acts as though struck against a bolder, the spear snaps, thoughts become fallacious, and the fantasy causes slips. 'You have seen many of them establishing friendship with the unbelievers. Vile is what their souls have achieved! They have invoked the wrath of Allah upon themselves and they will live forever in torment.' (5:80)

"In short, this being their condition, I, therefore, (finding no help) left them on their own (like throwing the camels reign on his neck, free of the control of the rider) and I have allowed them to carry their own burden. I dislike and detest their being jealously envious about it (leadership after the Holy Prophet). Therefore it is a dishonor, like a cutoff nose and legs. May the unjust ones be crushed and destroyed.

"Woe on them! Why do they try to displace it (leadership after the Holy Prophet) from the firmly established pillars and foundations (house) of the messenger-ship and the basis of Prophet–hood and the location of the descent of [the trusted spirit] divine revelation, who is trusted and is the healer of the worldly ills and religion. This indeed is the most manifest loss! It certainly is the great loss. What has made them hostile toward abu al-Hassan is only their dislike toward his sword (against the enemies of the religion of Allah), his daring death, his firm feet, dislike of his status and position, his bullying (the enemy) just for the sake of Allah, most Majestic, most Glorious.

"[By Allah were they to deviate from the well-established guidelines or slip away from accepting the clear authority, he (abu al-Hassan) would bring them back and make them to shoulder their obligations] then lead them smoothly. It (the reign of the government, the nose piece of the reign of the camel) would not make it to sustain any injuries and its [company] rider would not feel [tired], any jolts, [fed up].

He would lead and show them the waterhole, for a clear, pleasant, thirst quenching drink, with great openness on both sides of the pathway to the waterhole and would lead them out, with their bellies full and providing vital instructions both in public and in private. He would not indulge in the worldly gains more than barely quenching his pressing thirst and eating to survive.

They would recognize and distinguish between the restraining ones (from indulgence in the worldly matters. Those interested in it would become manifest as well as the truthful ones and those who speak lies. 'Had the people of the towns believed (in Our revelations) and maintained piety, We would have certainly showered on them Our blessings from the sky and the earth. But they called Our revelations lies, thus Our torment struck them for their evil deeds.' (7:96) Allah will hold them responsible for what they have done.

"You must take notice that if you live longer time will show you strange and astonishing things. If this remark is astonishing, then what has happened must make you more astonished.

"On what basis they have based what they have done and to what kind of protective ring do they hold for support and to which generation they have moved for sustenance. [Turning to the unjust for support is indeed an evil alternative.] They have turned the tail, by Allah, to where the head is and the rear to where the withers (ridge between shoulder bones of a horse). Despite their failure (to follow the instructions of the Holy Prophet) they think that they have done a good deed, in reality, they have done something evil and corrupt but do not realize it. Woe is on them.

"'...Say, "Only Allah guides to the Truth." Is the one who guides to the Truth a proper guide or one who himself cannot find guidance unless he is guided (by others)? What is wrong with you that you judge (so unjustly)?' (10:35)

"May Allah grant you long life, you just wait; only inception has taken place, until it gives birth then they will fill the bowl with the fresh blood instead of milk and with bitter poison, then the followers of the falsehood will suffer a great loss. The later generations will face the (awful) consequences deeds of which the previous ones had done.

"You then can become certain to prepare yourselves for the emergence of mischief and the rise of the cutting sword, complete chaos and the tyranny which will reduce your windfall profits to very little and your plantations harvested (totally lost).

"Woe is on you. 'Noah replied, "My people, do you think that - if my Lord has sent me a miracle and granted me mercy but your ignorance has obscured them from your sight - we can force you to believe when you do not want to?'" (11:28)

"And where will you live. Your hearts have turned blind."

Suwayd ibn Ghafalah has said that the women then repeated the words of Fatimah, 'Alayha al-Salam, before their men. A group of people from Muhajir (immigrants) and al-Ansar (people of al-Madinah) then came to Fatimah, 'Alayha al-Salam, requesting for forgiveness and to say that had abu al-Hassan had brought it to their attention before their pledging allegiance they would not turn to other instead of him (abu al-Hassan Ali).

Fatimah, 'Alayha al-Salam, then said, "You can keep it to yourselves and away from me. There is no justification, for making yourselves helpless and there is no task left after your shortcomings."

H 186, Ch. 7, h 10
'Amali al-Tusi:

Al-Haffar has narrated from 'Isma'il ibn Ali Di'bali from Ahmad ibn Ali al-Khazzaz from abu Sahl al-Daqaq from 'Abd al-Rzzaq and Di'bali has said that narrated to us Ishaq ibn Ibrahim al-Dayri from 'Abd al-Razzaq from Mu'ammar from al-Zuhri from 'Ubayd Allah ibn 'Abd Allah ibn 'Utbah ibn Mas'ud from ibn 'Abbas who has said the following:

A group of women of Muhajir (immigrants) and al-Ansar (people of al-Madinah) visited Fatimah, 'Alayha al-Salam, daughter of the Messenger of

Allah, during her illness. They offered her *Salam* (the phrase of offering greeting of peace) and asked her, "How are you doing this morning, O daughter of the Messenger of Allah, *O Allah grant compensation to Muhammad and his family worthy of their services to your cause?*"

Fatimah, *'Alayha al-Salam*, replied, "I have entered upon this morning in dislike to your world with anger at your men. (Similar to the dates (the fruit) after exposing its stones found to have been spoiled), I have discarded them. I reject them after my examining them. Hideously ugly is indeed [weakness of thoughts and fallaciousness of words] when the cutting-edge turns dull, seriousness turns into gimmicks and it acts like striking against a bolder, the spear snaps, thoughts become fallacious, and the phantasy causes slips. "You have seen many of them establishing friendship with the unbelievers. "Evil is what their souls have achieved! They have invoked the wrath of Allah upon themselves and they will live forever in torment." (5:80)

In short, this being their condition, I, (by Allah) therefore, (finding no help) left them on their own (like throwing the camels reign on his neck, free of the control of the rider) and I have allowed them to carry their own burden. I dislike and detest their being jealously envious about it (leadership after the Holy Prophet). Therefore it is a dishonor (like a cutoff nose and legs). May the unjust ones be crushed and destroyed.

Woe on them! Why have they displaced it (leadership after the Holy Prophet) from (abu al-Hassan) the firmly established pillars and foundations (house) of the messenger-ship and the basis of prophet–hood and the location of the descent of [the trusted spirit] divine revelation, who is trusted and is the most intelligent one in dealing with the worldly and religious matters. This indeed is the most manifest loss? It certainly is the great loss. What has made them hostile toward abu al-Hassan is only their dislike toward his sword (against the enemies of the religion of Allah), his daring death, his firm feet in the battle field, dislike of his status and position, his bullying (the enemy) just for the sake of Allah, most Majestic, most Glorious.

[By Allah were they to deviate from the well-established guide lines or slip away from accepting the clear authority, he (abu al-Hassan) would bring them back and make them to shoulder their obligations]

By Allah, had they left the reign (the post of leadership) where the Messenger of Allah had left he would shoulder it lovingly then lead them smoothly. It (the reign of the government, the nose piece of the reign of the camel) would not make it to sustain any injuries and its [company] rider would not feel [tired], any jolts, [fed up]. He would lead and show them the water hole, for a clear, pleasant, thirst quenching drink, with great openness on both sides of the path way to the water hole and would lead them out, [providing vital instructions both in public and in private. He would not indulge in the worldly gains more than barely quenching his pressing thirst and eating to survive. The restraining (from indulgence the worldly matters and those interested in it) one and the ones interested would become manifest as well the truthful ones and those who speak lies] with their bellies full due to the abundance of the water to a degree of being more than the needed amount unless its use is reduced just to calm down the blaze of hunger. "Had the people of the towns believed (in Our revelations) and maintained piety, We would have certainly showered on them Our blessings from the sky and the earth [But they called Our revelations lies, thus Our torment struck them for their evil deeds. (7:96)." (7:96) Allah will hold them responsible for what they have done.

You must take notice that if you live longer time will show you strange and astonishing things. If this remark is astonishing then what has happened must make you more astonished.

On what basis they have based what they have done and to what kind of protective ring they hold for support and to which generation they have moved one for sustenance. [Turning to the unjust for support is indeed an evil alternative.]They have turned the tail, by Allah, to where the head is and the rear to where the withers (the shoulder, the chief of a tribe), Despite their failure (to follow the instructions of the Holy Prophet) they think that they have done a good deed, in reality, they have done something evil and corrupt but do not realize it. Woe is on them.

"Say, 'Only Allah guides to the Truth.' Is the one who guides to the Truth a proper guide or one who himself cannot find guidance unless he is guided (by others)? What is wrong with you that you judge (so unjustly)?" (10:35)

May Allah grant you long life, you just wait; only the inception has taken place, until it gives birth then they will fill the bowl with fresh blood instead of milk and with bitter poison, then the followers of the falsehood will suffer a great loss. The posterior (later generations) ones will find what the previous ones have done.

You then can become certain to prepare your selves for the emergence of mischief and the rise of the cutting sword, complete chaos and tyranny which will reduce your wind fall profits to very little and your plantations harvested.

Woe is on you. "Noah replied, 'My people, do you think that -if my Lord has sent me a miracle and granted me mercy but your ignorance has obscured them from your sight - we can force you to believe when you do not want to?" (11:28)

Suwayd ibn Ghafalah has said that the women then repeated the words of Fatimah, 'Alayha al-Salam, before their men. A group of people from Muhajir (immigrants) and al-Ansar (people of al-Madinah) then came to Fatimah, 'Alayha al-Salam, requesting for forgiveness and to say that had abu al-Hassan had brought it to their attention before their doing pledge allegiance they would not turn to other instead of him (abu al-Hassan Ali).

Fatimah, 'Alayha al-Salam, then said, "You can keep it to yourselves and away from me. There is no justification, for making yourselves helpless and there is no task left after your shortcomings."

H 187, Ch. 7, h 11
Kitab Ibn Faddal 'Imam (leader) al-Imamah of al-Tabari:

It is narrated from Muhammad ibn Harun ibn Musa al-Tal'akbari from his father from Muhammad ibn Hammam from Ahmad al-Barqiy from Ahmad ibn Muhammad ibn 'Isa from 'Abd al-Rahman ibn abu Najran from ibn Sinan from ibn Muskan from abu Basir from 'Abu 'Abd Allah, 'Alayhi al-Salam who has said the following:

Fatimah, 'Alayha al-Salam, died on a Tuesday, the third of the month of Jamdi al-akhir in the year eleven (A.H) The cause of her death was the injuries caused to her by Mawla of 'Umar called Qunfudh who struck her with the bottom part of the sword by the command of 'Umar. It caused miscarriage of her child, Mohsin and she then fell seriously ill. She then did not allow any one of those who had troubled her to visit her.

Two men of the companions of the Holy Prophet had asked 'Amir al-Mu'minin, Ali, to intercede on their behalf before her to allow them to visit her. 'Amir al-Mu'minin, *'Alayhi al-Salam* then asked her and when they visited they asked, "How are you doing O daughter the Messenger of Allah?" She said, "I am good and I am thankful to Allah." She then asked the two of them, "Had you heard the Messenger of Allah, say, 'Fatimah, is a part of myself, whoever troubles her has troubled me and whoever troubles me has troubled Allah?" They both replied, "Yes, we have heard it from him, (the Messenger of Allah)." She then said, "Both of you, by Allah, have troubled me." He (the narrator) has said that they both left her place and she was angry with them both.

Muhammad ibn Hammam has said that she died on the twentieth of the month of Jamadi al-Awwal and on the day of her death she was eighteen years old. She died eighty five days after the death of her father. 'Amir al-Mu'minin, *'Alayhi al-Salam* prepared her for funeral and no one except al-Hassan and al-Husayn, *'Alayhim al-Salam*, Zaynab, 'Umm Kulthum and Fizzah, and her housemaid, 'Asma' daughter of 'Umays were present. She was taken to al-Baqi' during the night and along with him were al-Hassan and al-Husayn, *'Alayhima al-Salam*. He performed the *Salat* (prayer) for funeral for her and no one was told about it and no one attended her funeral and no one performed the funeral *Salat* (prayer) for her other than the people just mentioned. Fatimah, *'Alayha al-Salam*, was buried in *al-Rawdah* and the marks of her grave were obscured.

In the next morning forty new graves were found. When the Muslims learned about her death they gathered in al-Baqi' cemetery where they found forty new graves and it became difficult for them to find out which one was the grave of Fatimah, *'Alayha al-Salam*. People crowded and blamed each other saying that your Prophet had left no more than one daughter among you. She dies, is buried and you did not attend her funeral or perform *Salat* (prayer) for funeral and you do not know where her grave is.

Their authorities told them to call the Muslim women to exhume these new graves to find her out and then we perform funeral *Salat* (prayer). This reached 'Amir al-Mu'minin, *'Alayhi al-Salam*. He came out angry with his eyes turned red in anger and his veins swelled wearing his yellow gown which he would wear in critical conditions, leaning on his sword Dhulfaqar. He arrived in al-Baqi' and it was a warning for the people. They said, "This is Ali ibn abu Talib coming as you see swearing that if even one stone is displaced from these graves he will place the sword at the end of the last one."

'Umar with his company met him and asked, "What has happened to you O abu al-Hassan? By Allah we will exhume her grave to perform funeral *Salat* (prayer)." Ali, *'Alayhi al-Salam* then grabbed him by his collar, shook him and then struck him against the ground and said, "O son of the black. I gave up my rights for fear that people may turn to apostasy. About the grave of Fatimah, *'Alayha al-Salam,* however, keep in mind, and I swear by the one in whose hands is the soul of Ali, that if you or your company think to do something, I will make the ground drenched with your blood. If you wish then oppose me O 'Umar!"

Abu Bakr then came forward and said, "O abu al-Hassan, I swear you by the rights of the Messenger of Allah and by the rights of the one on the Throne to allow him to leave. We will not do anything that you may dislike."

He (the narrator) has said that he let him go and people dispersed and they did not repeat such demand.

H 188, Ch. 7, h 12
'Amali al-Tusi:

Ibn Hamawayh has narrated from abu al-Husayn from abu Khalifah from al-'Abbas ibn al-Fadl from Muhammad ibn abu Raja' from Ibrahim from Sa'd from abu Ishaq from 'Abd Allah ibn Ali ibn abu Rafi' from his father from Salmah wife of abu Rafi' who has said the following:

Fatimah, *'Alayha al-Salam,* became ill, then on the day when she died she told me to ready some water for her. I then poured water and she took a shower as best as she would do. Then she asked me to bring her new clothes, which she then wore then came to her room. She then asked me to spread the floor covering in the middle of the room. She then lied down facing *al-Qiblah* (al-

Ka'bah) placing her hand under her cheek and said, "My soul is about to be taken away. You must not uncover me because I have already taken a bath."

She (the narrator) has said that she then died and when Ali, *'Alayhi al-Salam* came I informed him. He said, "You must not uncover her. He raised Fatimah, *'Alayha al-Salam* to wash her."

H 189, Ch. 7, h 13
'Amali of al-Saduq:

Al-Daqaq has narrated from al-Asadi from al-Nakha'i from al-Nawfali from ibn al-Bata'ini from his father from ibn Jubayr from ibn 'Abbas in a lengthy narration which we have recorded in the section on the Ahadith of the Holy Prophet about the injustice committed against *Ahl al-Bayt, 'Alayhim al-Salam.*

The Holy Prophet, *'Alayhi al-Salam* has said, "My daughter Fatimah, *'Alayha al-Salam,* is the leader of the women of the worlds, of the past and future generations. She is a part of myself, the light of my eyes, the fruit of my heart and she is my spirit that exists between my sides. She is *al-Hawra'* human being. Whenever she stands up in her place of *Salat* (prayer) before her Lord her light shines for the angels of the sky just as the stars shine to the people of the earth. Allah, most Majestic, most Glorious, then says to His angels, "O my angels, look to my female servant Fatimah, *'Alayha al-Salam,* the leader of my female servants standing before me with her body muscles shaking for having realized my greatness. She has to worship me with her heart present before me. I assign you as witness that I have given protection to her and her (*Shi'a,* followers of *Ahl al-Bayt*) against the fire."

The Holy Prophet, *'Alayhi al-Salam* then said, "When I see her I am then reminded of the (injustice) that will be done to her after I will die. It is as if I see her coming home humiliated, her dignity violated, her rights usurped, her share of inheritance is denied, her unborn child is miscarried (because of injuries) and she calls, 'O Muhammad!' But no one answers her, she pleads for help but no one comes to her aid, she remains grief stricken and weeping. She is reminded of the cutting off of divine revelation from her home suddenly, then she is reminded of her separation from me. She feels frightened at night because of missing to hear my voice that she would hear during the night when

I would say my *Tahajjud* (*Salat* (prayer of eleven Rak'at) during the last part of the night) and recite al-Quran. Then she finds herself humiliated after being glorified in her father's lifetime.

"At such time Allah, most Majestic, most Glorious, provides her solace through the angels who calls her as Maryam (Mary) daughter 'Imran was called, and says, 'O Fatimah, *'Alayha al-Salam,* "Behold," [the angels told Mary], "Allah has chosen you, purified you, and given you distinction over all women. (3:42) Mary, you should pray devotedly to your Lord, prostrate yourself before Him and bow down with those who bow down before Him." (3:43)' She then falls ill with pains and Allah, most Majestic, most Glorious, sends Maryam (Mary) for her to comfort her in her illness and at such time she says, 'O Lord, I am depressed in life and I have become fed up with people of the world, please join me with my father.' Allah, most Majestic, most Glorious, then joins her with me and thus she is the first to join me from my *Ahl al-Bayt* (family). She comes to me sad, depressed, and sorrowful with her rights usurped, and herself murdered.

"I then say, 'O Lord, please condemn those who have done injustice to her and punish those who have usurped her rights and humiliate those who have humiliated her and throw in the fire those who have crushed her sides until she lost her miscarried child and the angels will say, "Amin!"'"

H 190, Ch. 7, h 14
'Amali of al-Saduq:

Ibn al-Mutawakkal has narrated from Muhammad al-'Attar from ibn abu al-Khattab from Hammad ibn 'Isa from Al-Sadiq, 'Alayhi al-Salam from his father who has said the following:

Jabir ibn 'Abd Allah has said that he heard the Messenger of Allah, *O Allah grant compensation to Muhammad and his family worthy of their services to your cause,* say to Ali ibn abu Talib, *'Alayhima al-Salam,* just three days before his death, "May Allah grant you peace, O father of two sweet young basil plants, (my grandsons). I recommend you to take good care of the delight for my eyes in the world; very soon your two corners will be no more. Allah is my successor about you."

When the Messenger of Allah, *'Alayhi al-Salam* died Ali, *'Alayhi al-Salam* said, "He was one of my corners (stones) about which the Messenger of Allah, *'Alayhi al-Salam* had spoken." When Fatimah, *'Alayha al-Salam,* died, Ali, *'Alayhi al-Salam* said, "This was my second corner about which the Messenger of Allah had spoken."

Ma'ani al-Akhbar:

My father has narrated from Sa'd from ibn 'Isa from Muhammad ibn Yunus from Hammad a similar Hadith.

H 191, Ch. 7, h 15

I ('Allamah Majlisi) say that I have found in certain books a narration about the death of Fatimah, *'Alayha al-Salam,* and I like to mention it here, even though I have not taken it from dependable sources:

Warqah ibn 'Abd Allah al-Yazdi has said, "I travelled for al-Hajj of Bayt Allah al-Haram seeking rewards from Allah Lord of the worlds. During Tawaf I saw a young woman of brownish complexion, of a charming face, sweet talking, who pleaded in her eloquent words, "O Lord, of al-Ka'bah al-Haram and honorable protectors, Lord of Zamzam and the station and the great reminders (of Allah), Lord of Muhammad the best of all people, I plead before you to raise me with my masters, the purified ones and their sons, the blessed ones who possess marks of nobility. O group of pilgrims for al-Hajj and al-'Umrah take notice that my masters are the best of the chosen ones, the purest of virtuous ones. They are the ones whose values are above all values, who are spoken of in other cities as dressed in the gown of pride."

Waraqah ibn 'Abd Allah has said that he asked her, "O young lady, I think you must be of the friend of *Ahl al-Bayt* (family of the Holy Prophet). Am I correct?" She replied, "Yes, that is correct." I (the narrator) then asked, "Who are you. Are you one of their Mawali?" She replied, "I am Fizzah, the housemaid of Fatimah, *'Alayha al-Salam,* daughter of Muhammad al-Mustafa' (the purified one), *O Allah grant compensation to her, her father, Muhammad and her husband and sons.*"

I then said "You are most whole-heartedly welcome. I had a great yearning to hear your speech and the manners you speak, so I request you to give me an hour time to answer my question that I will ask you. So when you finish Tawaf please wait for me in the food market until I come and Allah will grant you reward for it." We then parted each other.

When I completed my Tawaf and I wanted to return to my lodging I then made my path through the food market and I found her sitting a little away from the people. I then went to her and I then sat a little away from the people and I presented to her a gift. I did not think it was Sadaqah (charity). I then said, "O Fizzah, please tell me about your Mawlat (owner, guardian) Fatimah, *'Alayha al-Salam*."

Waraqah has said that when she heard my words her eyes became flooded with tears then she sobbed and wailed and said, "O Waraqah ibn 'Abd Allah, you just have disconcerted my calmed down sorrow and grief and the pain that existed in my heart. Now listen to what I had observed from Fatimah, *'Alayha al-Salam.*

"Take notice that when the Messenger of Allah, *'Alayhi al-Salam* passed away, the small as well as the grownup people suffered shock, weeping for him became a great deal, but very little solace; the loss was greater for the near ones, companions, well-wishers and friends, the relatives and non-relatives, everyone you would meet was weeping, or wailing. There was no one of the people of the earth, the companions, relatives, and friends suffering more intense grief, weeping and sobbing than my Mawlat, Fatimah, *'Alayha al-Salam.* Her sadness and grief would renew, and increase her weeping. For seven days her wailing did not calm down and her compassionate feelings did not become quiet. With every new day her weeping would become more intense than the day before. On the eighth day she expressed her grief when her patience snapped. She came out and cried as if from the mouth of the Messenger of Allah, *'Alayhi al-Salam*, she was speaking. Women hurried toward her, children came out and people grumbled weeping and sobbing. People came from all directions; the lamps were extinguished so that no one can see the faces of the women. Women thought as if the Messenger of Allah, *'Alayhi al-Salam*, has risen from the grave. People were freighted and confused because of the difficult condition with which they were faced. She would call and wail for her father, 'O father, O the chosen one, O Muhammad! O abu al-Qasim, O the spring for the widows and orphans. Who is there after you for *al-Qiblah* (al-Ka'bah) and the place of *Salat* (formal prayer) and who is for your grief stricken wailing daughter!'

"She then moved forward but stumbled over the back piece of her garments while unable to see anything because of the tears continuously following until she was close to the grave of her father, Muhammad, *O Allah grant compensation to Muhammad and his family worthy of their services to your cause.* When she looked at the room she also saw the minaret. She then made her steps shorter and continued sobbing and weeping until she fell unconscious. The women then rushed toward her sprinkled water on her chest and forehead until she regained consciousness then she stood up saying, 'My power has diminished, my self-control, has betrayed me, the enemy rejoice seeing my condition and aggravation kills me. O father, I am left in grief all alone disoriented and lonely. My voice has subsided; backing for me is cut off. My life has become unpleasant my environment has become depressing. After you, O dear father I do not find any comforter for my fearfulness, or a helper in my weakness. After you there is no more clear divine revelation as well as the descent of Jibril, and the coming of Michael. After you, O dear father the means have turned backward and the doors are shut before me. After you I dislike the world and for you I breathe with tears, my yearning for you does not diminish as well as my grief and sadness.' She then called, 'O father, O my intelligence!' She then said:

My sorrow for you is new, my heart, by Allah, pour down persistently,

Every day my anxiety increases and my pains do not diminish,

My bitterness has become great and solace has become contrary, so my weeping every time is new,

The heart that joins patience for you or solace indeed is icy cold and daring.

"She then called, 'O dear father, the world has cut off its light with (your passing away) and its shine has diminished; its beauty, and grace was because of you. Its days have become black so its wet and dry copy its darkest night.

'O dear father, I continue living sorrowful for you until I meet you, O dear father my endurance has vanished after my separation from you. O dear father, there is no one for the widows and the destitute and there is no one for the nation (followers) up to the Day of Judgment. After you O dear father every day we live as the suppressed ones, O dear father, people turn away from us; with you we were great among the people. Now we are the suppressed ones. What kind of tears are they that because of separation from you give a chance and what kind of grief is it that after you does not remain continuous, what kind of eyelash is it that after you rest for sleep.

'You were the spring of religion, the light of the Prophets. Why the mountains do not pass flying and the oceans do not dry up and the earth does not quake.

'Your passing away has caused great bitterness and the sorrow has not been of a small degree. Your passing away has brought great tribulations and gross neglect.

'The angels have wept for you, O dear father and the orbits are as if stopped. Your pulpit after you is dreadful, and the place of your *Salat* (formal prayer) is devoid of your whispering to Allah, your grave is happy to hide you, the garden (paradise) is yearning to have you and for your prayers and *Salat* (formal prayer).

'O dear father, how great has become the darkness of the place where you would sit. Alas, we are sorrowful until very soon I will meet you.

'Abu al-Hassan is bereaved, the trusted one and the father of your grandsons, al-Hassan and al-Husayn, *'Alayhima al-Salam,* your brother, your friend, the beloved one to you whom you brought up since his childhood, and chose as your brother when he grew up, the most sweet one among your beloved ones and among your companions of earlier Muhajir (immigrants) and al-Ansar (people of al-Madinah). Bereavement has encompassed us all and weeping has become murderous for us and sorrowfulness has gripped us.'

"She then kept breathing hard and groaned with which her spirit almost left her body. She then said, 'My patience is reduced to very little and solace is moved away from me after my eyes have missed the seal of the Prophets. O eyes you must shed tears a great deal, fie up on you if you did not allow blood to flow instead of tears. O Messenger of Allah, O the choice of Allah, O refuge for the orphans and the weak, mountains have wept for you as well as the wild animals, the birds, the earth as well as the sky. Al-Hajun, the corner, al-Mash'ar and al-Batha' (names of certain holy locations) have all wept for you as well as the place for *Salat* (formal prayer), the classrooms of al-Quran for the public in the morning and in the evening. Al-Islam has wept for you because of its becoming stranger to the people like the other strangers.

'If you see the pulpit on which you would climb, on it darkness has climbed after the light. O Lord, please make my death to come quicker because life has turned a blind eye, O my master.'"

She (the narrator) has said that she then returned to her home but continued weeping and wailing day and night and she could not reduce her stressful breathing.

"The elders of the city of al-Madinah came to Ali, *'Alayhi al-Salam* saying, 'O abu al-Hassan, Fatimah, *'Alayha al-Salam,* weeps day and night because of which no one of us is able to sleep in our beds at night or during the day we live restless on our works for our living. We like to ask you to ask her to weep either in the night or during the day only.'

"Ali, *'Alayhi al-Salam* said, 'I will do so with love and honor.' Ali, *'Alayhi al-Salam* then came to Fatimah, *'Alayha al-Salam,* who was not able to recover from weeping and solace could not help. When she saw him she felt a little comfort. Ali, *'Alayhi al-Salam* then said, 'O daughter the Messenger of Allah, *'Alayhi al-Salam,* the elders of the city of al-Madinah requested me to ask you to weep only in the night or during the day only.'

"She said, 'O abu al-Hassan, the time for my living in their neighborhood is very short and very soon I will disappear from among them. By Allah I cannot remain calm in the nights or during the day until I join my father, the Messenger of Allah, *'Alayhi al-Salam.*' Ali, *'Alayhi al-Salam* then said, 'You can do, O daughter of the Messenger of Allah, as you like.'

"Then he, Ali, prepared a room for her in al-Baqi' cemetery away from the city, called 'the house of grief.' In the morning she with al-Hassan and al-

Husayn, *'Alayhima al-Salam,'* in front of her would leave for al-Baqi' weeping and remained amongst the graves weeping. In the evening 'Amir al-Mu'minin, Ali, *'Alayhi al-Salam* would go to al-Baqi' and lead them back to her home.

"She continued in such condition for twenty-seven days, then she became ill with the illness from which she died. She then lived up to the fortieth day. 'Amir al-Mu'minin, Ali, *'Alayhi al-Salam,* had just performed *al-Zuhr Salat* (formal prayer) then moved to the house when he came face to face with the girls weeping in intense grief. He (the Imam) asked them, 'What is the matter? Why do I see this change in your faces and conditions?' They said, 'O 'Amir al-Mu'minin, please help the daughter of your uncle al-Zahra' and we do not think you will find her alive.'

"'Amir al-Mu'minin, then moved quickly and found her lying on the floor covering which was a *Qibty* gown and saw her get hold of the right or stretch to the left. He then threw aside his gown which was on his shoulders, and his turban from his head, opened his buttons came forward until he held her head in his lap and called, 'O al-Zahra'' but she did not respond. He then called, 'O daughter of Muhammad al-Mustafa' (the purified one).' She did not respond. He then called, 'O daughter of the one who would carry Zakat in his gown for the needy.' She did not respond. He then called, 'O daughter of the one who lead *Salat* (formal prayer) for the angels in the sky twice and twice.' She did not respond. He then said, 'O Fatimah, *'Alayha al-Salam,* speak to me I am your cousin, Ali ibn abu Talib.'

"He (the narrator) has said that she then opened her eyes, at his face, looked at him and wept and he also wept. He asked, 'How do you feel. I am your cousin Ali ibn abu Talib.' She said, 'O son of my uncle, I feel and find myself dying from which there is no escape. I know that after me you will not be able to wait without marriage. If you will marry then please stay one day with her and one day with my children, O abu al-Hassan. Please do not be loud with them to make them feel as two orphans, strange, and broke. Yesterday they lost their grandfather and today they lose their mother. Woe is on the nation (followers) who will murder them and hate them.' She then read the following lines:

It makes me weep if you weep, O the best guide,

Allow the tears to flow because it is the day of separation,

O partner of al-Batul, follow my will about the children;

They are left with their wish, which has not yet come true,

Which makes me weep and you also weep for the orphans but you must not forget the one who is murdered in *al-Taf* (tragedy of Karbala) in al-Iraq,

They are separated (from their mother) they are orphans, and disoriented, by Allah such is the day of separation.

She (the narrator) has said that Ali, *'Alayhi al-Salam,* then asked, "How do you know this, O daughter of the Messenger of Allah, when coming of divine revelation has discontinued from us?"

She replied, "O abu al-Hassan, in this hour I was overcome by sleep and I saw my beloved one, the Messenger of Allah, *'Alayhi al-Salam,* in a palace of white pearls. When he saw me he said, "Come to me, O dearest daughter; I am yearning for you so much." I then said, "My yearning to be with you is more intense." He then said, "This night you will be with me," he is truthful and he keeps his promise when he makes a promise. When you recite Yasin then I will be dead. Wash me but do not uncover me because I am clean and purified. Only people of my family closer and closer relatives should perform *Salat* (formal prayer) for my funeral and those who receive payment from me. Bury me during the night because this is how my beloved one, the Messenger of Allah, has informed me."

Ali, has said that he undertook the task of her funeral matters and washed her in her shirt without having uncovered her. By Allah she was a blessing, clean and purified. He then applied camphor left from that, which was applied to the Messenger of Allah during his funeral tasks. He then shrouded her and when he wanted to tie down the overall sheet he called, "O 'Umm Kulthum, O Sakinah, O Fizzah, O al-Hassan, al-Husayn, come and see your mother for the last time; it is the departing time and the meeting will be in the garden (paradise)."

Al-Hassan and al-Husayn, *'Alayhima al-Salam,* then came forward saying, "How great is the grief and sorrow which do not go away because of the death of our grandfather, Muhammad al-Mustafa' (the purified one) and our mother Fatimah, al-Zahra' *'Alayha al-Salam*. O mother of al-Hassan and al-Husayn, when you meet our grandfather Muhammad, al-Mustafa' (the purified one), convey our *Salam* (the phrase of offering greeting of peace) to him and say to him that we have remained as orphans in the world after him."

'Amir al-Mu'minin has said, "I assign Allah as a witness that she expressed compassion and groaned then extended her hands then held both of them against her chest gently and at such time a caller from the sky called, 'O abu al-Hassan, raise them up from her, they, by Allah have made the angels of the sky weep. The loving is yearning for the beloved one.'

He, Ali has said, I then picked them up from her chest and began to tie down the overall sheet reciting these lines:

Separation from you, O Fatimah, *'Alayha al-Salam,* is a great tragedy and bereaving,

I will weep in sorrow, lament in pain, for the beloved one who has passed away, to the exalted path.

O eyes generously shed tears and help me; my grief is perpetual to weep for my beloved one.

He (the Imam) then raised her in his hands and brought her to the grave of her father calling, "*Salam* (the phrase of offering greeting of peace) is with you O Messenger of Allah, O beloved one to Allah, O selected one by Allah, from me, and also *Salam* (the phrase of offering greeting of peace) with you and blessings to remain continuous to you and before you and from your daughter who has just disembarked in your location. The trust is returned and the security is taken back. O how severe is the sorrow for the Messenger of Allah and then for al-Batul. The land has turned black before my eyes and far away has gone the greenery from me. How great is the sorrow and grief?"

He then turned to *al-Rawdah*, performed *Salat* (formal prayer) for the funeral amongst his family, friends, servants, and a group of Muhajir (immigrants) and al-Ansar (people of al-Madinah). When he buried her in her grave he recited these lines:

I see the illness of the world a great many on me and the one suffering these illnesses is ill until death. Between every two friends there is separation and my living with you is for a very little time. My losing Fatimah, *'Alayha al-Salam,* after the loss of Ahmad is proof that the loved ones cannot live together forever.

H 192, Ch. 7, h 16
Manaqib of ibn Shahr Ashub:

When the Holy Prophet, *O Allah grant compensation to Muhammad and his family worthy of their services to your cause,* passed away Fatimah, *'Alayha al-Salam,* was eighteen years and seven months old. She lived after her father for seventy-two days. It is also said that she lived for seventy-five days also it is said that it was four months.

Al-Qurbani has said that it is said that she lived for forty days and this is the correct viewpoint. She died on a Sunday night on the thirteenth of the month of al-Rabi' al-Akhar in the year eleven (A.H) and her grave is in al-Baqi'.

They have said that she was buried inside her house and they also have said that her grave is between the grave of the Messenger of Allah and his pulpit.

Al-Sam'ani in al-Risalah, abu Nu'aym in al-Hulyah, Ahmad in Fada'il of al-Sahabah, al-Natanzi in al-Khasais, ibn Mardwayh in Fada'il of 'Amir al-Mu'minin, al-Zamakhshari in al-Fa'iq has narrated from Jabir who has said the following:

The Messenger of Allah, *O Allah grant compensation to Muhammad and his family worthy of their services to your cause,* before his death said to Ali, you must take good care of the two sweet smelling flowers. I advise you to take good care of my sweet smelling flower in the world. Very soon your two corner stones will come apart on you.

He (the Imam) has said that when the Messenger of Allah, passed away, Ali, said, "This is one of my corner stones." When Fatimah, *'Alayha al-Salam,* passed away, Ali, said, "This is my second corner stone."

Al-Bukhari, Muslim, al-Hulyah, Musnad of Ahmad ibn Hanbal has narrated from 'A'ishah that the Holy Prophet, called Fatimah, *'Alayha al-*

Salam, during his complaints from his illness from which he died. He whispered to her with something and she began to weep. Then he called her closer, whispered something to her and she laughed. I then asked about it. She said that the Holy Prophet has informed her that he will die very soon and she wept then he informed her that she will be the first one from his family to join him then she laughed.

The book of ibn Shahin:

'Umm Salamah and 'A'ishah have said that when Fatimah, *'Alayha al-Salam,* was asked about her laughing and weeping she replied, "The Holy Prophet informed me that he will die very soon and that after me my children suffer great hardships, thus I wept, then he informed me that I will be the first one from his family to join him and for this reason I laughed."

In the narration of abu Bakr al-Ja'abi, abu Nu'aym al-Fadl ibn Dukayn, al-Sha'bi from Masruq, in al-Sunan from al-Qazwini, al-Ibanah from 'Akbari, Musnad from al-Musuli, Fada'il from Ahmad through the chains of their narrators, from 'Urwah, from Masruq from 'A'ishah who has said the following:

Fatimah, *'Alayha al-Salam,* came walking exactly as the Messenger of Allah walked. The Messenger of Allah, *O Allah grant compensation to Muhammad and his family worthy of their services to your cause,* said welcome to her and made her to sit on his right side then whispered something to her and she began to weep, then he whispered something to her and she laughed. I then asked her about it and Fatimah, *'Alayha al-Salam,* said, "I do not make public the secrets of the Messenger of Allah." When he (the Messenger of Allah) died then I asked her about it and she said, "At first he whispered to me and said that Jibril would present al-Quran to me once every year but this year he has presented al-Quran to me twice. I see nothing other than the fact that my time to leave this world has come and that you are the first one from my family to join me. I am a good precedent for you. For this reason I wept. He then said, "Will you not be happy to be the leader of the women of the believing people?" I then laughed.

It is narrated that Fatimah, *'Alayha al-Salam,* after her father, always tied her head, with a weak body, broken corners, weeping eyes, broken heart, would lose conscientiousness hour after hour and would ask her two children,

"Where is your father who would honor and carry you time after time? Where is your father who was intensely compassionate to you and would not allow you to walk on the ground? I will never see him open this door or carry you on his shoulder as he would always do."

Fatimah, 'Alayha al-Salam, then became ill and remained ill for forty days. Then she called 'Asma' the daughter of 'Umays and Ali, and she made a will to Ali, about three matters, 1, to marry the daughter of her sister, 'Amamah because of her love for her children, 2, to prepare a coffin because she had seen the angels made a picture of it and explained to her about it, 3, and that no one of those who had done injustice to her must be allowed to attend her funeral or perform funeral Salat (formal prayer) for her.

Muslim has mentioned from 'Abd al-Razzaq from Mu'ammar from al-Zuhri from 'Urwah from 'A'ishah and in the narration of al-Layth ibn Sa'd from 'Aqil from ibn Shihab from 'Urwah from 'A'ishah in a lengthy Hadith in which it is mentioned that Fatimah, 'Alayha al-Salam, sent for abu Bakr to ask for her inheritance from the Messenger of Allah, 'Alayhi al-Salam.

In short she kept away from him and did not speak to him until she died and abu Bakr was not given permission to perform Salat (formal prayer) for her funeral.

Al-Waqidi has said that when Fatimah, 'Alayha al-Salam, was about to die she made a will to Ali not to allow abu Bakr and 'Umar to perform Salat (formal prayer) for her funeral and her will was executed.

'Isa ibn Mehran has narrated from Mikhwal ibn Ibrahim from 'Umar ibn Thabit from Ishaq ibn Jubayr from ibn 'Abbas who has said the following:

Fatimah, 'Alayha al-Salam, made a will which said, "If I die abu Bakr and 'Umar must not be informed about it and they must not be allowed to perform funeral Salat (formal prayer) for me." Ali buried her in the night and did not inform the two of them about it.

History of abu Bakr ibn Kamil:

He (the author) has said that 'A'ishah has said that Fatimah, 'Alayha al-Salam, lived for six months after the death of the Messenger of Allah, 'Alayhi al-Salam. When Fatimah, *'Alayha al-Salam,* died Ali buried her in the night and performed funeral *Salat* (formal prayer) for her.

It is narrated in this book from Sufyan ibn 'Uyaynah from al-Hassan ibn Muhammad and 'Abd Allah ibn abu Shaybah from Yahya' ibn Sa'id Al-Qattan from Mu'ammar from al-Zuhri who has said the following:

Fatimah, *'Alayha al-Salam,* was buried in the night.

It is narrated from the narrator of the previous Hadith in this book:

'Amir al-Mu'minin, al-Hassan and al-Husayn, *'Alayhim al-Salam,* buried Fatimah, *'Alayha al-Salam,* in the night and made her grave to remain hidden.

History of al-Tabari:

Fatimah, *'Alayha al-Salam,* was buried in the night and no one attended her funeral except al-'Abbas, Ali, al-Miqdad, and al-Zubayr. In our narration it is said that 'Amir al-Mu'minin, al-Hassan, al-Husayn, *'Alayhim al-Salam,* 'Aqil, Salman (Rh), abu Dharr, al-Miqdad, 'Ammar, and Burayd performed funeral *Salat* (formal prayer) for her. In a narration it is said that al-'Abbas and his son al-Fadl also were present. In another narration it is said that Hudhayfah and ibn Mas'ud were also there.

It is narrated from al-'Asbagh ibn Nabatah that he asked 'Amir al-Mu'minin, about the burial of Fatimah, *'Alayha al-Salam,* in the night. Ali, said that she was angry with a certain people and disliked their presence in her funeral matters. It is unlawful for those who love them to perform *Salat* (formal prayer) for her children.

It is narrated that her grave was leveled with the ground. They have said that around her grave other false graves were made numbering about seven so that her grave can remain unidentified, so they cannot perform funeral *Salat* (formal prayer) on it.

'Abu 'Abd Allah, ibn Battah through their chain of narrators has narrated from 'Umm Salma' wife of abu Rafi' who has said the following:

Fatimah, *'Alayha al-Salam,* suffered the illness because of which she died. I served her as a nurse. One morning she felt a degree of comfort more than before and Ali left for some of his chores. Fatimah, *'Alayha al-Salam,* then asked me to arrange a shower for her. I then helped pour water and she took a shower as best as it can be then she put on her new clothes and told me to spread some floor covering in the middle of the room. She then facing the *al-Qiblah* (al-Ka'bah) lied down and said, "My spirit is about to be taken away from my body. I have just taken a shower so no one must uncover me." She then placed her cheek on her hand and died.

'Asma' the daughter of 'Umays has said that Fatimah, *'Alayha al-Salam,* made a will that said that no one must wash her except I or Ali, *'Alayhi al-Salam.* I then helped Ali, if he was washing her.

The book of al-Biladhuri:

'Amir al-Mu'minin, Ali washed the upper parts and 'Asma' the daughter of 'Umays washed the rest.

Abu al-Hassan al-Khazzaz al-Qumi in al-Ahkam al-Shari'ah has said that 'Abu 'Abd Allah, was asked about washing Fatimah, *'Alayha al-Salam.* He (the Imam) replied, "'Amir al-Mu'minin, Ali washed her because she was a Siddiqah (truthful) who can only be washed by a truthful one.

It is narrated that 'Amir al-Mu'minin, at the time of her burial said, "*Salam* (the phrase of offering greeting of peace) be with you. . ." as it will be mentioned quoting from Al-Kafi.

It is narrated that when he approached the grave with her a hand came out from the grave to receive her and he then turned back.

'Abd al-Rahman al-Hamadani and Hamid al-Tawil have said that he recited these lines while at the edge of the grave:

I remembered the one, who cherished my love,

I passed the night as if I am assigned to return the grief and the concerns of the past,

My losing Fatimah, *'Alayha al-Salam,* after Ahmad,

Is proof that friends do not remain together forever.

A caller then responded:

The youth does not want the beloved one to die,

But there is no other way except death. Death is not avoidable and trial is unavoidable, however, my living after you is very short. If one day of life passes, then the weeping of those who weep is very little.

You will soon disregard speaking of me and forget my love and after me for the beloved a substitute will come into being.

H 193, Ch. 7, h 17
Manaqib of ibn Shahr Ashub:

Abu Ja'far al-Tusi has said that most probably Fatimah, *'Alayha al-Salam,* was buried in her house or in *al-Rawdah* (the area between the grave and the pulpit of the Holy Prophet, *'Alayhi al-Salam*). A proof for this is the words of the Holy Prophet, *'Alayhi al-Salam*: "The area between my grave and my pulpit is a garden of the gardens of the garden (paradise).

In al-Bukhari it is said, "between my house and my pulpit". In al-Muwattah, al-Hulyah, Tirmizi, and Musnad of Ahmad ibn Hanabal it is said, "between my house and my pulpit".

The Holy Prophet, *O Allah grant compensation to Muhammad and his family worthy of their services to your cause,* has said, "My pulpit is on a hill of the hill of the garden (paradise)."

They have said that the limits of *al-Rawdah* are the area between the grave and the pulpit of the Holy Prophet to the pillars that are next to the compound of the Masjid.

Ahmad ibn Muhammad ibn abu Nasr has said that he asked abu al-Hassan about the grave of Fatimah, *'Alayha al-Salam.* He (the Imam) replied, "Fatimah, *'Alayha al-Salam,* was buried inside her house. When the Amawides expanded the Masjid her house became part of the Masjid."

Yazid ibn 'Abd Malik has narrated from his father from his grandfather who has said the following:

"I visited Fatimah, *'Alayha al-Salam*. She initiated *Salam* (the phrase of offering greeting of peace) then she asked what brings you here this morning?" I replied, "The quest for blessing has brought me." Fatimah, *'Alayha al-Salam*, then said, "My father informed me of something and it is this: 'Whoever says *Salam* (the phrase of offering greeting of peace) to him or to me for three days Allah makes the garden (paradise) necessary for him." I (the narrator) then asked, "Is it during his and your lifetime?"

She replied, "Yes, and also after we die."

H 194, Ch. 7, h 18
Kashf al-Ghummah:

Abu Ja'far once opened a box or a basket and took out a document from it and then read it. It was the will of Fatimah, *'Alayha al-Salam,* that said, *Bismillah,* (in the name of Allah, most Beneficent, most Merciful). This is the will of Fatimah, *'Alayha al-Salam,* the daughter of Muhammad, *O Allah grant compensation to Muhammad and his family worthy of their services to your cause.* She has made this will to transfer the ownership of the seven walls (the gardens encompassed by walls) to Ali ibn abu Talib. When he passes away then they will belong to al-Hassan and when he passes away then they will belong to al-Husayn, *'Alayhi al-Salam.*

Witnessed by al-Miqdad ibn al-Aswad

Al-Zubayr ibn al-'Awwam

Documented by

Ali ibn abu Talib, *'Alayhima al-Salam.*

It is narrated from 'Asma' the daughter of 'Umays who has said the following:

Fatimah, *'Alayha al-Salam,* made a will to me that said, "No one must wash her for her funeral except I ('Asma' the daughter of 'Umays) and Ali, *'Alayhi al-Salam.*" Ali and I washed her for her funeral.

It is said that Fatimah, *'Alayha al-Salam,* said to 'Asma' the daughter of 'Umays when she made wudu for *Salat* (formal prayer), bring for me the perfume which I wear and my clothes in which I perform *Salat* (formal prayer)." She then made wudu then placed her head (on the ground for rest) and told me to sit near her head and when it becomes time for *Salat* (formal prayer) wake me up. If I woke up then it will be fine, if not then send for Ali, *'Alayhi al-Salam*. When the time for *Salat* (formal prayer) came I called O daughter of the Messenger of Allah, it is time for *Salat* (formal prayer), but she had passed away.

Ali came and she informed him that the daughter the Messenger of Allah, Fatimah, *'Alayha al-Salam,* has passed away. Ali asked, "When did she pass away?" She replied, "It happened when I sent for you. He (the narrator) has said that he Ali commanded 'Asma' and she washed her for funeral and commanded al-Hassan and al-Husayn, *'Alayhima al-Salam,* to pour water. He buried her in the night and leveled the grave for which he was admonished, and reproached. He Ali said, "This is how she had said in her will."

It is narrated that Fatimah, *'Alayha al-Salam,* lived after her father for forty days and when she was about to die she made a will to 'Asma' that said: "Jibril came to the Holy Prophet, when he was about to pass away, with some camphor from the garden (paradise) and he divided it into three parts, one third for himself, one third for Ali, and one third for me and it was forty dirham (in weight). Fatimah, *'Alayha al-Salam,* said to 'Asma', "Bring for me the remaining of *Hunut* of my father from such and such place and leave it near my head." I ('Asma') then did as she had said to do. She then shrouded herself with her clothes and told me to wait for a while and call her. If she responded then is fine, otherwise, you must take notice that I have moved forward to my father, *'Alayhi al-Salam.* I waited for a while then called her but she did not respond. She called her, "O daughter of Muhammad al-Mustafa' (the purified one), O daughter of the one who was carried by women, O daughter of the best of those who walked on the sand, O daughter of the one who went near to his Lord by a distance of the length of one bow or even closer."

He (the narrator) has said that she did not respond. She then removed the clothes from her face and found out that she had passed away. She fell on her, kissing and said, "O Fatimah, *'Alayha al-Salam,* when you meet your father, the Messenger of Allah please convey to him *Salam* (the phrase of offering greeting of peace) from 'Asma' the daughter of 'Umays." In such time al-

Hassan and al-Husayn, *'Alayhima al-Salam,* came in and asked, "O 'Asma' what has made our mother sleep at this time?"

She then said, "O children of the Messenger of Allah, your mother is not sleeping, she has passed away." Al-Hassan then fell on her, kissing and said, "O dearest mother speak to me, before my soul departs my body."

She has said that al-Husayn, moved forward and began kissing her feet and saying, "O dearest mother I am your al-Husayn, please speak to me before my heart bursts apart and I die."

'Asma' then said to them, "O children of the Messenger of Allah, please go to your father, Ali, to inform him of the death of your mother." They then left and when they arrived near the Masjid they raised their voices weeping. All the companions of the Holy Prophet rushed toward them and asked about what has made them to weep, O children of the Messenger of Allah, may He never make your eyes weep. Perhaps you looked the place of your grandfather and wept because of your love for him. They replied, "No, it is because our mother, Fatimah, *'Alayha al-Salam,* has just died."

He (the narrator) has said that Ali fell on his face saying, "With who will I find solace, O daughter of Muhammad. I would find solace with you and after you with who can I find solace."

He, Ali then said, "In every gathering of two friends, there is separation and those who are without separation are very little in number. My losing Fatimah, *'Alayha al-Salam,* after Ahmad is proof that friends do not remain together."

He, Ali, then said, "O 'Asma' wash, apply *Hunut* (camphor), and shroud Fatimah, *'Alayha al-Salam.*" They then washed, shrouded, applied *Hunut* (camphor), performed funeral *Salat* (formal prayer) and buried Fatimah, *'Alayha al-Salam,* in al-Baqi'. Fatimah, *'Alayha al-Salam,* died after al-'Asr.

Ibn Babwayh (r.h) has said that this narration has also come as it is. The correct narration in my opinion is that she was buried in her house and when the Amawides expanded the Masjid it became part of the Masjid.

I ('Allamah Majlisi) say that apparently according to the popular view that people have narrated and the historians maintain, she was buried in al-Baqi' as mentioned before.

In *a marfu' manner* it is narrated to Salmah mother of banu Rafi' who has said that she was with Fatimah, *'Alayha al-Salam,* the daughter of Muhammad, during her illness from which she passed away. One day Fatimah, *'Alayha al-Salam,* felt better and Ali ibn abu Talib went for certain chores seeing that she was feeling better.

Fatimah, *'Alayha al-Salam,* then asked me saying, "O female servant of Allah, please arrange for a shower for me and pour water." I followed her instructions and she took a shower in the hardest way that I had ever seen then she asked me to bring her new clothes, which I then brought for her and she wore them. She then asked me to make her bed and help her to face *al-Qiblah* (al-Ka'bah). She then said I have made my soul free so do not uncover me; my spirit is being taken away at this time. She then made her right hand as her pillow and turned toward *al-Qiblah* (al-Ka'bah) and she died.

Ali came when we were crying. He asked about Fatimah, *'Alayha al-Salam,* and I informed him. He then said, "If so then by Allah you must not uncover her. She was taken in her clothes and was made to disappear.

I ('Allamah Majlisi) say that ibn Babwayh (r.h) has narrated as you see. Ahmad ibn Hanbal in his Musnad has narrated from 'Umm Salma' who has said that Fatimah, *'Alayha al-Salam,* felt ill with the illness because of which she died and I served as a nurse. One day she felt better and Ali then went after some of his chores and Fatimah, *'Alayha al-Salam,* said to me, "O female servant of Allah, arrange for a shower for me and pour water." I then following her instructions poured water and she took a shower as best as she would do. Then she said, "O 'Ummah, give me my new clothes." I gave her clothes which she wore then said, "O 'Ummah, bring my bed in the middle of the room." I did as I was told to do. She then lied down facing *al-Qiblah* (al-Ka'bah) placing her hand under her cheek, then she said, "'Ummah, my spirit is being taken away at this time. I have cleansed myself so no one must uncover me." She died in her place. She has said that Ali came and she informed him about her.

The concordance about this according to both *Shi'a* and Sunni group despite the fact that the rule of fiqh (Islamic laws) is against it is very strange.

Fuqaha (Scholars of Islamic laws) both *Shi'a* and Sunni do not consider it lawful to bury a dead body without washing unless it is of the exceptional cases and the above case is not of the exceptional ones. Thus, why is it that the two have narrated this Hadith without reasoning of lawful and unlawful conditions. Perhaps her case is exceptional. *Fuqaha* (Scholars of Islamic laws) have argued that a husband is allowed to wash the dead body of his wife and it is the popular view.

Ibn Babwayh (r.h). in *a marfu' manner* has narrated from al-Hassan ibn Ali, who has said that Ali, washed Fatimah, *'Alayha al-Salam*. It is narrated from Ali that he performed funeral *Salat* (formal prayer) for Fatimah, *'Alayha al-Salam*, in which he said five *Takbir* (Allah is great beyond description) and buried her in the night.

Note:

In the book of al-Mazar we have explained that on the basis of the correct facts Fatimah, *'Alayha al-Salam*, is buried in her house. That she was not washed requires an explanation. She was not uncovered because she did not need cleansing. But for her funeral Ali, washed her from over her shirt as mentioned earlier also the narration of Waraqah should be considered.

H 195, Ch. 7, h 19
Kashf al-Ghummah:

It is narrated from the book al-Zuryah al-Tahirah of al-Dulabi about the death of Fatimah, *'Alayha al-Salam*. He has narrated from his narrators and has said that Fatimah, *'Alayha al-Salam*, lived for three months after the Holy Prophet, *'Alayhi al-Salam*. Ibn Shihab has said that she lived for six months. Al-Zuhri has said that she lived for six months; also from 'A'ishah and 'Urwah ibn al-Zubayr a similar Hadith is narrated.

It is narrated from abu Ja'far, Muhammad ibn Ali, *'Alayhima al-Salam*, that Fatimah, *'Alayha al-Salam*, died ninety-five days after the death of her father in the year eleven (A.H).

Ibn Qutaybah in Mu'arifah has said that she died one hundred days after the death of her father.

It is also said that she died in the year eleven on a Tuesday night on the third of the month of Ramadan and at that time she was twenty-nine years old.

It is also said that al-'Abbas visited Ali ibn abu Talib, *'Alayhima al-Salam,* and Fatimah, *'Alayha al-Salam,* the daughter of the Messenger of Allah when one of them said to the other, "Who is older of the two of us?" Al-'Abbas then said, "You were born several years before the building of the al-Ka'bah and she (my daughter) was born when al-Quraysh was building al-Bayt (the holy house) and the Messenger of Allah, at that time was thirty five years old, five years before the Prophet-hood.

It is narrated that she made a will to Ali, and 'Asma' daughter of 'Umays to wash her.

It is narrated from ibn 'Abbas who has said the following:

Fatimah, *'Alayha al-Salam,* became seriously ill. She said to 'Asma' the daughter of 'Umays, "As you see my condition and what has become of it. You must not carry me on an open bed." She then said, "No, by Allah, however, I will make a coffin as I had seen in Ethiopia." Fatimah, *'Alayha al-Salam,* then asked her to show how it looks. I, 'Asma' then sent for wet twigs then bent them on a bed that formed a *Na'sh* (a box with its open side downward on the bed) and it was the coffin used in that place. Fatimah, *'Alayha al-Salam,* after looking at it smiled. She was not seen smiling except on that day. We then carried her and buried in the night. Al-'Abbas ibn 'Abd al-Muttalib performed the funeral *Salat* (formal prayer) and she was taken down in her grave; he, Ali, and al-Fadl ibn 'Abbas climbed down in the grave.

It is narrated from 'Asma' the daughter of 'Umays who has said that Fatimah, *'Alayha al-Salam,* the daughter of the Messenger of Allah, said, "I detest people's placing a sheet on the women from behind which people can see the figure of the women." Asma' then said, "O daughter of the Messenger of Allah, I can show something which I have seen in Ethiopia." She has said that she then sent for palm tree twigs and formed a 'u' shaped structure facing down by bending the twigs then spread a sheet over it. Fatimah, *'Alayha al-*

Salam, said, "This is very good and beautiful, one cannot see the figure if it is a man or a woman."

He (the narrator) has said that Fatimah, *'Alayha al-Salam,* said, "When I die you must wash me and do not allow anyone else to come in." When Fatimah, *'Alayha al-Salam,* died 'A'ishah came to see her. 'Asma' said, "You cannot go in where Fatimah, *'Alayha al-Salam,* is." 'A'ishah then spoke to abu Bakr about it saying, "This al-Khath'ami woman is preventing me from seeing the daughter of the Messenger of Allah, and she has made for her something like the carriage of a bride (on the back of the camel)." 'Asma' then said to abu Bakr, "Fatimah, *'Alayha al-Salam,* commanded me not to allow anyone to come in to see her and the structure is what I showed her in her lifetime and she commanded me to make one for her."

Abu Bakr said, "You can make what you are commanded to make," and he went back. Ali, and 'Asma' then washed Fatimah, *'Alayha al-Salam.*

Al-Dulabi has narrated the narration about washing and the shower that Fatimah, *'Alayha al-Salam,* took before her death and that she was buried with that shower and that she was not uncovered and it was mentioned before. It is narrated from others that abu Bakr and 'Umar reproached Ali for not allowing them to perform the funeral *Salat* (formal prayer) for Fatimah, *'Alayha al-Salam,* and apologized because of her will which she had made as such and he swore before them and they excused him and accepted his words.

Ali at the time of burying, as though whispering to the Messenger of Allah, said near his grave, "*Salam* (the phrase of offering greeting of peace) be with you, O Messenger of Allah, from me and from your daughter who has just disembarked in your neighborhood . . ." to the end of the narration that will be mentioned.

Ali ibn 'Isa then has said that the story is painful as a certain one of the companions of Qadi abu Bakr ibn abu Quray'ah has composed:

O you who persevere to ask about every knotty and ridiculous issue,

Do not uncover the hidden; you may uncover a carcass,

Some veiled thing may appear,

Like a drum from under the sheet,

The answer is ready,

But I am afraid of fear,

Had the subject not transgressed,

Khalifa, (the caliph) would drop his sword,

The swords of the enemy,

By which our skulls would become split,

I would have made public certain secrets,

Ale (family of) Muhammad, certain unique statements,

Enough is for what Malik and abu Hanifah have narrated,

I could show that al-Husayn, was murdered on the day of Saqifah,

And for what reason honorable Fatimah, *'Alayha al-Salam,* was buried in the night,

For what reason did your two Shaykhs not protect the house of Fatimah, *'Alayha al-Salam,* from being violated, Alas the daughter of Muhammad died with her anger and sorrow.

There are narrations of Fatimah, *'Alayha al-Salam,* in her own words during her illness which reveal the intensity of her sorrow, pain and grief, the greatness of the degree of injuries to her feelings, her complaints against those who did injustice to her, and denying her rights which I have disregarded to mention them all, because my goal is to record the documents about their (*Ahl al-Bayt* (family of Muhammad), excellence and their distinguished merits and to awaken the neglectful ones about the love for them perhaps they may wake up and speak of their attributes which Allah has granted them and to no one else beside them. Speaking of evil and good is not of the goals of this book and such issues are left for the day of reckoning. To Allah all issues move.

H 196, Ch. 7, h 20
Rawdatul Wa''izin:

Fatimah, *'Alayha al-Salam,* became ill severely and she remained ill for forty days until she died. When Fatimah, *'Alayha al-Salam,* was told about her death approaching she called 'Umm Ayman and 'Asma' the daughter of 'Umays and sent for Ali, *'Alayhi al-Salam.* Fatimah, *'Alayha al-Salam,* said to him, "O son of my uncle, considering my condition what I see is that every hour I am getting closer to joining my father. I like to make a will to you about a few things." Ali said, "Make your will about whatever you like, O daughter of the Messenger of Allah, *'Alayhi al-Salam.*" He then sat near her head and asked everyone to leave the room. Fatimah, *'Alayha al-Salam,* said, "O my cousin (I hope) you have not found me lying to you, betraying or opposing you since the time we have lived together." Ali said, "I seek protection with Allah. You have been most knowledgeable about Allah, more virtuous than others, more pious, more honorable and of more intense fear from Allah than you can be reproached by saying that you have opposed me. It is very difficult for me to become separated from you and lose you. However, it is a matter which is not avoidable. I swear by Allah that my grief for the Messenger of Allah has renewed itself. Your death and loss has greatly weighed on me." He then said *Istirja'* (the expression, to Allah we belong and to Him we all return). "How painful is this affliction, and tribulation of grief, sadness and an irreplaceable loss."

They both then wept for an hour holding her head against his chest and he then said, "Please make your will to me for whatever you like and you will find me following them as you command me and I will give the priority to your will over my own affairs." Fatimah, *'Alayha al-Salam,* then said, "May Allah grant you on my behalf best compensations, O son of the uncle of the Messenger of Allah, *'Alayhi al-Salam.* One part of my will is that after me you should marry the daughter of my sister, Amamah, because she will be like me to my children. Obviously men need women."

He (the narrator) has said that for this reason 'Amir al-Mu'minin, has said, "There are four things from which I cannot remain separate. The Daughter [of abu al-'As] Amamah because of the will of Fatimah, *'Alayha al-Salam,* the daughter of Muhammad, *'Alayhi al-Salam.* "

Fatimah, *'Alayha al-Salam,* then said, "O son of my uncle another part of my will is that you should prepare a casket, a coffin, because I saw the angels showing me its picture.

Ali then said, "Please describe it for me." She then described it and Ali made it ready for her and this was the first coffin on the face of the earth. No one before had see.n it and no one had made it.

Fatimah, *'Alayha al-Salam,* then said, "Another part of my will is that no one of those who have done injustice to me and have usurped my rights must be allowed to attend my funeral procession; they are my enemies and the enemies of the Messenger of Allah, and no one of them or their followers must be allowed to perform funeral *Salat* (formal prayer) for me. You must bury me in the night when the eyes calm down and they go to sleep."

Fatimah, *'Alayha al-Salam,* then passed away. O Allah grant compensation to her, her children, her husband and sons.

Inhabitants of al-Madinah wept all at once, the women of banu Hashim gathered in her house and they sobbed all at once, as such that the city of al-Madinah almost underwent a quake because of their wailing and saying, "O our leader, O daughter of the Messenger of Allah." People like the mane of horse came to Ali while he was sitting with al-Hassan and al-Husayn in front of him weeping. People wept because of their weeping. 'Umm of Kulthum came out veiled with the back part of her gown dragging on the ground with which she covered herself and said, "Oh father, O Messenger of Allah, Now indeed we have lost you after which we cannot meet you."

People gathered tumultuously in turmoil waiting to be called for funeral services of the daughter of the Messenger of Allah, *'Alayhi al-Salam.*

Abu Dharr came out and he told them to go home because the funeral service for the daughter of the Messenger of Allah is delayed this evening. People then went back. When the eyes became calm and some part of the night passed, Ali, al-Hassan, al-Husayn, 'Ammar, al-Miqdad, 'Aqil, al-Zubayr, abu Dharr, Salman (Rh), Buraydah and a few people from banu Hashim, and his special people performed the funeral *Salat* (formal prayer) for Fatimah, *'Alayha al-Salam,* and buried her in the night, with seven false graves around her gravesite so that her grave could not be identified. Some of the special people said, "The grave was leveled with the ground to make it indistinguishable."

H 197, Ch. 7, h 21
Al-Kafi: [H 1236, Ch. 114, h 3, from al-Kafi]

Ahmad ibn Mihran, may Allah grant him blessing, has narrated in a marfu' manner and Ahmad ibn Idris has narrated from Muhammad ibn 'Abd al-Jabbar al-Shaybani who has said that narrated to me al-Qasim ibn Muhammad al-Razi who has said that narrated to him Ali ibn Muhammad al-Hurmuzani from abu 'Abd Allah al-Husayn ibn Ali, 'Alayhi al-Salam, who has said the following:

"Abu 'Abd Allah al-Husayn ibn Ali, 'Alayhim al-Salam, has said, 'When Fatimah, 'Alayha al-Salam, passed away Amir al-Mu'minin Ali, 'Alayhi al-Salam, buried her secretly, camouflaged her gravesite and then stood up facing the grave of the Messenger of Allah and said, "O Messenger of Allah, may Allah grant you blessings on my behalf and on behalf of your daughter who is visiting you and will pass this night in the soil of your location. Allah chose to make her join you the fastest. O Messenger of Allah, my patience has reached its limits and I miss so much your chosen one (daughter) and my self-control has vanished due to the departure of the leader of the ladies of the world. The only solace for me is to follow your tradition and be mournful for your own departure from us. A little while ago I placed you in your grave and your spirit left your body between my own throat and chest. Yes, in the book of Allah (for me) there is the best example for expressing acceptance of Allah's decision, 'We are the servants of Allah and to Him we shall all return.'" (2:156)

'The trust is returned, the commitment is recalled and al-Zahra' is taken away from us. How sad, O Messenger of Allah, the green skies and the dusty earth seem to us. My sadness has become perpetual and my nights have become sleepless. There is an anxiety that will not relieve my heart until Allah will choose for me a dwelling like that where you are. I have a heart bleeding, sorrowful, and a restlessess and anxiety. How quickly the separation took place. Before Allah I lament, and your own daughter will explain to you how your 'Umma (followers) succeeded in committing injustice against her. You may ask her questions and find information about the case from her. How great was her sorrow for which she could not find a place for expressing, but now she has found a place and an ear to express it to. She would say, 'Allah will judge because He is the best judge'. I offer my prayer to Allah to grant you blessings as a note of farewell, but not because of disappointment and desperation. If I return it is not because I have become tired and if I stand up it will not be because of pessimism toward the promise of Allah to those who exercise patience. Indeed to exercise patience is more safe and fruitful. Had I not feared the mischief of the enemies I would have liked to turn the place into a place of worship, to keep my worship continuous and to cry like the mothers for the death of their son, for the great loss. In the sight of Allah your daughter is buried secretly, her rights are taken away unjustly, her inheritance is withheld for no valid reason. It all happened just after you left and your memories are still fresh. To Allah, O Messenger of Allah, we lament and from you, O Messenger of Allah, we seek condolences. May Allah grant blessings to you and to her. May the peace and happiness from Allah be with you.'"

H 198, Ch. 7, h 22
Al-Kafi: [H 633, Ch. 40, h 5, from al-Kafi]

Muhammad ibn Yahya has narrated from Ahmad ibn Muhammad from ibn Mahbub from ibn Ri'ab from abu 'Ubayda who has said the following:

"People from our group asked abu 'Abd Allah, *'Alayhi al-Salam*, about *Jafr* and the Imam said, 'It is the skin of a bull which is full of knowledge.' They then asked the Imam about *al-Jami'ah*. The Imam replied, 'It is a parchment that is seventy yards long with the width of a hide like that of the leg of a huge camel. It contains all that people may need. There is no case for which there is not a rule in it. In it there is the law even to settle the compensation for a scratch caused to a person.'

"I (the narrator) then asked the Imam, 'What is the Mushaf of Fatimah?' The Imam waited for quite a while. Then he said, 'You ask about what you really mean and what you do not mean. *Fatimah, 'Alayha al-Salam*, lived after the Messenger of Allah for seventy-five days. She was severely depressed because of the death of her father. Jibril (peace be upon him) would come to provide her solace and condolence due to the death of her father. Jibril would comfort her soul, inform her about her father, his place, of the future events and about what would happen to her children. At the same time Ali, *'Alayhi al-Salam*, would write all of them down and thus has come to be the Mushaf of *Fatimah, 'Alayha al-Salam.'*"

H 199, Ch. 7, h 23
Al-Kafi: [H 10298, Ch. 10, h 2, from al-Kafi]

A number of our people have narrated from Ahmad ibn Muhammad from al-Qasim ibn Yahya from his grandfather al-Hassan ibn Rashid from abu Basir who has said the following:

"Abu 'Abd Allah, *'Alayhi al-Salam,* has said, 'My father narrated to me from my grandfather that `Amir al-Mu'minin has said, 'Name your children before they are born: and if you do not know they are male or female, then name them with such names that are good for both male and female. In case a child is miscarried, when that child will meet you on the Day of Judgment, whom you had not given a name, it will say to his father, 'I wish you had named me.' The Messenger of Allah had named Muhsin before his birth.'"

H 200, Ch. 7, h 24
Al-Kafi: [H 8090, Ch. 9, h 3, from al-Kafi]

A number of our people have narrated from Ahmad ibn Muhammad from al-Husayn ibn Sa'id from Al-Nadr ibn al-Suwayd from Hisham ibn Salim who has said the following:

"I heard abu 'Abd Allah, *'Alayhi al-Salam,* say, 'Fatimah, *'Alayha al-Salam*, lived for seventy-five days after the death of the Messenger of Allah. During this time, she was never seen laughing or smiling. Every week she would go twice to the gravesites of the martyrs, once on Monday and on Thursdays, and say, 'There was the Messenger of Allah, O Allah, grant compensation to Muhammad and his family worthy of their services to Your cause, and there were the pagans.'"

In another Hadith, Aban has narrated from those whom he has mentioned from abu 'Abd Allah, *'Alayhi al-Salam,* who has said the following:

"She would perform salat (prayer) there and pray until she died."

H 201, Ch. 7, h 25
Al-Kafi: [H 15011, h 564, from al-Kafi]

Humayd ibn Ziyad has narrated from al-Hassan ibn Muhammad al-Kindiy from Ahmad ibn al-Hassan al-Mithamiy from Aban ibn 'Uthman from Muhammad ibn al-Mufaddal who has narrated the following:

"I once heard abu 'Abd Allah, *'Alayhi al-Salam*, say that Fatimah, *'Alayha al-Salam*, came to one of the pillars in the Masjid and addressing the Holy Prophet, *O Allah grant compensation to Muhammad and his family worthy of their services to your cause*, said, 'After you great differences have taken place. If you had been present the issue would not increase this much. We have missed you just as the land loses its drenching rain. Your nation is in disorder; you must bear witness and do not remain absent.'

H 202, Ch. 7, h 26
Iqbal al-'A'mal:

We have narrated from a group of our people who we have mentioned in Kitab al-Ta'rif about the graceful birth, that Fatimah, *'Alayha al-Salam,* died on the third of the month of Jamadi al-Akhar.

H 203, Ch. 7, h 27
Manaqib of ibn Shahr Ashub:

After the death of her father, Fatimah al-Zahra' 'Alayha al-Salam, recited the following lines:

We have suffered a great loss of his pure essence, clear value, lineage and relationships,

You were the full moon, and the light to shine,

To whom came the books from the owner of majesty,

Jibril and the Holy Spirit were our visitors,

From us all goodness has disappeared,

I wish death had met us before it met you,

When you passed away there is a curtain between us and you,

We have suffered by something which no pain sufferer has done,

Of all people Arabs and non-Arab ones,

The whole area has become congested despite being vast,

Your two grandsons have become weary, and disconsolate in the town and for me is more sorrow,

You, by Allah were the best of all the creatures,

And the most truthful in matters of truth and falsehood,

We weep for you as long as we live,

And as long as our eyes can shed any tears.

'Umar ibn Dinar has narrated from Al-Baqir, 'Alayhi al-Salam who has said the following:

Fatimah, *'Alayha al-Salam,* was never seen laughing from the day the Holy Prophet, died to the time Fatimah, *'Alayha al-Salam,* herself passed away.

H 204, Ch. 7, h 28
Al-Ihtijaj:

Of the matter of argumentation of al-Hassan, against Mu'awiyah and his people is his words to al-Mughiah ibn Sha'bah, "You struck Fatimah, *'Alayha al-Salam,* the daughter of the Messenger of Allah to make her bleed and caused her to miscarry her child. It was your intention to humiliate the Messenger of Allah, and disobey his commandment, to disregard his honor and dignity, despite the fact that the Messenger of Allah had said, 'You, O Fatimah, *'Alayha al-Salam,* are the leader of the women of the garden (paradise),' by Allah, your destination is the fire (of hell)."

H 205, Ch. 7, h 29

I ('Allamah Majlisi) have found the following in the book of Sulaym ibn Qays al-Hilali in the narration of Aban ibn 'Iyash from him from Salman (Rh) and 'Abd Allah ibn al-'Abbas who have said the following:

The Messenger of Allah, *O Allah grant compensation to Muhammad and his family worthy of their services to your cause,* passed away on the day that he did. He was not yet placed in his grave that people turned back to become apostates. They agreed to oppose. Ali remained busy with the burial issues of the Messenger of Allah, until he completed washing, shrouding, *Tahnit* (applying camphor), then placed him in his grave. He then moved to compile al-Quran, according to the will of the Messenger of Allah, which kept him occupied.

'Umar said to abu Bakr, "O you, people have pledged allegiance to you except this man and the people of his family." You must send for him (to come to pledge allegiance to you). He then sent a cousin of 'Umar called Qunfudh and told him, "O Qunfudh, go to Ali, and tell him to answer the call of *Khalifah* (Caliph) of the Messenger of Allah, '*Alayhi al-Salam.*" They sent him several times but each time Ali refused to go to them. 'Umar then sprang up with anger and called Khalid ibn Walid and Qunfudh. He commanded them to prepare firewood and fire. He then came to the door of the house of Fatimah and Ali, '*Alayhima al-Salam.* Fatimah, '*Alayha al-Salam,* was sitting behind the door with her head swathed. She had become very weak physically because of grief after the death of the Messenger of Allah, '*Alayhi al-Salam.* 'Umar came forward and hit the door then called, "O son of abu Talib, open the door." Fatimah, '*Alayha al-Salam,* said, "O 'Umar we have nothing to do with you. Why do you not leave us alone in our condition?" He said, "Open the door or else I set it on fire at you." She said, "O 'Umar, why is it that you are not pious before Allah, most Majestic, most Glorious. You want to enter in our house by force and attack it." He refused to go back. 'Umar then asked for the fire and set the door on fire. The door burned, then 'Umar shoved it. Fatimah, '*Alayha al-Salam,* came in front of him crying, "O father, O the Messenger of Allah!" He raised the sword which was in its sheath and poked with its tip on her side. She screamed. He then raised the whip and hit her arm with it, and she screamed, "O father!"

Ali then sprang and grabbed 'Umar by the collar of his shirt, shook him and struck him on the ground and poked his nose and neck intending to kill him but he remembered the words of the Messenger of Allah, *O Allah grant compensation to Muhammad and his family worthy of their services to your cause,* and his will to remain patient and to obey. He then said, "I swear by the one who has honored Muhammad with prophet-hood, O son of Sahak, had it not been documented in the book of Allah previously, you would learn that you cannot enter my house."

'Umar then sent word pleading for help. People came until they entered the house, overpowered him and threw a rope around his neck. Fatimah, *'Alayha al-Salam,* then came between them and Ali at the door of the house. Qunfudh the condemned one hit Fatimah, *'Alayha al-Salam,* with the whip - because of which she then died when she died - and the whip formed a coil around her arm and Fatimah, *'Alayha al-Salam,* sought to find support with the door jamb but he pushed her, broke her ribs on her side and her baby was miscarried. From that time Fatimah, *'Alayha al-Salam,* remained in bed until she died, *O Allah grant compensation to Fatimah, 'Alayha al-Salam, worthy of her services to your cause and for her becoming a martyr.*

He (the narrator) has continued the story of the great tragedy and the huge suffering until he has said that ibn 'Abbas has said that Fatimah, *'Alayha al-Salam,* was informed that abu Bakr has confiscated Fidak plantations.

Fatimah, *'Alayha al-Salam,* along with the women of banu Hashim went out to the office of abu Bakr and said to him, "Why do you intend to take away from me the land which my father, the Messenger of Allah, had assigned for me?"

Abu Bakr asked for ink and paper to write to give the land back to Fatimah, *'Alayha al-Salam.* 'Umar came in and said, "O *Khalifah* (caliph) of the Messenger of Allah, *'Alayhi al-Salam.* You must not write anything for her before she presents witnesses to prove her case. Fatimah, *'Alayha al-Salam,* said, "Ali, and 'Umm 'Ayman are my witnesses." 'Umar said, "The testimony of a non-Arab woman who cannot speak is not admissible. However, Ali, pulls the fire to bake his own bread."

Fatimah, *'Alayha al-Salam,* came back depressed and she became ill. Ali would perform his *Salat* (formal prayer) in Masjid five times and abu Bakr and 'Umar would ask, "How is the daughter of the Messenger of Allah doing," until the illness became heavy on Fatimah, *'Alayha al-Salam.* They asked about how she was doing and they said, "There was something between us and Fatimah, *'Alayha al-Salam,* as you know. Consider giving us permission to visit her and apologize." Ali said that is up to you. They then moved and at the door they sat down. Ali entered the house and said to Fatimah, *'Alayha al-*

Salam, "O free one, so and so is at the door and they want to say *Salam* (the phrase of offering greeting of peace) to you. What do you say about it?"

Fatimah, *'Alayha al-Salam,* said, "This is your house, and the free one is your wife. You can do what you like. Ali then said, "Put on your gown please and she then did so but Fatimah, *'Alayha al-Salam,* turned her face away from them to the wall. They came in said *Salam* (the phrase of offering greeting of peace) and asked not to be unhappy with them, and then Allah will be happy with you. Fatimah, *'Alayha al-Salam,* asked, "What has made you to ask for such thing?" They said, "We confess that we have done bad things against you and we hope you will accept our apology."

Fatimah, *'Alayha al-Salam,* said, "If you are truthful then you must answer what I am going to ask you, because I will not ask you anything unless I know that you are fully aware of it. If you spoke the truth then I will learn that you are truthful in your coming."

They said, "You can ask whatever you like."

Fatimah, *'Alayha al-Salam,* said, "I swear you to Allah to answer me this: Did you hear the Messenger of Allah, say, 'Fatimah, *'Alayha al-Salam,* is a part of myself. Whoever, harms and hurts her has harmed and has hurt me'?"

They both replied, "Yes, we have heard it." Fatimah, *'Alayha al-Salam,* then raised her hands to the sky and said, "O Lord, these two have harmed and hurt me, I complain against them before you and your messenger. No by Allah, I will never become happy with you until I will meet my father, the Messenger of Allah, and complain before him against you and inform him about what you have done to me and he will be the judge against you."

At that time abu Bakr expressed, regret for being subjected to destruction and punishment. He expressed a great deal of disappointment and distress.

'Umar then said, "You must not express disappointment and distress because of the words of a woman, O *Khalifah* (caliph) of the Messenger of Allah."

He (the narrator) has said that after the death of her father, Fatimah, *'Alayha al-Salam,* lived for forty days. When her illness became severe she called Ali

281

and said, "O son of my uncle, as you can see my condition as it is I make a will to you to marry Amamah, daughter of my sister Zaynab because to my children she will be like myself, and prepare for me a coffin because I have seen it as the angels have described it for me and no one of the enemies of Allah must be allowed to attend my funeral, the burial and *Salat* (formal prayer)."

Ibn 'Abbas has said that on the day Fatimah, *'Alayha al-Salam,* passed away the city of al-Madinah shook with weeping of the men and women. People became afraid like the day the Holy Prophet passed away. Abu Bakr and 'Umar came to offer condolences to Ali and said, "O abu al-Hassan, please do not perform *Salat* (formal prayer) for the funeral of the daughter of the Messenger of Allah before us."

When it was night Ali then called al-'Abbas, al-Fadl, al-Miqdad, Salman (Rh), abu Dharr and 'Ammar. Al-'Abbas moved ahead and performed *Salat* (formal prayer) and they buried her. In the morning when the people woke up then abu Bakr and 'Umar and the people wanted to take part in performing *Salat* (formal prayer) of funeral for Fatimah, *'Alayha al-Salam,* but al-Miqdad told them, "We buried Fatimah, *'Alayha al-Salam,* last night." 'Umar then turned to abu Bakr and said, "Did I not tell you that they will do it?"

Al-'Abbas said, "She had made a will that the two must not be allowed to perform funeral *Salat* (formal prayer) for her."

'Umar then said, "You, O people of banu Hashim do not leave your old grudge against us, the jealousy in your hearts will never go away. By Allah, I must exhume her grave to perform funeral *Salat* (formal prayer)."

Ali said, "By Allah, O son of Sahak, if you think of it you must keep in mind that your right (hand) will not return to you. If I draw my sword I will not place it back in its sheath without destroying your soul."

'Umar (with his courage) broke, remained silent, knowing that when Ali swears he makes it true.

Ali then said, "Are you not the one, O 'Umar whom the Messenger of Allah, intended to destroy and sent me then I came with my sword ready and moved forward to you to kill you but Allah, most Majestic, most Glorious, sent divine revelation that said, "Do you not realize that We have sent Satan to incite the unbelievers to sin (withhold *Khums* and *zakat).* (19:83) Muhammad), do not be hasty; We count it for them exactly (how many times can they breathe). (19:84) On the Day of Judgment, when the pious people will be brought in the presence of the Beneficent as the guests of honor (19:85) and the criminals will be driven and thrown into hell, (19:86) no one will benefit from the intercession except those who establish a covenant with the Beneficent before they die. (19:87)"

I ('Allamah Majlisi) say that the rest of this narration and other accounts of what had happened to Fatimah, *'Alayha al-Salam,* is what I have recorded in the book al-Fitan.

H 206, Ch. 7, h 30
Al-Misbah al-Anwar:

It is narrated from Ja'far ibn Muhammad from his ancestors *'Alayhim al-Salam* that Fatimah, *'Alayha al-Salam,* died between the time for al-Maghrib and al-'Isha'.

It is narrated 'Abd Allah ibn al-Hassan from his father from his grandfather who has said the following:

When Fatimah, *'Alayha al-Salam,* was about to pass away she looked sharply and said, "*Salam* (I offer you peace and serenity), O Jibril, *Salam* (I offer you peace and serenity) to the Messenger of Allah, *'Alayhi al-Salam.* O Lord, keep me with your messenger, O Lord, with your happiness, in your neighborhood, in your home the house of peace." Then she asked, "Do you see what I see?" She was asked, "What do you see?" She then said, "This is the procession of the inhabitants of the skies. This is Jibril and this is the Messenger of Allah who says, "My dearest daughter come; ahead of you there is all good for you."

It is narrated from Zayd ibn Ali, who has said the following:

When Fatimah, *'Alayha al-Salam,* was about to pass away she said, "*Salam* (I pray for you to have peace and serenity) to Jibril, to the Holy Prophet, and to the angel of death." They felt the presence of the angels, of very sweet smelling perfumes as best as it can be.

It is narrated from abu Ja'far, who has said the following:

Fatimah, *'Alayha al-Salam,* lived for six months after her father.

It is narrated from abu Ja'far, who has said that Fatimah, *'Alayha al-Salam,* remained ill for fifteen days after which she passed away.

It is narrated from abu Ja'far, who has said the following:

Present at the funeral services of Fatimah, *'Alayha al-Salam,* were Salman (Rh) al-Farsi, al-Miqdad, abu Dharr al-Ghifari, ibn Mas'ud, al-'Abbas ibn 'Abd al-Muttalib and al-Zubayr ibn al-'Awwam.

It is narrated from abu Ja'far, who has said the following:

Fatimah, *'Alayha al-Salam,* the daughter of the Messenger of Allah lived for six months after the death of her father. She was not seen laughing (during this time).

It is narrated from the narrator of the previous Hadith who has said the following:

Fatimah, *'Alayha al-Salam,* was shrouded in seven pieces of fabrics.

It is narrated from Husayn ibn 'Ulwan from Sa'd ibn Trif from abu Ja'far, who has said the following:

The beginning of the illness of Fatimah, *'Alayha al-Salam,* was fifty days after the death of the Messenger of Allah, *'Alayhi al-Salam.* She found it to be leading to her death. She then began to ready herself for it and called 'Amir al-Mu'minin, Ali, so she make her will to him and asked him to promise to do certain things for her. 'Amir al-Mu'minin, expressed distress but obeyed her in all of her will and whatever she commanded.

Fatimah, *'Alayha al-Salam,* said, "O abu al-Hassan, the Messenger of Allah, promised me and told me that I will be the first one from his family to join him. What is not avoidable is not avoidable, so you must exercise patience about the command of Allah, most High, and be happy with His decision."

He (the Imam) has said that Fatimah, *'Alayha al-Salam,* made a will to wash her, prepare for burial and bury her in the night which he followed. He (the Imam) has said that she made a will about her charities and her legacy. He (the

Imam) has said that when 'Amir al-Mu'minin completed her burial tasks the two men met him and asked, "What made you to do what you have done?" Ali replied, "It was because of her will and her trust."

H 207, Ch. 7, h 31
'Ilal al-Shara'i':

Narrated to us Ali ibn Ahmad saying that narrated to us abu al-'Abbas Ahmad ibn Muhammad ibn Yahya' from 'Amr ibn abu al-Miqdam and Ziyad ibn 'Abd Allah who have said the following:

A man came to 'Abu 'Abd Allah, *'Alayhi al-Salam*, and asked, "Is it permissible to carry fire or something for light in a funeral procession?" He (the narrator) has said that the color of the face of 'Abu 'Abd Allah, changed. He (the Imam) then sat straight and said, "One of the wicked ones came to Fatimah, *'Alayha al-Salam*, daughter of the Messenger of Allah, and said, 'Do you know that Ali, has proposed marriage with the daughter of abu Jahl?' She then asked, 'Are you telling the truth.' He said, 'Yes, indeed I speak the truth.' He said it three times.

She then felt protective emotions, and ardor because of which she could not control herself; Allah, most blessed, most High, has placed this feeling in women and in man He has placed the ability for *Jihad* (hard work). Those (women) who bear patience to expect reward from Allah, He then grants them the reward which is equal to the reward for those who guard the borders and those who migrate in the way of Allah.

He (the narrator) has said that sadness became intense in Fatimah, *'Alayha al-Salam*, because of it and she remained thinking about it until the evening. The night fell and she then carried al-Hassan on her right shoulder and al-Husayn on her left shoulder, held the left hand of 'Umm Kulthum in her right hand and then moved to the room of her father. Ali, *'Alayhi al-Salam*, came and entered the room but he did find Fatimah, *'Alayha al-Salam*, and he became very intensely sad which weighed very heavy on him and he did not know what the reason was. He felt shy to call her from the house of her father. He then went out to the Masjid and performed *Salat* (formal prayer) there as much as Allah willed. He then collected something of the sand on the floor of the Masjid then leaned on it. When the Holy Prophet, observed the condition of Fatimah, *'Alayha al-Salam*, he sprayed water on her and then wore his

285

clothes, then entered the Masjid and continued performing *Salat* (formal prayer) doing *Sujud* (prostrations) and *Ruku'* (bowing down on one's knees). After each two *Rak'at* he prayed to Allah to remove the sad feeling from Fatimah, *'Alayha al-Salam,* and her depressions, because when he left her she was breathing fast and hard. When the Holy Prophet, found her unable to sleep and restless he then said, "My dearest daughter stand up to go. The Holy Prophet, then picked up al-Hassan, Fatimah, *'Alayha al-Salam,* picked up al-Husayn and held the hand of 'Umm Kulthum in her hand until they reached where Ali, was sleeping. The Holy Prophet, then pressed the foot of Ali with his foot and said, "Get up, O abu Turab, how many are the peaceful ones whom you have made restless. Call abu Bakr from his home and 'Umar from the meeting of Talhah." Ali then went and brought them out from their homes and they gathered before the Messenger of Allah, *'Alayhi al-Salam.* He (the Messenger of Allah) said, "O Ali, did you not know that Fatimah, *'Alayha al-Salam,* is a part of myself and I am from Fatimah, *'Alayha al-Salam,* whoever, harms and hurts her has harmed and has hurt me and whoever harms and hurts me has harmed and has hurt Allah. Whoever hurts and harms her after my death is just as he has harmed and has hurt Fatimah, *'Alayha al-Salam,* in my lifetime, and whoever harms and hurts her in my lifetime is just as he has harmed and has hurt her after my death." Ali said, "Yes, O Messenger of Allah." He (the Messenger of Allah), then asked, "What then has made you to do what you have done?" Ali said, "I swear by the one who has sent you in truth as His Prophet, I have not done anything such as what she has heard; I have not even thought of it in my soul." The Holy Prophet, said, "You have spoken the truth and she also has spoken the truth."

Fatimah, *'Alayha al-Salam,* then became happy and smiled as such that her front teeth became visible. One of them then said to his friend, "It is strange, what made him to call us at this hour?"

He (the narrator) has said that the Holy Prophet, then held the hand of Ali, and then crisscrossed their figures, then the Holy Prophet, picked up al-Hassan, Ali, picked up al-Husayn, and Fatimah, *'Alayha al-Salam,* picked up 'Umm Kuthum and the Holy Prophet, made them to enter their home, placed a sheet on them, entrusted them with Allah then moved out and performed *Salat* (formal prayer) for the rest of the night.

When Fatimah, *'Alayha al-Salam,* became ill from which she died, the men came to pay a visit as people suffering from illness are visited; she refused to allow them to visit her. Abu Bakr then promised not to stay in the shadow of a roof until she becomes happy with him. He spent the night in the frost, without anything providing him shelter. 'Umar came to Ali and said that abu Bakr is an old tender-hearted man. He was in the cave with the Messenger of Allah, *'Alayhi al-Salam.* We have come several times before also to visit her but she refuses to allow us a visit and ask her to accept our apology. Please consider to get permission from her for us to visit her. Ali said, "Yes, I will ask her." Ali then went to Fatimah, *'Alayha al-Salam,* and said, "O daughter of the Messenger of Allah, the two of them did what they did and they have been coming and going several times but you have refused to allow them. Now they ask me to ask you to give them permission for a visit."

Fatimah, *'Alayha al-Salam,* said, "By Allah, I will not allow them and I will not speak to them a word from my head until I meet my father and complain before him against them for what they have done and (the sin) they have committed." Ali said, "But I have guaranteed them to get permission from you." Fatimah, *'Alayha al-Salam,* said, "The house is your house and women follow men. I do not want to oppose you. You can give permission to come to our home whomever you want." Ali came out and then gave them permission to come inside his house. When they looked at Fatimah, *'Alayha al-Salam,* they said *"Salam"* (the phrase of offering the greeting of peace) but she did not respond. Instead she turned her face away from them. They moved to the place where she had turned her face several times but each time she turned away. She said, *"jafa al-thawb* (the dress has dried or rotted [a metaphorical expression perhaps about the devestaed relation]). " She then said to the women around her to help turn her face away and when they did so the two of them also turned to that direction. Abu Bakr then said, "O daughter of the Messenger of Allah, we have come to make you happy and to avoid your anger. We ask you to forgive us and for what we done against you." Fatimah, *'Alayha al-Salam,* said, "I do not want to speak to you from my head not even one word until I meet my father and complain against you and what you have done and your deeds and what you have committed against me."

They said, "We have come apologizing and asking you to be happy with us so forgive us kindly and do not hold us responsible for what we have done."

Fatimah, *'Alayha al-Salam,* then turned to Ali, and said, "I do not want to speak to them not a word from my head until I asked about something that they have heard from the Messenger of Allah, if they confirm what I ask then I will see to my decision."

They said, "O Lord, that is for her. We will say nothing but the truth and will not testify to anything but the truth."

Fatimah, *'Alayha al-Salam,* then said, "I swear you to Allah and ask you this: Do you remember when the Messenger of Allah, called in the night about something that was related to Ali, *'Alayhi al-Salam?"* They replied, "O Lord, yes, we remember." Fatimah, *'Alayha al-Salam,* then asked, "Did you hear the Messenger of Allah, saying, 'Fatimah, *'Alayha al-Salam,* is a part of myself and I am from Fatimah, *'Alayha al-Salam,* whoever harms and hurts her has harmed and has hurt me and whoever harms and hurts me has done so to Allah and whoever harms and hurts her after my death is just like harming and hurting her in my lifetime and whoever harms and hurts her in my life is just like hurting and harming her after I will die?" They both said, "O Lord, yes, we heard it all." Fatimah, *'Alayha al-Salam,* then said, *Tahmid,* (all praise belongs to Allah). Fatimah, *'Alayha al-Salam,* then said, "O Lord, I assign you as witness and all those who are present here that these two have harmed and have hurt me in my life and at the time of my death. By Allah I will not speak to them from my head not even one word until I will meet my Lord and complain against them before Him about what they have done [to him] and to me and what you have committed against me."

Abu Bakr then expressed distress because of destruction and punishment and said, "I wish my mother had not given birth to me."

'Umar then said, "It is strange, why people have entrusted you with their leadership when you have become a decrepit old mean, express distress because of the anger of a woman and become happy because of her happiness. So what can happen if one makes a woman angry?"

The two then got up and left.

He (the narrator) has said that when Fatimah, *'Alayha al-Salam,* was informed of leaving this world and she then sent for 'Umm 'Ayman who was the most trusted among the women to her and told her, "O 'Umm 'Ayman my soul has informed me of my death. Call Ali for me."

When Ali came Fatimah, *'Alayha al-Salam,* said, "O son of my uncle I like to make my will to you about a few things please remember them for me." Ali, *'Alayhi al-Salam,* said, "You can say in your will whatever you like." Fatimah, *'Alayha al-Salam,* then said, "You should marry so and so because she will be caring for my children like myself after me. You must prepare a coffin for me the picture of which the angels showed me." Ali, *'Alayhi al-Salam,* then asked her to describe its picture. Fatimah, *'Alayha al-Salam,* then described for him as it was shown to her and as she was commanded to do so. Fatimah, *'Alayha al-Salam,* then said, "When I will die take me for the funeral in whatever hour of the day or night but no one of the enemies of Allah and the enemies of His messenger must be allowed to perform the funeral *Salat* (formal prayer) for me." Ali, *'Alayhi al-Salam,* said, "I will follow your will."

When Fatimah, *'Alayha al-Salam,* passed away, Ali, *'Alayhi al-Salam,* performed funeral *Salat* (formal prayer) for her. Ali, *'Alayhi al-Salam,* in the night prepared for the funeral tasks in the hour as she had said in her will. When Fatimah, *'Alayha al-Salam,* was prepared he took out the body, set fire on palm tree twigs and used its light to find the way and until he performed *Salat* (formal prayer) and completed the burial tasks in the night.

In the morning abu Bakr and 'Umar came to visit Fatimah, *'Alayha al-Salam,* and they met a man from al-Quraysh. They asked, "Wherefrom are you coming?" He replied, "I just offered condolences to Ali, *'Alayhi al-Salam,* because of the death of Fatimah, *'Alayha al-Salam.*" They asked, "Is she dead?" He replied, "Yes, and she is buried in the night." They expressed great concerns then they came to Ali, *'Alayhi al-Salam,* met him and said, "By Allah you have not left any scourge and evil without using against us and it is only because of what you have in your heart against us. This is just like your washing the Messenger of Allah, in our absence and without including us with you and the yelling of your son at the face of abu Bakr to 'climb down the pulpit of my father.'"

Ali, *'Alayhi al-Salam,* said, "Will you believe if I swore before you?" They said, "Yes, we believe you." He swore and then took them to the Masjid and

289

said, "The Messenger of Allah, *O Allah grant compensation to Muhammad and his family worthy of their services to your cause,* had said in his will to me not to allow anyone to see his privacy except the son of his uncle. I was washing him, angels turned his body from side to side and al-Fadl ibn al-'Abbas gave me water and his eyes were blindfolded with a piece of rug. I wanted to remove his shirt but someone shouting shouted at me from the house, whose voice I heard but did not see the figure, 'do not remove the shirt of the Messenger of Allah,' and I heard the voice repeating it on me. I then extended my hand in between, under the shirt then washed him, then the shroud was brought before me and I placed him in the shroud then I removed the shirt after shrouding him.

"About al-Hassan, my son, you know and the people of al-Madinah know well that he would walk on rows of people to reach the Holy Prophet, when he would perform Sajdah (prostration). He (al-Hassan) then would climb on his back. The Holy Prophet would stand up with his hand on the back of al-Hassan and his other hand on his knee until he would complete the *Salat* (formal prayer)."

They both said, "Yes, we already know it."

Ali, *'Alayhi al-Salam,* then said, "You and the people of al-Madinah know well that al-Hassan would climb on the shoulders of the Holy Prophet, then hang his legs down on the chest of the Messenger of Allah. The people could see, from the far corners of the Masjid, his anklets shining, while the Holy Prophet delivered his speech and al-Hassan was still on his neck until the Holy Prophet completed his speech and the child was still on his neck. When the child saw someone else on the pulpit of his father it became difficult for him to bear. By Allah, I did not command him and he did not do because of my command.

"Fatimah, *'Alayha al-Salam,* is the person from whom I got permission for you to visit her and you both saw (learned) her words addressed to you. By Allah, she in her will to me had said that I must not allow you to attend her funeral or perform funeral *Salat* (formal prayer). I was not supposed to act against her will to me."

'Umar then said, "Leave your lullabying speech aside; I must exhume her grave so we can perform funeral *Salat* (formal prayer)." Ali, *'Alayhi al-Salam,* said, "By Allah, if you went with the intention to do such a thing you must take notice that you cannot reach such a point before the banishment of that in which is your eyes; I will not deal with you by anything else other than the sword before you reach such point."

Words were exchanged between Ali, *'Alayhi al-Salam,* and 'Umar until utterance of expressing acts of bravery became public from them and the people of Muhajir (immigrants) and al-Ansar (people of al-Madinah) gathered who said, "We will not be happy with such words said against the cousin and brother of the Messenger of Allah, *'Alayhi al-Salam.*" A disorder was about to take place but they departed each other.

H 208, Ch. 7, h 32
'Ilal al-Shara'i':

My father has narrated Ahmad ibn Idris from ibn 'Isa from al-Bazanti from 'Abd al-Rahman ibn Salim from al-Mufaddal who has said the following:

I (the narrator) asked 'Abu 'Abd Allah, saying, "I pray to Allah to keep my soul in service for your cause, who washed Fatimah, *'Alayha al-Salam,* for burial?" He (the narrator) has said that it seemed as if I considered it a great thing. He (the Imam), said, "It is as if you are stressed by what I informed you of." I (the narrator) replied, "Yes, indeed that was the case, I pray to Allah to keep my soul in service for your cause." He (the Imam), said, "You must not feel stressed because she was a *Siddiqah* (truthful one); no one other than one of such quality must have washed her. Did you not know that Maryam (Mary) was not washed by anyone other than 'Isa, *'Alayhi al-Salam.*"

Al-Kafi:

Muhammad ibn Yahya' has narrated from ibn 'Isa from 'Abd al-Rahman a similar Hadith.

H 209, Ch. 7, h 33
Qurb al-Asnad:

Ibn Tarif has narrated from ibn 'Ulwan from Ja'far from his father 'Alayhima al-Salam, who has said the following:

Ali, *'Alayhi al-Salam,* washed, for burial, Fatimah, *'Alayha al-Salam,* the daughter of the Messenger of Allah, *O Allah grant compensation to Muhammad and his family worthy of their services to your cause.*

H 210, Ch. 7, h 34
'Ilal al-Shara'i':

Ali ibn Ahmad ibn Muhammad has narrated from al-Asadi from al-Nakha'i from al-Nawfali from al-Bata'ini from his father who has said the following:

I (the narrator) asked 'Abu 'Abd Allah, about the reason why Fatimah, *'Alayha al-Salam,* was buried in the night and not during the day. He (the Imam), replied, "It is because she made a will that the two Arab men must not perform funeral *Salat* (formal prayer) for her."

"The (desert-dwelling) Arabs are far worse than the others in their disbelief and hypocrisy and have more reason to be ignorant of the revelations that Allah revealed to His messenger. Allah is All-knowing and all-wise." (9:97)

H 211, Ch. 7, h 35
'Ilal al-Shara'i': 'Amali of al-Saduq:

Ibn Musa has narrated from ibn Zakariya Al-Qattan from ibn Habib from Muhammad ibn 'Ubayd Allah and 'Abd Allah ibn al-Salt al-Jahdari who both has said that ibn 'A'ishah narrated to them from 'Abd Allah ibn 'Abd al-Rahman al-Hamadani from his father who has said the following:

When Ali, *'Alayhi al-Salam,* buried Fatimah, *'Alayha al-Salam,* he stood at the brink of the grave and it was in the night because she was buried in the night then he recite the following lines:

For every gathering of two friends there is a departing,

Those who do not face blaming are very few,

My losing one after the other,

Is proof that friendship does not remain forever,

You will soon avoid speaking of me and forget,

My love and after friendship a friendship comes into being.

H 212, Ch. 7, h 36
Kitab al-Dala'il of al-Tabari:

It is narrated from Ahmad ibn Muhammad al-Khashshab from Zakariya ibn Yahya' from abu Basir from 'Abu 'Abd Allah, 'Alayhi al-Salam, who has said the following:

When the Messenger of Allah, *O Allah grant compensation to Muhammad and his family worthy of their services to your cause,* passed away he did not leave anything other than the two heavy matters: the book of Allah and his descendants, his *Ahl al-Bayt* (family). He had whispered to Fatimah, *'Alayha al-Salam* that she will be the first one from his *Ahl al-Bayt* (family) to join him.

Fatimah, *'Alayha al-Salam,* has said that within few days after the death of her father, she in a condition of being fully awake, saw her father come to her. Fatimah, *'Alayha al-Salam,* has said, "When I saw him, I could not control myself and I called, 'O dear father, after you the news from the sky is cutoff from us.' In such condition rows of angels came to me, led by two angels, until they took me and ascended with me to the sky. I raised my head and there were the palaces all well-built, with gardens and streams flowing. There were palaces after palaces, gardens after gardens, and from those palaces maidens came out playing, who congratulated me laughing and saying welcome is the one for whom the garden (paradise) is created and for whose father we are created. The angels continued ascending with me until they admitted me in a *dar* (dwelling area) where there were palaces and in every palace there were such homes that no eyes had ever seen. There were thrones (couches) covered with silk and silk brocades with coverings of many colors of silk, and utensils of silver and gold, tables of many kinds of food. In those gardens there was a flowing stream with a substance whiter than milk and of the finer fragrance than al-Adhfar musk. I then asked, 'To who does this dwelling area belongs, and what is in this stream?'

"They replied, 'It is called *al-Firdaws al-'A'ala'* (the high paradise) after which is no other garden (paradise) and it is the home of your father with the Prophets and those whom Allah loves.' I then asked, 'What is this stream, canal?' They replied, 'This is al-Kawthar which Allah has promised to give to him.' I then asked, 'Where is my father?' They replied, 'He is about to visit you in this hour.'

"I was in that condition that palaces of intense whiteness appeared which were whiter than those ones and with better furnishings. There was a furnishing high on the thrones and my father was sitting on it and along with him there was a group. When he saw me he held me to himself and kissed between my eyes. He said, 'Welcome My dearest daughter.' He made me sit in his lap and said, 'O my dearest one, did you see what Allah has prepared for you and to what kind of place you are headed?' He showed me shining palaces with unique colors, decorated with ornaments. He said, 'This is your home and the homes of your husband and your two sons and those who love them. Allow your soul to enjoy that to which you are coming in few days.'"

Fatimah, *'Alayha al-Salam,* has said, "My heart almost flew, my yearning became intense and I woke up from my sleep frightened."

'Abu 'Abd Allah has said that Ali, *'Alayhi al-Salam,* has said that when she woke up she called me and I asked about the reason for her complaints. She then told me about her vision and then made me to promise as if promising the Messenger of Allah that when she will die no one should be informed except 'Umm Salamah, wife of the Holy Prophet, 'Umm 'Ayman, Fizzah, and of men, her two sons, 'Abd Allah ibn 'Abbas , Salman (Rh) Farsi, 'Ammar ibn Yasar, al-Miqdad, abu Dharr and Hudhayfah and she said, "I give you permission to look at me after my death and you must remain with the women who will wash me, you must not bury me in any time except in the night and no one must know the location of my grave."

When it was the night in which Allah willed to honor her and take her soul away she began to say, "'Alay*kum al-Salam* (to you I offer greeting of peace)." She said to me, "O dear cousin, Jibril has come offering, '*Salam*' (the phrase of offering peace and serenity), saying also that *al-Salam* (one of the names of Allah) offers you '*Salam*' (the phrase of offering the greeting of peace), O the beloved one to the one who is beloved to Allah and the fruit of his heart, today you are joining the friend of the high place, in the garden (paradise) of al-Ma'wa, then he went back." We then heard Fatimah, *'Alayha al-Salam,* for the second time say, "'Alay*kum al-Salam* (to you I offer greeting of peace)." She then said to me, "O my cousin, this was Michael who said to me what his companion, Jibril had said to me."

We then heard Fatimah, *'Alayha al-Salam,* say, "''Alay*kum al-Salam* (to you I offer greeting of peace)." We saw this time Fatimah, *'Alayha al-Salam,* opened her eyes bigger and said, "O son of my uncle, this is the truth. This by Allah is 'Izrael, the angel of death, who has spread his wings over the east and the west and he is just as my father had described him for me." We then heard Fatimah, *'Alayha al-Salam,* say, "''Alay*ka al-Salam* (to you I offer greeting of peace), O the one who takes away the spirits. Please be quick and do not punish me." We then heard Fatimah, *'Alayha al-Salam,* say, "To you O Lord, and not to the fire." She then closed her eyes and she then relaxed her hands and feet as if she was never alive."

H 213, Ch. 7, h 37
'Amali of al-Saduq:

Al-Maktab has narrated from al-'Alawi from al-Fazari from Muhammad ibn al-Husayn al-Zayyat from Sulayman ibn al-Hafs al-Marwazi from ibn Tarif from ibn Nabatah who has said the following:

'Amir al-Mu'minin Ali ibn abu Talib, *'Alayhima al-Salam,* was asked about the reason why Fatimah, *'Alayha al-Salam,* was buried in the nigh? He (the Imam), replied, "It is because Fatimah, *'Alayha al-Salam,* was angry with a people and she disliked that such people take part in her funeral matters and it is unlawful for all of those who have friendship with such people to perform funeral *Salat* (formal prayer) for any one of her children."

H 214, Ch. 7, h 38
'Amali al-Tusi:

Al-Mufid has narrated from Muhammad ibn Ahmad al-Mansuri from Salman ibn Sahl from 'Isa ibn Ishaq al-Qarashi from Hamdan ibn Ali al-Khaffaf from ibn Humayd ibn 'Ammar ibn Yasar from his father who has said the following:

When Fatimah, *'Alayha al-Salam,* the daughter of the Messenger of Allah, became ill with the illness because of which she died, and when her illness became grave, al-'Abbas ibn 'Abd al-Muttalib came to visit her. He was told that her illness has become grave, so no one is allowed to visit her. He went back and sent someone to Ali, *'Alayhi al-Salam,* to tell him, "O son of my brother your uncle sends you "*Salam*" (the phrase of offering the greeting of peace). He says that grief has suddenly overpowered him because of the complaints of the beloved daughter of the Messenger of Allah, and the delight of his eyes as well as the delight of his (Imam Ali, *'Alayhi al-Salam)* eyes, Fatimah, *'Alayha al-Salam,* has threatened him and he thinks that she is the first among us to join the Messenger of Allah, who chooses her, gives gifts to her and prepares her for her Lord. If the inevitable in her case takes place then I gather - may I be your ransom - the Muhajir (immigrants) and al-Ansar (people of al-Madinah) so that they can gain the reward for attending her funeral *Salat* (formal prayer) and in this there is the beauty for the religion."

Ali, *'Alayhi al-Salam,* said to his messenger, when I (the narrator) was present with him, "Convey my "*Salam*" (the phrase of offering the greeting of peace) to my uncle that I appreciate his compassionate feelings and greetings and I have noted his advice and that there is merit in his opinion. Fatimah, *'Alayha al-Salam,* the daughter of the Messenger of Allah, continues to remain oppressed, barred from her rights, pushed back from her legacy and the will of the Messenger of Allah is not followed about her and his rights as well as the rights of Allah, most Majestic, most Glorious, about her is not respected.

"That Allah is the Judge who exacts due compensation from the oppressors, is sufficiently comforting. I ask you, O dear uncle to excuse me for asking you to disregard your plans about the funeral arrangements for Fatimah, *'Alayha al-Salam,* because she has made a will to me to keep her affairs a secret."

He (the narrator) has said that when the messenger delivered the words of Ali, *'Alayhi al-Salam,* to al-'Abbas, al-'Abbas said, "May Allah grant forgiveness to the son of my brother who is being granted it already. His opinion cannot be criticized, because of the children of 'Abd al-Muttalib no one is created of the greatest blessing more than Ali, *'Alayhi al-Salam,* except the Holy Prophet, *'Alayhi al-Salam.* Ali, *'Alayhi al-Salam,* continues to be the foremost among them in every honorable matter and the most knowledgeable of every virtuous issue, the most brave one in difficult conditions and the strongest among them in acts of *Jihad* (hard work against the enemies) in defending the true religion, and the first one among those who believed in the Messenger of Allah *O Allah grant compensation to Muhammad and his family worthy of their services to your cause.*"

H 215, Ch. 7, h 39
Al-Khisal:

Muhammad ibn 'Umayr al-Baghdadi has narrated from Ahmad ibn al-Hassan ibn 'Abd al-Karim from 'Abbad ibn Suhayb from 'Isa ibn 'Abd Allah al-'Amri from his father from his grandfather from Ali, who has said the following:

"The earth is created for the sake of seven people because of whom they receive sustenance, rain and support and they are: abu Dharr, Salman (Rh), al-Miqdad, 'Ammar, Hudhayfah and 'Abd Allah ibn Mas'ud. Ali, *'Alayhi al-Salam,* has said that he is their Imam and they were the ones who attended the funeral *Salat* (formal prayer) for Fatimah, *'Alayha al-Salam.*

Rijal al-Kashshi:

Jibril ibn Ahmad has narrated from al-Husayn ibn Khurzad from ibn Faddal from Tha'labah from Zurarah from abu Ja'far from his father from his grandfather *'Alayhim al-Salam* a similar Hadith.

H 216, Ch. 7, h 40
Majalis al-Mufid: 'Amali al-Tusi:

Al-Mufid has narrated from al-Saduq from his father from Ahmad ibn Idris from Muhammad ibn 'Abd al-Jabbar from al-Qasim ibn Muhammad al-Razi from Ali ibn Muhammad al-Haramrazi from Ali ibn al-Husayn from his father al-Husayn, who has said the following:

When Fatimah, *'Alayha al-Salam,* the daughter of the Messenger of Allah, became ill she made a will to Ali ibn abu Talib, *'Alayhima al-Salam,* to keep her funeral affairs secret and keep the news about it away from the public and he must not allow anyone to visit her during her illness. Ali, *'Alayhi al-Salam,* followed her will. He alone would nurse Fatimah, *'Alayha al-Salam,* with help from 'Asma' the daughter of 'Umays (r.h) according to her will for secrecy. When Fatimah, *'Alayha al-Salam,* was about to die she said in her will to Ali, *'Alayhi al-Salam,* to undertake personally the tasks of her funeral matters, bury her in the night and conceal the traces of her gravesite. 'Amir al-Mu'minin followed her will thoroughly then concealed the traces of the gravesite.

When removing the dust of the gravesite from his hands waves of grief surged in him. He then allowed his tears to flood on his cheeks. Then he turned to the grave of the Messenger of Allah, saying such words which are recorded in Al-Kafi as follows:

[H 1236, Ch. 114, h 3, from al-Kafi]

Ahmad ibn Mihran, may Allah grant him blessing, has narrated in a marfu'
manner and Ahmad ibn Idris has narrated from Muhammad ibn 'Abd al-
Jabbar al-Shaybani who has said that narrated to me al-Qasim ibn
Muhammad al-Razi who has said that narrated to him Ali ibn Muhammad al-
Hurmuzani from abu 'Abd Allah al-Husayn ibn Ali, 'Alayhi al-Salam, who has
said the following:

"Abu 'Abd Allah al-Husayn ibn Ali, *'Alayhim al-Salam*, has said, 'When Fatimah, *'Alayha al-Salam*, passed away Amir al-Mu'minin Ali, *'Alayhi al-Salam*, buried her secretly, camouflaged her gravesite and then stood up facing the grave of the Messenger of Allah and said, "O Messenger of Allah, may Allah grant you blessings on my behalf and on behalf of your daughter who is visiting you and will pass this night in the soil of your location. Allah chose to make her join you the fastest. O Messenger of Allah, my patience has reached its limits and I miss so much your chosen one (daughter) and my self-control has vanished due to the departure of the leader of the ladies of the world. The only solace for me is to follow your tradition and be mournful for your own departure from us. A little while ago I placed you in your grave and your spirit left your body between my own throat and chest. Yes, in the book of Allah (for me) there is the best example for expressing acceptance of Allah's decision, 'We are the servants of Allah and to Him we shall all return.'" (2:156)

'The trust is returned, the commitment is recalled and al-Zahra' is taken away from us. How sad, O Messenger of Allah, the green skies and the dusty earth seem to us. My sadness has become perpetual and my nights have become sleepless. There is an anxiety that will not relieve my heart until Allah will choose for me a dwelling like that where you are. I have a heart bleeding, sorrowful, and a restlessess and anxiety. How quickly the separation took place. Before Allah I lament, and your own daughter will explain to you how your 'Umma (followers) succeeded in committing injustice against her. You may ask her questions and find information about the case from her. How great was her sorrow for which she could not find a place for expressing, but now she has found a place and an ear to express it to. She would say, 'Allah will judge because He is the best judge'. I offer my prayer to Allah to grant you blessings as a note of farewell, but not because of disappointment and desperation. If I return it is not because I have become tired and if I stand up it will not be because of pessimism toward the promise of Allah to those who exercise patience. Indeed to exercise patience is more safe and fruitful. Had I not feared the mischief of the enemies I would have liked to turn the place into a place of worship, to keep my worship continuous and to cry like the mothers for the death of their son, for the great loss. In the sight of Allah your daughter is buried secretly, her rights are taken away unjustly, her inheritance is withheld for no valid reason. It all happened just after you left and your memories are still fresh. To Allah, O Messenger of Allah, we lament and from you, O Messenger of Allah, we seek condolences. May Allah grant blessings to you and to her. May the peace and happiness from Allah be with you.'"

H 217, Ch. 7, h 41
'Uyunu al-Mu'jizat by Al-Sayyid al-Murtada' (r.h):

It is narrated that Fatimah, *'Alayha al-Salam,* died and on the day of her death she was eighteen years old. She lived seventy-five days after the death of the Holy Prophet, *'Alayhi al-Salam.* It is also narrated that she lived forty days thereafter. 'Amir al-Mu'minin, *'Alayhi al-Salam* prepared her for her funeral and no one except al-Hassan and al-Husayn, *'Alayhima al-Salam* were present. She was taken to al-Baqi' during the night. He performed the *Salat* (prayer) for funeral and no one was told about it. She was buried in al-Baqi'. He formed forty new graves there. People found forty new graves and it became difficult for them to find out which one was her grave. People crowded and blamed each other saying that your Prophet had left no more than one daughter among you. She dies, is buried and we did not attend her funeral or perform *Salat* (prayer) for her funeral and we do not know where her grave is so we can visit.

Their authorities told them to call the Muslim women to exhume these new graves to find out Fatimah, *'Alayha al-Salam,* and then we perform funeral *Salat* (prayer) and visit her grave. This reached 'Amir al-Mu'minin, *'Alayhi al-Salam.* He came out angry with his eyes turned red in anger leaning on his sword, Dhulfaqar, until he arrived in al-Baqi' where the people had gathered. Ali, *'Alayhi al-Salam,* said to them, "If you exhumed even one of these graves I will place the sword in you." People then turned back from al-Baqi'.

H 218, Ch. 7, h 42
Tahdhib:

Salmah ibn al-Khattab has narrated from Musa ibn 'Umar ibn Yazid from Ali ibn al-Nu'man from ibn Muskan from Sulayman ibn Khalid from 'Abu 'Abd Allah, who has said the following:

I (the narrator) asked 'Abu 'Abd Allah, *'Alayhi al-Salam*, about the first person for whom a coffin was prepared. He (the Imam) said, "That person was Fatimah, *'Alayha al-Salam*, the daughter of the Messenger of Allah, *Allah grant compensation to Muhammad and his family worthy of their services to your cause.*"

H 219, Ch. 7, h 43
Al-Tahdhib:

Salmah ibn al-Khattab has narrated from Ahmad ibn Yahya' ibn Zakariya from his father from Humayd ibn al-Muthanna from abu 'Abd al-Rahman al-Hadhdha' from 'Abu 'Abd Allah, who has said the following:

The first coffin which was introduced in the Muslim community was the one prepared for Fatimah, *'Alayha al-Salam*. Fatimah, *'Alayha al-Salam*, complained because of the illness from which she died. Fatimah, *'Alayha al-Salam*, said to 'Asma', "I have become very weak because of this illness. Can you prepare a device that can keep me out of the public sight?" 'Asma' said, "When I was in Ethiopia I had seen something and if you like I can show it to you." Fatimah, *'Alayha al-Salam*, said, "Please do prepare one for me." 'Asma' then turned a bed frame upside down then by running twigs from one of its legs to the other leg then to the one next and the next until all four was connected then she covered it with a sheet of fabric saying, "This is what I had seen they would do there." Fatimah, *'Alayha al-Salam*, then told her. "Prepare one to keep me out of public sight and may Allah keep you out of the fire."

H 220 Ch. 7, h 44
It is from old books of al-Manaqib (virtues):

The narrations are different about the time of death of Fatimah, 'Alayha al-Salam:

In one narration it is said that Fatimah, *'Alayha al-Salam*, lived for two months after the death of the Messenger of Allah, in another narration it is three months and still in another one it is one hundred days and in another one it is eight months.

It is narrated from Ali ibn Ahmad al-'Asemi through the chain of his narrators from Musa ibn Ja'far, from his ancestors 'Alayhim al-Salam, from Ali, who has said the following:

When the Messenger of Allah, passed away, Fatimah, *'Alayha al-Salam,* would say, "Alas, O beloved father, how close he is from his Lord, Alas, O father, the garden (paradise) of eternity has become his home, Alas, O father, his Lord honors him when he goes to Him, Alas, O father to whom his Lord and the messengers offer *"Salam"* (the phrase of offering the greeting of peace) when he meets them."

When Fatimah, *'Alayha al-Salam,* died, 'Amir al-Mu'minin, recited the lines:

"All intimate friends one day depart. . ."

Al-Hakim has said that when Fatimah, *'Alayha al-Salam,* died Ali, *'Alayhi al-Salam,* composed these lines:

My soul is holding on to its deep breaths,

I wish it were to come out with its deep breaths,

There is nothing good in life after you,

I only weep for fear of my living longer.

It is narrated from al-Sayyid al-Huffaz abu Mansur al-Daylami through the chain of his narrators from 'Abd Allah ibn al-Hassan who visited Hisham ibn 'Abd Malik when al-Kalbi was with him. Hisham asked 'Abd Allah ibn al-Hassan saying, "O abu Muhammad, at what age did Fatimah, *'Alayha al-Salam,* daughter of the Messenger of Allah, die?" He replied, "She died at the age of thirty years." Al-Kalbi then said, "It was thirty-five." 'Abd Allah then said, "O 'Amir al-Mu'minin, you can ask me about my mother because I am more knowledgeable about my mother and ask al-Kalbi about his mother, because he is more knowledgeable about his mother."

It is narrated from al-'Asem ibn Hamid through the chain of his narrators from Muhammad ibn 'Umar who has said the following:

Fatimah, *'Alayha al-Salam,* the daughter of Muhammad, *O Allah grant compensation to Muhammad and his family worthy of their services to your cause,* died on the third of the month of Ramadan and she was twenty nine or so years old.

Abu 'Abd Allah ibn Mandah Isfahani in the book al-Ma'rifah has said that Ali, *'Alayhi al-Salam,* married Fatimah, *'Alayha al-Salam,* one year after the migration of the Holy Prophet and his wedding took place one year afterward. Al-Hassan, al-Husayn, al-Muhsin, 'Umm Kulthum al-Kubra' and Zaynab al-Kubra' were born to them.

Muhammad ibn Ishaq has said that Fatimah, *'Alayha al-Salam,* died at the age of twenty eight years. It is said that she died at the age of twenty seven years and in another narration it is said that she was born when the Holy Prophet, was forty one years old and on this basis she must have lived for twenty three years. The majority is of the opinion that she was twenty nine or thirty years old.

Wahab ibn Manbah has narrated from ibn 'Abbas who has said that she lived only forty days after the death of the Holy Prophet, *'Alayhi al-Salam.* He has said that when she died 'Asma' tore her shirt and came out then she met al-Hassan and al-Husayn, who asked her, "Where is our mother?" She remained silent, they entered the house and found their mother lying down, al-Husayn, wiggled her but found out that she was dead. He said, "O brother, may Allah grant you your reward; your mother is dead." The two of them came out weeping, "Alas, O Muhammad, Alas, O Ahmad, today our grief for your death is renewed because our mother has died."

They then informed Ali, *'Alayhi al-Salam,* who was in the Masjid. He fainted and water was sprinkled on him until he regained conscienceness. He took both of them until they arrived at the house of Fatimah, *'Alayha al-Salam.* They found 'Asma' near her head weeping saying, "O Allah, most High, these are the orphans of Muhammad. We sought solace with Fatimah, *'Alayha al-Salam,* after the death of your grandfather and now from whom can we find solace?" Ali, *'Alayhi al-Salam,* uncovered her face and near her head he found a sheet with the following writings on it:

Bismillah, (in the name of Allah, most Beneficent, most Merciful)

This is the will of Fatimah, *'Alayha al-Salam,* the daughter of the Messenger of Allah, who has said, "I testify that only Allah deserves worship, He is one and has no partners and I testify that Muhammad is His servant and Messenger, that the garden (paradise) is true and the fire is true and that the hour inevitably comes and Allah will raise those who are in the graves. O Ali, *'Alayhi al-Salam,* I am Fatimah, *'Alayha al-Salam,* the daughter of Muhammad. Allah has given me in marriage to you so I am for you in the world and in the next life. You are for me before others. Apply *Hunut* to me, wash, shroud me and perform funeral *Salat* (formal prayer) for me and bury me in the night and do not inform anyone. I leave you in the trust of Allah and please convey my "*Salam*" (the phrase of offering the greeting of peace) to my two sons. With "*Salam*" (the phrase of offering the greeting of peace) until the Day of Judgment.

When it became night he washed her then placed her on the bed frame, then told al-Hassan to call for him abu Dharr. They then carried her to the place for *Salat* (formal prayer) and performed the funeral *Salat* (formal prayer) for her, then performed two Rak'at *Salat* (formal prayer). He then raised his hands to the sky and called. "This is Fatimah, *'Alayha al-Salam,* the daughter of your Holy Prophet, you have taken her from darkness to light. Then the land became bright one mile by one mile. When they wanted to bury her they were called from a location in al-Baqi', "Come to me, come to me, her soil is raised from me." They looked there and there was a grave already made. They carried the coffin to the edge of the grave and said, "O soil I entrust you with my security, this is the daughter the Messenger of Allah. A call then came from inside it saying, "O Ali, *'Alayhi al-Salam,* I am more kind and gentle to her than you. You can go back without worries." He then returned and closed the grave and leveled the ground. No one was able to find out where she was until the Day of Judgment.

H 221 Ch. 7, h 45

I ('Allamah Majlisi) say that abu al-Faraj in Muqatil al-Talibiyin has said that Fatimah, *'Alayha al-Salam,* died after the death of the Holy Prophet, with in a time about which there are different narrations. The maximum of which is eight months and the minimum is forty days. However, what is established is what is narrated from abu Ja'far, Muhammad ibn Ali, *'Alayhima al-Salam,* that she died after three months.

This was narrated to me by al-Hassan ibn Ali narrated to me from al-Harith from ibn Sa'd from al-Waqidi from 'Amr ibn Dinar from abu Ja'far Muhammad ibn Ali, *'Alayhima al-Salam*.

H 222 Ch. 7, h 46
Misbah al-Kufah'ami: al-Misbahayn:

Fatimah, *'Alayha al-Salam*, passed away on the third of the month of Jamadi al-Akhar, in the year eleven. (A.H).

H 223 Ch. 7, h 47
Al-Misbahayn:

Fatimah, *'Alayha al-Salam*, died on the twenty first of the month of Rajab according to the words of ibn 'Abbas.

Note: The accounts about the date of birth and death of Fatimah, *'Alayha al-Salam*, as mentioned from the historical narrations are not reconcilable.

According to the authentic narration Fatimah, *'Alayha al-Salam*, lived for seventy five days after the death of the Messenger of Allah, *'Alayhi al-Salam*. . .

H 224 Ch. 7, h 48
I ('Allamah Majlisi) say that in *al-Diwan* (a booklet) ascribed to Ali, *'Alayhi al-Salam*, the following lines are recorded. He recited these lines after the death of Fatimah, *'Alayha al-Salam*:

Is there a way to a long life,

Where can it be found when this death does not change?

Even though I am certain of death,

Still I have hope beyond it which is very long,

Time has its colors that change mornings and evenings,

And souls in between get flooded,

The true destination cannot be diverted,

For every man from it (colors) there is a path,

I have passed such days that to make a mention of them is precious,

However, every cherished mater is humble here,

I see the worldly illnesses are many on me,

But the friends of the world until death is ill,

I yearn for those whom I love,

Is there a path to the ones I had loved?

Although my household matters are scattered and being displaced,

But before me beautiful ones have died because of separation,

In proverbs on separation what has been said,

I repeat, "separation announces a departure",

For every gathering of two friends there is a departing,

All those who can remain without separation are very few,

My losing Fatimah, *'Alayha al-Salam,* after Ahmad,

Is proof that friends cannot remain together all the time,

How is life thereafter losing them,

By your life is something, to which there is no way to know,

Speaking of me will be disregarded,

My love will be forgotten and after me friends will appear as substitutes,

My friend is not saddened and not as such that,

If I remained absent someone else instead of me can make him happy,

However, my friend is one, whose accessibility continues,

His heart protects my secret as a sanctuary,

If I pass a day from life,

The weeping of the weepers is very little,

The youth wants his beloved one not to die,

But there is no way to reach what he wants,

The loss of property is not a great thing,

However, the loss of honorable ones is a grave thing,

For this reason my side does not rest on the bed,

And in my heart there is boiling because of the heat of separation.

Also of his lines are the following after the death of Fatimah, *'Alayha al-Salam*:

Why am I standing on the graves offering "*Salam*" (the phrase of offering the greeting of peace),

To the grave of the beloved one who is not responding to me,

O beloved one, what is the matter, you do not respond to us,

Have you forgotten the intimacy of the beloved ones?

Answering himself he has said on behalf of Fatimah, *'Alayha al-Salam*:

The beloved one has said: How can I respond to you,

When I am buried under the bolders and soil,

The soil has consumed my beauty so I have forgotten you,

And I am barred from my family and peers,

From me to you is "*Salam*" (the phrase of offering the greeting of peace),

But the intimate relations friendship between us has become cut off.

H 225 Ch. 7, h 49
Al-Misbah al-Anwar:

It is narrated from abu Ja'far, who has said the following:

Fatimah, *'Alayha al-Salam,* the daughter of the Messenger of Allah, *O Allah grant compensation to Muhammad and his family worthy of their services to your cause,* lived only for sixty days after the death of the Messenger of Allah, she then became ill and it became grave and she would recite this prayer:

"O the living, the guardian I plead for your mercy, please respond to my plea. O Lord, keep me away from the fire and admit me in the garden (paradise) and join me with my father, Muhammad, *O Allah grant compensation to Muhammad and his family worthy of their services to your cause.*" 'Amir al-Mu'minin, would say, "May Allah grant you good health and give you long life." Fatimah, *'Alayha al-Salam,* would say, "O abu al-Hassan, how fast is arriving in the presence of Allah." Fatimah, *'Alayha al-Salam,* then made her will about her charity and the household belongings. In the will Fatimah, *'Alayha al-Salam,* said that he should marry Amamah daughter of abu al-'As because as the daughter of her sister she will be compassionate to her children.

He (the narrator) has said that he (Ali) buried Fatimah, *'Alayha al-Salam,* in the night.

It is narrated from ibn 'Abbas who has said that Fatimah, *'Alayha al-Salam,* in her dream saw the Holy Prophet, *'Alayhi al-Salam.* She has said, "I complained before him against things that has happened to us after him." Fatimah, *'Alayha al-Salam,* has said that the Messenger of Allah, said to me, "For you there is the next life which is prepared for the pious ones and that you will be coming to us very soon."

It is narrated from Ja'far ibn Muhammad from his ancestors 'Alayhim al-Salam who has said the following:

When Fatimah, *'Alayha al-Salam,* was about to leave this world she wept and Ali, *'Alayhi al-Salam,* asked, "What has made you to weep, O my *Sayyidah* (madam)?"

Fatimah, *'Alayha al-Salam,* replied, "After me you will face great hardships and that is what has made me to weep." Ali, *'Alayhi al-Salam,* said, "You must not weep; such suffering for the sake of Allah is a very small thing to me."

He (the narrator) has said that Fatimah, *'Alayha al-Salam,* had said in her will not to allow the two Shaykhs to attend her funeral and Ali, *'Alayhi al-Salam,* executed her will thoroughly.

H 226 Ch. 7, h 50
Kitab al-Dala'il of al-Tabari:

It is narrated from abu Ishaq al-Baqirji from Fala''ijah from 'Abu 'Abd Allah, from abu Ahmad from Muhammad ibn Baghdan from Muhammad ibn al-Salt from 'Abd Allah ibn Sa'id from abu Jarih from Ja'far ibn Muhammad from his father from Fatimah, 'Alayha al-Salam:

Fatimah, *'Alayha al-Salam,* bequeathed to each of the wives of the Holy Prophet, twelve *Awqiyah* and a similar amount to each of the women of banu Hashim and something to Amamah daughter of abu al-'As.

Through another chain of narrators from 'Abd Allah ibn al-Hassan from Zayd ibn Ali it is narrated that Fatimah, *'Alayha al-Salam,* gave her belongings in charity to banu Hashim and banu 'Abd al-Muttalib and that Ali, *'Alayhi al-Salam,* gave them as charity but included others also.

Chapter 8 - Pleading of Fatimah, *'Alayha al-Salam*, for justice on the Day of Judgment and the manner of her coming to the location of resurrection

H 227 Ch. 8, h 1
'Amali of al-Saduq:

Al-Taliqani has narrated from Muhammad ibn Jarir al-Tabari from al-Hassan ibn 'Abd Wahid from 'Isma 'il ibn Ali al-Sadi from Muni' ibn al-Hajjaj from 'Isa ibn Musa from Ja 'far al-Ahmar from abu Ja 'far Muhammad ibn Ali Al-Baqir, 'Alayhi al-Salam who has said the following:

I (the narrator) heard Jabir ibn 'Abd Allah al-Ansari say the following:

He (the narrator) has said that the Messenger of Allah, has said that when it will be the Day of Judgment my daughter Fatimah, *'Alayha al-Salam,* will come on a camel of light decorated on both sides, with a harness of fresh pearls, legs of green emerald, a tail of al-Adhfar saffron, eyes of two red rubies, with a dome of light on it, transparent totally, inside with pardoning of Allah and outside with the mercy of Allah. She will have a crown of light on her head with seventy corners decorated with pearls and rubies that shine like a bright star in the horizon of the sky, seventy thousand angels on each of the right and left sides, Jibril holding the harness of the camel announcing to the peak of his voice: "Cast down your eyes until Fatimah, *'Alayha al-Salam,* the daughter of Muhammad passes by." On that day no one of the Prophets, messengers, and martyrs will remain without casting down their eyes until Fatimah, *'Alayha al-Salam,* passes by. Fatimah, *'Alayha al-Salam,* will move until she arrives parallel to the Throne of her Lord, and leaves the camel and will say, "O Lord, my master, please judge between me and those who have done injustice to me. O Lord, judge between me and those who murdered my children."

A call then will come from the Lord, most Majestic, most Glorious, saying, "My beloved one, the daughter of my beloved one, ask me and you will be granted and intercede, it will be granted, by my majesty and glory, no injustice of the unjust ones can bypass me." Fatimah, *'Alayha al-Salam,* will say, "My Lord, my master, my descendants, my (*Shi'a*, followers of *Ahl al-Bayt*), *Shi'a* of my descendants and those who honored me and those who loved my descendants."

A call will come from Allah, most Majestic, most Glorious, "Where are the descendants of Fatimah, *'Alayha al-Salam,* her *Shi'a* and those who honored her and those who loved her descendants?" They will come forward surrounded by the angels of mercy then Fatimah, *'Alayha al-Salam,* will lead them until they enter the garden (paradise).

H 228 Ch. 8, h 2
'Yun Akhbar al-Rida':

Ahmad ibn abu Ja'far al-Bayhaqi has narrated from Ahmad ibn Ali al-Jurjani from 'Isma'il ibn abu 'Abd Allah al-Qattan from Ahmad ibn 'Abd Allah ibn 'Amir al-Ta'i from Ali ibn Musa al-Rida', from his ancestors, 'Alayhim al-Salam, who has said the following:

The Messenger of Allah, *O Allah grant compensation to Muhammad and his family worthy of their services to your cause,* has said, "My daughter Fatimah, *'Alayha al-Salam,* will be resurrected on the Day of Judgment and with her there will be clothes stained with blood. They will be shown on the pillars of the Throne and she will say, "O justice, judge between me and the murderers of my children."

Ali ibn abu Talib, *'Alayhima al-Salam,* has said that the Messenger of Allah, has said, "By the Lord of al-Ka'bah, Allah will issue His Judgment in favor of my daughter."

H 229 Ch. 8, h 3
'Yun Akhbar al-Rida':

Through the three chains of narrators it is narrated from al-Rida', from his ancestors, *'Alayhim al-Salam,* who have said that the Messenger of Allah, has said, "My daughter Fatimah, *'Alayha al-Salam,* will be resurrected on the Day of Judgment and with her there will be clothes stained with blood. They will be shown on a pillar of the Throne and she will say, "O justice, judge between me and the murderers of my children."

He (the narrator) has said that the Messenger of Allah, has said, "By the Lord of al-Ka'bah, Allah will issue His Judgment in favor of my daughter. Allah, most Majestic, most Glorious, is angry because of the anger of Fatimah, *'Alayha al-Salam,* and He is happy because of the happiness of Fatimah, *'Alayha al-Salam.*"

Sahifah al-Rida':

It is narrated from al-Rida', from his ancestors *'Alayhim al-Salam* a similar Hadith.

H 230 Ch. 8, h 4
'Yun Akhbar al-Rida':

Through the three chains of narrators it is narrated from al-Rida', from his ancestors, *'Alayhim al-Salam,* who have said that the Messenger of Allah, has said, "On the Day of Judgment an announcer will announce, 'O the community of creatures cast down your eyes until Fatimah, *'Alayha al-Salam,* daughter of Muhammad, passes by.'"

H 231 Ch. 8, h 5
Sahifah al-Rida':

It is narrated from al-Rida', from his ancestors who have narrated a similar Hadith.

In another narration he (the Imam), has said that on the Day of Judgment it will be announced, "O all those present in the gathering you must cast down your eyes until Fatimah, *'Alayha al-Salam,* the daughter of the Messenger of Allah, passes by." She will pass by with two pieces of fine red fabrics on her.

H 232 Ch. 8, h 6
'Yun Akhbar al-Rida':

Through the three chains of narrators it is narrated from al-Rida', from his ancestors *'Alayhim al-Salam* who have said that the Messenger of Allah, has said, "My daughter Fatimah, *'Alayha al-Salam,* will be raised on the Day of Judgment with the dress of honor which is combined (made marvelous) with the water of the life of eternity. The creatures will look to her in astonishment. Thereafter she will dress in a thousand dresses of the garden (paradise) on each of which it will be written in green, "Admit the daughter of Muhammad in the garden (paradise) in the best form, the best honor, and with the best appearance." Fatimah, *'Alayha al-Salam,* will be escorted (hurried) to the garden (paradise) as a bride is escorted with seventy thousand angels as her maidens (guards).

Sahifah al-Rida':

It is narrated from the narrator of the previous Hadith from his ancestors a similar Hadith.

H 233 Ch. 8, h 7
Thawab al-'A'mal:

Majiluwayh has narrated from Muhammad al-'Attar from al-Ash'ariy from Muhammad ibn al-Husayn from Muhammad ibn from certain ones of his people from 'Abu 'Abd Allah, who has said the following:

The Messenger of Allah, has said, "On the Day of Judgment a dome of light will be established for Fatimah, *'Alayha al-Salam.* Al-Husayn, *'Alayhi al-Salam,* will move forward with his head in his hand. When Fatimah, *'Alayha al-Salam,* will see him she will sob and moan because of which no one in the gathering of the close angels, messenger Prophet, or the believing people remain without weeping. Allah, most Majestic, most Glorious, then will delegate a person of the best form as the attorney to prosecute his murderers (of the plaintiff without head). Allah then will summon all of his murderers, those who prepared them and those who took part in his murder. They will all be killed to the end, then they will be raised again and 'Amir al-Mu'minin will punish them with capital, punishment, then they will be raised again, and al-Hassan will punish them with capital punishment, then they will be raised again, and al-Husayn, will punish them with capital punishment, then they will be raised again, Ali ibn al-Husayn, will punish them with capital punishment, then they will be raised again, and no one of our descendants will be left without punishing them with capital punishment. At that time Allah will uncover the intense anger and make the grief to become forgotten.

'Abu 'Abd Allah, then said, "May Allah grant mercy to our *Shi'a,* by Allah they are believing people. They certainly have taken part with us in the long lasting grief and sorrow."

H 234 Ch. 8, h 8
Thawab al-'A'mal:

Ibn al-Mutawakkal has narrated from Muhammad al-'Attar from al-Ash'ariy from ibn Yazid from Muhammad ibn Mansur from a man from Sharik in a marfu' manner has narrated the following:

The Messenger of Allah, *O Allah grant compensation to Muhammad and his family worthy of their services to your cause,* has said that on the Day of Judgment Fatimah, *'Alayha al-Salam,* will come in the group of her women. She will be asked to enter in the garden (paradise). She will say, "No, until I learn what was done to my son after me." It then will be said to her, "Look at the center of the resurrection." She will look at al-Husayn, standing without his head. She will sob a severe sobbing because of which I will sob and the angels will sob because of our sobbing and Allah, most Majestic, most Glorious, is angry at that time and He commands the fire called *Hab Hab* which is being blown into for a thousand years until it turns black. No happiness ever enters there and no sadness ever comes out of it. It then will be commanded to snatch the murderers of al-Husayn, *'Alayhi al-Salam,* who carried al-Quran also.

When they turn into its crop it will snort, whinny as they also do so, it will sob and they also will do so, it will breathe and they also will do so. They will speak with smooth and clear tongue, "O Lord, how is it that you have placed us in the fire before the worshippers of the idols?"

The answer will come from Allah, most Majestic, most Glorious: "Those who know are not equal to those who do not know."

H 235 Ch. 8, h 9
Thawab al-'A'mal:

Ibn al-Barqiy has narrated from his father from his grandfather from his father from Muhammad ibn Khalid in a marfu' manner from 'Anbasah al-Ta'i from abu Khayr from Ali ibn abu Talib, 'Alayhima al-Salam, who has said the following:

The Messenger of Allah, *O Allah grant compensation to Muhammad and his family worthy of their services to your cause,* has said that the head of al-Husayn, stained in his blood will be portrayed for Fatimah, *'Alayha al-Salam,* and she will sob, "Alas, my son! Alas, the delight of my heart!" The angels will also moan because of the sobbing of Fatimah, *'Alayha al-Salam.* The population of the field of resurrection will call, "May Allah destroy the murderers of your son, O Fatimah, *'Alayha al-Salam.*"

He (the narrator) has said that Allah, most Majestic, most Glorious, will say, "This is what I do for him, for his *Shi'a* and friends and his followers." Fatimah, *'Alayha al-Salam,* on that day will be on a camel of the camels of the garden (paradise) decorated on both sides, of clear forehead, of *shahla* (a mix of black and blue colors) eyes, with its head made of pure gold, its neck made of musk and ambergris, its reign made of green emerald, its seat made of pearls decorated with gems. On the camel there will be a carriage covered with the light of Allah, its filling made of the mercy of Allah and its reign will be three miles of the worldly miles. The carriage will be surrounded by seventy thousand angels reciting *Tasbih* (Allah is free of all defects), *Tahmid,* (all praise belongs to Allah), *Tahlil,* (no one deserves worship except Allah), and *Takbir* (Allah is great beyond description) and praise of Lord of worlds.

Then a caller will call from under the Throne, "O inhabitants of the field of resurrection cast down your eyes. This is Fatimah, *'Alayha al-Salam,* the daughter of Muhammad, the Messenger of Allah, crossing the bridge." Fatimah, *'Alayha al-Salam,* and her *Shi'a* will cross the bridge like lightening.

The Holy Prophet, has said that the enemies of Fatimah, *'Alayha al-Salam,* and the enemies of her descendants will be thrown in hell.

H 236 Ch. 8, h 10
Manaqib of ibn Shahr Ashub:

Al-Sam'ani in Resalah al-Qawamiyah, al-Za'farani in Fada'il al-Sahabah, al-Ashnahi in 'I'tiqad of Ahl al-Sunnah, al-'Akbari in al-Ebanah, Ahmad in Fada'Imam (leader), ibn al-Mu'adhdhin in al-Arba'in through the chains their narrators from al-Sha'bi from abu Juhayfah, from ibn 'Abbas, al-Asbagh from abu Ayyub, from Hafs ibn al-Bakhtariy ibn Ghiyas from al-Qazwini from 'Ata' from abu Hurayrah all from the Holy Prophet, have narrated the following:

The Holy Prophet, has said that on the Day of Judgment all creatures will stand before Allah, most High. A caller will call from behind the curtain, "O people, cast down your eyes and bow down you heads because Fatimah, *'Alayha al-Salam,* the daughter of Muhammad, *O Allah grant compensation to Muhammad and his family worthy of their services to your cause,* crosses the bridge." In the narration of abu Ayyub it is said, "Then along with her seventy thousand maidens of *al-Hawra' al-'in* she will cross the bridge like a lightning-bolt."

H 237 Ch. 8, h 11
Majalis al-Mufid:

Al-Saduq has narrated from his father from Ali from his father from ibn abu 'Umayr from Aban ibn 'Uthman from 'Abu 'Abd Allah, 'Alayhi al-Salam, who has said the following:

'Abu 'Abd Allah, has said that on the Day of Judgment all the people of the past and the last generations will be assembled on one ground. An announcer will announce, "Cast down your eyes and bent down you heads, until Fatimah, *'Alayha al-Salam,* the daughter of Muhammad, *O Allah grant compensation to Muhammad and his family worthy of their services to your cause,* crosses the bridge. The creatures then will cast down their eyes then Fatimah, *'Alayha al-Salam,* comes on a noble camel of the noble camels of the garden (paradise) escorted by seventy thousand angels. She will take her honorable place of the stations of resurrection. She will then disembark the noble carrier and hold the shirt of al-Husayn ibn Ali, *'Alayhima al-Salam,* stained with his blood and will say, "O Lord, this is the shirt of my son and you know what was done to him." At that time a call will come from Allah, most Majestic, most Glorious, saying, "O Fatimah, *'Alayha al-Salam,* I want your happiness." Fatimah, *'Alayha al-Salam,* will say, "I ask for your support against his murderers." Allah will then command a part of the fire which will come out therefrom and pick up the murderers of al-Husayn, just as birds pick up grains. The part of the fire will return with them and they will be punished there with various kinds of punishment. Fatimah, *'Alayha al-Salam,* then will embark the noble carrier with the angels escorting her descendants and their friends of the people on the right and left to enter the garden (paradise).

H 238 Ch. 8, h 12
Tafsir of Furat ibn Ibrahim:

Abu al-Qasim al-'Alawi al-al-Hassani has narrated in Mu'an'an manner from ibn 'Abbas who has said the following:

On the Day of Judgment a caller will call, "O the community of the creatures, cast down your eyes until Fatimah, *'Alayha al-Salam,* the daughter Muhammad, *O Allah grant compensation to Muhammad and his family worthy of their services to your cause,* passes by."

Fatimah, *'Alayha al-Salam,* will be the first one to dress up and to receive the welcome from twelve thousand *al-Hawra' al-'in.* No one before and no one after Fatimah, *'Alayha al-Salam,* had received such welcome on the noble carriers with their wings made of rubies and reigns of pearls. On the carrier there will be reclining areas furnished with carpets of thickly woven silk. The stirrups of the carrier are made of emerald.

They along with Fatimah, *'Alayha al-Salam,* will pass the bridge until they arrive along with her at al-Firdaws and the inhabitants of the garden (paradise) receive the glad news. In al-Firdaws the garden (paradise) there are white palaces and yellow palaces made of pearls consisting of one single bead. The white palaces have seventy thousand chambers which are the dwellings of Muhammad and *Ale* (family of) Muhammad, *'Alayhim al-Salam.* The yellow palaces have seventy thousand chambers which are the dwellings of Ibrahim, and *Ale* (family of) Ibrahim, *'Alayhi al-Salam.* Fatimah, *'Alayha al-Salam,* will sit on a chair of light and they *al-Hawra' al-'in* sit around her. An angel who is not sent to anyone before or after her will be sent to her who will say, "Your Lord conveys '*Salam*' (the phrase of offering the greeting of peace) to you and says, 'You can ask me for whatever you like and I will give it to you.'" Fatimah, *'Alayha al-Salam,* will say, "He has already completed His bounties on me, made His grace pleasant for me, He has made His garden (paradise) permissible for me but I ask Him for my children and descendants and those who loved them." Allah will grant Fatimah, *'Alayha al-Salam,* her descendants, children and those who loved them and protected them for her sake. He will say *Tahmid*, (all praise belongs to Allah who has removed grief and has made my eyes delighted.

Ja'far has said that my father would say that whenever ibn 'Abbas would remember this Hadith he would recite the following verse of al-Quran:

"(The bountiful) paradise is for the pious ones) and for the believers and their offspring who have followed them (their parents) in belief, whom We shall join with their parents therein. We shall reduce nothing from their deeds. Everyone will be responsible for his own actions." (52:21)

H 239 Ch. 8, h 13
Tafsir of Furat ibn Ibrahim:

Sulayman ibn Muhammad has narrated Mu'an'an manner from ibn 'Abbas who has said the following:

I (the narrator) heard 'Amir al-Mu'minin, Ali ibn abu Talib, *'Alayhima al-Salam,* say, "One day the Messenger of Allah, visited Fatimah, *'Alayha al-Salam,* and found her sad. He then asked her about the reason for her sadness. She said, "You have spoken of resurrection and that people will be naked on the Day of Judgment." He then said, "My dearest daughter that will be a great day, however Jibril has informed me from Allah, most Majestic, most Glorious, that the first one for whom the ground will be made to split apart on the Day of Judgment will be myself then Ibrahim, then your husband Ali ibn abu Talib, *'Alayhima al-Salam.* Thereafter Jibril will be sent for you with seventy thousand angels who will establish seven domes of light then Israfil will come with three dresses of light and will stand near your head and call you, "O Fatimah, *'Alayha al-Salam,* the daughter of Muhammad, rise for the resurrection." You then will rise safe from fear, all covered then Israfil will give you the dresses which you will wear then Zuqael will come with a noble carrier of light, with its reign made of fresh pearls with a comforter of gold on it and you will embark on it and Zuqael will lead it with seventy thousand angels in front of you with the banners of *Tasbih* (Allah is free of all defects) in their hands. When the journey will seem wearying to you then seventy thousand *al-Hawra' al-'in* will welcome you who receive the glad news of having permission to look at you with a tray of incense of light in the hands of each one of them from the fragrance of *'Ud* (a certain kind of perfume) will rise without fire. They will have crowns of gems on them decorated with green emerald. They will travel on your right side and when you travel a similar distance from your grave I will meet you, and Maryam (Mary) daughter of 'Imran will receive you along with the same number of *al-Hawra' al-'in* as those with you. She will offer you *"Salam"* (the phrase of offering the greeting of peace) then she and those with her will travel on your left side.

Then your mother Khadijah *'Alayha al-Salam* daughter of Khuwaylid will welcome you. The first believing female in Allah and His messenger and with her there will be seventy thousand angels with banner of *Takbir* (Allah is great beyond description) in their hands and when you will arrive near the gathering Eve along with Asiyah the daughter of Muzaham will receive you and you will travel with her and those with her until you arrive in the middle of the

317

gathering, it is because Allah gathers all creatures on one ground where their feet remain straight. Then a caller will call from under the Throne which all creatures will hear, "Cast down your eyes until Fatimah, *'Alayha al-Salam,* the truthful, daughter of Muhammad and those with her pass by." No one on that day, except Ibrahim the close friend of Allah, the beneficent, and Ali ibn abu Talib, *'Alayhima al-Salam,* will be able to look at you. Adam, *'Alayhi al-Salam,* will search for Eve and will see her with your mother Khadijah, *'Alayha al-Salam*, in front of you.

Then a pulpit of light will be set for you with seven steps and from one step to the other step there will be rows of angels with the banners of light in their hands, the *al-Hawra' al-'in* will line up on the right side of the pulpit and on its left. The nearest to you from your left will be Eve, and Asiyah. When you will arrive on top of the pulpit Jibril, will come to you and say, "O Fatimah, *'Alayha al-Salam,* ask for whatever you want." You will say, "O Lord, show to me al-Hassan and al-Husayn, *'Alayhima al-Salam.'"* They both will come to you but the veins of al-Husayn, will be pouring out blood, and he will say, "O Lord, take my right back from those who did injustice to me."

At such time the Glorious is angry and because of His anger hell become angry as well as all angels. Hell then roars, then an army of fire comes out and snatch the murderers of al-Husayn, their children and children of their children who will say, "O Lord, we were not present during the murder of al-Husayn, *'Alayhi al-Salam."* Allah will say to a shooting flame of the fire to "Take them by their complexion, their blue eyes, and black faces. Take them by their foreheads then throw them in the lowest depth of the fire; they were stern against the friends of al-Husayn, more than their ancestors who fought al-Husayn, and murdered him."

Jibril then will say, "O Fatimah, *'Alayha al-Salam,* ask for whatever you want." You will say, "O Lord, my *Shi'a,* (followers of *Ahl al-Bayt)."*

Allah, most Majestic, most Glorious, will say, "I have granted them forgiveness." You then will say, "The *Shi'a* of my *Shi'a."* Allah will say, "You can go and whoever, sought protection and safety with you is forgiven." At that time the creatures would love to have been *Fatimiyin* (belonging to the party of Fatimah, *'Alayha al-Salam.)* You will move along with your *Shi'a* and the *Shi'a* of your children and the *Shi'a* of 'Amir al-Mu'minin in safety from the horror with the privacies all covered leaving the suffering and hardship behind them with their arrival safely. People will face horrors but they will not face horror, people will feel thirsty and they will not face it.

When you will arrive at the gate of the garden (paradise) twelve thousand *al-Hawra' al-'in* will receive you who had not received any one before or after you with the spears of light in their hands on the noble carriers of light with reclining seats made of yellow gold and ruby with their reigns made of fresh pearls with a carpet of double layers of woven silk.

When you will enter the garden (paradise), inhabitants of the garden (paradise) will be congratulated and they will spread tables of gems on the pillars of light and they will eat from them while people will present their accounts and they (your *Shi'a*) will live forever in everything that they may desire.

When friends of Allah will settle in the garden (paradise) Adam, *A'layhi al-Salam*, and those after him will visit you. Inside al-Firdaws there will be two pearls from one root, one white and one yellow in both of them there will be palaces, and homes, seventy thousand in each one. The white will be the homes for us and our (*Shi'a*, followers of *Ahl al-Bayt*) and the yellow will be the homes for Ibrahim and *Ale* (family of) Ibrahim, *'Alayhi al-Salam.*"

Fatimah, *'Alayha al-Salam,* then said, "O dear father I love to see your day and I do not like to live after you." The Messenger of Allah, *O Allah grant compensation to Muhammad and his family worthy of their services to your cause,* said, "My dearest daughter, Jibril has informed me from Allah, most Majestic, most Glorious, that you will be the first one from my *Ahl al-Bayt* (family) to join me."

"Woe is upon those who do injustice to my *Ahl al-Bayt* (family) and woe is on those who do injustice to you and great triumph is for those who support you."

'Ata' has said that ibn 'Abbas on remembering this Hadith would recite this verse of al-Quran.

"(The bountiful paradise is for the pious ones) and for the believers and their offspring who have followed them (their parents) in belief, whom We shall join with their parents therein. We shall reduce nothing from their deeds. Everyone will be responsible for his own actions." (52:21)

Chapter 9 - The children of Fatimah, *'Alayha al-Salam*, her descendants, their issues, excellence and that they are the children of the Messenger of Allah, *O Allah grant compensation to Muhammad and his family worthy of their services to your cause*, in a real sense

H 240 Ch. 9, h 1

I ('Allamah Majlisi) found in certain books of al-Manaqib (virtues) narrated to us Ali ibn Ahmad al-'Asemi, from 'Isma'il ibn Ahmad al-Bayhaqi from his father Ahmad ibn al-Husayn from 'Abu 'Abd Allah, al-Hafiz from abu Muhammad al-Khurasani from abu Bakr ibn abu al-'Awwam from his father from Hariz ibn 'Abd al-Hamid from Shaybah ibn Nu'amah from Fatimah, the daughter of al-Husayn, from Fatimah, *'Alayha al-Salam,* al-Kubra' who has said the following:

The Messenger of Allah, *O Allah grant compensation to Muhammad and his family worthy of their services to your cause,* has said that all children of a mother is related to their paternal kinship except the children of Fatimah, *'Alayha al-Salam,* in whose case I am their father and their paternal kinship.

Abu al-Hassan ibn Bishran al-'Adl Baghdad has narrated from abu 'Amr ibn al-Sammak from Hanbal ibn Ishaq from Dawud ibn 'Amr from Salih ibn Musa from 'Asem ibn Bahdalah from Yahya' ibn Ya'mur al-'Amiri who has said the following:

Once al-Hajjaj summoned me and said, "O Yahya' are you the one who thinks the children of Ali from Fatimah, *'Alayha al-Salam,* are children of the Messenger of Allah, *'Alayhi al-Salam?*" I said, "If you grant me protection I will speak." He said, "You are granted protection."

I then said to him, I can recite al-Quran, the book of Allah for you:

"We gave (Abraham) Isaac and Jacob. Both had received Our guidance. Noah received Our guidance before Abraham and so did his descendants: David, Solomon, Job, Joseph, Moses, and Aaron. Thus is the reward for the righteous people. (6:84) We also gave guidance to Zacharias, John, Jesus, and Elias, who were all pious people, (6:85) and Ishmael, Elisha, Jonah, and Lot whom We exalted over all people. (6:86) From their fathers, descendants, and

321

brothers, We chose (certain) people and guided them to the right path. (6:87) Such is the guidance of Allah by which He guides whichever of His servants He wants. If people worship idols, their deeds will be turned devoid of all virtue." (6:88)

"'Isa is the word of Allah and His spirit whom He placed in *al-'Azra' al-Batul*, Allah, most High, has called him of the descendants of Ibrahim, *'Alayhi al-Salam*."

Al-Hajjaj then asked, "What has made you to publicize it?"

I replied, "It is the fact Allah, most Majestic, most Glorious, has made it obligatory on people of knowledge about their knowledge:

"When Allah made a covenant with the People of the Book saying, 'Tell the people about it (prophesy of Muhammad) without hiding any part therefrom, they threw it behind their backs and sold it for a very small price. What a miserable bargain!' (3:187)

Al-Hajjaj then said, "You have spoken the truth but you must never speak of this again to publicize it."

In a mursal manner this Hadith is narrated with greater length than this from 'Amir al-Sha'bi who has said the following:

One night al-Hajjaj summoned me and I became afraid. I then stood up, made wudu, made my will then I went to him. With him there were produce leaves spread around and the sword drawn out of its sheath. I offered him "Salam" (the phrase of offering the greeting of peace) and he responded likewise and said, "Do not be afraid; I have granted you protection for tonight and tomorrow." He made me sit with him then he hinted to his people and a man in chains and shackles was brought in and placed in front of him.

Al-Hajjaj then said, "This old man says that al-Hassan and al-Husayn, *'Alayhima al-Salam*, were sons of the Messenger of Allah, *'Alayhi al-Salam*. He must prove it from al-Quran, otherwise, I cut off his neck."

I then said, "You must release him from the chains and shackles; if he gives good argumentation he will become free to go anyway but if he loses then the sword will not be able to cutoff the iron around his neck." They then released him and I then looked at him found him to be no one other than Sa'id ibn Jubayr. I became very sad and I said, "How can he find proof for this issue from al-Quran." Al-Hajjaj then told him to present his proof in support of his claim; otherwise, his neck will be cut off. He said to him to wait, and he waited for an hour (while) then al-Hajjaj again told him to present his proof and he said to al-Hajjaj to wait, who remained silent for an hour (while) then al-Hajjaj told him the same thing again and he then recited, "I seek refuge with You against Satan, condemned to be stoned. *Bismillah*, (in the name of Allah, most Beneficent, most Merciful). We gave (Abraham) Isaac and Jacob. Both had received Our guidance. Noah received Our guidance before Abraham and so did his descendants: David, Solomon, Job, Joseph, Moses, and Aaron. Thus is the reward for the righteous people." (6:84) He asked al-Hajjaj to recite what is next which he read. "We also gave guidance to Zacharias, John, Jesus, and Elias, who were all pious people." (6:85) Sa'id asked, "How can 'Isa (Jesus) be placed here?" He said, "It is because he is of his descendants." He Sa'id then said, "If 'Isa is of the descendants of Ibrahim who did not have a father because he was the son of his daughter and for this reason he is called of his descendants then al-Hassan and al-Husayn, as a matter of greater preference must be called descendants of the Messenger of Allah, because of being very near to him." Al-Hajjaj then commanded to give him ten thousand dinar and that it must be transported for him to his home and he was given permission to go home.

Al-Sha'bi has said that in the morning I said to myself that it is necessary for me to visit this Shaykh to learn from him the meanings of al-Quran, because I was thinking that I know them and in fact I do not know them. I went and found him in the Masjid with those dinars in front of him which he was dividing ten by ten dinars to give as charity. He then said, "This is all because of the blessings of al-Hassan and al-Husayn, *'Alayhima al-Salam.* If we have saddened one person but a thousand persons are made happy. We have made Allah and His messenger happy."

Kitab al-Dala'il of Muhammad ibn Jarir al-Tabari:

It is narrated from Ibrahim ibn Ahmad al-Tabari from Muhammad ibn Ahmad al-Qadi al-Tanukhi from Ibrahim ibn 'Abd al-Salam from 'Uthman ibn abu Shaybah from Jarir from Shaybah ibn Nu'amah from Fatimah, al-Sughra' from Fatimah, al-Kubra' who has said the following:

The Holy Prophet *O Allah grant compensation to Muhammad and his family worthy of their services to your cause,* has said that every prophet has an ancestral lineage to which they are related. Fatimah, *'Alayha al-Salam,* is my ancestral lineage to which she is related (to me)."

H 241 Ch. 9, h 2
Ma'ani al-Akhbar:

Al-Husayn ibn Ahmad al-'Alawi and Muhammad ibn Ali ibn Bashshar both from Muzaffar ibn Ahmad al-Qazwini from Salih ibn Ahmad from al-Hassan ibn Ziyad from Salih ibn abu Hammad from al-Hassan ibn Musa al- Washsha' al-Baghdadi who has said the following:

I (the narrator) was in Khurasan with Ali ibn Musa al-Rida', *'Alayhima al-Salam,* in his meeting place where Zayd ibn Musa was also present who had turned to a group of people expressed pride and boastfulness saying, "We are . . . and we are so excellent." Abu al-Hassan was busy with a group of people talking to them. He (the Imam) heard the words of Zayd then he turned to him and said, "O Zayd, the words of the merchants of al-Kufah have tempted you. Fatimah, *'Alayha al-Salam,* maintained chastity thus, Allah made her descendants unlawful to the fire, but this is for al-Hassan and al-Husayn, only and those to whom she gave birth only.

"There is Musa ibn Ja'far, *'Alayhima al-Salam,* who obeys Allah fasting all days and stands for *Salat* (formal prayer) all night and you disobey Him and you both come on the Day of Judgment with equal position, you will be more important to Allah, most Majestic, most Glorious, than him. Ali ibn al-Husayn, *'Alayhima al-Salam,* would say, 'Those of us who do good deeds will have double as much reward and for those of us who do bad deeds will face double as much punishment.'

Al-Hassan al-Washsha' has said, "He (the Imam) then turned to me and said, "O al-Hassan, how do you read this verse of al-Quran: 'His Lord replied, "He is not one of your family; he is a man of unrighteous deeds. . . ."' (11:46)'

I, al-Washsha' replied, "Certain people read it as 'He has done an unrighteous deed.' Certain others read it as, 'He is the result of an unrighteous deed,' in which case it means that he is not the son of his father."

He (the Imam) said, "Certainly he was the son of his father, however, he disobeyed Allah, most Majestic, most Glorious, so Allah refused to recognize him to be a son of Noah. So also is the case with us. Those of us who disobey Allah are not one of us. If you obey Allah you are one of us, *Ahl al-Bayt* (family of Muhammad *'Alayhi al-Salam*)."

'Yun Akhbar al-Rida':

Al-Sinani has narrated from al-Asadi from Salih ibn Ahmad a similar Hadith.

H 242 Ch. 9, h 3
Ma'ani al-Akhbar:

My father has narrated from Sa'd from al-Barqiy from his father from ibn abu 'Umayr from Jamil ibn Salih from Muhammad ibn Marwan who has said the following:

I (the narrator) once asked 'Abu 'Abd Allah, *'Alayhi al-Salam*, if the Messenger of Allah, *'Alayhi al-Salam*, has said, "Fatimah, *'Alayha al-Salam*, maintained chastity, therefore, Allah made her descendants prohibited for the fire." He (the Imam) *'Alayhi al-Salam*, said, "Yes, meaning thereby, al-Hassan al-Husayn, *'Alayhi al-Salam*, Zaynab and 'Umm Kulthum, *'Alayhima al-Salam*."

H 243, Ch. 9, h 4
Ma'ani al-Akhbar:

Ibn al-Walid has narrated from al-Saffar from ibn Ma'ruf from Ali ibn Mahziyar from Muhammad ibn al-Qasim ibn al-Fudayl from Hammad nm 'Isa who has said the following:

I (the narrator) once asked 'Abu 'Abd Allah, *'Alayhi al-Salam*, saying I pray to Allah to keep my soul in service for your cause, What is the meaning of the words of the Messenger of Allah: "Fatimah, *'Alayha al-Salam*, maintained chastity, therefore, Allah made her descendants prohibited for the fire." He (the Imam) *'Alayhi al-Salam*, said the ones free from the fire are only the ones to whom she gave birth like, al-Hassan al-Husayn, *'Alayhima al-Salam,* Zaynab and 'Umm Kulthum."

H 244, Ch. 9, h 5
'Yun Akhbar al-Rida':

Through the chain of the narrators of al-Tamimi from al-Rida', from his ancestors *'Alayhim al-Salam* who have said that the Messenger of Allah, *'Alayhi al-Salam,* has said, "Fatimah, *'Alayha al-Salam,* maintained chastity, therefore, Allah made her descendants prohibited for the fire."

Al-Misbah al-Anwar:

It is narrated from 'Abu 'Abd Allah, from the Holy Prophet, *'Alayhi al-Salam,* a similar Hadith.

H 245 Ch. 9, h 6
'Yun Akhbar al-Rida':

Majiluwayh and ibn al-Mutawakkal and al-Hamadani have narrated from Ali from his father from Yasar who has said the following:

Zayd ibn Musa brother of abu al-Hassan, *'Alayhi al-Salam,* made an uprising in al-Madinah, he burned (houses of certain people) and killed (certain people). He was called 'Zayd of fire.' Ma'mun dispatched (his forces) against him and he was captured and sent to Ma'mun and Ma'mun commanded to take him to abu al-Hassan, *'Alayhi al-Salam.* Yasar has said that when he was admitted in the presence of abu al-Hassan, *'Alayhi al-Salam,* he said, "O Zayd, it seems the words of the lowly people of al-Kufah have misled you: 'Fatimah, *'Alayha al-Salam,* maintained chastity, therefore, Allah made her descendants prohibited for the fire.' That applies to al-Hassan and al-Husayn, *'Alayhi al-Salam,* particularly. If you think that you disobey Allah and enter the garden (paradise) and Musa ibn Ja'far, *'Alayhi al-Salam,* obeys Allah so he also enters the garden (paradise), in such case you become more honorable in the sight of Allah, most Majestic, most Glorious, than Musa ibn Ja'far. By Allah no one can achieve what is with Allah, most Majestic, most Glorious, except by showing obedience to Allah and if you think that you can receive it by disobedience to Him then it is a bad thinking." Zayd then said to him, "I am your brother and the son of your father." Abu al-Hassan, *'Alayhi al-Salam,* said, "You are my brother but have not obeyed Allah, most Majestic, most

Glorious. Noah *'Alayhi al-Salam,* said, 'Noah prayed to his Lord, saying, "Lord, my son is a member of my family. Your promise is always true and you are the best Judge." (11:45) His Lord replied, "He is not one of your Family; he is a man of unrighteous deeds. . . ."' (11:46) Allah has excluded him from his family because of his disobedience."

H 246 Ch. 9, h 7
Manaqib of ibn Shahr Ashub:

History of Baghdad and Kitab of al-Sam'ani and al-Arba'in of al-Mu'adhdhin and Manaqib of Fatimah, of ibn Shahin through the chain of narrators from Hudayfah and ibn Mas'ud who have said the following:

The Holy Prophet, *'Alayhi al-Salam,* has said, "Fatimah, *'Alayha al-Salam,* maintained chastity, therefore, Allah made her descendants prohibited for the fire." Ibn Mandah has said that this applies particularly to al-Hassan and al-Husayn, *'Alayhima al-Salam.* It is said that they are those to whom she gave birth and it is narrated from al-Rida', *'Alayhi al-Salam.* According to the priority basis it applies to all of her descendants who are believing people.

H 247, Ch. 9, h 8
Al-Ihtijaj:

It is narrated from abu al-Jarud from abu Ja'far, 'Alayhi al-Salam, who said to him:

"O abu al-Jarud what do they say about al-Hassan and al-Husayn, *'Alayhima al-Salam?*" I (the narrator) said, "They reject our saying that they are the sons of the Messenger of Allah, *'Alayhi al-Salam.*" He (the Imam), *'Alayhi al-Salam,* then asked, "What kind of proof do you present against them?" I replied, "We bring to their notice the words of Allah about 'Isa ibn Maryam (Mary) who is of the descendants of Dawud:

"We gave (Abraham) Isaac and Jacob. Both had received Our guidance. Noah received Our guidance before Abraham and so did his descendants: David, Solomon, Job, Joseph, Moses, and Aaron. Thus is the reward for the righteous people." (6:84) We also gave guidance to Zacharias, John, Jesus, and Elias, who were all pious people." (6:85)

"'Isa (Jesus) is called of the descendants of Ibrahim. We also bring to their notice the words of Allah: 'If anyone disputes (your prophesy) after that knowledge has come to you, say, "Let each of us bring our children, women, our people, and ourselves to one place and pray to Allah to condemn the liars among us."' (3:61)"

He (the Imam), then asked, "What do they say then?" He (the narrator) has said, "I then said that they say, 'Sometimes the sons of a daughter also is called one's sons but they are not from one's seeds.'"

He (the narrator) has said that abu Ja'far, *'Alayhi al-Salam*, then said, "By Allah O abu al-Jarud, I will show a verse from al-Quran which calls them of the seeds of the Messenger of Allah, *'Alayhi al-Salam*, and no one except an unbeliever denies it."

I (the narrator) then asked, "I pray to Allah to keep my soul in service for your cause, where is it?" He (the Imam), said, "It is this verse: 'You are forbidden to marry your mothers, daughters, sisters, paternal aunts, maternal aunts, nieces, You are forbidden to marry the wives of your own sons . . .' (4:23)

"You can ask them, O abu al-Jarud, 'Is it lawful for the Messenger of Allah, *'Alayhi al-Salam*, to marry the wives of al-Hassan and al-Husayn, *'Alayhima al-Salam*? If they say yes then they have rejected the words of Allah but if they say, "No, it is not lawful for him," then they are the sons of the Messenger of Allah, *'Alayhi al-Salam*, from his seeds and it has not become prohibited except because of their being of his seeds.'"

I ('Allamah Majlisi) say that their being called sons and of his children have many examples. Detailed Ahadith in the section on the debate between al-Rida', the in court of Ma'mun were mentioned and they will also be mentioned in the debates of Musa ibn Ja'far against the rulers of his time. More details will be mentioned in the section on al-Khums (tax on net savings) by the will of Allah.

H 248, Ch. 9, h 9
Tafsir of Ali ibn Ibrahim:

My father has narrated from Zarif ibn Nasih from 'Abd al-Samad ibn Bashir from abu al-Jarud from abu Ja'far, 'Alayhi al-Salam, who has said the following:

Abu Ja'far, *'Alayhi al-Salam,* asked me, "O abu al-Jarud, what do they say about al-Hassan and al-Husayn, *'Alayhima al-Salam?*" I (the narrator) replied, "They reject our saying that they are the sons of the Messenger of Allah, *'Alayhi al-Salam.* He (the Imam), *'Alayhi al-Salam,* then asked, "What kind of proof do you present against them?" I replied, "We bring to their notice the words of Allah about 'Isa ibn Maryam (Mary) who is of the descendants of Dawud: 'We gave (Abraham) Isaac and Jacob. Both had received Our guidance. Noah received Our guidance before Abraham and so did his descendants: David, Solomon, Job, Joseph, Moses, and Aaron. Thus is the reward for the righteous people. (6:84) We also gave guidance to Zacharias, John, Jesus, and Elias, who were all pious people.' (6:85) 'Isa (Jesus) is called of the descendants of Ibrahim.

He (the Imam), *'Alayhi al-Salam,* then asked, "What do they say then?" I (the narrator) replied, "They say that sometimes the sons of one's daughter are called one's sons, but they are not from one's seeds."

He (the Imam), *'Alayhi al-Salam,* then asked what other argumentation do you then make?" I replied, "We also bring to their notice the words of Allah: 'If anyone disputes (your prophesy) after knowledge has come to you, say, "Let each of us bring our children, women, our people, and ourselves to one place and pray to Allah to condemn the liars among us."' (3:61)"

He (the Imam), then asked, "What do they say then?" He (the narrator) has said, "I then said that they say, 'Sometimes in Arabic language one son is called our sons, but in fact they can be only one son.'"

He (the narrator) has said that abu Ja'far, *'Alayhi al-Salam,* then said, "By Allah O abu al-Jarud, I will show a verse from al-Quran which calls them of the seeds of the Messenger of Allah, *'Alayhi al-Salam,* and no one except an unbeliever denies it."

I (the narrator) then asked, "I pray to Allah to keep my soul in service for your cause, where is it?" He (the Imam), said, "It is this verse: 'You are forbidden to marry your mothers, daughters, sisters, paternal aunts, maternal aunts, nieces,. . . You are forbidden to marry the wives of your own sons . . .' (4:23)

"You can ask them, O abu al-Jarud, 'Is it lawful for the Messenger of Allah, *'Alayhi al-Salam,* to marry the wives of al-Hassan and al-Husayn, *'Alayhima al-Salam?'* If they say, 'Yes,' then they have rejected the words of Allah but if they say, 'No, it is not lawful for him,' then they are the sons of the Messenger of Allah, *'Alayhi al-Salam,* from his seeds and it has not become prohibited except because of their being of his seeds."

Al-Kafi:

Al-'Iddah has narrated from al-Barqiy from al-Hassan ibn Zarif from 'Abd al-Samad a similar Hadith.

H 249, Ch. 9, h 10
Manaqib of ibn Shahr Ashub:

Al-Hassan, *'Alayhi al-Salam,* was born when Fatimah, *'Alayha al-Salam,* was twelve years old. [See H 1, Ch. 1, h 1, about the special rate of growth of Fatimah, *'Alayha al-Salam.*] The children of Fatimah, *'Alayha al-Salam,* were al-Hassan and al-Husayn, *'Alayhima al-Salam,* and al-Muhsin who was miscarried and according to Ma'arif of al-Qutaybi Muhsin was miscarried because of the injuries caused to her by Qunfudh al-'Aadwi, Zaynab and 'Umm Kulthum are daughters of Fatimah, *'Alayha al-Salam.*

Appendix

'Abd al-Hamid ibn abu al-Hadid in the interpretations of Nahj al-Balaghah about the words of 'Amir al-Mu'minin, during the days of the battle of Siffin on seeing his son al-Hassan advance in the fighting said, "Hold back this young man for my sake, it does not rise me in splendor; I treat them, al-Hassan and al-Husayn, *'Alayhima al-Salam,* more valuably than allowing them to die and that the offspring of the Messenger of Allah, *'Alayhi al-Salam,* must not discontinue."

If you ask, "Is it permissible to call al-Hassan and al-Husayn, *'Alayhima al-Salam,* and their children sons of the Messenger of Allah, *'Alayhi al-Salam,* his children and descendants and the offspring of the Messenger of Allah?" I will say yes, it is permissible; Allah has called them sons of the Messenger of Allah in His words: '. . . 'Let each of us bring our children, women, our people, and ourselves to one place and pray to Allah to condemn the liars among us.' (3:61) This is a reference to al-Hassan and al-Husayn, *'Alayhima al-Salam.* If one bequeaths a certain amount of property for certain children, then it applies to the children of daughters also. Allah, most High, has called 'Isa of the descendants of Ibrahim, *'Alayhi al-Salam,* and the people of a language do not reject the fact that children of daughters are of the descendants of a man.

"If you ask, 'What do you say about the words of Allah: 'Muhammad is not the father of any of your males. He is the Messenger of Allah and the last Prophet. Allah has the knowledge of all things.' (33:40)

"I then ask you about his fathering Ibrahim son of Maria. Whatever answer you give it is the answer about al-Hassan and al-Husayn, *'Alayhima al-Salam.* The conclusive answer is that it is a reference to Zayd ibn al-Harithah because the Arabs would call him Zayd in Muhammad based on their tradition of calling the slaves their sons. Allah has invalidated that custom and has prohibited practicing the tradition of the age of ignorance. The verse says that Muhammad is not the father of any of the grown up man among you. This does not exclude small children like Ibrahim, al-Hassan and al-Husayn, *'Alayhima al-Salam.*"

I ('Allamah Majlisi) say that he has answered other objections which do not fit in this chapter.

Chapter 10 - The Endowments and Charities of Fatimah, *'Alayha al-Salam*

H 250, Ch. 10, h 1
Al-Kafi: [H 12927, Ch. 35, h 1, from al-Kafi]

Muhammad ibn Yahya has narrated from Ahmad ibn Muhammad who has narrated the following:

"I once asked abu al-Hassan, al-Thani, *'Alayhi al-Salam,* about the seven walls (gardens) which were of the legacy of the Messenger of Allah, *O Allah, grant compensation to Muhammad and his family worthy of their services to Your cause,* for Fatimah, *'Alayha al-Salam.* He (the Imam) said, 'No, they were endowments. The Messenger of Allah would take thereof for his guests and maintenance as needed. When he (the Messenger of Allah) passed away, al-'Abbas came to dispute Fatimah, *'Alayha al-Salam,* about it. So she presented Ali, *'Alayhi al-Salam,* and others who testified that they were endowments and she, *'Alayhi al-Salam,* was the beneficiary thereof. The gardens are called al-Dalal, al-'Awaf, al-Husna', al-Safiyah, Mali 'Umm Ibrahim, al-Maythab and al-Burqah.'"

H 251, Ch. 10, h 2
Al-Kafi: [H 12928, Ch. 35, h 2, from al-Kafi]

Ali ibn Ibrahim has narrated from his father from ibn abu 'Umayr from Hammad ibn 'Uthaman from 'Ubayd Allah al-Halabiy and Muhammad ibn Muslim who has narrated the following:

"We once asked abu 'Abd Allah, *'Alayhi al-Salam,* about the charities of the Messenger of Allah, *O Allah, grant compensation to Muhammad and his family worthy of their services to Your cause,* and the charities of Fatimah, *'Alayha al-Salam.* He (the Imam) said, 'Their charities are for banu Hashim and banu al-Muttalib.'"

H 252, Ch. 10, h 3
Al-Kafi: [H 12929, Ch. 35, h 3, from al-Kafi]

It is narrated from the narrator of the previous Hadith from his father from ibn abu Najran from 'Asem ibn Humayd from Ibrahim ibn abu Yahya al-Madiniy who has narrated the following:

"Abu 'Abd Allah, *'Alayhi al-Salam,* has propounded the following. 'Al-Maythab is that garden upon which Salman contracted for his freedom; then Allah, most Majestic, most Glorious, granted it to His messenger, *O Allah, grant compensation to Muhammad and his family worthy of their services to Your cause,* as properties captured from the enemies; and it is in her charity.'" (The Messenger of Allah planted the garden. *O Allah, grant compensation to Muhammad and his family worthy of their services to Your cause,* Amir al-Mu'minin, and Salam for the Jewish slave master which miraculously grew immediately as payment for the freedom of Salman)

H 253, Ch. 10, h 4
Al-Kafi: [H 12930, Ch. 35, h 4, from al-Kafi]

Muhammad ibn Yahya has narrated from Ahmad ibn Muhammad from ibn Faddal from Ahmad ibn 'Umar from his father from abu Maryam who has narrated the following:

"I once asked abu 'Abd Allah, *'Alayhi al-Salam,* about the charities of the Messenger of Allah, *O Allah, grant compensation to Muhammad and his family worthy of their services to Your cause,* and the charities of Ali, *'Alayhi al-Salam.* He (the Imam) said, 'It is lawful for us.' He (the Imam) said, 'Fatimah, *'Alayha al-Salam,* left her charities for banu Hashim and banu al-Muttalib.'"

H 254, Ch. 10, h 5
Al-Kafi:[H 12931, Ch. 35, h 5, from al-Kafi]

Ali ibn Ibrahim has narrated from his father from ibn abu Najran from 'Asem ibn Humayd from abu Basir who has narrated the following:

"Once abu Ja'far, *'Alayhi al-Salam,* decided to inform us about an important fact. He (the Imam) said, 'Do you like if I read the will of Fatimah, *'Alayha al-Salam,* for you?' I replied, 'Yes, I like to hear.' He (the Imam) then took out a box or a basket from which he took out a book (a letter) and read, 'In the name of Allah, the Beneficent, the Merciful. This is the will of Fatimah, daughter of Muhammad, the Messenger of Allah, *O Allah, grant compensation to Muhammad and his family worthy of their services to Your cause.* She; bequests all of her seven walls (gardens enclosed by walls), al-'Awaf, al-Dalal, al-Burqah, al-Maythab, al-Husna', al-Safiyah and Ma li 'Umm Ibrahim to Ali ibn abu Talib, *'Alayhi al-Salam.* When Ali passes away it then is for al-Hassan, when al-Hassan passes away then it is for al-Husayn and when al-Husayn passes away then it is for the eldest of my children. Allah is witness thereof, al-Miqdad ibn Aswad, al-Zubayr ibn al-'Awam and Ali ibn abu Talib are the scribes.'"

From the narrator of the previous *Hadith* from his father from ibn abu 'Umayr from 'Asem ibn Humayd a similar *Hadith* is narrated in which he has not mentioned box or basket and has said . . . 'to the eldest of my children other than [not] your children.'

Addendum

The Speech of Fatimah, *'Alayha al-Salam,* in the Masjid

(From Volume 29 of Behar al-Anwar)

Hadith No. 8

Shaykh Ahmad ibn abu Talib al-Tabarsi has narrated in the book al-Ihtijaj in a Mursal manner. We write down according to his words then will point out the areas of differences of the narrations when explaining certain passages:

He (rh) has said that 'Abd Allah ibn al-Hassan through the chain of his narrators, narrated from his ancestors, *'Alayhim al-Salam,* that abu Bakr decided to prevent Fatimah, *'Alayha al-Salam,* from the benefits of Fidak and when she was informed about it, she then dressed up herself as such that covered her from head down to the ground and in the company of a group of women of her relatives and helpers moved toward the Masjid and the train of their dresses touched the ground. Her walking did not miss even slightly the way the Messenger of Allah walked, *O Allah, grant compensation to him and his family worthy of their services to your cause,* until she arrived in the office of abu Bakr where he was in a crowd of Muhajir (immigrants) and al-Ansar (people of al-Madinah) and others. A curtain was then put in place between her and the people present. She then sighed deeply struggling with tears that made the whole gathering shake in sobbing and wailing. She then remained calm for a while until the sobbing of the crowd settled in calmness from the outburst of moaning, weeping and gasping.

She then commenced her speech with thanking and praising Allah and praying to Allah to grant blessings upon His Messenger, *'Alayhi al-Salam.* The people turned to weeping again and when they held back their weeping she resumed her speech and said, "All praise belongs to Allah who has granted bounties, and all thanks are due to Him for his granting inspiration. He is admired for His universal grants which He initiated, which are abundantly pleasant gifts that are there all in continued manners. Such bounties which are greater than can be enumerated and attaining the limits of compensation for the same is far away, beyond reach and beyond comprehension. He has instructed to appreciate the same to receive additional ones in continuation and that the creatures must praise Him for His grants and admire Him for similar ones. I testify that no one other than Allah alone, who has no partners, deserves worship and I testify no one deserves worship except Allah. This is the statement for which He has set sincerity as its interpretation which is placed in the hearts, and has placed light in the heart to understand it. It is not possible for the eyes to see Him, for the tongues to describe Him, and for the imagination to figure out how is He.

"He has invented things but not from something that existed before, and without any models to follow its example. He brought them in existence by His power, then spread them as He wished without being in need of inventing them or any benefit to give their shape, except to establish His wisdom and to provide awareness for the need to obey Him and to submit to His Lordship and cherisher-ship and to honor His call (praying before Him). He has placed the rewards in obedience to Him and suffering in disobedience to Him, to keep His servants away thereby from His anger and to attract them to His Paradise.

"I testify that Muhammad, my father, is His servant and His messenger, who He had chosen and selected before sending him to the people (for their guidance). He had named him before creating him, and had chosen him before sending him (as His messenger) in which time the creatures were hidden in the unseen, safe from the covering of fears, and very close to the limits of nothingness, while knowledge of Allah is thorough and complete about the limits of all things, encompassing the events of all times and with the locations of the measured things thoroughly distinguished in His knowledge.

"Allah, most High, sent him as His messenger to complete His commandments by His firm decision to approve His wisdom and to execute inevitably what He had measured.

"He saw the nations forming sects in their religion, attending the fires of their religion, worshipping their idols, denying the existence of Allah despite knowing Him.

"Allah through Muhammad, *O Allah, grant compensation to him and his family worthy of their services to your cause,* made the light to shine to turn its darkness to light and to bring ease against its difficulties and clear up the saddened, clouded eyes. He rose with guidance among the people, saved them from misguidance, gave them eyesight in blindness, taught them the upright religion, and called them to the straight path.

"Allah then took him to His self with compassion and choice, interest and His preference for Muhammad, *O Allah, grant compensation to him and his family worthy of their services to your cause,* to relieve him from the fatigue of this world to receive comfort, surrounded by the virtuous angels and the pleasure of the forgiving Lord, in the neighborhood of the powerful King. May Allah, grant compensation to my father, His Holy Prophet, trustee of His revelation, His chosen one and His selected from among the people, the accepted one. May the greeting of peace, kindness and blessings of Allah be with him."

She then turned to the people in the gathering and said, "You are the people who are addressed by His commandments and prohibited, the carriers of His religion and revelations and the Trustees of Allah over your own souls and His preachers among other nations. You believe that all of this belongs to you; in fact, all of this is a covenant from Allah which He has presented to you, with that which remains as successors among you. There is the speaking book of Allah, the truthful al-Quran, the shining light, the blazing brightness in which understanding is evidently clear, with open secrets, out worldly clear (face meaning), whose followers are proud of it and it leads its followers to His pleasure and listening to which takes one to salvation. With it the bright authority of Allah is gained as well as His interpreted commands, His warned off prohibited matters, His clear evidence, His sufficient argumentations, His preferred excellence, His allowable gifts, and His written laws.

"Allah has made belief to cleanse you from paganism, the Salat (formal prayer) to keep you away from arrogance, Zakat, (charity) to cleanse the soul (self) and to increase wealth, fasting to establish sincerity, al-Hajj to propagate the religion, justice to harmonize the hearts, *obedience to us to keep the nation organized, our Imamat (leadership with divine authority) for protection against schism.*

"Jihad (working hard for the cause of Allah) for strengthening al-Islam, exercising patience for deserving rewards, commanding the people to do good and prohibiting them from doing unlawful things for general wellbeing, being kind to parents for protection against the anger of (Allah), maintaining good relations with relatives for the growth of the number of relatives, retaliation

339

and compensations for suffering wrong doing to save lives, fulfilling vows for deserving forgiveness, giving and taking by complete measures for avoiding losses, prohibiting the drinking of wine to avoid filth, avoiding false accusation for protection against remaining away from the mercy of Allah, stopping stealing for establishing chastity and Allah has prohibited considering things as partners of Allah for establishing sincere belief in His Lordship, 'Believers, be pious before Allah as you should and die only as Muslims (having submitted to the will of Allah).' (3:102)

"'Only Allah's knowledgeable servants fear Him. Allah is Majestic and All-pardoning.' (35:28)"

She then said, "O people, you must take notice that I am Fatimah, *'Alayha al-Salam* and my father is Muhammad, *O Allah, grant compensation to him and his family worthy of their services to your cause.* I said so initially as well as repeatedly. I do not speak that which is wrong and do not do that which is conflicting, 'A messenger from your own people has come to you. Your destruction and suffering are extremely grievous to him. He really cares about you and is very compassionate and merciful to the believers.' (9:128)"

She then said, "If you like to find out about his relationship (with me) you will find him to be my father and not the father of anyone of your women and the brother of my cousin and not the cousin of anyone of your men. How excellent is it to be related to him, *O Allah, grant compensation to him and his family worthy of their services to your cause.* He preached the message prohibiting the people by means of warning. He kept away from the path of the pagans, striking in their middle, holding their breathing passage and calling to the path of his Lord with wisdom and good advice, smashing the idols headlong until all were defeated. They (the enemy pagans and others) turned on their heels and until the night moved away from its morning and the pure truth became public, the leader of religion spoke and the bluffing of the devils turned dumb. Hypocrisy in lowliness fell a part, the knot of disbelief and schism turned loose. You then asserted the statement of sincerity along with a few slim white ones. 'You were at the brink of the pit of fire' easily could have been snatched away and targeted or trampled readily by the others. You could only find polluted water to drink and leaves to eat, weak and failing (afraid of being snatched away by other people around you) but then Allah, most High, rescued you through Muhammad, *O Allah, grant compensation to him and his family worthy of their services to your cause,* after a number of upward and downward turns of events and after his facing some of the daring ones among men and the Arab thieves and beggars who did not have any wealth or credentials and the arrogant ones of the people of the books, ('Whenever they kindle the fire of war, Allah extinguishes it. They try to spread evil in the land but Allah does not love the evildoers' (5:64)) or a devil raised his horn (showed his power) or a serpent from the pagan Arabs opened wide his jaws to attack, he (the Messenger of Allah) threw his brother at their throat and he would not turn back without trampling their faces under his sole and extinguishing the fire of war with his sword working hard for the cause of Allah and striving to follow the commands of Allah. As a person very close to the Messenger of Allah, the master of His appointed guardian with divine authority with his belt tightened in the service of Allah to give good advice seriously, working hard, while you enjoyed an easy life entertaining yourselves in safety and comfort waiting and expect everything's turning against us but you followed only the news, turned back from the battle and fled away from the fighting grounds.

"When Allah chose for His Prophet the dwelling of His Prophets and the houses of His friends animosity and hypocrisy emerged from among you and the outer dress of religion became old, the silence of tyranny spoke out, the timid minority showed up as if being the genius, the cherished as noble camel began to bluff which then showed up in your courtyards then Satan then stuck out his head from hiding to call you to his self, then found you responding to his call positively, looking for an opportunity to come by. He then made you to rise and then he found you to be very light but not heavy, he enraged you then found you very angry. You have marked something which is not your camel and have arrived to that which is not your water hole.

"The era (of the Messenger of Allah) is very near, the injury is very wide (large) and the wound is not yet healed, the Messenger of Allah is not yet buried, but you quickly assumed the leadership for fear (as you have said) from the test (discord): ('Some of them ask you, "Make us exempt from taking part in the battle and do not try to tempt us by telling us what we may gain from the battle; many people have died in the battle." Hell certainly encompasses the unbelievers.' (9:49)) This condition must have remained away from you and how could you do so, and where have you turned to? The book of Allah is among you. Your issues spoken of therein are clear, its rules blossom, its landmarks are astonishing, its prohibitions are openly stated, its commandments are clear, but you have left it behind your backs. Is it that because you are interested in moving away from it or it is because you want to issue Judgment on the basis on something other than al-Quran ('How terrible will be the recompense that the wrong doers will receive!' (18:50) 'Whoever follows a religion other than Islam will be lost on the Day of Judgment.' (3:85) You then made its blazing (misguidance) to increase responding to the call of the misleading Satan positively to extinguish the light of the bright religion and to change the traditions of the chosen Prophet, showing to do good and in reality you secretly had a destructive intention behind, and you walk against his family and children from behind the bushes and ditches. We exercise patience to tolerate the pain of the cutting of the sharp knife and the piercing spears into the internal organs of the body.

"You think that there is no legacy for us, 'Do they want judgments that are issued out of ignorance? Who is a better judge for the people whose belief is based on certainty, than Allah?' (5:50) Is it because you do not know? No, that is not the case. You know it very well as clear as the midday sun that I am his daughter, O Muslims. Why am I overpowered about his (my father's) legacy?

"O ibn abu Quhafah, does the book of Allah say that you inherit from your father but I cannot inherit from my father? '…this is indeed a strange thing.' (19:27) Have you intentionally abandoned the book of Allah and have thrown it behind your backs? Al-Quran says, 'Solomon became the heir to David. He said, "People, we have been taught the language of the birds and have been granted a share of everything. This indeed is a manifest favor (from Allah)."' (27:16) About the case of Yahya' and Zakariya it says, 'Lord, grant me a son (19:5) who will be my heir and the heir of the family of Jacob. Lord, make him a person who will please you' (19:6) 'Relatives have priority to each other according to the Book of Allah. Allah has knowledge of all things.' (8:75) 'This is a commandment from Allah: After the payment of debts or anything bequeathed, let the male inherit twice as much as the female. . .' (4:11) 'If one of you facing death can leave a legacy, he should bequeath it to his parents and relatives, according to the law. This is the duty of the pious.' (2:180)

"You have thought that I have no share and I cannot inherit my father and there is no relationship between us. Is there a verse (in al-Quran) which excludes my father particularly? Or, you say that people of two different religions cannot inherit each other. Are my father and I not of the people of the one and the same religion? Or is it because you are more knowledgeable in the matters of the meanings of the general and particular terms of al-Quran than my father and my cousin? There it is (Fadak) harnessed and saddled for the two of you. It will meet you on the day of resurrection, before Allah the best judge, the leader is Muhammad, the time is the Day of Judgment and the hour of doom in which if you suffer any losses, regretting will not be of any benefit for you, 'and that for every prophecy (about you which comes from Allah) there is an appointed time (for coming true) and that they will soon experience it.' (6:67) 'You will soon learn who will face a humiliating punishment and will be encompassed by an everlasting torment.' (11:39)"

She then turned the side of her eyes to al-Ansar (people of al-Madinah) and said, "O community of the younger generation, the supporters of the nation, the helpers of al-Islam, what is this disregard on your part of my rights and slumbering in the matters of injustice done to me? Did the Messenger of Allah, *O Allah, grant compensation to him and his family worthy of their services to your cause*, my father not say that a man is preserved in his children? How quickly you have shown your disregarding (your Obligations toward the rights of Ahl al-Bayt (family of Muhammad)) and how soon you have shown weakness in the matter! You have the ability to overcome what I am trying to deal with and you have the power to settle the case in which I am caught.

"Is it not the fact that you say Muhammad, *O Allah, grant compensation to him and his family worthy of their services to your cause,* has died and it is a great issue, the gap has become wide, the crack is expanding, the rapture is widening, the land has become dark because of his disappearing, the stars have become eclipsed because of the tragedy of his death, hopes have diminished, the mountains have become humble, respect is lost and dignity and honor is taken away because of his death. This by Allah is the great tragedy and a sudden cause of huge sorrow. It is like no other hardship and tragedy. The book of Allah, most Majestic, most Glorious, has announced it in your courtyards in your evenings and mornings, loud and clearly, in recitations and in sweet sounding manners of reading and what has happened before him to the Prophets of Allah and His messengers. It is a distinct judgment and an inevitable determination.

"'Muhammad is only a Messenger. There lived other Messengers before him. Should (Muhammad) die or be slain, would you then turn back to your pre-Islamic behavior? Whoever does so can cause no harm to Allah. Allah will reward those who give thanks.' (3:144) How can, O members of the tribe of al-Qayla (al-Aws and Khazraj) my legacy be devoured before your very eyes and hearing, your gathering and presence? How can the call (my claim) remain confusing before you and the information remain hidden when you are great in numbers and means, resources and power and you have the weapons and shields, even though the call for help reaches you but you do not answer, the crying for support reaches you but you do not respond to the pleading for help while you are qualified to defend, well known for your doing good in matters of wellbeing, as the noble ones by birth and the chosen selected ones. You fought the Arabs enduring hardships and fatigue, challenged the nations, defended (yourself) against a great many of your enemies. We continued to command you and you complied with our commands until the mill of al-Islam started to spin and the days provided us milk, the boundaries of paganism crumbled, the boiling of falsehood subsided, the fire of disbelief extinguished, the call for anarchism silenced, the system of religion took roots, then where are you headed, after the issues are made clear and why do you hide what is already declared. Have you turned back after coming forward and have become pagans after accepting the faith? 'Why will you not fight against a people who have broken their peace treaty with you, have decided to expel the Messenger (from his home town), and who were the first to disregard the peace treaty? If you are true believers, you should have fear only of Allah.' (9:13)

The fact is that I see you are headed toward seeking the worldly comfort forever, moved away from the ones who have the right to expand and reduce (namely, 'Amir al-Mu'minin, *'Alayhi al-Salam*). You have sought pleasures and you are found to live affluently after poverty. You have thrown away what you had heard, swallowed after what you chewed after regurgitation. 'Moses told his people, "If you and everyone on the earth turn to disbelief, know that Allah is self-sufficient and praiseworthy."' (14:8)

"I have said what I have said knowing well by acquaintance and the betrayal that I have noticed from your hearts but it is a flow (from consciences) and a deep breath due to anger, due to weakness of the spear, to relax the chest and to present the evidence.

"You can package it in your luggage of disgrace marked with the anger of Allah and an everlasting defect reaching to, 'It is a fierce fire created by Allah (104:6) to penetrate into the hearts.' (104:7) 'The unjust will soon know how terrible their end will be.' (26:227)

"I am the daughter of the warner who warned you of the 'severe punishment ahead of you', 'You can do what you like and we also work', you can wait and so will we."

Abu Bakr 'Abd Allah ibn 'Uthman then responded to her saying, "O daughter of the Messenger of Allah, your father had been very compassionate and gracious to the believing people, very affectionate and kind. He was to unbelievers as a painful punishment and a great chastisement. If we find out about his relationships we find him to be your father not the father of other women, a cousin of you husband, instead of the of friends, whom he gave preference over all other close friends and helped him in all great issues, no one loves you except the ones who are fortunate, and no one dislikes you except those who are wicked. You are the descendants of the Messenger of Allah, the fine ones, the best and the select ones, who are our guide to what is good and our leaders to the garden (paradise). Yourself, O the best among the women, the daughter of the best of the prophets, are truthful in your words, the first in your great power of reason and you are not turned away from your rights or prevented from expressing your truthful words. By Allah I have not bypassed the words of the Messenger of Allah, *O Allah, grant compensation to him and his family worthy of their services to your cause,* and I have not acted without his permission, because the leader does not speak lies to whom he leads. I take Allah as the witness who is sufficient as witness that I heard the Messenger of Allah, *O Allah, grant compensation to him and his family worthy of their services to your cause,* say, 'We the community of the Prophets do not leave as our legacy gold, silver, a house, or properties except books, wisdom, knowledge and prophet-hood and whatever belongings we leave is for the person in command of the affair after us about which he judges by his judgment.' We have placed what I have possessed, in the means and weapons with which the Muslims do Jihad against the unbelievers and fight against the rebels the sinful ones and this is based on the consensus of the Muslims in which I alone have not done anything by an arbitrary opinion of my own. These are my conditions and belongings all for you and at your disposal of which we do not keep away from you or keep in hiding from you. You are the master of the nation (followers) of your father and the blessed tree for your children. What belongs to you is not blocked and nothing of your original of branches is deducted. Your command is effective on whatever belongs to me. Do you see me opposing your father, *O Allah, grant compensation to him and his family worthy of their services to your cause*, in this matter?"

She then said, "Tasbih (Allah is free of all defects), the Messenger of Allah, *O Allah, grant compensation to him and his family worthy of their services to your cause*, would never act against the book of Allah. He never opposed the laws of the book of Allah. He, in fact, would follow its rules and act according the instructions in its chapters. Are you forming consensus of betrayal on the basis of lies against him which is just like the transgressions committed against him in his lifetime. This is the book of Allah the most just justice that says, '...who will be my heir and the heir of the family of Jacob. Lord, make him a person who will please you.' (19:6) 'Solomon became the heir to David. He said, "People, we have been taught the language of the birds and have been granted a share of everything. This indeed is a manifest favor (from Allah)."' (27:16) Allah, most Majestic, most Glorious, has explained the manner of the distribution of the shares and He has sanctioned the rules of inheritance, assigned the shares of male and female persons. He has moved aside the objections of the people of falsehood as well as the pessimism and the confusions that existed among the people of the past. This has never been the case: 'Your souls have tempted you in this matter. Let us be patient and beg assistance from Allah if what you say is true.' (12:18)"

Abu Bakr then said, "Allah, His Prophet and the daughter of His Prophet have all spoken the truth. You are the mine of wisdom, the location of guidance and kindness, the pillar of religion, the very fact of proof. I do not move away your correct words; I do not deny (the facts) in your speech. These are the Muslims between you and I. They have made me responsible for the responsibility which they have placed on my shoulder by their consensus I have undertaken what I have undertaken without exaggeration, dictatorship or giving preference to a certain choice and they are witness thereof."

Fatimah, *'Alayha al-Salam* then turned to the people and said, "O people; the ones who quickly follow the false words, close the eyes before the evil deeds, '. . . Is it that they do not think about the Quran or are their hearts sealed?' (47:24)

"In fact, your hearts have become stained. How evil are your deeds! Your hearing and vision are seized. How evil is your interpretation, how detestable is what you have purchased, how evil is what you have gained in exchange. You by Allah will find it to be a very heavy load, and its consequences debilitating, when the cover will be moved aside and what is of the degree of loss behind it is made apparent and you will find with your Lord what you did not expect. 'When Allah's decree of punishment comes to pass, He will judge truthfully and the supporters of the falsehood will perish (fail).' (40:78)"

She then turned to the grave of the Holy Prophet and said:

> After you there has been a mix-up in conflicting news,
>
> Had you been present the assertions would not become large,
>
> We have missed you just like the land misses rain,
>
> Your nation (followers) has become deceitful and you can see them deviant,
>
> The close relatives of a man who are of high status,
>
> In the sight of Allah are the closest relatives,
>
> Certain men have made public to us what was inside their chest,
>
> After you passed away and the soil curtained you from us,
>
> Certain men have attacked to insult us,
>
> When they found you absent then all lands are usurped,
>
> You were the moon and the light that gave brightness,
>
> On to you Allah, most Majestic, most Glorious, would reveal the book,
>
> Jibril with the verse would give us comfort,
>
> You are missed now, all good is curtained,
>
> We wish that before you death had encountered us,

This should have taken place before the piles of sands stand in between,

Sorrow has griped us like no sorrowful has experienced,

Of all the people, the Arabs and non-Arabs.

She then returned home and 'Amir al-Mu'minin, *'Alayhi al-Salam,* was expecting her return and he was looking forward.

The author has said that when Fatimah, *'Alayha al-Salam,* returned from the court of abu Bakr she turned to Ali, 'Amir al-Mu'minin, *'Alayhi al-Salam* and said, "O ibn abu Talib you have adopted the manner of the baby (fetus), and you have sat in the room like a suspect, you have been able to crush your opponent armed to the teeth but now the unarmed opponent has tricked you. Ibn abu Quhafah has snatched away the gift that I had received and it was for the sustenance of my children. He has been very loud against me and I found him to persistently oppose me. People of the tribe of Qaylah (al-Ansar (people of al-Madinah)) held back their support from me and Muhajir (immigrants) showed themselves as his (abu Bakr) relatives, people in the gathering kept looking down instead of supporting me, there was no defender for me to prevent injustice (from affecting me). I left home with intense anger but I have returned defeated and there is no choice for me. I wish I had died before being insulted and before being (wrongfully) made to fall. O Allah grant me pardon for crossing my limits. From you is support. Woe is me in every morning and woe is me, the support I once had is dead, and the shoulder is weakened. I take my complaint before my father and my Lord. O Lord, you are the strongest power."

'Amir al-Mu'minin, *'Alayhi al-Salam* then said, "Woe is not on you. Woe is on those who are against you. Restrain your emotions, O daughter of the chosen one, the surviving child of the Prophet-hood. I have not neglected my religion and I have not miscalculated my abilities. You wanted sustenance, rest assured it is guaranteed for you and your guardian is trusted. What He has prepared for you is better than what is cut off from you. You must count it on Allah."

She then said, "Allah is enough support for me and the best attorney."

www.ingramcontent.com/pod-product-compliance
Lightning Source LLC
Chambersburg PA
CBHW062359090426
42740CB00010B/1336